Yardbird Suite

Yardbird Suite:
A Compendium of the Music and Life of Charlie Parker

Lawrence O. Koch

Bowling Green State University Popular Press
Bowling Green, Ohio 43403

Cover Design and Art by Gary Dumm

Acknowledgements

My sincere and appreciative thanks go to the following people who helped immeasurably in the preparation of this book:

Michael Goldsen of *Atlantic Music Corporation* for allowing the use of the material used in the many examples.

Down Beat Magazine and author Don Heckman for the use of a substantial portion of the article "Bird in Flight."

Althea "Sam" Buchanan and Val Lizak for typing the manuscript.

Martin Williams of the Smithsonian Institute for encouraging me through the many years I worked on the project.

Chuck Nanry, Dave Cayer, and Dan Morgenstern of the *Rutgers Journal of Jazz Studies* for publishing the initial study that gave birth to the book.

Marilu and Kerri Koch for their patience.

Charles Parker, Jr. for his music.

Contents

PREFACE

An insight into a jazz artist's work can only be gained by listening; his recordings are preservations of spontaneous acts that will never occur again. Perhaps this is why recordings are more important to jazz than to other types of music. This work, therefore, has been concentrated on Charlie Parker's recorded out-put.

Nevertheless, much biographical material has been included as an introduction to Parker's life for those readers that are not familiar with it; this material also has the purpose of setting certain events in his life in the proper place in relationship to the music. Much of the biographical information was drawn from three sources:

Bird: The Legend of Charlie Parker by Robert Reisner.
Bird Lives! by Ross Russell.
"Charlie Parker Chronology" by Gordon Davies which appeared in *Discographical Forum* in 1970-71.

The Reisner book is made up of statements by friends, relatives, sidemen, and wives, but there is no attempt made to put these together in an orderly chronological fashion or to solve the discrepancies between the different comments. Russell, on the other hand, does put some of the statements together, but distorts time, place, and accuracy in order to present a dramatic picture of the black artist in a white society. Neither work spends any significant time on the music itself. The music, however, as mentioned before, is the primary concern of this work, and many events, therefore, that were covered in great detail in the aforementioned books are purposely done with less detail here unless this author had a much different view or had some original thoughts to add. The biographical material is complete in itself, however, and should provide a clear picture of Parker's life.

Furthermore, this work is meant to act as a synthesizer—to collect much Parker material of different types (biographical, discographical, and analytical) in one place. Both novice and musician, therefore, should find the work useful, for enjoyment or for research and reference. For example, the accounts of each recording session, which are, for the most part, done in a descriptive rather than analytical manner (although *some* technical material was necessary), can help the non-musician to follow the Parker lines and to tell the various "takes" apart. Moreover, throughout the descriptions, various "quotes" (portions of other pieces of music that are blended into an improvisation) are given, so that identification of various "takes" can be done by ear alone. The musician, however, can also benefit from the descriptions since they do contain *some* technical references, and in addition, he should find the detailed analysis section at the end of the work (not meant for laymen, except

1

for the music examples, which are not, for the most part, duplicated in the main text) a useful guide to the study of Parker's music.

As to the use of the book, it is probably best to read the biographical material first—taking note of the recording descriptions and skim-reading them—and to then use the descriptions as reference for detailed listening. For the descriptions are best understood when one is hearing the music; this was the writer's intention. They can also be useful, however, in helping one to decide which Parker recordings one would like to obtain.

In regard to Parker recordings, the discographical listings in this work generally list only one source, although at this writing many and varied reissues are being done. In Appendix VI—*Labelogy*, however, the writer has listed as many of the new issues as possible.

Although there are many uses for this work, it serves its primary purpose if it only stimulates the reader to *listen*; for it is listening that will keep the virile, spontaneous art of Charlie Parker alive.

NOTES ON FORM (For the Novice)

and

NOTES ON NOTATION (For the Musician)

FORM

Most of the form descriptions found in this work will be easy to follow if the listener has a knowledge of the standard AABA song form and the twelve-measure blues. The song form is usually 32 measures in length and generally consists of four eight-measure sections: three that are the same (A) and a "bridge" section which is different (B). When the song form being described is different from this form, it is either stated, or, when deemed too complicated, simply referred to as section 1,2,3, etc., even if the relationship is a bit more technical. A good universal example of the standard form is *Rudolph the Red Nosed Reindeer*; the section that begins with "Then one foggy Christmas eve." and ends with "Won't you guide my sleigh tonight" is the bridge (B), and the other familiar sections, of course, are the "A", or main, sections.

The blues can also be best thought of in a vocal way by the non-musician, and an example that most readers would be familiar with is the traditional blues, *Kansas City*. The twelve-measure form is usually divided into three four-bar vocal sections—a statement, its repeat, and a complementary phrase; or "Goin' to Kansas City—Kansas City here I come," the repeat of this, then "Got the crazy little women there and I'm gonna get me one." If the novice listener keeps this pattern in mind it will be a great aid in following even the most complex Parker blues.

The *I Got Rhythm* AABA form that formed a frame for many a Parker "bop" line can be understood by humming the "We-Want-Cantor" chant or the *Heart and Soul* chords that almost everyone pounds out on the piano. These familiar chord changes make up most of the "A" section. This is a bit over-simplified, to be sure, but it is a simple way for the average listener to become acquainted with Parker's inventiveness.

Both the standard song form and the blues are, of course, repeated in the whole (or in part, in some cases) and each full repeat is referred to as chorus. The opening theme or melody can also be called the exposition; this is usually followed by improvised or "blowing" sections by several players until the theme returns for an ending in the recapitulation or "out-chorus." A basic understanding of this format makes jazz listening an easy and intellectually pleasing activity.

NOTATION

The basic unit of rhythm in Parker's music is the eighth note, but the interpretation of two eighth notes is generally read as long-short ($\sJ$ = $\sJ^3\sr$), or in other words, the beat is subdivided into three instead of two. The original eighth note notation is used throughout this work and as a general jazz practice, in order to simplify the reading aspect. When the long-short value is especially pronounced, however, the dotted eight and sixteenth pattern is used ($\sJ\sJ$). There are times, of course, when the feeling changes from uneven to even for a specific portion of a tune. *Hot House* (May 11, 1945) and *Blues for Alice* (Aug. 8, 1951) are two examples from the Parker recordings.

Because of the uneven, long-short feel, interpretation of anticipated notes ($\sr\sJ$) is also a problem. The "legitimately" trained musician often tries to read the anticipation *exactly on* the up-beat when in effect it should be played *after*, close to the next beat. Thinking of the subdivision of three easily shows this ($^3\!\!\sJ\sJ$). It also points out the "dirt" that would be added to the reading should the "exact" notation be adopted. If this seems like an unscholarly remark, an investigation of the notational and interpretive practice of dotted eights and sixteenths during the Baroque period (written $\sJ\sJ$ —played $\sJ.\,^3\!\!\sr$) can be very revealing.

There is one example in the text where the change of time signature ($\frac{2}{2}$ to $\frac{2}{4}$) is meant to show the exact doubling of the time (metric modulation) in a rubato section (*Charlie's Wig*—introduction—November 4, 1947). This is strictly a quirk of the author's and not a universal practice.

If anything, the above explanations, or the fact that they were necessary, should point out the *inexactness* of notation. Moreover, if it is to be used practically, notation must depend on the ready recognition of a relatively small number of familiar symbols that can vary in interpretation according to the style of music.

The chord symbols used in this work are the author's choice, selected by the implications in the melodic line and by a great amount of experimentation. They are not always exactly the same as the harmonization used on the original record, but they are usually close to the originals in functional purpose.

INTRODUCTION

THE MUSICIAN
Many Things Was He

Music was a thing of the soul—a rose-lipped shell that murmured of the eternal sea—
a strange bird singing the songs of another shore.
J.G. Holland—Plain Talks on Familiar Subjects. Art and Life.

Much has been written about Charlie Parker's eccentric behavior, his sexual
appetite, his drug addiction, and his compulsive drinking. Although some "Bird-
stories" are completely true, many others are exaggerated; the inflations make good
copy, and often make Parker something he was not. If we are to look at him as
a genius, it is, perhaps, best to see him as a human one; for he utilized talents
developed by human striving to deliver the message ingrained in him by fate. He
was neither a black messiah nor an inhuman god, but rather a *man* with very
human problems that he could solve and express only through music. His personal
failings, which illuminate universal ones, pointedly magnify human imperfection,
but the music itself gives many a clue to his *higher* nature: Is it possible to listen
to *The Gypsy* and not know that Bird could cry unashamedly? Can we not hear
an intrapersonal sermon—a soul search, if you will—in his *Parker's Mood* solo?
And do we not find in *all* of Bird's finest solos some abstract emotions that we
ourselves have felt, but could not express? Perhaps, then, it is best to speak about
the *man* in terms that can be related to the *music*.

Indeed, his personal life was sprinkled with extremes, ranging from open
tenderness with children to cheap trickery with friends and sidemen. There were
examples of vengefulness and selfishness, but others of extreme generosity and
sensitivity. The passions that raged within him seemed to be mutable; they could
be turned in either direction—good or bad. The music could swing to extremes
also, as evidenced by the orderliness of the late Dial recordings and the free-wheeling,
sometimes chaotic atmosphere of some "live" recordings such as *Bird at St. Nick's*
and the wild recording made at the International Jazz Festival at Paris.

The underlying discipline, however, that Parker achieved in even his musical
flights was not present in his personal life. In fact, his lack of personal discipline
created most of his difficult situations. His emotions and senses governed his personal
approach to the world, but his musical genius was rooted in his ability to
communicate these emotions and "sense-impressions" in a disciplined, intellectual
manner. Even when he was under the influence of drugs or alcohol, or both, the

4

basic scales, chord resolutions, fingerings, and other technical aspects of musical creativity stayed firmly in his "automatic pilot" and allowed him to create freely, without having to *think* about these basics. In other words, he could concentrate completely on the development of his improvisational ideas because the groundwork of musical discipline was already under his fingers. Unfortunately, there was no such groundwork for his *personal* discipline.

But if a stronger set of values had been absorbed during his youth, his life may have been as orderly as his music. A stronger father-figure and a less permissive mother might easily have saved him from many of his troubles, for most of his wildest acts were those of a spoiled child who always got his way, rather than the rational rebellion of an anti-social genius. Being forced to choose his own values at an immature age, he made many mistakes—most of them costly.

He seems to have been bent on self-destruction, but only as a reaction to his self-gratifying actions. The higher part of his personality (the musician), it seems, viewed these actions with disgust; and to further degrade the lower-end personality (the sensualist), he indulged in more self-gratification, thus creating a self-destructive circle. His guilt was the parent; his hedonism, the child; and so the circle continued.

The circle was further reinforced by the weight of being a black innovator in a white man's world, but the criticism leveled at him by other black jazzmen possibly hurt him most of all. He was accused of breaking with the traditions of jazz, playing gibberish, being unmelodic, and lacking in rhythmic strength (the "You can't dance to it" syndrome), but in retrospect we see exactly the opposite: Parker was a strong blues player, coming straight from the blues tradition of Kansas City; his improvisations always related to the basic chord and were complete melodies with developments and climaxes; his rhythmic sense was so strong that it, too, could go on "automatic pilot" and allow him to freely create phrases over the bar lines. No matter how revolutionary it seemed then, his music is actually only an *expansion* of traditional boundaries.

Nevertheless, the criticism of traditionalists is probably what goaded Parker to state in a *Down Beat* interview (Sept. 9, 1949) that "Bop is no love-child of jazz." This response seems to be an angry reaction rather than an explicit attempt at definition, for if we examine the music we find that it has all the elements of traditional jazz, but developed further and shifted in importance: The driving jazz four-beat became mainly the function of the bass, leaving the drummers right foot free for accents, or "bombs", as they were called—this created a lighter pulse, but retained the drive, making it more "felt" than heard; the improvisations were based on tunes and forms used by traditional jazzmen, but refitted with new themes and extended substitute harmony; the soloist, a jazz fixture since Louis Armstrong, was given more room than ever before, an obvious reaction to the tight structure of the big band era, directly preceding the "bop" age. All in all, the music seems to us now a logical extension of mainstream jazz.

Furthermore, with his searing emotional qualities, Parker can truly be viewed as the culmination of the "hot" style pioneered by Louis Armstrong. Although this was not at all clear at the time of his greatest records, we now—standing back and looking at a greater distance—easily see the proper perspective. It does not stop there, however, for he was also, intellectually, the beginning of the new. He developed the ideas of extended chords and linear improvisation, the building blocks of later jazz, and paved the way for further refinements. He was truly the end of one style and the beginning of another rolled into one—both the *Omega* and the *Alpha*.

Intellect and emotion, as seen above, both played an important part in Parker's music; they were, in fact, wound around its very core. Although the emotional quality came from Bird's childish openness and his black sub-culture roots, his intellect was stimulated by innovations in the arts and sciences from the white man's world: His blues-playing, for instance, contained soulful melodic lines with sophisticated harmonic implications. This blend of head and heart produced Bird's wonderful approach to music, with his torrid emotions pouring forth in intellectual phrases, swinging back and forth from earthiness to extreme coolness in the course of a few measures. Both ingredients, intellect and emotion, are necessary for every artistic endeavor, but Parker found his own unique combinations—some balanced, some extreme, some undulating—to express his humanity.

Indeed, this writer grew to manhood loving Parker's music—and hence loving Bird's humanness—for it expressed perfectly the rebelliousness of a difficult adolescence, plagued with indecision and doubt. It gave direction to musical knowledge, confidence to the ego, and self-acceptance to the soul. Considering Bird's appeal, one can suppose that large numbers of amateur and professional musicians had the same experience.

The appeal, however, should continue. It will not, to be sure, if we only hear occasional references to Bird through secondary sources, such as the scoring of his lines or the use of one of his themes for an improvised excursion. Depending as it does upon improvisation, jazz cannot be viewed, regarding its permanence, in the same light as "classical" music. We can enjoy Beethoven's "Pathetique" piano sonata in performances by many artists, or sit and make our own attempt at an interpretation (those of us who play the piano); the sonata is a complete creation; a whole work of art. To do the same to a jazz composition, however, is to experience only a small part of a work of art, for much of the creativity lies in the original improvisation on the theme. A different player using a Parker line as a vehicle for improvisation is giving a personal creation-interpretation; this is the wonderful uniqueness of jazz. It does not, however preserve Parker's *original* improvisation. To do this, his *records* must be *played*; a jazz *recording* is the equivalent of a "classical" *score*.

Parker's musical reputation, although far-reaching among music-oriented people, is not well known to the man on the street. Armstrong is a household name, even to people who have never heard his early innovative recordings, but Parker remains cloudy to the general public. This is sad, for some Parker material, such as the "Bird with Strings" recordings, can be programmed *anywhere*—even on Muzak stations. The public can only "know" music it hears, and it hears very little Bird.

The confusion, however, over "takes", titles, and recording dates obviously did not help Parker's general popularity, although it did fascinate researchers and musicologists. Thanks to many dedicated efforts, the chaos is becoming order, but probably many mysteries will always remain; this is part of the Parker mystique.

Mystique it is! Strange, fatalistic incidents followed Bird. Although most of them have been spoken of to the exclusion of the music, making him a mini-god, the incidents, nevertheless, continue to happen, even after his death. The music-related ones, which concern us here, show—if anything—mysterious human communication. This writer, working on the "motif" of *Embraceable You* in the wee morning hours, had such an experience: The television set had been absently playing as the writer worked; directly before sign-off time, one of those strange commercials that are only seen at that time of the morning appeared on the screen—it was for a spiritual center, on an independent New York channel; a harp softly strummed arpeggios, and suddenly, as the writer wrote the notes on the manuscript paper, a guitar played the opening "motif" phrase of Bird's solo. Coincidence? Possibly, but still unnerving. The writer has seen the commercial once since, so it was not the result of too much ale imbibing or working too long. The incident was, however, fascinating. Other "Bird-stories" of the same type (there are many) suggest the same conclusion: an ESP (for want of a better term) experience. At the moment of Bird's death, for instance, Carmen McRae was performing *Yardbird Suite* on stage at Carnegie Hall; the words are especially relevant and can be heard on Carmen's Decca recording (8173) of 1953:

> It's hard to learn
> how tears can burn one's heart
> But that's the thing that I found out
> too late, I guess
> 'cause I'm in a mess...

Another possible coincidence? This could be—but it does set one to speculating. Further judgements here, however, would be inappropriate; they are beyond the scope of the writer. Let the mystique continue, then, as part of Parker's many-sided nature.

Mystique or not, many sides of the music are evident, as recounted before, and so are many sides of the man. Both Doris Sydnor, his third wife; and jazz critic Leonard Feather, a close friend; agree that they rarely saw the wild side of him generally presented to the public. But in Robert Reisner's *Bird: The Legend of Charlie Parker*, which offers direct quotes from people who knew Bird, the conflicts of opinion regarding Parker's personality, life style, views, and other facets are alarming and create much confusion; one can find a counter-argument for almost every opinion on the man. Perhaps this is close to the truth, for the Bellevue Hospital report of September 10, 1954—after his attempted suicide—gave a psychological diagnosis of "latent schizophrenia." The report after his next admission, two and a half weeks later, gave the report of "undifferentiated schizophrenia", a further jump of the monkey on his back. The point is that Bird may have really been different people at different times, most especially in his own self-view. Two opinions on his racial views are enlightening:

George Wallington, bop pianist who knew Parker on 52nd Street in the mid-Forties:

Bird seemed to avoid the subject of race. About the South, he said, "The only way to get around there is with a gun. Why should anyone live down there while there's a place like New York?" Statements like those were rare. Usually, when someone brought up the topic, Bird would smile and say: "Why discuss these things? Let's get high."[1]

Hampton Hawes, west coast pianist, speaking of opening night at Berg's in 1945:

He talked to us about things I wasn't to read until years later in books by Malcolm X and Cleaver. I heard all that in his music...Bird felt deeply about the black-white split. He was the first jazz musician I met who understood what was happening to his people. He couldn't come up with an answer. So he stayed high.[2]

It is possible that Parker was reticent on the race issue with Wallington, a white man, on the grounds that there could be no real understanding. With Hawes, a young black man, however, Bird may have felt more affinity and opened up. The pianists' views may also have been colored by each one's self-image, unconsciously reflected—Wallington's white, Hawes's black. Both men, however, recognized drugs as an escape route, a way that Bird would not have to think about the subject.

A friend of Bob Reisner's, all the same, mentions that Bird tried to "put him on" about race by intimating that musicians were a race in themselves.[3] Perhaps this was partly "put-on" and partly what Bird believed: Humanness is certainly greater than blackness or whiteness, and the expression of intangible, universal truths through personal creation—specifically, in music—is the gift of few humans; this may have been the message in Bird's "put-on". A statement by Art Blakey, a black musician, underlines this: "A symbol to the negro people? No. They never heard of him and care less. A symbol to the musicians, yes."[4]

Here again, in conclusion, we see the ever-present relationship of the man to the music, for it is the musicians who most easily recognize Bird's human imperfection as a causative factor—a reason for the creation of great music. It is they, on their instruments, who continue to shout "Bird lives"—not by mere repetition, but by further development. The music, therefore, lives on, and so, symbolically, does the man—or rather, *the musician*. Through his music, perhaps, all humanity, in time, will see him as a symbol, just as it views Beethoven; then Bird will be truly free.

* * *

Bird was "gone"; Bird was "gone" they said.
But what they meant, now that he is,
is that he was never more "here."
...And this...is part of Bird's
contribution to you.

Al "Jazzbeau" Collins, New York Disc Jockey
Spoken Introduction to
Charlie Parker Memorial Album   *Savoy 12014*

CHAPTER I

THE EARLY BIRD
Out of Nowhere
(1920-1939)

Perhaps there lives some dreamy boy, untaught
In Schools, some graduate of the field or street,
Who shall become a master of the art,
An admiral sailing the high seas of thought
Fearless and first, and steering with his fleet
For lands not yet laid down in any chart.
Longfellow—Possibilities

In the aftermath of World War I, burdened by an incapacitated president and a national melee over alcohol prohibition, America slowly moved toward the "jazz age." Louis Armstrong was performing on the riverboats with Fate Marable; King Oliver was at the Dreamland in Chicago; and Charles Parker, Jr. was soon to be born. While touring the Midwest during the last years of the war, Charles Parker, Sr., a nomadic vaudeville-minstrel performer from Memphis, Tennessee, had been stranded in Kansas City. Soon after establishing himself as a local entertainer, he met and married Addie Boyley,[1] a girl of seventeen. When Charles, Jr. was born on August 29, 1920, little did the couple realize that they had created the genius who, within three decades, would restructure the American music then just beginning.

Because of the small income and heavy drinking of Charles, Sr., Addie was forced to seek menial jobs almost immediately after her son's birth; her most frequent duties were those of a domestic cleaning woman. During his early years, therefore, young Charles spent most of his time in a Catholic day school. Indeed, he thought of himself as a Catholic throughout his childhood even though the family was Baptist.

The Parkers, residing at 852 Freeman Street in Kansas City, Kansas, across the Kaw River from metropolitan Kansas City, Missouri, moved to the larger city to open further opportunities for the senior Parker's career. His questionable talent as a dancer, pianist, and singer, however, probably worked against him, for he only played occasional tours with local circuses; consequently, he became a railroad chef. Nevertheless, the move across the river in 1927 was a significant one; the

9

rented house at 1516 Olive Street lay in the urban black section of Kansas City proper and was within walking distance of Twelfth and Vine, the heart of the entertainment district. The nearness of such a musical environment later became an important factor in the career choice of young Charles.

As the depression crowded American history, the elder Parker paid less and less attention to his family and spent more time at his after-hours role—a small-time gambler and occasional pimp. In 1929, the Parker couple separated completely, and Addie became the lone supporter of both their nine-year-old son and her husband's son, John, who was two years older than Charles. John had been with the family since his infancy, but the exact facts of his informal adoption are unknown. Probably, Charles, Sr. had also abandoned John's mother; eventually, having no means of support for her child, she probably found the Parkers and gave them the responsibility for John's upbringing. Whatever the case, the half-brothers apparently related well, for Addie was to state later, "I treated them both equally. John has always loved Charles."[2] There is no further documented evidence, however, of a close relationship during their later years. In adulthood, John became a postal employee in Kansas City, Kansas.

After the move across the river, young Charles had entered the Crispus Attucks Elementary School (named for the black hero killed in the Boston Massacre) where his grades were good and he was well-behaved. He went on to Lincoln High School's junior division where his scholastic interest began to wane. He did, however, show an interest in music, and the school band director, Alonzo Lewis, persuaded him to try the baritone horn (his mother referred to it later as a "tuba", but in recorded interviews Parker himself stated it was the baritone). But the young man was disappointed; he had wanted a saxophone. Professor Lewis, however, faced the problems of band balance (baritones, like football linemen, are necessary but unappreciated) and instrument availability (the saxophone being non-essential to a military band, was not usually stocked by schools); Parker, therefore, became a baritone player.

Nevertheless, Addie Parker, procuring a regular job at the Western Union telegraph office as a cleaning woman, indulged her son's wish for an alto saxophone as she did most of his desires. In school, however, he was stopped again; the band did not need a saxophone player. The young musician, therefore, continued to play baritone horn in the marching and concert bands, but convinced Professor Lewis to give him some instruction on the traditional beginning woodwind—the clarinet. The transference of fingering system from clarinet to saxophone is comparably easy, of course, and the young man used his meager clarinet instruction as a jumping-off point and learned the saxophone through self-study and determination. Although the embouchures (mouth formation) for playing the clarinet and saxophone, both being woodwinds, are almost identical, the brass baritone embouchure is quite different. Parker's instruction on the baritone, however, did provide the basic breath control needed for all wind instruments, a background in reading and interpreting music, and a slight knowledge of scales—all of which helped his progress on the alto sax.

Although it seems incredible that Parker should later cite Rudy Vallee as the influence which made him lean toward the alto saxophone, it makes sense when one considers the national popular music scene about 1930 (Parker's fifth grade year). Crooners (a word coined by Vallee himself) and "sweet" bands (groups with syrupy saxophones) dominated. Crooner Russ Columbo's *Prisoner of Love* and saxophonist Wayne King's *Goofus*, two pop tunes of the day, illustrate the point. There is even a reference to the saxophone in the words to *Goofus*. The alto sax was so popular, in fact, that many standard piano sheets included a special part for the instrument. Even Louis Armstrong had gone to the popular "sweet" band format; he was the featured "hot" soloist with the Les Hite band and was spotlighted on popular tunes such as *Body and Soul*. Vallee, a national radio figure with his Fleishmann's Yeast Hour, was a combination of crooner and sweet sax stylist— the popular style personified. Furthermore, a young boy of age ten or eleven receives music as a whole. He is drawn to certain sounds and certain instruments, his choice usually being influenced by the popular trend, but specific fields of music are generally not a part of his thinking until later. Charlie was no exception; he heard Vallee's national radio broadcasts and also the strong, eight-to-the-bar piano style favored by popular Kansas City pianists, such as Pete Johnson—the style generally known as "boogie-woogie." The influences pushed him toward a general love of music, rhythm, and the saxophone; his *jazz* influences were to come later.

It is interesting that *Honeysuckle Rose* and *I Got Rhythm*, both of which Parker was to transform many different times later in his life as vehicles for improvisation, bear the copyright dates of 1929 and 1930 respectively. Ethel Merman's show-stopping version of *I Got Rhythm*, occurring directly before the first act finale of the George Gershwin show *Girl Crazy*, was the talk of Broadway and eventually the nation; and the ebullient *Honeysuckle Rose*, written by Fats Waller, was also extremely popular, especially among blacks. These strongly rhythmic pieces, important to a young man falling in love with music, were to prove *more* important later.

As he moved into high school proper (1934), Parker began playing his alto sax with a group of older high school boys in a band called the Deans of Swing. Lawrence Keyes, the pianist, was the leader, and the group consisted of a sax section, trumpet player, and rhythm section. Walter Brown, who later became well known as a blues singer with Jay McShann, was the group's vocalist. The instrumentation lends itself well to "stock" orchestrations, and the repertoire of the group probably consisted of some of these plus some "heads" (memorized arrangements). Personnel changes are common in groups led by struggling high school youngsters and the Deans obviously followed the same pattern. A job calling for less men would find the group paring down to the minimum—say, perhaps, sax, trumpet, and rhythm. It could also be expanded for a better paying "gig."

Paying jobs were hard to come by in the beginning, however, and school functions and "fun" rehearsals were the prime purposes of the band. James Ross was the main-stay on trumpet; Parker, Freddie Culliver, Franz Bruce, and Vernon Walker comprised the saxes; and Ernest Daniels was the drummer. Charlie seems to have been the young hanger-on who wanted to attend rehearsals and discuss music. His horn of the period was described by Keyes as "raggedy as a pet monkey, rusty and patched up with rubber bands."[3] He carried it in a homemade bag made from pillow ticking. Gene Ramey, a Kansas City bassist who was a few years older than Charlie, recreated Parker's role in the Deans for the English magazine *Melody Maker*: "...Bird wasn't doing anything, musically speaking, at that period. In fact, he was the saddest thing in the band, and the other members gave him something of a hard time."

Parker, however, was determined to withstand the musical tests of his new-found world. He began to question Lawrence Keyes about chords and tried to relate the answers to his small knowledge of scales and music basics gleaned in the studies at Lincoln High. He also found his personal "hero" in the person of Robert Simpson, an older trombonist at Lincoln. Simpson, having great technique, was a logical choice for a young man who had spent his apprenticeship as a baritone horn player, for the baritone and trombone are closely related—so closely that many players "double" on both instruments. The trombone uses a slide to produce its tones and the baritone a set of three valves, but the sound is in the identical register and the mouthpieces are almost interchangeable. It is easy to see why young Parker could relate to the strong musicianship of the older player.

Simpson, participating in many of the "fun" sessions with Parker and Keyes, also served as a "father figure" to young Charlie. Perhaps, Simpson did not ridicule Parker's early efforts at playing; perhaps he was the only older male who accepted him as he was. Whatever the reason, Charlie was extremely fond of him, and when Simpson died, near the age of twenty, Parker was broken up. He was to remark almost twenty years later to his friend Ahmed Basheer: "Once in Kansas City I had a friend and a sorrowful thing happened...he died."[4] He said this to Basheer to explain why he did not want people close to him.

Charlie's truancy record at Lincoln was appalling; he hardly ever attended a full week and paid no attention at all to academic activities or homework. Music was his all consuming interest, and he lived to learn more about it. His moral discipline, already weakened by a doting mother, was given even greater lee-way by the lack of supervision created by Mrs. Parker's working hours. She performed her duties as a Western Union char-woman through the night, giving Charlie complete freedom to sample the temptations of the nearby nightclub district.

Most musicians, of any era, are thrown into the nightclub world at quite young ages, but most also have steadier home influences than Parker had. His all-night freedom allowed him to find the underworld elements that always seem to lurk in the background of the nightclub world. He learned of nutmeg "highs", achieved by mixing this substance with a coke or orange soda; of marijuana cigarettes; of cocaine sniffing; and finally, of heroin. As he learned the secrets of the music trade, he also picked up the traits of the underworld. A great many boys begin to smoke at about age fifteen—some to project manhood, some to experience something new, some as a childish whim, and some for a combination of these reasons. The habit generally continues, however, for life. Charlie's reasons were probably the same, but he was fooling with much more dangerous habits. In his own words for a *Metronome* interview in 1948:

It all came from being introduced too early to night life. When you're not mature enough to know what's happening—well, you goof. It was so sudden. I was a victim of circumstances. High school kids don't know any better. That way, you can miss the most important years of your life, the years of possible creation.

The nightclub circuit, however, provided a wealth of knowledge for a young man interested in learning music. Charlie heard Lester Young, Count Basie's tenor soloist; and Buster Smith, the altoist and arranger with Basie. He also heard Dick Wilson, the tenorist with Andy Kirk; and the "boogie-woogie" piano of Pete Johnson. The Basie band was entrenched at the Reno Club, near Twelfth and Cherry Streets, until Basie's recording success in 1936, and Johnson was the house pianist at the Sunset Club. The Reno became legend through its boisterous, all-night "cutting" sessions (tests of improvisational skill and endurance), and the Sunset, also, was an "after-hours" place.

Parker's later comments on Lester Young are interesting. Commenting in Leonard Feather's *Inside Be-Bop* he said, "I was crazy about Lester; he played so clean and beautiful. But I *wasn't* influenced (italics author's) by Lester. Our ideas ran on differently." The implication is probably that his *mature* style was much removed from Youngs, for his *early* records with Jay McShann *do* sound very Young-influenced. The vibratoless sound of Young obviously left a mark on Parker's tone, and even the improvisational ideas of the McShann days sound like Lester with an original twist. Perhaps the original twist is what Parker meant in his statement. Interestingly, the sound of Parker on *tenor* saxophone in 1947 predicts the future. He sounds like the young black tenors that were to emerge during the Fifties (influenced, of course, by Bird's alto style), and one can look long and hard to find any Young influence.

The years 1935-1936 form a hazy history in the Parker story. The facts are all there, documented the same way by different people, but dates are different in each documentation. The facts can be reconstructed by logical assumption, but it is perhaps best to think of the events as happening in the *general period* of these formative years. Parker, remember, was a teenager trying to break into the music business. He associated mainly with older musicians both in school and in his night wanderings. There is a human tendency to remember people who are older than one's self and to easily forget those that are younger unless there is an extremely close connection (think of those ahead of you in school and then try to recall those behind you). The established musicians with whom Charlie tried to run during these years paid him little heed and as a result the dates are unsure.

The Deans of Swing began getting some paying jobs, and as is common among musicians, members took jobs with other groups. Indeed, "pick-up" jobs were common activity in these years with amateurs as well as seasoned professionals; therefore, Parker had a variety of experiences. Buster Smith sums up Parker's attitude during this period:

Charlie would run by himself. He wouldn't stay with anyone for over a night or two, and then, tomorrow, he would be with somebody else. He wanted to play in small groups where he could solo like he wanted to, when he wanted to.[5]

His early engagements were dance jobs at the Panama and the Florida Blossom. The usual fare of young musicians for commercial work consisted of lead parts to stock orchestrations being played with a rhythm section—usually piano and drums. Sometimes, when economics and availability permitted, a bass could be added to strengthen the rhythm. The players did not have to "know" tunes or be able to improvise; for the most part, they simply read the music.

"Knowing" a tune, in musicianese, means to know its melody line and chord construction well enough to perform it without music—on the spot. Most musicians build themselves a repertoire as they gain experience, allowing their "inner ear" to develop, until they finally become adept at "faking" tunes that they have heard only once or twice. There are also the so-called "natural" players, found in every field of music from jazz to polka, whose inner ear is so intuitive that they can spontaneously—without attempts at craftsmanship—recreate melodies they have heard. Parker seems a blend of the two types; he did not play completely naturally in the sense that a gypsy violinist does, but developed his natural abilities through intellectual means. His genius was as *creator* not a melodic *recreator*; the melodies which he heard were his own—surging to come forth.

In describing his own first attempts at jamming, Parker stated that he only "knew the first eight bars of *Lazy River* and the whole tune of *Honeysuckle Rose*."[6] Attempting to play without further knowledge seems unbelievable to the novice, but a little musical thought helps to elucidate things: It is possible to improvise on tunes which one does not "know"; it is done all the time in amateur circles, many times with disastrous results; the musician creates a melody intuitively, listening for the chords as he goes. Secondly, the tunes which Parker "knew" were useful ones in the sense that they contain chord progressions used in many other "standard" tunes: The first eight-bar section of *Lazy River* is based on the cycle of fifths, a standard harmonic device, and *Honeysuckle Rose* contains the ii7 to V7 progression, plus a bridge or "B" section so common harmonically that it became known among musicians as the "Sears and Roebuck Bridge."

Parker also stated that he was badly humiliated on the tune *Body and Soul* when he tried doing double time; the musicians literally laughed him off the bandstand. Again, a little musical analysis gives some insight into what *might* have happened. Both *Honeysuckle Rose* and *Body and Soul* begin on the ii7 chord and move through the dominant (V7) chord to the tonic or "home" chord. They do this at different speeds, however, *Honeysuckle* repeating the pattern several times (ii7 to V7) over four measures and *Body and Soul* once over two measures. Parker's ear may have intuitively diagnosed the chord changes correctly from his familiarity with *Honeysuckle*; realizing the tonic was coming sooner, he may have attempted to "double-time" to get there in time. Parker stated, however, that he knew little about keys or progressions at the time, so the diagnosis would have had to be intuitive.

A good example of Parker in a similar situation is a recording of him "sitting-in" with the Woody Herman Band about sixteen years later. He improvises on Jimmy Giuffre's *Four Brothers* and does not know the bridge. By his final attempt on the tune he has learned it and is able to improvise well on it. The bridge is, incidentally, constructed of ii7-V7-I patterns in a succession of distantly related keys. By the time of the Herman recording, however, Parker had put all of his musical elements and experience together; nevertheless, the recording is still instructive.

The *Body and Soul* fiasco happened at the High Hat at 22nd and Vine, where the band was led by Jimmy Keith, a tenor saxophonist. The group also included James Ross, the trumpeter from the Deans of Swing; and pianist Robert Wilson (these men and others from the band would form the nucleus for the later bands of Tommy Douglas and Harlan Leonard). The humiliation pushed Charlie to tears, but it only strengthened his determination to play music. He was not allowed to "sit-in" on the sessions that were so prevalent; he was laughed at and ridiculed; but he went on studying. He hung around the clubs, listening outside or trying to force his way into the sessions. He was considered a "goat", and the established musicians kept chiding him about his appearance and his horn. Some of them, however, were not so harsh. Gene Ramey, a member of Parker's general circle of acquaintances during this period, stated: "An alto player called Professor (Buster) Smith used to help Bird get to his horn better. Efferge Ware, a guitarist, coached a whole group of us, teaching us cycles, chords, and progressions."[7] He also said of Ware in the English magazine *Melody Maker*: "Ware was a great chord specialist, although he did no solo work. He had lots of patience and explained everything to Bird, after which, of course, Bird expanded on his own." Parker's *mature* style certainly suggests that he was fundamentally drilled by a chordal player, for his ideas are always harmonically perfect; his beautiful melodic lines are inspired by the underlying harmony. He was surely a chordal player, perhaps the last truly great one.

Another humiliating session occurred at the Reno Club, before Basie left Kansas City. Charlie, forcing his way into a session, awaited his turn to blow. Just as he began, Jo Jones, Basie's talented drummer, hurled his cymbal to the floor, sounding the gong signifying that the "amateur show" was over. Charlie again was forced from the stand.

Parker's nickname began to emerge about this time. One origin could have been his "goat" image—the boy standing in the alley looking for a way to force his way into the man's world—a yardbird. He was fond of chicken, which he sometimes referred to as "yardbird", and his use of the colorful pseudonym probably added emphasis to his own tag. Parker himself claimed it evolved through a Charlie-Yarlie-Yarl-Yard-Yardbird-Bird line. A combination of these stories seems to be the best explanation; they seem to reinforce each other, causing the nickname to remain.

Although his contemporaries had little respect for him at this time, Bird managed to find some jobs throughout the circuit. The pay was low, as little as seventy-five cents a night, at times, and the hours were long, but he was happy—he was playing music.

The Deans of Swing continued to work as a group, and the pay began improving slightly. At the urging of singer George E. Lee the band joined Local 627 of the Musicians' Protective Association; they became a "union band." Lee had worked a job with the musicians, obviously liked them, and helped them with a down payment for their initiation fees. Mrs. Parker later stated that Charlie falsified his age for the purpose of joining the union. This practice was common, however, with young musicians of the period. An under-age musician applying to the national secretary for membership was usually accepted, but most young musicians and local union officials simply sidestepped the application and falsified the age. Even after their "unionization", however, the Deans only worked occasionally together; most of the young men spent time in the bands of older, experienced musicians.

A stint with Tommy Douglas's band helped to improve Parker's musicianship. Douglas, a classically trained clarinetist and an excellent altoist, had assumed the leadership of the Jimmy Keith group, and many of Parker's friends, including James Ross, were usual members. The band normally consisted of seven men, probably three saxes, trumpet, and rhythm. In this type of work it was usual for the sax players to double on clarinet in some of the arrangements, especially with the leader being proficient on the instrument. Although Charlie had had some clarinet training in his music studies at Lincoln High, he certainly was not a clarinetist; he didn't even own a clarinet. Douglas comments on this in Reisner's *Bird: The Legend of Charlie Parker*: "I took a Boehm system clarinet over to him one day and he came back the next and played all the parts, he was that brilliant." As mentioned before, there is a degree of similarity between the two instruments, and Parker did have *some* clarinet training, but one must still marvel at the statement. He continued to double clarinet with the Douglas band and began gaining technique on the instrument. His drug habit continued to gain, also, throughout this period, and Douglas helped him to get his horn out of hock several times. The "monkey" was beginning to tighten its grip.

Nevertheless, the Charlie Parker of this time can generally be described as "happy-go-lucky." He was fond of practical jokes and often did imitations of movie cartoon characters, especially Popeye. He was also learning to wise-crack back at his detractors and gaining a healthy aggressiveness. The area around 18th and Vine became his hangout—his base of operations—and here he met Eddie ("Little Phil") Phillips, a drummer, who became his drug "connection." Phil lived on Paseo Boulevard and was present at the many all-night outdoor sessions in Paseo Park. Bird soon was tolerated, if not accepted, by the established musicians at the sessions in the Park and at the after-hours clubs around the city. He was beginning to build his "chops."

He did some playing at the Mayfair, owned by Tutti Clarkin, a genial man who was friendly to musicians. Bird's general pattern of consistent lateness and horn-hocking continued; sometimes he did not show up at all. Clarkin bought him a better horn and Charlie proceeded to hock it almost immediately. He borrowed small amounts of money from owners and other musicians—amounts that could be easily forgotten; he was learning to "con"—out of his need for drugs. He loved taxi cabs and took them everywhere—even places within easy walking distance—often running up bills he could not pay. He would then be forced to give his horn to the driver until he could come up with the money. Once he sold his mother's iron for fifty cents in order to get cab fare for an "appointment." Whether this "taxi quirk" was a show of imagined royalty—an enjoyment of having people chauffeur and wait on him—or a jab back at Jim Crow, we will never know, but his love of cabs continued throughout his life.

In his sixteenth year, Bird dropped out of Lincoln High and married Rebecca Ruffin, a girl four years older, whom he had been dating throughout his high school years. Rebecca's mother and the six other Ruffin children also moved into the upstairs of the Parker household. Charlie, already hampered by drugs and the insecurity of growing up, certainly was too young for the responsibility of marriage. Soon after the marriage, however, Rebecca announced she was pregnant; and if some speculation may be permitted, the pregnancy—or the fact that Rebecca and Bird suspected it—may have been the main reason for Parker abandoning his high school education in favor of an early marriage.

On Thanksgiving night in 1936, Parker was hired for a job in Eldon, Missouri. Eldon is located about 15 miles southwest of Jefferson City, at the upper rim of the Ozarks; it is approximately 115 miles from Kansas City in a southeasterly direction. The job was at a rural roadhouse that was owned by a man named Musser. In late afternoon, Musser met the musicians in Kansas City to lead them to his place. As the two-car caravan neared its destination, the trailing car skidded on a patch of ice and overturned, throwing out the three passengers. George Wilkerson, the bassist, was killed, and Ernest Daniels, the drummer and driver of the car, was hospitalized with multiple bruises and a punctured lung. Bird, who was riding in the back seat with the bass and drums, broke several ribs, but, according to Daniels, was not hospitalized.[8] The two other members of the group (probably Carrie Powell, piano; and Efferge Ware, guitar) were riding with Musser. Musser paid all the expenses and replaced the mangled instruments. Bird received enough money to purchase a new Selmer alto sax, and Daniels was given a new drum set and overcoat. Without much problem, Bird recovered and set about finding additional musical work. For him, with a pregnant wife, work had become a necessity.

Fortunately, his alto idol, Buster (Prof.) Smith, returned to Kansas City after leaving the Basie group and decided to form a new band. Charlie jumped at the chance to play third alto under his hero. The saxes also included Odel West on second tenor and an unknown fourth tenor player. There were three trumpets, including Buddy Anderson; Fred Beckett was the trombonist; and the rhythm section had Jay McShann, piano; Willie McWashington, drums; Bill Hadnott, bass; and a guitarist named Crooke—twelve pieces in all. Smith used this large group for dances and the like, but kept just six pieces, he and Parker plus a rhythm section, for steady club work. For a great part of 1937 the small group worked at *Lucille's Band Box*, located on 18th Street, and did occasional local broadcasts from the club; the pianist was usually Emil Williams after McShann left to form his own group. Bird continued his all-night blowing sessions and obviously did some record listening, for he spoke strongly to Jay McShann about saxophonists Jimmy Dorsey, Frankie Trumbauer, and Lester Young. A good example of the Dorsey influence can be heard on Parker's recording of *Dream of You* done with Trummy Young's group in 1945.

Rebecca Parker gave birth to a son, Leon Francis, during 1937. The birth brought a welcome moment of joy to the Parker household, for the marriage itself was going badly. Bird saw a mother-image in Rebecca and rebelled accordingly. There were violent eruptions, often physical, and he stayed away from home more and more to avoid the confrontations.

During the summer, he left the city with a group formed by George E. Lee, the singer that befriended the Deans of Swing, for a resort job at Lake Taneycomo. The resort is located deep in the south Ozarks, about ten miles north of the Arkansas border. In this placid atmosphere, with his afternoons free, he was able to think and work and study. There were no "pushers" to bother him; no jibes to counteract; no mothers to nag him. He had taken with him harmonic instruction books, saxophone studies, and perhaps some records of Lester Young and other great saxophonists. The group's pianist was Carrie Powell, an excellent chord man, and Buster Smith and Efferge Ware were also on the band. The tutelage of the older musicians was an invaluable aid in Parker's investigation of music theory. Bird studied triad and seventh chord construction and also the *relationship* between chords. The concept of tonality began making sense to him, as did the rules of tone resolution. He could soon put his intuitive ear to practical use and begin to see music as a working whole. The blues he had been hearing all his life were not only emotional, he found, but could also give much room for intellectual experimentation. The *I Got Rhythm* form, so prevalent as the all-night sessions, related to the cycle of fifths; scale patterns could be used with related chords; everything related to everything else. The standard patterns were all there, since Bach's time, waiting for something different to happen to them.

Upon his return to Kansas City, no one could believe the transformation that had taken place in the young musician. He was soon *accepted* at *all* the sessions. Perhaps it was not a transformation, but rather a coming together of elements which were already there—an *understanding*. In his studies of Lester Young, he probably gleaned the *how* of Lester's solos rather than the *what*. If he memorized Young's choruses, he probably did so as an exercise in technique and understanding, for Parker was too strong a voice to use someone else's concept, except to build on it. There is, however, an amount of influence that takes place unconsciously in a musician listening to another over a period of time—that is to say, a process of absorption.

To see the achievements that Parker realized during his stay in the Ozarks is also to see how much circumstances and environment affected his life. He absorbed the harmony lessons and advice of the older musicians like a sponge, ready to pour it out later. He had, however, already absorbed the workings of drugs, gamblers, pimps, and whores. With a different early environment, of course, his life may have been much different, but then, perhaps it was not meant to be. Genius sees better than normalcy and is put here to improve the sight of normalcy; it must, then, see the evil as well as the good. Bird not only saw it, but experienced it as well. The experiences improved his artistic sight, but degenerated his physical and mental well-being.

In early 1938, Buster Smith went to New York to find employment as an arranger and to seek work for his large group. Charlie, meanwhile, joined Jay McShann, who had formed his own band. The McShann band opened at Martin's-On-The-Plaza in Kansas City and remained there for approximately three months. At the end of the engagement, McShann, flustered by Charlie's drug habit and consistent lateness, was forced to let him go. Moreover, the atmosphere in the Parker home had been getting worse; the violent eruptions between Rebecca and Charlie were becoming more frequent and more physical. One evening at the end of one of his frequent taxi jaunts, Bird again could not pay the fare. The driver challenged him, and Bird struck back with a knife. He was arrested, and his mother, furious at his conduct, made him sit out the sentence (another reinforcement of his nickname?). Upon his release from prison, he heeded his mother's advice and left the scene for awhile. Setting his sights on New York, where he could find Buster Smith, Bird hoboed his way to Chicago.

The 65 Club in Chicago had a "breakfast dance" one day a week, with a floor show starting about six-thirty in the morning. King Kolax, the trumpeter, led the group, which included "Goon" Gardner, alto and clarinet; John Simmons, bass; and Kansas Fields, drums. Billy Eckstine reports on Bird's entrance to the Chicago music scene:

> We were standing around one morning when a guy comes up that looks like he just got off a freight car, the most raggedy guy you'd want to see at this moment. And he asks Goon, "Say man, can I come up and blow your horn?"...And this cat gets up there, and I'm telling you, he blew the bell off that thing! It was Charlie Parker, just come in from Kansas City on a freight train. I guess Bird was no more than eighteen then, but playing like you never heard...[9]

Later that day, Gardner befriended Bird and loaned him some clothes and a clarinet. Gardner also introduced him to a few musicians and got him some work throughout Chicago. A few weeks later when Gardner tried to find Bird he found he had disappeared—clothes, clarinet, and all!

His destination was probably Kansas City, for his mother stated that she located him in Chicago when his father was killed; the elder Parker had been fatally stabbed by a woman during a drunken brawl. Mrs. Parker gives Bird's age as seventeen at the time of his father's death, and this would be correct for most of 1938, his birthday not coming until the end of August. Bird attended his father's funeral and remained in Kansas City for most of the year. Rebecca negotiated a divorce, gaining alimony payments of five dollars a week from Charlie, and Addie Parker took the responsibility of raising their son, Leon. In the latter part of the year, Bird worked in Harlan Leonard's Rockets (a band made up of many of Parker's cronies) for a period of about five weeks. His dismissal was the result of his perennial habits—drugs and lateness.

The funeral had been a rather shocking experience for the young man. He had not seen his father since 1929, when the elder Parker deserted the family, and the body was so emaciated from loss of blood that it was hardly recognizable. It is possible that he thought of Buster Smith, his musical father, who later recalled:

> He used to call me his dad, and I called him my boy. I couldn't get rid of him. He was always up under me. In my band, we'd split solos. If I took two, he'd take two; if I took three, he'd take three; and so forth. He always wanted me to take the first solo. I guess he thought he'd learn something that way...[10]

Charlie appeared in New York at Buster Smith's apartment in late 1938 or early 1939 and moved in with him.[11] He had hoboed all the way, and his legs and feet were extremely swollen. During the day, he would sleep in Smith's bed, but spend his nights trying to find sessions and trying to make contacts for jobs throughout the city. When his search for musical employment proved fruitless, however, Bird accepted a job as a dishwasher at Jimmy's Chicken Shack in Harlem. The restaurant was owned by pianist Mary Lou Williams' husband, John, an altoist himself; and the feature attraction was the great pianist Art Tatum. Probably Parker and Smith knew the owner previously, as both Mary Lou and John were with Andy Kirk in Kansas City and were present at many "blowing" sessions. The kitchen job held Parker over for three months, as he tried to find his way into the tough New York musical circle, even though the pay was only a meager nine dollars per week plus meals. He slept wherever he could and lived the life of a roustabout as he absorbed the environment that would eventually become the capital of his brand of music.

Some friendly musicians, frequenters of sessions, managed to get Parker a horn and some job contracts. He worked at the Parisien Dance Hall, at Broadway and 48th Street, and also at the Kew Gardens, on the outskirts of Harlem; the latter job lasted about four months. As his economics improved slightly, he began living at the Woodside Hotel where he remained for the rest of his stay in New York.

Clark Monroe's Uptown House was a session, after-hours club on W. 134th Street that did not have a pay scale, but worked on a percentage of the "take". Charlie became a regular and soon was in the basic group that began each evening's session. His colleagues included Dave Riddick, trumpet; and Ebenezer Paul, bass. The basic group also included two or three other men. On a *good* night each musician could expect about six dollars.

Another favorite hangout was Dan Wall's Chili Parlor on Seventh Avenue, between 139th Street and 140th Street, where Bird and a guitarist named Biddy Fleet often "jammed" in the backroom of the restaurant. One night when working over *Cherokee* Parker hit upon his theory of using the higher chordal tones as important melody tones and backing them with substitute harmony. Parker told Leonard Feather later: "For instance, we'd find that you could play a relative major, using the right inversion against a seventh chord and we played around with flatted fifths."

The "relative major" (related major triad is clearer) he spoke of is the triad formed by the three highest chord intervals—the ninth, augmented eleventh, and thirteenth (Example (A) below).

Ex. 1 (A) and (B)

The "flatted fifth" relationship is that two seventh chords a flatted fifth apart, each having a flatted fifth in the chord, contain exactly the same notes. In example (B) above the F-flat is enharmonically the same as E and the D-double-flat is enharmonically the same as C. The other two notes of each chord are also the same. The "flatted fifth" of one of the chords is the root of the other and vice-versa. One chord could be substituted at random for the other and variations built on either at a given spot in a tune. By using the principle at (A) against the substitute (Gb7b5) in example (B) an even "further out" effect can be obtained.

Ex. 2 (C)

All effects give the feeling of polytonality or "many keys". At (A) we have D Major against a C Seventh; at (B) a Gb7b5 against a C7b5; and at (C) a Gb7 against an Ab major triad; each a substitution for a simple C7 chord! The augmented eleventh and the flatted fifth of a chord are enharmonically the same, and the best practice is to label them as to *usage*. If the principle is as at (A) or (C), an augmented eleventh is the most correct terminology, but if used as at (B), the best nomenclature is a "flatted fifth."

The above principles and others based upon them were the harmonic foundation of the music later to be dubbed "BeBop." Perhaps the most important thing to see at this point in Bird's life is that his music was formulated from a *harmonic* basis; his lovely melodies were born from the underlying harmony and from the substitute principles mentioned above.

Indeed, the young Bird was gingerly trying his jazz wings. He seemed to have come from nowhere, but in truth, he had jumped from a tree that had deep jazz roots. Most birds, real and metaphorical, moreover, usually carry seeds to new places; the new tree, because of conditions, sometimes appears slightly different form the old, but the roots retain the same general characteristics. The early Bird followed the usual ornithological pattern—the seed was sown.

CHAPTER II

KANSAS CITY ROOTS
The Jay McShann Band
(1939-1942)

One of the best methods of rendering study agreeable is to live with able men, and to suffer all those pangs of inferiority which the want of knowledge always inflicts.

Sydney Smith—Second Lecture on the
Conduct of Understanding

In late summer, 1939, Bird left New York for a hotel job in Annapolis, Maryland, with entertainer Banjo Burney. At the conclusion of the engagement, he returned to Kansas City and soon after rejoined Jay McShann. Sometime in this period, while World War II began in Europe, a session took place at the Booker T. Hotel; John Birks "Dizzy" Gillespie, then on the Cab Calloway band, was the trumpet player, and Parker was the altoist. Kansas City, which had spawned so much jazz, was an apt place for the first meeting of the two titans who were later to become fast friends, sometime rivals, and leading exponents of a new jazz style. In all probability, some of the ideas that would become bebop's harmonic foundation were first discussed at the piano of the Kansas City hotel.

The reason for Bird's return to Kansas City is unclear. Some sources say that McShann sent for him; others, as has been mentioned (notes—Chapter I), place the funeral at this time. It seems logical, however, that Parker, having little monetary or artistic success in New York, would return home, where his musical reputation and contacts would present better opportunities for finding satisfying work. McShann, in later interviews, makes no mention of "sending" for Parker, but does mention that he remembers him being with Harlan Leonard for about a year before he joined the McShann Band. McShann places the Harlan Leonard stay as coming after Bird's New York excursion, but places the date as "the last of 1938." As the Leonard band was a usual "stop" for Bird when he was home, however, it is quite probable that he was on the band for short periods during both 1938 and 1939. He became a regular member of McShann's group in early 1940.

The McShann band was the last of the excellent groups to emerge from Kansas City, or from the Middle Southwest, in the 1925-1945 period. Some of these groups, however, are unknown to the casual jazz listener or to the person mainly interested in Parker's music. A brief historical account is necessary, therefore, to familiarize the reader with some of the names and to set the background of Parker's music.

Bennie Moten, born in 1894, was the pioneer of Midwest big band music. He began as a baritone player in his high school band, although he had also studied piano during his early years. Later the piano became his main instrument, and in 1918, he was leading a ragtime Joplinesque trio. In 1923, he jumped to a six-man New Orleans-type format with three horns (trumpet, clarinet, trombone) and three rhythm (piano, drums, and banjo). About half of the repertoire was blues, as substantiated by their Okeh recordings, and the style can be related to the King Oliver band, then in Chicago. In 1924, Moten added a tuba and also brought in Harlan Leonard on saxophone. The 1925 recordings are instructive; they reflect the New Orleans influence, but make more use of the saxophone. Four years later, after the band had expanded to a "big band" format of eleven men, William (Count) Basie and Eddie Durham (of later Jimmy Lunceford fame) left Walter Page's Oklahoma Blue Devils, another Midwest band, and joined Moten. Basie can first be heard with Moten on recordings made in October, 1929. In 1930, trumpeter Oran (Hot Lips) Page and blues-bawling vocalist Jimmy Rushing joined the group. Moten toured the east in 1931, and in December, 1932, he made a group of innovative records. Walter Page had given up his own band and joined Moten, giving the group the drive of his pulsating bass. The light four-four swing generated mainly by the bass began a new concept that has since influenced all jazz; this rhythmic concept certainly laid the groundwork for Parker and the "boppers." The prime example of the 1932 Victors is *Toby*, a swinging riff tune. Roughly contemporary with Moten was the Alphonse Trent group, which toured mainly in Texas, Arkansas and Oklahoma. The best known sidemen were Stuff Smith, jazz violin; and Snub Mosely, trombone.

In 1935, Count Basie took over the Moten band; this was the group that young Parker heard in his nightly rounds. The 1936 recordings featuring Lester Young—*Shoeshine Boy, Evenin', Boogie-Woogie*—obviously influenced Parker, as did the *Honeysuckle Rose* recorded for Decca in 1937. After the recording of *One O'Clock Jump*, in July, 1937, Basie went on to national fame.

Walter Page, who played bass and doubled on tuba and baritone sax, formed his Oklahoma Blue Devils in 1926, and Count Basie joined the group in 1928. The group recorded in 1929 and featured solos on both alto and clarinet by Buster Smith. Willie Lewis was the piano player as Basie had left earlier to join Moten. Page disbanded his group in 1931 and joined Moten also. In addition to working with Page and leading his own group, Buster Smith was a sideman with Basie and later wrote arrangements for Gene Krupa and Harlan Leonard.

George E. Lee, the singer-leader who befriended Parker, was on the local music scene from about 1924. He recorded in 1927 with nine pieces—including his sister, Julia, on piano—and also in 1929 with a group that included Budd Johnson on tenor and Clarence Taylor on alto. His recorded material sounds very "progressive" for the period, and careful listening makes one understand Lee's sympathy for Bird's early efforts. A good example is *Ruff Scufflin'* from 1929, which gives an insight into how Lee's "Ozarks" band, a few years after, sounded.

The Kansas City Rockets were first led by Jimmy Keith, the tenorist. Parker's infamous first attempt at jamming was with this group and he ran in the same general circles. The band was taken over and drilled by the conservatory-trained Tommy Douglas (Parker's clarinet experience came at this time) in 1936. Because of Douglas's constant hassles with the union, however, the group was relatively unsuccessful until 1938, when Harlan Leonard took the helm. Many of the same musicians, including Bird, were with the band—on and off—throughout the various leaderships. In 1940, Leonard took his Rockets to New York as one of the six bands that opened the Golden Gate Ballroom in Harlem. The Rockets' 1940 recordings show solo examples of Bird's early associates—trumpeter James Ross and trombonist Fred Beckett. Both men display good improvisational skill and, as was the case with most Midwest musicians of the period, a strong command of their instruments. Tadd Dameron, a later associate of Bird, did many of the arrangements.

Another great Midwest band, which lasted from 1929 to 1948, was Andy Kirk's Twelve Clouds of Joy. Tenorist Dick Wilson and pianist Mary Lou Williams were mainstays. *Zonky*, a recording by a splinter group from the band, Six Men and a Girl, in 1940, shows a good example of typical Kansas City small group playing and gives a nice look at Wilson's tenor style. During the mid-Thirties, when Basie's group was at the Reno, the Kirk band spent much of each summer season at Fairyland Amusement Park.

The McShann band was heavily blues-oriented and featured the boogie-woogie-tinged, barrelhouse piano style of the leader. Nicknamed "Hootie" because of his fondness for "hootch," McShann was an amiable man and a good musician. The band comes through in its early recordings as very clean in the section work and very vibrant in the jazz solos. Besides Parker, William Scott (tenor), John Jackson (alto), and Buddy Anderson (trumpet) were also capable soloists, as was the rough-toned Bob Gould on trombone. The bulk of arranging and composing was done by Scott, and the lead trumpet work was handled by Orville "Piggy" Minor, who was also a competent soloist. The band totaled eleven pieces—four saxes four brass, and a rhythm section held down by Gene Ramey, bass, and Gus Johnson, drums. The fourth saxophone was Bob Mabane, a Herschel Evans-type soloist, and the third trumpet chair was held by Harold Bruce, basically a "section" player. The almost all-blues vocals were done by Walter Brown, Bird's colleague from the Deans of Swing.

Upon joining McShann's group, Parker told the pianist that the old habits were gone; that he had "straightened up." McShann placed Parker in charge of the four-man saxophone section and Bird did a creditable job of rehearsing them and taking charge. He insisted on promptness and was prompt himself. He began trying some arranging and composing, and his *Yardbird* Suite, then titled *What Price Love*, became a standard "chart" in the McShann book. The fact that he attempted some writing serves as a good reminder of how much he had learned from his studies in the Ozarks.

Parker was also the "joker" of the band, keeping everyone happy with clever coined phrases, practical jokes, and musical humor. He was also the initiator of the constant sparetime jam sessions that took place almost anywhere; he was eager to transmit his new-found ideas to others.

After spending the first half of 1940 at the Century Room and the summer at Fairyland Park, both controlled by McShann's agent, John Tumino, the band began a tour of Missouri, Kansas, and Oklahoma. While in Wichita, McShann was contacted by the manager of radio station KFBI, Fred Higginson, a past acquaintance. Higginson suggested that the band make some broadcast transcriptions for KFBI and McShann agreed. The group was scaled down to an octet, probably for financial reasons, and on the Saturday and Monday following Thanksgiving made their first recordings.

* * *

Recording—November 30, 1940—Station KFBI, Wichita, Kansas— Jay McShann Band—Orville Minor, B. Anderson (tp); Bud Gould (tb); C. Parker (as); William Scott (ts); J McShann (p); Gene Ramey (b); Gus Johnson (d).

I Found A New Baby	Onyx 221
Body and Soul	Onyx 221

The first tune is taken at a brisk tempo and opens with the leader's piano plus the rhythm section; McShann only hints at the melody while playing a barreling chorus. Next comes Minor with the saxes playing a legato riff behind him; at the end of the bridge, he shows a Parker influence—a whole tone scale. Bird plays the third chorus backed by staccato brass, and his ideas are very linear and fast; in the bridge one can hear the patterns based on the major scale, a familiar Parker device, emerging for the first time; his phrases begin after the beat at times—another device for which he later became famous. Gould plays a rough-edged solo, exhibiting some lip trills, and Scott sounds like a typical "Kansas City" tenor. McShann returns for the sixth chorus, and the whole group joins in on the last eight bars for a riffing ending.

Parker has the first chorus of *Body and Soul* to himself, at a ballad tempo. He stays close to the melody in the first "eight" (this term will be used throughout this work for eight-bar section), but uses double time in the second. The bridge is fairly straight, but the final eight contains beautiful double time ideas that all seem to hang together. This final eight is the most mature-sounding effort out of all the tunes recorded in Wichita; even someone familiar with his work could mistake this section for a much later effort. During Minor's chorus the rhythm doubles until the final eight, which returns to the original tempo; McShann takes the ballad home with an extra eight bars of the "A" section.

The general feeling of the tunes recorded in Wichita—this set and the next— is that of a small "jump band"; there is plenty of solo room and an over-all feeling of freedom. This is not to say that the performances are slip-shod, however, for the band is very "together" and the riffs and the solo order seem well-discussed. The recordings are good jazz of the period—not merely commercial trivia; they are well worth owning as a representation of Kansas City jazz, as well as a documentation of Parker's playing during this period.

Recording—December 2, 1940—Radio Station KFBI—Wichita, Kansas—Jay McShann Band—C. Parker (as); Bob Mabane (ts); B. Anderson, Orville Minor (tp); Bud Gould (trb, vln); Jay McShann (p); Gene Ramey (b); Gus Johnson (d).

Moten Swing	Onyx 221
Coquette	Onyx 221
Lady Be Good	Onyx 221
Wichita Blues	Onyx 221
Honeysuckle Rose	Onyx 221

The opening ensemble chorus, following the piano introduction, on *Moten Swing* is undoubtedly arranged. Bird plays the first solo and sounds a bit Lesterish, but still original. He employs a wild group of triplets at one point with excellent effect. There is something of an older era in his sound, but his turns of phrase predict the future. Anderson and Mabane follow Parker, with Minor splitting Mabane's offering, and the ensemble takes it out, complete with tag. Anderson, usually considered an early exponent of new sounds, seems to be under a Roy Eldridge influence, at least on this tune.

Parker opens *Coquette* with a relaxed theme statement for sixteen bars; he sounds not unlike Willie Smith. Anderson blows the bridge, and Bird returns with more melody until the turn-around bars, where he tries some nice variations. Gould plays a chorus after which McShann returns to the bridge. The tune goes home with Minor blowing over a "head" riff.

Lady Be Good is essentially a succession of solos with a riff out-chorus. Bird plays the third chorus, following Mabane and Minor, and plays an excellent solo. He pays a small debt to Lester Young and also tries a phrase that later became famous as *Opus de Funk* during the late Fifties; the same phrase also became the main motif of *Mr. Chips*, a tune done by the Billy Eckstine band during the period that Parker was with them.

The main soloist in *Wichita*, a twelve-bar slow blues, is Gould, in a Teagardenish mood. Beneath the trombone, the band intones the melody that Parker, in 1947, used as his theme to *The Hymn*. Parker does not solo.

Honeysuckle Rose opens with a humorous "louder and funnier" band chant alternating with drums. This type of routine was originated by Alphonse Trent; and Gould, as Dan Morgenstern states in the album notes, sounds very much like Trent's violinist, Stuff Smith, complete with double-stop effects. Parker plays the fourth chorus and again gives us a glimpse of his use of the major scale in improvisation. There is a coolness to Bird's sound on this tune, predicting the altoists of the Fifties. In the final chorus, Bird plays the bridge, sandwiched between the riffing "A" sections, and on the final dominant, he intones a whole-tone scale based on Gb against C7 (flatted fifth principle). Hearing it in this context lets the listener know what Bird's contemporaries meant when they accused him of "running out of the key"; he was truly ahead of his time. The full-chorus solo contains the same opening phrase used by Lester Young on the 1937 Basie recording of *Honeysuckle*, and is the strongest early example of the young influence on Parker.

Don Schlitten and Onyx Records deserve congratulations for the reissue of these long-unavailable Wichita transcriptions; they fill a void in the Parker record legacy. A similar issue was done in England by Tony Williams (Spotlite 120), but the Onyx issue is recommended for the excellent notes of Dan Morgenstern.

* * *

Following the Wichita recordings, the McShann Band continued throughout the Southwest, playing ballroom dates and college dances. In the early spring of 1941, the band returned to Kansas City and worked for six weeks at Casa Fiesta, a site McShann had played occasionally during his formative period.

During April, a tour of one nighters throughout the Southeast culminated in New Orleans. Meanwhile, John Tumino—with the promotional help of Dave Dexter, *Down Beat* magazine's Midwest correspondent—had turned the band into a successful, saleable product. While in New Orleans, McShann received word that the Decca label had asked Tumino to have the band record a group of sides during their swing through Dallas, within a week or so after the New Orleans stint. Gene Ramey speaks of the news of their first recording contract in Reisner's *Bird: The Legend of Charlie Parker*:

> We were at a club in New Orleans on one occasion,...when we were informed by Decca that we were due for a record session in a couple of weeks. McShann suggested that we do something real quick. After beginning with a little jam session, we began to improvise. I believe we succeeded in less than forty-five minutes in completing *Jumpin' Blues*. It had been [after the rehearsal] entirely orchestrated by Bird...[1]

The Jumpin' Blues, however, was not recorded until 1942. Ramey, therefore, could have been referring to *Hootie Blues*, although Parker is listed as the composer as well as the arranger (McShann is given co-composer credit, but it was customary for band leaders—in return for the exposure they could give the composition— to share composing rights with their sidemen-composers). *Jumpin'* is the type of tune that could have originated as a "head," however, and McShann is listed as the sole composer (it was also customary for leaders to assume rights to "head" arrangements). Another possibility, therefore, is that *Jumpin'* developed as Ramey says it did, but was rejected by Dave Kapp, Decca recording supervisor, for the first session, as happened, according to McShann,[2] with *Yardbird Suite*.

* * *

Recording—April 30, 1941—Dallas, Texas
Jay McShann Band—H. Bruce, B. Anderson, O. Minor (tp); John Jackson, C. Parker (as.); H. Ferguson, B. Mabane (ts.); Jay McShann (p.); G. Ramey (b); Gus Johnson (dr.); Walter Brown (vcl.).

Swingmatism	Decca DL (7) 9236
Hootie Blues	Decca DL (7) 9236
Dexter Blues	Decca DL (7) 9236

Swingmatism and *Dexter Blues* were composed by William Scott, who played tenor on the first Wichita recording. Scott had left the band during the last Kansas City stay to pursue a career as a radio technician. Parker solos on *Swingmatism*, an intriguing tune that begins it's sixteen-bar sections in the minor and modulates to the parallel major, through the use of a diminished chord, for the final cadence.

The Parker solo is sixteen bars long, and although not spectacular, it is charming in its simplicity and exacting in its harmonic implications. McShann, making allusions to *Topsy*, is the only other soloist on *Swingmatism*.

Hootie Blues contains a Walter Brown vocal, and is a traditional Eb blues. Bird's one chorus is spare blues playing, but is broken by sixteenth-note patterns that are uncharacteristic of the period; in the fourth bar of the blues, the solo also contains a phrase used extensively by later improvisors:

Ex. 3 Hootie Blues - Bar 4

The phrase is built from the "blues scale" (containing the flat 3rd, flat 5th, and flat 7th) and is notable for the double timing effect of the sixteenth notes. The theme to *Hootie* is carried by the brass, with a sax riff in the background, and even in this simple arrangement, Parker showed his penchant for moving the rhythm at unexpected places.

John Jackson and McShann solo on *Dexter Blues*, a traditional C Blues written for jazz writer Dave Dexter, who helped McShann obtain the Decca contract (Parker and Dexter were old adversaries, as Dexter had been the butt of some of Bird's practical jokes in Kansas City: hot foots, wallet snatches, and false rumors). Jackson's alto sound is more liquid than Bird's and his ideas are less adventurous, but his solo is well played in his own blues style. Orville Minor opens the tune with a rough-toned growling solo that sets the mood for the other soloists.

In addition to the big band cuts, McShann also recorded *Hold 'Em Hootie* and *Vine Street Boogie* with just the rhythm section and featured Walter Brown on *Confessin' the Blues*, with rhythm accompaniment. *Confessin'* was a surprise hit with its earthy lyrics and its "stop time" effects in the first four bars of each vocal chorus; this tune, moreover, put the "blues band" label on McShann and made Walter Brown a potential "seller" for Dave Kapp and Decca Records. *Confessin' the Blues* was backed by *Hootie Blues* on the original 78 rpm record, and Decca 9236 contains the most recent reissue of the McShann-Brown classic.

In the Dallas set, we hear McShann's group in the classic "big band" format for the first time, and it is delightful. There is an unpretentious earthiness to the band, enhanced by the good musicianship of the players. Both blues (*Hootie* and *Dexter*) are fine examples of the transference of this form to the big band medium, and *Swingmatism* adds an original touch to this group of tunes. The set is a very healthy example of big band jazz, but is rarely heard by the general public or mentioned in jazz history.

* * *

In Texas, McShann "discovered" young Al Hibbler, the talented vocalist, who was then working with Boots and His Buddies, a local territorial band based in San Antonio. Parker and Hibbler became great friends, and Bird remained a Hibbler fan for the rest of his life. The acquisition of Hibbler gave McShann three competent vocalists, for he had also added Bill Nolan, an adequate balladeer, who was usually overshadowed by Brown's earthy blues-bawling. Hibbler, however soon was doing the majority of the ballad work, and Nolan, therefore, left the band.

During the summer of 1941, the band stayed in the Midwest, touring the Kansas and Missouri summer spots. In the meantime, at the urging of Kapp, the powerful General Amusement Corporation had assumed the band's booking management. Consequently, the band traveled to Chicago in mid-autumn for its second Decca session; the set was to heavily feature Brown, in an attempt to capitalize on the popularity of *Confessin' the Blues*. Eight tunes were planned, all featuring Brown's blues vocals. Parker is heard on one of the titles—*One Woman's Man*—and two others, with rhythm only, are also found on the Decca LP 9236—*Red River Blues* and *Hootie's Ignorant Oil*. Brown's *Red River Blues* is pleasant but trite, although *Hootie's Ignorant Oil* (a colloquialism for whiskey) is a virile, boogie-woogie stomper, with excellent and original drum work by Gus Johnson. An earlier "live" version of the *One Woman's Man* is rumored to exist, but has never been issued commercially.

* * *

Recording—November 18, 1941—Chicago
Jay McShann Band—J. McShann (p), Gene Ramey (b), Gus Johnson (dr), Walter Brown (vcl), Chas. Parker (as), Orville Minor (tp), probably J.T. Baird (tb).

One Woman's Man   Decca DL (7) 9236

McShann opens the tune with a piano introduction, and the three horns then state a simple hymn-like blues theme (usually there is no trombone player listed in the personnel, but careful listening will reveal one in the ensemble). Brown sings four blues choruses, with piano obligato on the first two, alto backing the third, and trumpet backing the fourth. Parker is subtle in his backing, starting with an octave jump on the fifth of the scale and intoning the flat 7th in the classic place—the fourth bar. In the eighth bar, Bird uses an ascending phrase of the *type* that he used in the ninth bar of *Hootie Blues*; each spot involves the implied harmony of a minor-seventh chord, and Bird's melody ascends the chord to its ninth and then drops back a step to the root. Listening to these two spots will give the listener some insight into Bird's harmonic thinking at this early stage.

* * *

After the November session for Decca, the band remained in Chicago for an engagement at the Regal Theatre; they were continuing eastward for a prestigious engagement at the Savoy Ballroom in New York City. Parker drove the instrument truck, with Hibbler for a companion, for the whole eastward trek. Two weeks into the tour, however, the McShann group, along with the rest of the world, was shocked at the Pearl Harbor attack and America's subsequent war declaration. Nevertheless, on Friday, January 10, 1942, the band opened at the exclusive 140th Street ballroom and alternated the bandstand with Lucky Millinder's Orchestra. Dizzy Gillespie was in the Millinder trumpet section, and he and Bird resumed their discussions from the Kansas City hotel and experimented with their new ideas both on and off the bandstand. Gene Ramey states "...Gillespie practically worked with the band. We always kept a seat on the bandstand for him. . . ."³ Some good recorded examples of Gillespie with Millinder are *Mason Flyer* and *Little John Special* (the riff from this piece later became *Salt Peanuts*), which were done in July.

Parker worked after-hours at Monroe's, his old haunt from his previous New York visit, and began receiving some recognition from other musicians. Kenny Clarke, one of the fathers of modern drumming, states, "We went to listen to Bird at Monroe's for no other reason except that he sounded like Pres [Lester Young]. That is, until we found out that he had something of his own to offer."⁴

The feature numbers for Bird with the McShann band were *Cherokee* and *Clap Hands, Here Comes Charlie. Cherokee*, a Ray Noble tune copyrighted in 1938 and later made famous by Charlie Barnet, was a difficult tune for improvisation, especially in the bridge or "B" section, which went through several distantly related keys. The chords were all logical ii7-V7-I progressions in the different keys, however, and Bird's theoretical studies in the Ozarks made them easy to hear and to execute. One can also relate Bird's early studies to *Clap Hands*, a novelty with an "A" section harmonically based on *I Got Rhythm* and a "B" section containing the harmony of the *Honeysuckle Rose* bridge. Unfortunately, no recordings of these showpieces exist with the McShann Band, but there is a version of *Cherokee* recorded most likely at Monroe's around this period.

* * *

Recording—circa 1942—probably at Monroe's, New York
C. Parker (as), unknown piano, bass, drums, clarinet, trumpet.
    Cherokee   Onyx 221
    As the horns state the theme in harmony, the piano moves through obligato improvisations; the piano has the bridge alone, and then the beginning format returns. Bird begins his improvisation with the second chorus, and on the third chorus, he alternates his ideas during the "A" sections with a riff from the other horns. His solo, although innovative for the time, is surely not the multi-noted excursion that he would take on *KoKo*, based on the same chords, only three years hence. In fact, when comparing this version to the 1945 cut, one must marvel at the rapid blossoming of conception that had taken place in the short period.

Bird seems to be reaching for something in this solo which he never finds. Perhaps his own statement about his early efforts, "I could hear it, but I couldn't play it," is the best way to explain his efforts on this particular tune. The chunk-chunk, "two" feeling of the rhythm section (despite the fact that the bass player plays in four) does not help the overall feel of the tune, and the recording, originally a "home-mader" of the Jerry Newman collection, is noisy.

Dan Morgenstern suggests in the notes to the Onyx LP that a good guess on the recording date would be after Parker left McShann, because of the presence of an arrangement with a feature spot. The arrangement, however, is very simple and could have been either "learned" or sketched out and read in a very short time. Regardless, this track, especially when compared with the later (1945) version, is an interesting study for improvisors who are just beginning.

* * *

While in New York, during the winter of 1942, McShann and his group worked at the Apollo Theatre. The group then embarked on a Midwestern tour and returned to New York for a quick recording session in July. The recording ban of the American Federation of Musicians, which was to be imposed in August because of a royalty dispute with the record companies, sent a last minute panic through the industry, and caused much recording activity.

The country was also in a panic, as the American forces in the Philippines had been forced to surrender, and the draft was uprooting many families. Parker, however, is rumored to have been classified as 4-F (unacceptable) by the Selective Service. This is hard to substantiate, but with his many dissipations, surely, he probably would not have been able to pass a stringent physical examination. Another possibility, of course, is that he simply sidestepped the draft, as he did with all unpleasant matters.

Interestingly, the McShann band as a whole was relatively unaffected by the draft. Since the 1941 recordings, there had been only two replacements: Bob Merrill on trumpet for Harold Bruce; and Freddy Culliver, the tenorist from the Deans of Swing, for Harry Ferguson. Jimmy Coe, baritone sax; Lucky Enois, guitar; and Lawrence Anderson, trombone; however, were added to the basic personnel.

* * *

Recording—July 2, 1942—New York
Jay McShann Band—B. Merrill, B. Anderson, Orville Minor (tp); L. Anderson, J. Baird (tb); John Jackson, C. Parker (as); Fred Culliver, Bob Mabane (ts); James Coe (bs); McShann (p); Lucky Enois (g); G. Ramey (b); Gus Johnson (dr); Walter Brown, Al Hibbler (vcl).

Lonely Boy Blues	Decca DL (7) 9236
Get Me On Your Mind	Decca DL (7) 9236
The Jumpin' Blues	Decca DL (7) 9236
Sepian Bounce	Decca DL (7) 9236

The Jumpin' Blues—the "head" that Bird orchestrated—begins with a twelve-bar chorus by McShann and then moves to a sax melody with brass responses for two choruses. The fourth chorus is Bird's improvisation, and he starts it with the phrase that later became the opening of *Ornithology*, his composition harmonically based on *How High the Moon*. Indeed, the solo is short, but the ideas are cohesive; there is no better example of a medium tempo Bird improvisation in the McShann recordings. After Bird's solo, Walter Brown sings three full blues choruses and is followed by a "dog fight" chorus, with saxes and brass interchanging. The final chorus, echoing the beginning, is saxes with brass responses again, and a short coda ends the tune.

If one judges from the few clues in the introduction, the alto soloist on *Lonely Boy* seems to be Parker, but the solo itself is based on simple blues phrases, with almost no space-filling embellishments. Therefore, one cannot eliminate the possibility of John Jackson being the soloist. The reference that Ross Russell makes in his book, *Bird Lives*, to this particular solo is ludicrous. Russell states: "...Charlie overblew F Sharp, half a step above the natural register of the Saxophone, with striking results. It was another first."[5] A few facts, however, prove this statement false: *Lonely Boy* is in the key of D concert (unusual for a blues tune—probably Eb, but sounding lower because of recording procedures), and the highest note in the concert key is F sharp. But on the alto saxophone—a transposing instrument—the note is D sharp, well within the acceptable range (even in the higher key of Eb concert, it is still only an E on the saxophone). The solo itself, moreover, is so bland that one cannot positively attribute it to Parker on hearing alone, and yet Russell perpetuates a myth about it! In fact, many saxophonists use false fingerings to achieve notes outside the normal range—notes called harmonics—but there is absolutely no evidence of this technique on *Lonely Boy*.

Get Me On Your Mind is Al Hibbler's first example on record. It contains no Parker solo, but there is a good 24-bar McShann stride solo. In the first chorus, the "A" sections have saxes backing the vocal along with piano obligato, and the bridge accompaniment is by muted brass. The second chorus is McShann's until the final eight-bar section, which returns to the vocal, with Hibbler ending on the major 7th of the scale.

Bird plays two separate eight-bar solos on *Sepian Bounce*, an *I Got Rhythm* derivative; his tone is lighter than the big sound associated with him in his later work. The effect, however, is pleasant, and the solos speak of things to come. In the Parker legacy, this tune is the first example of Bird blowing on the chords that later would become a standard part of his vocabulary.

After the McShann recordings, we do not hear Bird again on record until the September, 1944 recording with Tiny Grimes, over two years later. Although we only have small solos from the McShann period from which to judge, a comparison of the two dates (they both contain a blues and an *I Got Rhythm* derivative) shows an incredible amount of development towards his mature playing.

* * *

Recording—probably circa 1942—Chicago
Jay McShann Band—Personnel probably like preceding recording.

You Say Forward, and I'll March	Spotlite (Eng.) 120
Lonely Boy Blues	Spotlite (Eng.) 120
Vine Street Boogie	Spotlite (Eng.) 120
Jump the Blues (The Jumpin' Blues)	Spotlite (Eng.) 120
Theme (One O'Clock Jump)	Spotlite (Eng.) 120
Sweet Georgia Brown	Spotlite (Eng.) 120
Wrap Your Troubles in Dreams	Spotlite (Eng.) 120
Bottle It	Spotlite (Eng.) 120
Theme (One O'Clock Jump)	Spotlite (Eng.) 120

These recordings are difficult to date; they were originally done, however, for Armed Forces Radio Service, Discs No. 71 and 72. The two-date set seems to be from 1942, if one considers the low numbers on the AFRS discs, but it is listed on the Spotlite issue as "circa 1943." The alto soloist could be either Jackson or Parker, as they admired each other's musicianship and learned from each other. If it is Parker, the recording date, of course, would be prior to mid-1942. There is too little solo space, however, to make a positive judgement.

There are alto solos on *Lonely Boy, Jump the Blues*, and *Bottle It. Lonely Boy* sounds much the same as the "studio" alto solo recorded in July—a bit too bland for positive identification. The *Jump the Blues* solo, however, starts with the *Ornithology* phrase—or rather a hint at it—and has phrases beginning after a beat, as Bird was prone to do. On *Bottle It*, the alto also sounds a bit like Parker, especially the scalar passage that ends the solo; the "biting" quality, which Jackson did not have in his sound, is present on this tune. Incidentally, the key on *Lonely Boy* on this date is Eb concert, supporting the idea that recording procedures were responsible for the key sounding lower on the July date (a recording speed that is slightly slow would, of course, lower the pitch).

The band itself sounds excellent on this set, with McShann and a tenorist turning in some nice solos. *Vine Street* is a "boogie" piano solo that also features some bass work by Ramey; the final three choruses are saxes with answering brass in a constantly building crescendo. *Sweet Georgia Brown* is a tenor show-piece, and *Wrap Your Troubles in Dreams* features tenor, trumpet, and trombone improvisations, with a nice McShann solo and some fine sax section work. On the final *Theme*, guitar improvisations can be heard over the band (sometimes Les Paul is listed as the guitarist).

Included on the Spotlite issue are the Wichita transcriptions and the *Cherokee* cut from Monroe's.

* * *

When the July recordings in New York were completed, the McShann band embarked on a westward tour which would end back in Kansas City. Parker was beginning to revert to his old habits, however, and the "pushers" were beginning to follow him everywhere. Finally, at the Paradise Theatre in Detroit, things came to a head. Jay McShann remembered:

> He had a little too much that day and we had to carry him off the bandstand and lay him on a table....When he came to, I told him, "Bird, you done got back on your kick again, and so I've got to let you go." Andy Kirk gave him a lift to New York.[6]

The Detroit incident ended Parker's affiliation with McShann completely, but the McShann band and Kansas City jazz in general had already heavily influenced his jazz style and strengthened his musicianship. The time spent next to John Jackson, for instance, caused Bird to sharpen his reading ability; he had told McShann: "...I'm going to woodshed. This cat is makin' a fool out of me. If I miss a note at the performance you got the privilege of fining me."[7] Obviously, Jackson's solo style also influenced Parker (Bird's theories also rubbed off on Jackson, of course), as evidenced by the difficulty of identifying them on the McShann recordings. Bird, however, later expanded upon the basic style, although Jackson stayed relatively the same (the Jackson solos with the Billy Eckstine band in 1945 attest to this fact). Where musical discipline was concerned, however, Jackson was invaluable; he taught Bird the finesse of section playing and many other technical elements of big band craftsmanship.

Craftsmanship is indeed the key word where Kansas City jazz is concerned; the Midwesterners handed down the "tricks to trade" just as craftsman had done for centuries. Their pride in basic musical skills—from reading music to phrasing properly—is evident in all recorded examples, and the high level of individual and collective musicianship is amazing.

Furthermore, to gain an insight into Kansas City jazz, is to gain an insight into Charlie Parker; for the relaxed four-four time, the riff, the blues form, the "medium bounce" tempo, the *I Got Rhythm* and *Honeysuckle Rose* improvisational frames, and the over-all atmosphere of the Kansas City session all left an indelible mark on him as he moved ahead to new musical frontiers.

CHAPTER III

OUT OF THE APPLE
On the Road with Hines, Eckstine, and Others
(Late 1942-Fall 1944)

> The use of traveling is to regulate imagination by reality, and, instead of thinking how things may be, to see them as they are.

Samuel Johnson—Piozzi's Johnsonia

Back in "The Apple" Bird resumed his experiments. He shuttled between Monroe's at 198 West 134th Street, and Minton's Playhouse on 118th Street. Teddy Hill, a Thirties bandleader (Dizzy Gillespie made his earliest recording with him), was the manager at Minton's; he encouraged the sessions and gave the experimenters *carte blanche.* At Minton's, Bird's colleagues often included Kermit Scott, tenor sax; John Simmons, bass; Thelonious Monk, piano; and Kenny Clarke or Kansas Fields, drums.

New harmonic concepts were taking shape and being absorbed by men of the same kind of mind. Gillespie was a frequent visitor, as were Coleman Hawkins, Roy Eldridge, Charlie Christian, and other "oldsters" who were sympathetic with the new experiments. The atmosphere of a Kansas City jam session was recreated, but with new "blowing" tunes, such as *All The Things You Are*—tunes with difficult progressions that lent themselves well to substitute harmonies and extended improvisations. But the transition that was taking place was really a transformation of certain musical truths into a new way of stating them, rather than an abrupt revolutionary break from tradition. Nevertheless, while most of the general public danced to Goodman and Miller, new sounds were in the air. The underground, as usual, was years ahead of the times and was searching for directions that would allow jazz the freedom of movement it so desperately needed.

The men who forged the new music were interested in finding freedom for improvisation. A small group would give time for less arranged passages and more extended individual solos. This was, of course, a revolt against the large band format that had been the central movement of the "swing" period. Parker, Gillespie, and the other forerunners of the movement all gained their necessary foundations in

35

big bands, however, and learned their disciplines well. The constant reading of intricate arrangements honed their sight reading to a fine edge, and the ability to blend with other instruments was so natural from sectional playing that it became intuitive (the blending ability can be heard in the Parker-Gillespie unison lines recorded during 1945).

Parker spent his years from age 20 to 24 working with "name" bands (McShann, Hines, Eckstine—plus occasional stints with others) and his Kansas City days, during his teens, were also spent partly as a section player (Deans of Swing, Tommy Douglas, Buster Smith, Harlan Leonard). Gillespie came up with Teddy Hill and Cab Calloway and also did some time with Ella Fitzgerald (Chick Webb's Band), Lucky Millinder, and Les Hite before teaming with Bird on the Hines and Eckstine bands.

Indeed, the experimenters were coming from within the ranks to expand and develop what they had learned in their formative years. Unfortunately, this was not true of many of the musicians who later attached themselves to the new music. Some of them lacked experience at any other phase of music than "Bop" (the accepted name that evolved from the original "Bebop" label) and therefore had no relation to music as a whole. Instead of originating, they were merely copying what Parker and the other innovators played. It was this clichéd playing which led to "Bop's" criticism, but, as in every art, the truth remained and the rest vanished. Stan Kenton, much maligned by black-only oriented critics and over-idealized by the white middle-class hipsters, contributed a lot of the new music to the big band itself during these transitional years. Most revealing is that in 1941 Kenton recorded a transcription for MacGregor titled *Tribute to a Flatted Fifth*; Parker's seed had grown quickly from its "chili house" beginning.

As Christmas 1942 approached, Bird joined the Earl Hines Orchestra, replacing Budd Johnson on tenor sax. Benny Harris, Gillespie, and other "session buddies" of Bird's had been bugging Hines to get Parker for some time, and when he was dismissed from the McShann group in Detroit, Bird had spoken to Hines about coming on the band. When Johnson left, Hines bought Parker a tenor to fill the gap.

The Hines Band became a melting pot for those musicians interested in new musical developments. Bennie Green on trombone and Billy Eckstine on vocals were supporters of the "Bop" movement, as was drummer Shadow Wilson. Gillespie and Parker devoted much of their spare time to playing theoretical exercises together; they would then try to utilize parts of the exercise in actual music. Gillespie's famed minor excursion, *Night in Tunisa*, was composed during this period and titled by Hines—possibly because of the preponderance of North African "progress reports" in the daily war news (America had entered the African theater in November). The tune was later recorded by Sarah Vaughan using the title *Interlude* (so titled because of the difficult transition section in the composition).

Hines, the innovator of the twenties with his "horn style" piano and then-advanced harmonies, was sympathetic toward the developments of his young sideman, but a bit unsure as to what direction they were going to take. Lead altoist Scoops Carey rehearsed the band, however, and was well-liked by the younger musicians. Little can be said of Parker's tenor playing during this period, for no recorded evidence exists because of the recording ban imposed by the A.F. of M., but one can surmise from his two later recordings on the larger instrument (both with Miles Davis in 1947 and 1953) that he handled it well.

Hines himself said:

...I never heard so much tenor horn in my life...You know how the guy got all over that alto; you *know* that he was just as bad [meaning good] on tenor...Charlie was a good section man, and a very good reader...I mean, he was a *musician*.[1]

Parker's friend from the 1938 Chicago sessions, Andrew "Goon" Gardner, was the third alto player in the Hines band, and he and Bird exchanged many ideas. Gardner is spoken of by musicians as a creative thinker, but recorded documents are hard to find. Another experimenter was Benny Harris, one of the trumpet players, who collaborated with Parker in composing *Crazeology* and *Ornithology*.

Although an early experimenter himself (his duet with Louis Armstrong, *Weatherbird*, is a prime example), Hines had led conventional big bands throughout the Thirties. His 1943 band included a version of *The Easter Parade*, some violin and accordion solos by Angel Creasy, and a band vocal on *Down By the Old Mill Stream*. On the other hand, there were also some swinging riff tunes by Gillespie and some ballads and blues by Eckstine. The band seems to have been a pleasant mixture of the trite and the unique.

Hines, moreover, was something of a disciplinarian; he insisted on promptness, seriousness, and soberness. Bird, of course, resented the restrictions and rebelled against them; in fact, he never related well to Hines. Again, his lateness and bad habits plagued him; for example, he would sleep in the section during the show and need to be nudged awake for his featured solos. One well known "Bird-story" of this period is that Parker slept under the bandstand to avoid missing the matinee, but wound up sleeping through it instead! He was fined for the sleeping incidents and others, but it mattered little; he kept on with his undisciplined ways throughout his stay with Hines.

In mid-January 1943, the Hines group began its tour of the "theatre circuit" at the Apollo in New York. The band played a regular circuit, including Washington, Baltimore, Philadelphia, Detroit, and Chicago; and Bird and the other experimenters found many places to jam in each city. Two such sessions exist somewhere on tape, but as yet have not been issued to the public. They were both taped in Chicago, and one included Shorty McConnell, one of the Hines' trumpet players, along with Bird and an unknown rhythm section. Two of the titles on the McConnell session are rumored to be *Body and Soul* and *Shoe Swing*. The other session was at the Ritz Hotel featuring Diz, Bird, and Oscar Pettiford (on bass). This session was recorded by Red Cross, a friend of Billy Eckstine, and Parker later named a tune for Cross on his 1944 recording with Tiny Grimes.

The Hines band was lucky to be working so steadily, however, for most of the country was feeling the economic pinch of the war. Many commodities were rationed and others were not available at all. The crunch had even affected the nation's coinage: the steel penny, cursed by bartenders and storekeepers for its resemblance to the dime, was minted because of the shortage of copper, and silver had replaced nickel—another high-demand metal in wartime—in the five-cent piece.

In sports, Joe DiMaggio, the New York Yankee superstar, took a salary cut during the recently completed 1942 season, even though he had achieved an unbelievable feat during the preceding year—hitting safely in 56 consecutive games. Everything seemed to be affected by the wartime economy.

Parker's salary with Hines, however, was $105.00 per week, tops in his earnings so far. While in Washington at the Howard Theatre, during April, he met Geraldine Marguerite Scott and eventually married her. Geraldine was a pretty but irresponsible girl who slid into heavy drug use along with Bird. The two lived a wild, hotel-room marriage for a short time and then drifted apart without benefit of a legal divorce (after Parker's death, this short marriage would be the source of much entanglement in the estate settlement).

At the end of April, back in New York at the Apollo, a nineteen-year old girl singer named Sarah Vaughan became the featured girl vocalist; she also played "second" piano for Hines. Her rendition of *You Are My First Love* with Parker backing her received praise from many trade critics.

Parker's last days with the Hines band came during the summer on a package tour of army camps sponsored by Pabst Blue Ribbon Beer. The entourage was large, including comedians and several other acts; consequently, salaries suffered, and booking disputes cropped up quite often. Tiring of the constant hassles, Parker left Hines in August and worked for a short time with Sir Charles Thompson at the Crystal Caverns in Washington.

A mass exodus from the Hines band followed. Sarah Vaughan and Eckstine went out as singles, while Gillespie, with Oscar Pettiford, organized his own small group. Bird was originally in the group but had failed to gain an 802 (New York City) union card. He therefore returned home to Kansas City and formed a small group with Buddy Anderson, his trumpet-playing cohort from the McShann days. The group worked at Tutti Clarkin's Mayfair for the rest of the year.

While in Kansas City, Bird resumed his relationship with Rebecca, his former wife. There was good rapport—at least in the beginning—and when Parker decided to leave Kansas City for work in Chicago and St. Louis, Rebecca went with him.

In early 1944, the Gillespie-Pettiford group opened at the Onyx on New York's Fifty-Second Street with Don Byas, tenor sax; George Wallington, piano; and Max Roach, drums. Byas and Wallington, however, were later replaced by Budd Johnson and Clyde Hart.

Eckstine (the sign on the marquee said "X-stine") was across the street at the Yacht Club, alternating with Trummy Young's group. Gillespie, without Pettiford, moved his small combo to the Yacht Club, opposite Eckstine, in March. Diz had taught the singer trumpet during their tenure with Hines, and Eckstine sometimes "sat in" with the Gillespie combo for a tune or two. Diz and "B" (as Eckstine was known) formulated plans for a new band, fronted by Eckstine, that would use modern players exclusively. The band went into rehearsal, using as a nucleus the available New York modernists (many of the rehearsal musicians never became "road" members), and in April, they secured a record contract and did their first recordings; the label was DeLuxe.

Parker, meanwhile, had left Kansas City with Andy Kirk and then jobbed in Chicago and St. Louis with Carroll Dickinson and Noble Sissle, two big band leaders with their origins in the Twenties. In May, when the Yacht Club folded (it would soon reopen as the Downbeat), Eckstine contacted Parker and told him of the plans to take a band on the road. Bird, in turn, contacted some of the Midwest-based men that Eckstine wanted for his "dream band". The opening tour was to go to Texas, Kansas City, St. Louis and then return to the East. Some men, such as Buddy Anderson, and arranger Tadd Dameron, would join the band in Kansas City, and others such as Parker and drummer Art Blakey, would meet the group in St. Louis, where the band would go into serious rehearsal.

Gillespie was the "musical director" of the organization and Parker was to handle the reeds. The group was dedicated to the new sounds and harmonic structures that had been forged by Gillespie and Parker and the experimenters at Monroe's and Minton's. Tommy Potter, who was later to become one of Parker's regular bass players, was the mainstay of the rhythm section; Eckstine had met him at the Yacht Club when Potter was with Trummy Young.

Dameron's original compositions, arranged in his beautiful voicings, contributed another dimension to the band. *Cool Breeze* was one of his early charts, and later he did a memorable *Good Bait* in which he scored a Charlie Parker solo for the sax section. The other arrangers were trombonist Jerry Valentine and pianist John Malachi. Sarah Vaughan's singing, along with the leader's, contributed greatly to the band's success, and presented the new sounds in a different way—a vocal one. Eckstine had also learned the valve trombone (fingered the same as the trumpet) and he featured this instrument on certain tunes. Indeed, the band was truly representative of early modern sounds, but used an established medium—the big band—as a showcase.

In St. Louis, Buddy Anderson, ailing with tuberculosis, left the band and was temporarily replaced by 18-year old Miles Davis, who eventually became Parker's protegé and permanent trumpet player. Davis, from St. Louis, had been experimenting with the new sounds as he gigged with Eddie Randall's band; but he was far from a polished musician and he was shaken by playing with his heroes. After a few weeks in St. Louis, Davis was replaced by Marion Hazel. Davis's experience with the Eckstine band during July of 1944, however, pushed him to enter the Julliard School of Music in New York City for the fall term; conversations with Parker made Davis aware of the small-group opportunities that abounded on New York's Fifty-Second Street. Later, in 1945, Davis would further his jazz education under Parker on "The Street."

During the period that the Eckstine band was in St. Louis, Bird and Rebecca began quarreling again. He wanted her to move at his fast pace, but she was content to stay in the hotel room and read. When the band was ready to continue the tour, Rebecca and Bird decided their differences were irreconcilable and the couple split for the final time, with Rebecca moving back to Kansas City.

The band, however, continued east through Chicago and Detroit to New York. A *Down Beat* review of the Eckstine Band at the Regal Theatre in Chicago praised Parker's improvisations, especially his sixteen bars in the Sarah Vaughan vocal *I'll Wait and Pray*. Despite the excellence of the band, Bird longed for the greater solo freedom of the small group and the exciting atmosphere of New York; he gladly departed when the band returned to "The Apple" in August.

There is no recorded evidence of Parker with Eckstine. The "studio" records of the band which do exist were recorded in April, while Bird was still out West, and in December, after Parker had left the group. The DeLuxe records, however, show good examples of Gillespie's talent; he plays a fine solo in *I Stay in the Mood for You*, an Eckstine vocal, and the intro to *Good Jelly Blues* is the same intro and coda used by the Parker-Gillespie group on *All the Things You Are*, recorded nine months later. Gillespie was to leave the Eckstine group soon after Parker (early 1945) and join Boyd Raeburn's band. Trombonist Trummy Young, who was to become Gillespie's and Parker's compatriot in some of their 1945 recordings, was a principal soloist on the Raeburn band.

Eckstine filled the hole left by Gillespie with Theodore "Fats" Navarro, who had been with Andy Kirk for approximately a year. Navarro started as a Roy Eldridge imitator, as did Diz, but at the time of his Eckstine stint, he sounded like a lyrical version of Gillespie. The other gap, the one left by Parker, was filled by John Jackson, the excellent altoist from the McShann band.

Perhaps the best set of Eckstine recordings for setting the climate of the band during Parker's stay is the "live" set from the Plantation Club in Los Angeles from February 1945 (Alamac 2415). The set includes both Jackson and Navarro as soloists, and the remastering is well done. There is a great Navarro solo on *Love Me or Leave Me*, and the arrangement also shows off the extremely clean section work of the saxes and trombones. The Jackson solo on *Opus X* is surprising; it begins with Bird-like phrases and rhythms but peters out into simpler, scale-wise passages. Near the end of the solo one can hear that Jackson did not imply the underlying harmonies as well as Parker. There is a beautiful example of a Dameron composition-arrangement in *I Wanna Talk About You*, and some good vocals by both Eckstine and Sarah Vaughan. *Blowing the Blues* features a tenor "battle" between Budd Johnson and Gene Ammons. The set is a beautiful example of the first "Bop" big band.

After Bird's exit, the band hung on for two years, but then Eckstine, deep in debt, was forced to disband the group. The impact of the band was felt throughout the music world, however, especially by arrangers, and it is unfortunate that the recorded output was not greater and of better fidelity.

The Eckstine band was the only large group in the period of 1943-1944 that Parker joined for aesthetic rather than economic reasons, and, therefore, was a turning point in his career. He realized that his new concepts fitted a small combo better than a big band, and he never again would be a regular big band member. He moved on to freer avenues.

CHAPTER IV

FIFTY-SECOND STREET SCENE
—PART ONE
The Sideman (Fall 1944-Early 1945)

...into this background were cut myriads of brilliant parallelograms and circles and squares
through which glowed many colored lights. And out of the violet and purple depths ascended
like the city's soul, sounds and odors and thrills that make up the civic body.... Thus the
flavor of it came up to him and went into his blood.

O. Henry—The Duel

The Street, to the hip; Swing Lane, to the sophisticate; and Jive Alley, to the square,
were all designations for the block of Fifty-Second Street between Fifth and Sixth
Avenues during the Forties. The collection of brownstones lining the block had
once been evidence of societal wealth, but later became dingy clubs, catering to
the hip, with a preponderance of jazz and loose characters. The one-way traffic
(moving east) forced the people from the Broadway theater district to pass these
underground clubs and helped the attendance immensely. Furthermore, there were
two remnants of another era in the block, drawing the "class" dinner trade: Leon
and Eddie's at 33 West Fifty-Second Street, and The 21 Club. The "uppercrust",
therefore, occasionally frequented the jazz-oriented clubs as a "slumming" gesture.
Indeed, the audience was a true cross-section of New York City.

The block itself was approximately the length of a football field, and the jazz
clubs were centered near the west end of the block, towards Sixth Avenue. Their
addresses ranged from the fifties to the seventies. The east-west "divider" at this
point of Manhattan is Fifth Avenue, and the numbers go upwards to the west.
The classic "Street" block, between Fifth and Sixth Avenues, was numbered from
one through the two-digit numbers, and the block between Sixth and Seventh
Avenues, the "poor relation" whose only claims to fame were the Hickory House
and Kelly's Stables, began its street numbers with one hundred. The Hickory House's
address was 144 West Fifty-Second Street and Kelly's was directly across the street
at 137.

41

An interested observer traveling east on Fifty-Second Street from Sixth to Fifth Avenue would encounter the bulk of the jazz clubs on his right (the south side of the street) beginning with the Three Deuces. A look to the left would reveal the Onyx, and Jimmy Ryan's, the only Dixieland bastion. Continuing to concentrate on the right (south) side of the street, the traveler would find the Downbeat (called the Yacht Club until May 1944, and the Famous Door prior to that time), and the Spotlite, a new wartime addition. These clubs, gaily marqueed, served as the laboratory for the catalystic mixtures of the mid-Forties.

The clubs changed owners frequently and sometimes names and locations also. Competition ran high as to prices and "star" musicians, and most places featured a "headliner" plus another attraction, with the groups alternating sets. "Sitting-in" was common practice because of the proximity of all the clubs and the hour break that the musicians had between sets in their "home" club. Many rhythm-section musicians, in fact, doubled in two groups on the same night. Monday nights often featured special sessions involving members of many groups.

The piano trios that were popular on The Street included the groups of Art Tatum, Nat Cole, and Erroll Garner. Clyde Hart, Nat Jaffe, and Al Haig were all pianists of great talent, also, who could play with any type of group. Indeed, Haig at one time subbed for Tatum while the latter recovered from an operation. Hart, one of the first of the swing-based musicians to grasp the harmonic principles and rhythmic accompanying style of the new music, and Jaffe, a sensitive accompanist for vocalists, both died in 1945. Billy Taylor, then an up-and-coming jazz piano stylist, was also a frequent sideman and "sitter-in". The piano trio, which often used a guitarist rather than a drummer, gave rise to some fine quitarists along The Street, such as Tiny Grimes with Tatum, and Oscar Moore with Cole. Some other guitarists often present on the scene were Bill DeArango, Mike Bryan, Danny Barker, and Remo Palmieri.

Slam Stewart—the bassist of the Tatum trio, who was famous for his simultaneously hummed and bowed choruses—was the "dean" of the "Street" bassists. Curly Russell, Jimmy Butts, Oscar Pettiford, and Al Hall were also among the list of iron-armed sessioneers. Russell was later to become a regular with Parker's group. The other half of the jazz rhythmic foundation, the drummers, were only beginning to assimilate the new style pioneered by Kenny Clarke. The percussionists on The Street ran the gamut of styles. Sid Catlett, Max Roach, Stan Levey, J.C. Heard, Specs Powell, Cozy Cole and Doc West were among the usual coterie.

Woodwinds were great "Street" attractions, and the clubs fought to get the best "names." The main tenors were Colemans Hawkins, Don Byas, Ben Webster, and Budd Johnson, but Parker practically dominated the alto scene after his arrival on The Street. Before Parker the favorites had been Pete Brown and Benny Carter. Joe Marsala, the clarinetist, had the regular job at the Hickory House, with his wife Adele Girard on harp; and Tony Scott, then a struggling young clarinetist, made nightly rounds, sitting in wherever he could.

On the vocal scene, Billie Holiday was popular, as was Mildred Bailey, backed by her husband Red Norvo. Norvo, one of the major vibe voices in jazz history, was also a frequent after-hours player.

The brass players on The Street in the mid-Forties reflected the transition that was taking place: Roy Eldridge, Gillespie, Howard McGhee, Benny Harris, and Miles Davis were trumpet practitioners, although Davis was only a scared beginner at this time. Trummy Young fitted his mainstream trombone style into many of the 1945 sessions, but the only pure modern trombonist of the time, J.J. Johnson, did not appear on The Street until 1946.

George Wallington, Thelonious Monk, Teddy Wilson, Denzil Best, Sir Charles Thompson, Stuff Smith, Ray Brown, Dexter Gordon, George Shearing, and many other musicians of varying styles and ideas got their formative small-group training on Fifty-Second Street, both by working regularly and by sessioning with musicians of all types.

Jimmy Ryan's club basically held up the traditional end of The Street and would feature artists such as Jack Teagarden, Sidney Bechet, and Eddie Condon. The club was to become the longest-lived of all the jazz emporiums that lined Fifty-Second Street. By 1950, many of the clubs on the south side of the street had been torn down to make way for the Standard Oil Building extension of Rockefeller Center, and the rest of The Street gave way to "girlie club" clip joints, Chinese restaurants, and later to gigantic office buildings and parking lots. The Street's contribution as a jazz laboratory, however, will always be remembered in jazz history.

Upon leaving the Eckstine band, Bird sought employment on The Street; his earliest gigs were with Ben Webster in the early fall of 1944. Bird also jammed that fall and through the sessions became acquainted with Clyde Hart and Tiny Grimes. When Grimes procured a record contract with Savoy, Parker was hired for the date.

* * *

Recording—September 15, 1944—New York
Tiny Grimes Quintet—Parker (as), Clyde Hart (p), Tiny Grimes (vcl, g) Jimmy Butts (b), Doc West (dr).

Tiny's Tempo—Take 1	Savoy 12001—BYG (FR) 529.130
Tiny's Tempo—Take 2	Savoy 12001—BYG (FR) 529.130
Tiny's Tempo—Take 3—orig.	Savoy 12001—BYG (FR) 529.130
Romance Without Finance—Take 3	Savoy 9022—BYG (FR) 529.130
I'll Always Love You Just The Same—Take 2	Savoy 526—BYG (FR) 529.130
Red Cross—Take 1	Savoy 12001—BYG (FR) 529.130
Red Cross—Take 2—orig.	Savoy 12001—BYG (FR) 529.130

Savoy conceived this date as being a vocal session featuring Grimes, with the instrumentals being the "B" sides of the records. As time would have it, however, because of Parker's presence the instrumentals have become the sought-after items.

Both vocals (*I'll Always Love You Just The Same* and *Romance Without Finance*) were written by Grimes and are similar in harmonic construction. They both begin with the familiar I/17/IV/iv/, although the first is a serious ballad and the second a bouncy, nonsense novelty.

I'll Always Love You begins with rhythmic stop time—with Grimes bursting phrases into the breaks. Bird enters in a burst at the end of the introduction. Grimes's vocal is certainly not an example of vocal mastery, but Parker's sixteen-bar solo at the beginning of the second chorus is a valuable documentary in Bird's history.

It is one of the first mature efforts of ballad playing to be recorded by Parker (*Body and Soul*—or part of it—from Witchita is the other). The recording is difficult to find, however, except on the French BYG label listed above.

Romance is as inane as its title, but Parker plays three-fourths of the second chorus, with Hart taking the bridge. There is a full guitar chorus and another eight bars by Hart. The Grimes vocal then ends the fiasco with a "bop riff" coda tagged on by guitar and alto.

Tiny's Tempo is a "swing-oriented" blues frame by Grimes of which there are three takes. The tune opens with "hi-hat" rhythm being stated by West and the line being played in unison by guitar and alto.

Example 4 - Opening of *Tiny's Tempo*

Parker plays three fine choruses on both of the first two takes, but each take is cut off as soon as pianist Hart begins his solo. On the third take, however, which is faster than the others, Bird plays three blazing choruses, followed by Grimes on two choruses. Grimes's use of "echo phrases" in the beginning of his solo is pleasant. The guitar solo continues into the next chorus with a riff behind, and then the ensemble launches a chromatic riff. The "out-chorus" contains still another riff with a free-blown traditional ending.

Red Cross is a Parker composition suggesting *I Got Rhythm* harmonies, but the melody implies an ingenious twisting of the chords in bars five and six. This tune also gives the first look at the triplet figure that Parker was to use extensively in the future. The opening theme figure ends with a "mop-mop" lick that was pirated and used extensively by Coleman Hawkins and others. This is the tune that was named for Billy Eckstine's friend who taped the session at the Ritz Hotel in Chicago during 1943.

Ex. 5 - Opening "Mop Mop" figure

Ex. 6 - Chord Shifting - Authors Implied Chords

The usual chords in a frame of this type for bars five and six are /Bb Bb7/ Eb Ebm/ and the ones given above are the author's choice. Hart actually plays something simpler:/Bb/B7/.

Both takes of *Red Cross* begin with an oriental-sounding intro, then proceed to the theme, which is followed by a Parker solo. Both solos are cleanly conceived and speak of things to come, but Take 1 ends after the Bird solo. Bird's bridge melody implies the series of secondary dominants—the usual harmonization—being preceded by their related supertonics, and on Take 1, he leaps from the root (D) of the secondary dominant (D7) downward to the third (F#); on Take 2, however, he improves the figure by leaping from the third up to the root. The second is musically much better because the 7th (G) of the related supertonic (Am7) resolves naturally to the third (F#) of the secondary dominant (D7).

Ex. 7 Bridge Figure - Take 1 - Red Cross

Ex. 8 Bridge Figure - Take 2 - Red Cross

On *Red Cross*, one can also see the effect that the new music was having on older players, as Hart uses whole-tone scales against the bridge chords in his solo on the second take, and Grimes ends the bridge section of his solo with a flat five of the chord. On the final bridge Bird and Grimes exchange two-bar phrases.

The Grimes date readily shows the transition that was taking place in jazz during the early Forties; Parker is matched with players who are firmly rooted in the "swing" tradition of the preceding era, and it is interesting to hear the difference of conception, especially rhythmically, on familiar improvisational frames.

* * *

In January of 1945, Dizzy Gillespie and Trummy Young were in the Boyd Raeburn band based at the Apollo Theatre, while Parker was tiding himself over as a replacement for Eddie Vinson in the Cootie Williams band. Clyde Hart, the transitional pianist and frequent Fifty-Second Street jammer, was putting together a group to do some "black" recording for the independent Continental label, and the first date was to involve dancer and entertainer Rubberlegs Williams in a blues-based vocal session. A following session would feature Trummy Young in the same vocal role, but with somewhat more sophisticated material. Hart chose the young lions of the new movement as the horns, plus Don Byas, who—like Hart himself—was sympathetic with the new directions.

* * *

Recording—January 1945—New York City
Clyde Hart's All Stars—Rubberlegs Williams (vcl), D. Gillespie (tp), Trummy Young (tb), C. Parker (as), C. Hart (p), Mike Bryan (g), Al Hall (b), Specs Powell (d).

What's The Matter Now	Onyx 221
I Want Every Bit Of It	Onyx 221
That's The Blues	Onyx 221
4-F Blues—Take 1	Onyx 221
4-F Blues—Take 2 (G. I. Blues)	Onyx 221

Williams, not being accustomed to the new sounds, was a bit confused by some of the backings of the musicians. Furthermore, at a coffee break, Bird, who usually doctored his coffee with benzedrine, was true to form, and either by mistake or as a prank, also got some into Williams's coffee. This only made the proceedings more difficult, and Williams, floating away, barrel-housed his way through everything.

The material is all blues-based, but the first two are not in the traditional 12-bar form. Both tunes were written by Clarence Williams (no relation to the singer), and recorded by Bessie Smith in 1926. *Matter* begins with a guitar intro and after the Williams vocal, Parker plays a fine sixteen-bar solo, beginning with a phrase that later became one of his trademarks. Williams continues with Young backing, and then Byas plays a fine full chorus. Williams raucously takes it out with Diz backing and everyone joining for the finale.

On *Every Bit*, Byas backs Williams on the opening statement, and Diz does the second chorus accompaniment. Bird plays a flippant eight-bar solo, and Williams continues out, with Bird behind him and the other horns joining on the tag. All the bridges are done in stop-time by Williams.

Young introduces *That's the Blues*, a traditional blues with stop-time in the first four bars. Williams then sings four choruses, with guitar, alto, tenor, and horn-riff backgrounds, respectively.

4-F begins with a boogie-ish guitar figure, and Williams sings two choruses with Parker behind him. Byas plays a beautiful full-toned solo, followed by guitar, after which Diz builds a climactic chorus, punctuated with shouts from Williams. The horns riff behind Williams on the final twelve. *G.I.*, a different take of the same blues, contains the same format, but is not done as well.

Recording—January 1945—New York City
Clyde Hart's All Stars—Personnel the same as the preceding recording, excluding R. Williams.

Dream of You	Continental CLP 16004
Seventh Avenue	Continental CLP 16004
Sorta Kinda	Continental CLP 16004
Oh Oh, My, My	Continental CLP 16004

This date is more formal than the previous one; the ensemble passages are written, and Trummy Young does a vocal on all four tunes. On *Dream of You*, Bird plays a lovely ad-lib intro over sustained chords, and then launches into the theme with a tone that is reminiscent of Jimmy Dorsey. Diz plays a pretty bridge statement before Young's vocal, and there is an orchestrated out-chorus.

Seventh Avenue begins with a block-chord intro by Hart, and Young's vocal is backed by riffing horns. Parker wails behind Young on the bridge, and Byas and Diz split chorus two. Young returns to the bridge, with Parker backing again, and the ensemble goes out with a tag ending.

The romping exchanges between Gillespie and Parker on *Sorta Kinda* are a delight, but *Oh, Oh* is a typical "period" nonsense ditty that features Byas only.

Although the date does not offer much extended improvisation, it serves to point out the big band training of Parker and Gillespie. The ensemble passages are well played, even if Young's vocals are not exactly "show-stoppers".

Recording—February 12, 1945—Savoy Ballroom, New York City
Cootie Williams Orchestra—Cootie Williams (tp), C. Parker (as), Sam Taylor (ts) Arnold Jarvis (p), Carl Pruitt (b), Sylvester Payne (dr)

Floogie Boo   Onyx 221

Parker had been subbing since January for Eddie Vinson who had been drafted. This delightful small-band cut was made just before he left the Williams Orchestra. The big band was probably working the complete job, but certain tunes that were in the book were written for combo instrumentation and were performed as such. *Floogie* has an "A" section based on *I Got Rhythm* with the *Honeysuckle Rose* bridge. The line is performed very cleanly, and Taylor opens the solo proceedings with a growling chorus. Williams follows, opening his solo with an extremely long note. The piano chorus by Jarvis is wild! It contains parallel ninth chords running throughout—creating a feeling of shifting tonalities. In the last eight bars, Jarvis indulges in some two-handed, Latin-sounding unison figures. Bird enters during the Latin effects and plays a buoyant driving chorus, quoting *Paper Moon* at the beginning of the second eight and *Don't Be That Way* at the beginning of the final eight. The bare thirteenth (or sixth) at the end of the ensemble chorus seems a bit obnoxious as an ending.

* * *

During 1945, Bird met Doris Sydnor, a hat check girl in the Fifty-Second Street clubs. The relationship flourished and the couple lived together in Doris's apartment at 411 Manhattan Avenue near 117th Street. Doris was a simple but intelligent girl who learned about jazz only after meeting Parker. She and Bird were legally married in 1948. During their stay on Manhattan Avenue, Argonne Thornton, a piano player who was to figure in the confused November recordings, boarded with them.

Another female associate of this period was Chan Richardson, a sometime dancer and model whose mother ran the hat-check concession at the Cotton Club on Broadway at 48th Street. Chan grew up with and was familiar with the "hip" world of The Street: the musicians, the hustlers, the pushers, the photographers, and the girlie magazines. Her pad at 7 West Fifty-Second Street, near the northeast corner, next to the old Town Casino, became a hangout for the supporters of the new sounds.

An alto player, Dean Benedetti, dedicated himself to recording all of Parker's improvised excursions on a portable record cutting machine. Benedetti forced his way into men's rooms, upstairs apartments, spaces beneath band stands, anywhere that he could set a mike to record the evenings performances. He recorded only Parker choruses and followed Bird on all his jaunts. Benedetti was the start of the mythical cult that arose around Parker which, for better or worse, dominated the jazz world's remembrance of Bird. After Benedetti's death—in Italy during the late 1950s—the recordings were assumed lost until 1988 when Mosaic Records found them in the possession of his brother, Rick, and purchased them for release.

The "Bop" movement was not well accepted at first by jazz critics or the general public, but the young intellectual group, to which the new music appealed, became fanatic in their devotion. The new underground was taking shape with Fifty-Second Street as its headquarters.

An excellent picture of The Street can be found on the cover of album number 30 AM 6061, *Bird on 52nd Street*, on the French label, America. The photograph was taken facing east and one can readily see the marquees, the advertisements of featured musicians, and the names of many of the legendary clubs. Bird stands near the middle of the street; he is clad in beret, pin stripe suit, and tee-shirt, and is making a "cool" hand gesture! The material on the record is from 1948, but the picture seems to be earlier. Whenever it is from, it truly gives the feeling of the Fifty-Second Street scene.

CHAPTER V

FIFTY-SECOND STREET SCENE
—PART TWO
Bird and Diz (March-November 1945)

Iron sharpeneth iron; so a man sharpeneth the countenance of his friend.

Proverbs. XXVII 17

In March of 1945, Parker worked intermittently on The Street with a bass-less trio including Joe Albany, piano; and Stan Levey, drums. They worked Mondays at one of the clubs on the south side of the street—most likely the Spotlite. Soon Gillespie arrived on the scene to form a permanent group with Parker; Al Haig replaced Albany, and Curly Russell came in as the bassist. Albany had joined the Boyd Raeburn band as it embarked on a road tour, and Gillespie left the same group to remain with Parker in New York.

By April, the quintet was working regularly at the Three Deuces, and it was during this period that most of the classic Gillespie-Parker lines and arrangements were worked out. Gillespie was doing most of the composing and "head arranging," but Bird was emerging as the more logical and emotional soloist. The repertoire consisted mainly of variations on standard tunes, using altered chords; some of these variations Gillespie had been using as out-choruses for some time. Parker, of course, was already familiar with much of the material because of his association with Gillespie in the Hines and Eckstine bands. The themes, stated mostly in unison, were unbelievably clean, as evidenced by the recordings of the 1945 group, which stand as complete jazz classics of this period.

Tony Scott sums up the impact of the two giants on Fifty-Second Street:

...When Bird and Diz hit The Street regularly...everybody was astounded and nobody could get near their way of playing music. Finally, Bird and Diz made records, and then guys could imitate it and go from there![1]

* * *

Recording—February-March 1945—New York City

49

Dizzy Gillespie Sextet—Gillespie (tp), Parker (as), Clyde Hart (p), Remo Palmieri (g), Slam Stewart (b), Cozy Cole (dr).

Groovin' High	Savoy 12020
All The Things You Are	Savoy 12020
Dizzy Atmosphere	Savoy 12020

Groovin' High and *Dizzy Atmosphere* are both Gillespie tunes; the first is based on the *Whispering* chord sequence, and the latter is an *I Got Rhythm* derivative, with a chromatic bridge figure beginning on a D7 chord.

Ex. 9 *Groovin High* beginning of Theme

Ex. 10 *Dizzy Atmosphere* Theme

Diz and Bird open *Groovin'* with a two-bar unison figure, and then Stewart plays a bowed and hummed break after which the horns return for a two-bar lead-in to the theme. Alto, trumpet, and guitar state the theme in unison, with Hart answering the short two-note passages on piano. There is a smooth modulation from E-flat to D-flat at the end of the theme chorus, preceding Parker's ad-lib break. The modulation is achieved by consecutive major-seventh chords on the off-beat, with Stewart using the bow to advantage on the roots. Bird's break and chorus is, of course, in the new key.

Ex. 11 Modulation—Break—Beginning of Chorus—*Groovin High*

The Parker sixteen-bar solo is a lovely, logical melodic construction with constant rising and falling patterns alternating with each other. Stewart plays the back sixteen in his inimitable style, and at the end of the chorus, a short riff modulation moves the tune back to the higher key for Gillespie's solo.

Ex. 12 Modulation—Break to E flat—*Groovin High*

Gillespie plays excellently for sixteen measures, and then Palmieri solos adequately. The slow coda by Gillespie has become a jazz cliché, both in its melody and the chord pattern from which the melody was derived.

Ex. 13 End of Gillespie's Coda—*Groovin High* (octave lower than trumpet).

Gillespie shows his prima donna breath control on the high E-flat at the end, although there is just a *slight* lack of breath at the very end, causing a slight loss in intonation. (To realize the difficulty of this phase, listen to Conte Candoli's re-creation of it on *Super-Sax Plays Bird, Volume 2—Salt Peanuts*, Capitol 11271. Candoli, an excellent trumpet player, does not achieve the same amount of power and does not do as well with it as Gillespie.)

Dizzy Atmosphere opens with a trumpet "bop lick" over bass octave leaps. The horns state the riff-theme in unison, with the only harmony coming on the wild intervals at the final two bars of the bridge. Bird blows first again, superimposing a series of diminished chords over the familiar harmony on the second eight bars. The rhythmic effect—shifting of the normal accents—is as thrilling as the harmonic one. The bridge section of the solo has always been an enigma to this writer, the melody is beautifully constructed and sounds well to the ear, but when analyzed, seems to imply different tonalities than the ones implied by the chords. (See the analysis section for details.) Bird stays to this same type of construction on later versions of this tune, and so it is probably that he conceived in his mind a different progression than that of the actual tune. (Anti-intellectuals will probably laugh at this observation, but it is the only *unjustifiable* example that this writer has ever found of Parker's playing not logically fitting with the chords). Dizzy's chorus is indescribably good, and Stewart comes through with another pleasant "hummer." The fifth chorus is a running unison riff for twenty-four bars, played unbelievably clean, and then the theme is restated in the final eight. The coda is the same as the introduction, trumpet over leaping bass, with Bird joining on the closing bars.

The introduction and coda to *All The Things You Are* is the same one used by Gillespie on *Good Jelly Blues* with Eckstine, and was also to be used again by Parker in his later *Bird of Paradise*, based on the chords of the Jerome Kern ballad. Diz plays the melody with a lovely, singing sound for sixteen bars, and Parker's bridge is a miniature master-piece. He begins with a sequential phase based on the melody and proceeds to construct a lovely melody of his own. Stewart "bow-hums" the final eight of the first chorus passionately. Hart plays the front sixteen of the next chorus in a strident, cocktailish style that is not his best work. Palmieri plays well on the bridge, and Gillespie finished the tune with blowing, rather than a theme return. The introduction is repeated as a coda, where E-flat ends the tune as the raised ninth of a C7 chord (key of A-flat—actually in the F minor region at this point).

Ex. 14 Introduction/Coda to *All The Things You Are*

Recording—May 11, 1945—New York City
Dizzy Gillespie All Star Quintet—Gillespie (tpt), Parker (as), Al Haig (p), Curly
Russell (b), Sid Catlett (d), Sarah Vaughan (v),

Salt Peanuts	Savoy 12020
Shaw 'Nuff	Saga (English) ERO 8035
Loverman (v)	Everest FS—250
Hot House	Savoy 12020

Salt Peanuts and *Shaw 'Nuff* are both derived from the chords of *I Got Rhythm.*
Gillespie penned the first one and had been playing it since the Hines days. Both
he and Parker, however, are credited with *Shaw 'Nuff. Peanuts* contains a bridge-
base of/III7/III7/vi/vi/II7/II7/V7/V7/, but *Shaw 'Nuff* uses the more conventional
I Got Rhythm bridge, based on all secondary dominants. The only difference is
in bars three and four where the vi chord would be replaced by VI7.

Peanuts begins with Catlett stating the theme in an eight-bar drum introduction;
then comes a wild sequence of intervals by the two horns that sounds as fresh
today as it did in 1945. On the final two bars of this section, pianist Haig states
the *Salt Peanuts* octave jump, leading to the theme, which is stated in octave unison
by the horns.

Ex. 15 *Salt Peanuts* Theme

The first use of this riff on record is as the final chorus of a Lucky Millinder
tune, *Little John Special*, done in 1942. Gillespie is the featured trumpeter with
Millinder on this date, and the riff was probably his "brainstorm", although the
tune is credited to Millinder. On the Millinder recording, however, the four measure
riff is played three times as the theme of a blues and not as an *I Got Rhythm*
theme as used by Bird and Diz.

Although the "blowing choruses" use the conventional *I Got Rhythm* chords,
the theme is best harmonized by the variation shown above. This sequence is what
Haig states on the record (the second symbol merely means F chord-A bass) and
is a common substitution, almost at random, on tunes of this type. Following
the theme, there is an eight-bar transition section and then the theme returns, with
Bird stating the opening figure and Dizzy singing the *Salt Peanuts* figure. Bird
blows the bridge, and the theme again alternates between alto and voice. A walking

bass section of eight bars, based on the "A" section, is followed by a transition section, like the one in the introduction, but with Haig using the last two bars as a solo break into his chorus. Bird follows Haig and plays a beautiful solo, with a pleasant sounding Latin-tinged phrase opening the second eight-bar section. It is somewhat reminiscent of the *Peanut Vendor!*

Ex. 16 *Salt Peanuts*—Bird's Latin Lick

After Parker's solo, there is another transition section over "back-time," with alto-trumpet alternation. Dizzy uses his last alternation as a break into his solo and plays excellently throughout the improvisation. Catlett follows with twenty-four bars of drums, and the horn section of the introduction is repeated with the ensemble singing the *Salt Peanuts* lick for a close.

Shaw 'Nuff—named for Billy Shaw, the "boppers" favorite booker—begins with a conga-like introduction by the rhythm section that leads to a mid-Eastern sounding melody by the horns. After this strange introduction, the horns state the theme in octave unison, Haig's "comping" fits beautifully with the group, and in the bridge his statements of flat-five's in the chords lets the listener hear what all the talk about flatted fifths was about. This is the first example of a pianist that truly fit with Parker and Gillespie and understood their rhythmic and harmonic concept. The soloists are Parker, Diz, and Haig in that order, and all three turn in virile solos—classics of the era. The introduction is used as a coda, with the group exiting on a flat-five interval.

Sarah Vaughan's *Loverman* was her second time as solo artist on record; the first had come on New Year's Eve 1944, when she recorded with Gillespie, doing his tune *Interlude (Night In Tunisia)* along with three other compositions. Having been with the "boppers" in both the Hines and Eckstine bands, Miss Vaughan sounds quite at home here and possesses a gentle, naive quality that was present in all her work during this period.

After a five bar introduction on which Bird is heard to advantage on the last three, Miss Vaughan sings the first four bars with just rhythm. The horns enter behind her on the next four, ending the section with a flat-five interval on the dominant of the relative minor. The second eight follows the same format, only ending, of course, on the tonic. Diz does the accompanying on the bridge very tastefully, as does Bird on the beginning of the last eight. The tune then returns to the bridge for a Gillespie improvisation, and Sarah returns, singing the final eight. There is a tag ending culminating with staccato piano bass notes and two long harmonizing tones by the horns. The ensemble passages seem to be written, or at least cleanly worked out. This version is a worthwhile example of Miss Vaughan's work.

Hot House is a Tadd Dameron original composed specifically for this date. Dameron had begun to work on The Street during this period and was resuming his writing career. The base of the tune is *What Is This Thing Called Love,* but

Dameron's first twenty-four bar section is a continuous melody that forces altered chords at several points. The last eight-bar section echoes the first—the "signature" of the tune.

Ex. 17 *Hot House* opening of Theme

The "signature" is a chromatic melody punctuated by weird intervalic leaps of thirds landing on high chordal intervals. The first lands on the augmented eleventh (flat fifth) of the C7 chord, and the second leap culminates on the major-seventh of an Fm chord. At the end of the first sixteen bars Haig states the parallel chords that became characteristic of the period: (15)/ Cmaj. 7 Dm7 Em7 Fmaj.7/ (16)/ Em7 Dm7 Cmaj.7/.

The tune opens with Catlett's drums—an original solo. The horns state the line in unison, as usual, and Haig's comping is again outstanding. This is certainly the first example on record of fine, "be-bop" style comping and is a marvelous study for pianists. Bird creates an interesting solo; in the beginning of the second eight bars, he plays a curious melodic phrase that he often developed in later versions of these chords. It always sounds familiar to this writer, but never quite rings a bell.

Ex. 18 *Hot House* Parker Chorus beginning of 2nd eight

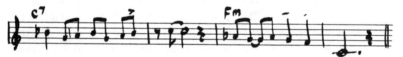

He uses the same type of idea in development at the beginning of the bridge, showing the compositional bent of his mind.

Ex. 19 *Hot House* Parker Chorus beginning of bridge

At the very end of his chorus, Parker uses the rhythmic figure that later became *Moose the Mooche*, and Diz immediately picks it up and uses it to start his chorus!

Ex. 20 *Hot House* Parker's Ending Figure

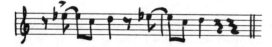

Haig solos ad-lib on the out-chorus bridge, but otherwise the ending chorus is like the first. This set of recordings is the definitive one to have of the early Gillespie-Parker Quintet, as it gives a true picture of this group at its best.

Salt Peanuts sums up in a nutshell (no pun intended) the Gillespie-Parker music. The line, composed by Gillespie, is riff-like, with humor injected into it. The piece is based on standard chord changes, with subtle changes, and the line must be harmonized differently from the improvisationary sections. Then there are the difficult transition sections, hard to execute and difficult to remember; the chunking off-beat piano chords; the hard-driving solos, coming together in swinging clockwork; and the hard-punched four-four rhythm, holding its own against solo syncopations and ensemble breaks in the tempo. There is a great balance of simplicity and complexity, of humor and seriousness, of harmony and dissonance, of logic and absurdity, of aloofness and emotion, and perhaps, of love and hate. The scales that measure all art need to be looked at, perhaps, as to their balance from time to time, and "be-bop" or whatever one chooses to call it would measure quite well when judged on this performance.

For the collector, the most difficult side to find of these four is *Shaw 'Nuff*. There are issues on foreign labels including the one cited, but domestic companies seem to have overlooked reissues of this particular track.

The original 78's were done for Guild, which went bankrupt and sold the rights to Musicraft. Later Savoy bought the rights, but probably never obtained *Shaw 'Nuff* and the Vaughan vocal. The latter had been issued fairly often on LP's under Miss Vaughan's name, with the Everest being the latest to date. Also contained on the Everest LP are her early sides with Freddy Webster, who was a major influence on the "cool" trumpeters.

Recording—May 25, 1945—New York City
Sarah Vaughan—D. Gillespie (tpt), C. Parker (as), Flip Phillips (ts.) Nat Jaffe (p), Tadd Dameron (p), Bill DeArango (gtr), Curly Russell (b), Max Roach (d).

What More Can A Woman Do	Palace PST—672
I'd Rather Have A Memory Than A Dream	Palace PST—673
Mean To Me	Palace PST—672

The introduction to *Mean To Me* is exquisite Parker—long-lined sixteenth notes. It is one of his earliest clear examples of the creative bursts for which he was to become famous. Phillips, in town with the Herman band, backs the vocal during the first chorus and does so tastefully. He continues with a sixteen-bar solo improvisation that is big-toned and buoyant, followed by some crisp Gillespie on the bridge. Bird plays the last eight of the second chorus beginning with an ironic, melodic statement. Sarah returns to the bridge and in the last eight is backed by the ensemble in parallel chord voicings that were to later become a "be-bop" cliché. Sarah alters the melody accordingly. This harmonization was first used by Tadd Dameron in his arrangement for the Eckstine band:/IMaj7/ii7/iii7/, etc.

The ensemble lines on *What More Can A Woman Do* are written, and Parker is heard briefly backing the first bridge. Phillips returns to the bridge after the first chorus. On the final vocal eight, DeArango's guitar can be heard improvising through the sustained background.

On *I'd Rather Have a Memory Than a Dream*, the interesting piano player is Dameron, an admirer of Miss Vaughan's art, who was later to do some of her most interesting arrangements, especially *A Hundred Years From Today* done with Georgie Auld's band a year later.

The fact that Dameron was present suggests that he wrote the arranged passages used on all three tunes.

* * *

In the month of June, Parker and Gillespie were featured at a Town Hall concert sponsored by an organization called the New Jazz Foundation. The concert was attended mainly by those people already interested in the new music and failed to draw many new fans. Many of the performers slated for the concert did not show for the performance and this turned the event into a minor fiasco. The publicity, however, kept Gillespie's name in the forefront, but the "hoopla" seemed only to detract attention from his musical ability and also to push Parker to the back of the public's mind.

The Gillespie-Parker group continued at the Three Deuces throughout the summer, but our only true documentation is the May 11th recordings. Gillespie was receiving much publicity, and at the end of June, plans were made for him to front a big-band with a show package entitled "Hep-Sations of 1945." Billy Shaw engineered a southern tour with a band that included Kenny Dorham, Charlie Rouse, and Max Roach, each destined for later fame on trumpet, tenor sax, and drums, respectively. Gil Fuller did the bulk of the arranging, and June Eckstine (B's wife) was the vocalist. The entourage also included comedy and show acts.

Bird remained at the Three Deuces for a short while, with Don Byas replacing Diz, and the rest of the group intact. In August Parker did a guest shot with the Elliot Lawrence band on WCAU, Philadelphia. This was his first encounter with a young trumpeter, Red Rodney, who was later to become his sideman and close companion. The Lawrence band eventually received recognition and took to the road.

Parker worked at the Downbeat Club next door to the Deuces with Sir Charles Thompson, piano; Miles Davis, trumpet; Dexter Gordon, tenor; Stan Levey, drums; and Leonard Gaskin, bass, for the month of September and moved to the Spotlite Club for October. Allen Eager and Haig were working the Deuces until October, when Haig left for the coast with the Charlie Barnet band. In early November, Bird worked a quick trip to Canada with Trummy Young and Slam Stewart and returned to find Gillespie back on the scene; the southern tour had been unsuccessful.

The free-wheeling June recordings for Comet by Bird and Diz were supervised by Red Norvo and are a good example of the variety of styles present on The Street. Sir Charles Thompson gathered a group including Bird and Dexter Gordon for another eclectic date for the Apollo label in September, and this set the scene for Bird's first recording under his own name in November.

* * *

Recording—June 6, 1945—New York City
Red Norvo Sextet—Norvo (vbs), C. Parker (as), Gillespie (tp) Flip Phillips (ts),

Teddy Wilson (p), Slam Stewart (b), Specs Powell (dr)—(first two tunes), J.C,. Heard (dr)—(both blues).

Hallelujah—Take 1	MGM (Ger) 65 106
Hallelujah—Take 2	Spotlite (Eng) 105
Hallelujah—Take 3—orig.	MGM (Ger) 65 106
Get Happy—Take 3	MGM (Ger) 65 106
Get Happy—Take 4—orig.	MGM (Ger) 65 106
Slam Slam Blues—Take 1	MGM (Ger) 65 106
Slam Slam Blues—Take 2—orig.	MGM (Ger) 65 106
Congo Blues—Take 1	MGM (Ger) 65 106
Congo Blues—Take 2	MGM (Ger) 65 106
Congo Blues—Take 3	MGM (Ger) 65 106
Congo Blues—Take 4	MGM (Ger) 65 106
Congo Blues—Take 5—orig.	MGM (Ger) 65 106

All three takes of *Hallelujah* contain a flippant Wilson intro and Diz stating the theme backed by a repeated four note counter-melody.

Ex. 21 Counter Melody— *Hallelujah*

Gillespie has each opening bridge to himself and then returns with the melody over the riff. The solo order on all takes is Norvo, Phillips, Wilson, Diz (Phillips riffing behind), Stewart, and Parker. The final chorus is a riff with a flamboyant "fall-off" bridge figure. The first take, although fluent, is not as well done as the other two. Parker is a bit redundant, although Gillespie comes on like a lion. Stewart comes through nicely with one of his "bow-hums," and the other soloists are pleasant, but not definitive. One can again notice the rhythmic *Moose the Mooche* motif in Bird's solo.

The second take, released as *Sing Hallelujah*, seems only to be available on the Spotlite LP. Diz plays a "cool" opening bridge and Norvo sounds fine, reflecting the new sounds with a whole-tone scalish figure at the end of the bridge. Phillips is driving and Wilson is flinging in modern ideas through his older style and swinging like the hammers of hell. Diz rears back and blows again; Stewart brings musical smiles, and Bird plays a wild solo before the riffing out-chorus.

The third take contains an excellent Wilson chorus and finds Diz beginning his solo quite riffishly (perhaps because of Phillips insistent backing). Stewart again displays both humor and good taste, and Bird is vibrant. The Parker solos on both Takes 2 and 3 are fine examples of his development during this period.

Get Happy also begins with a Wilson intro; it then goes to a unison theme statement by the horns, with Wilson taking the bridge. The solo order is the same as *Hallelujah*, but Stewart does not solo. On Take 1, Diz is "wholetone-y" after Norvo and Phillips, and Bird builds another wailer, with more reference to the rhythmic *Moose the Mooche* motif. On Take 2, Norvo, after his solo break, begins with a phrase reminiscent of *Limehouse Blues*, and Phillips sounds singing, but mediocre. Although the tune is played in the key of F, Norvo solos in Eb; the modulation back and forth is achieved by solo breaks by Norvo and Phillips. During Diz's statement, he reveals a lick in the final eight that was to become one of his "signatures," and Bird begins his solo with a melodic statement dripping with irony. The out-chorus on both takes is a riff with descending parallel wholetone harmony in the bridge, but the first take is incomplete.

Slam Slam is a slow blues and Stewart plays marvelously on the opening choruses of both takes, bending long notes and sounding mournful. Bird begins both solos with the same phrase, but expands on it on the second take. On both takes he is bluesy, but with Fifty-Second Street overtones; on the second take, for instance, he ends his solo on the major seventh. Diz is bluesy on the beginning of Take 1 but soon moves to wild intervals and incorporates the *Irish Washerwoman*. On Take 2, he is sophisticatedly modern and sequential. Wilson shows his modern influence as he approaches the chords to the middle of the blues on Take 1, but Bird and Diz, riffing behind Phillips, fail to help the cause. On Take 2, however, Phillips plays his best and the most logical solo of the date. Norvo's solos make for fine relaxed listening, in fact, so relaxed that one tends to forget the fine musical ideas contained therein. Both takes contain a Dixie-ish ending.

Congo starts with eight measures of Latin-tinged drums, then goes to a sixteen-bar lead-in statement by Gillespie. The first try is unclean by Diz, but he gets through the lead-in and into the improvised B-flat blues. On the second chorus, he removes the mute that he had been using since the opening, and the effect is unpleasant. Bird goes into his sixteen-bar lead-in, but stops in mid-blues-chorus. One can see that the form is thus: sixteen bars (minus rhythm), then two blues choruses (twelve bars each) for each soloist. The sixteen-bar section goes through the tonalities of E-flat—G-flat—A-flat—B-flat, at four bars apiece. The blues, of course, in B-flat, leads perfectly back to E-flat. The composition—or more truly—the form; for there is no line, is credited to Norvo. Take 2 has a better Diz intro, and he keeps the mute in all the way. Bird seems to have forgotten that there are to be two blues choruses apiece, for he plays only one, and the group stops in confusion. Take 3 has a relaxed trumpet call in Gillespie's intro, and Bird is "be-boppy". The group gets all the way through this take, but the ending riff has an unclean entrance. Gillespie retains the hunting call intro on Take 4, and Parker plays his best choruses on this take. The drum intro on Take 5 is not as virile as on the others, but the rest of the take is fine. Bird and Diz are both excellent, with Wilson showing some different left hand technique and Norvo playing fine ideas. Stewart plays an excellent break, and on this solo, as on some others on this date, he is impressive in that he does not play his "bow-hummers" in predictable phrases, but rather sings them out in a pure natural fashion. The ending ensemble riff on Take 4 is different than the one used on Takes 3 and 5.

All in all, the date was a successful blending of the old and the new, and anyone hearing these sides must admire the ideas, the technique, and musical blending ability of all players present.

* * *

Three days after this session, the Norvo group, without Diz and Bird, was the feature attraction at a Saturday afternoon concert at Town Hall. The concert was presented by critic Timme Rosenkrantz, who used the same personnel in recording under his own name in August. The Gillespie-Parker concert came later in the month.

The Bird-Diz Quintet, with Max Roach now its regular drummer, was the feature attraction of the June 22 concert, along with Coleman Hawkins. Buck Clayton, Sid Catlett, Don Byas, and the Erroll Garner Trio were also on the bill. Pearl Bailey provided the vocal-entertainment drawing card, and the event was emceed by "Symphony Sid" Torin, a prominent disc jockey.

Norvo and Parker had been associates since Bird's arrival on The Street in late August of 1944. It was the beginning of Parker's "Street" career and the end of Norvo's, who was playing out his final stand at the Downbeat on a bill with Billie Holiday. The Garner Trio was the second attraction at the Three Deuces when the Bird-Diz combo first arrived at the club in the spring of 1945, and, therefore, was a natural second attraction for the concert.

The *Esquire* magazine awards were then jazz status symbols, and Gillespie, Norvo, and Hawkins had been award winners during this time. One can clearly see that Parker was mainly thought of at this time as a sideman. He also continued with hard drugs and drink and often missed sets or was extremely late during the gig at The Deuces. The drugs, while seemingly not affecting his playing, made his personal life erratic and unpredictable. Gillespie stated:..."I'd get so mad. But then, oh man, he'd start playing, and I'd forget I was mad."[2]

At the end of June, Gillespie's "Hepsations of '45" tour took place, and at about this time, Miles Davis, who was then a student at Julliard, began sitting in regularly with Parker, as did Dexter Gordon. During this transitory period, Bird's only recording was with Sir Charles Thompson, his old friend from his Washington engagements who worked with him throughout the fall months on The Street.

* * *

Recording—September 4, 1945—New York City
Sir Charles Thompson All Stars—Parker (as), Thompson (p),
Dexter Gordon (ts), Danny Barker (g), Jimmy Butts (b), J.C. Heard (dr), Buck Clayton (tp).

Taking Off	Vogue (Fr) LDAP 769
If I Had You	Vogue (Fr) LDAP 769
20th Century Blues	Vogue (Fr) LDAP 769
The Street Beat	Vogue (Fr) LDAP 769

20th Century is a blues with a bridge, constructed 12—8—12. The bass begins by leaping octaves on the tonic, and the "strip-tease" type blues theme appears in the ensemble.

Ex. 22 *20th Century Blues* Motif

The theme has the blue seventh, complete with shake, as its important melodic tone, and the same pattern (with respective note changes, of course) continues on the subdominant and the dominant. The bridge is out of tempo, with some lovely melodic statements on it by Clayton (first four, theme chorus). The bridge moves into the subdominant key for the first two bars (ii7—V7—I) and the original melody (although it is not clearly stated) seems to have an augmented eleventh (b5) as important material on the secondary dominant. The bridge continues to the relative minor region and later to the dominant. The only soloist on the blues section is Bird, who is very "down-home" in his soulful one chorus. The format of this tune is refreshing, and composer credit goes to Thompson.

Sir Charles plays an introduction and the first sixteen of *If I Had You* in a relaxed swing style and Clayton plays the second half in a pleasant, but dated manner. Gordon breaks on the last two bars of the first chorus and uses four more measures—with appropriate stop-time chords from the rhythm section—to modulate from the key of B-flat to D-flat. He begins his solo in the new key at the bridge, based, of course, in the mediant minor region. Bird is not heard at all on this tune except for the cadence chords at the end of the tune (Ebm9—D7+9—Db6/9). The cadence is of the type that Stan Kenton used later in his now famous *Intermission Riff*.

The *Street Beat* is an *I Got Rhythm* derivative in A-flat that was later often confused with *Rifftide*, a Thompson original on *Lady Be Good*. The theme is a riff and ends with the tonic note being stated once, then twice, then three times, and finally on all four beats over sixteen bars.

Ex. 23 Street Beat—Theme and Tonic Endings

Thompson takes the bridge on the theme chorus and Bird lashes through the solo with quick ideas and a "cool" sound. Clayton follows with the saxes riffing behind him for sixteen and Gordon plays a masculine solo on the final sixteen. Thompson develops *Louise* during his solo for the first half of the next chorus and the bridge is a drum solo. The riff goes out with bass fills in the open spaces that end each pattern and Thompson noodles after the ending.

Takin' Off is another "Rhythm" offshoot in A-flat with the line basically being harmonized as/Ab/Bb7 Eb7/, etc. The bridge moves to the subdominant: /Db/ Ddim/Ab/Ab7/Db/Db/Bb7/Eb7/. In both instances the chords are altered on the spur of the moment to fit the soloist (common practice), and many slight variations occur throughout the choruses. Gordon blows a virile chorus followed by some tasty Thompson, and Clayton is masculine but still old-fashioned for the day. Bird emerges with solo honors, of course, with slick technique and flying ideas. The tune ends with the riff—harmonized this time—and the bass blowing the bridge, with Thompson tinkling above it.

This is not the best company, perhaps, for Bird, but the date does show the varying styles that were put together on The Street with no problems. The mutability of the musicians and their common respect for *all* music made this type of session fun and rewarding. The Apollo label, for which these sides were originally recorded, was a "black" label started in a Harlem record store in 1943.

* * *

In the late fall of 1945, Gillespie returned from his southern tour with many bad memories. "Jim Crow" had hit the "Hep-sations" tour hard and the band book had been labeled "undanceable" by the young ballroom crowd. On his return to The Street, he began putting together a compatible Bop group and the rehearsals and sessions included Bird, Thelonious Monk, Ray Brown (who arrived in New York that fall), and Stan Levey and Max Roach (the latter two alternating in the percussion department). Brown had just come off Snookum Russell's band and decided to try The Apple. Milt "Bags" Jackson, the vibes player of later MJQ fame, was also contacted by Gillespie to work in the group because of Parker's erratic habits. Gillespie was negotiating a five-man contract at Billy Berg's on the West Coast and wanted to be sure to have a five-man group. Jackson could also play passable piano for the rehearsals in New York, as could Gillespie himself.

November saw police "cleanups" and club closings on The Street, and Parker did a brief stint in Canada. For his up-coming record date on Savoy he had slated Curly Russell on bass, Roach on drums, and young Miles Davis on trumpet. Gillespie, after his return and organizational attempts, was naturally interested in the session (as Diz is in everything). Who the piano player was to be for this date is a mystery, for Bud Powell was recovering from a breakdown in Philadelphia, and the only other possibility seems to be Monk, who was making sessions and rehearsals with Diz and Bird.

On the day of the intended session, Monk was not to be found, and Bird located Argonne Thornton (later taking the Muslim name—Sadik Hakim), a boarder at Doris Sydnor's pad, to make the date; Thornton was a familiar figure on The Street. Gillespie wandered into the studio, and some quick "talk-overs" were discussed. During the morning hours, Bird had written two blues, and Gillespie expressed a desire to play piano on both of them. Miles was unsure on some of the difficult up-tempo lines (he was just nineteen years old), and Diz agreed to help out on some of these as the session went along. Savoy, because of union hassles (there were only three musicians with New York cards) and contract obligations (Gillespie was under contract to Musicraft) listed the pianist as "Hen Gates." More confusion evolved when the tracks were issued on LP because of John Mehegan's notes which cited Bud Powell as the pianist and suggested Gillespie to be the trumpet player on some of the selections on which Davis played (Diz plays only the introduction and coda an *Ko Ko* on trumpet). The session, which abounds in confusion, contains some of Parker's greatest improvisations and is probably the definitive Parker to own.

As Parker hunted around town for a better horn, Miles napped on the studio floor. The other musicians sent out for food and drinks and numerous hangers-on dropped by the studio. Finally, as things settled down, the music which oozed forth gave credibility to the whole absurd scene.

* * *

Recording—November 26, 1945—New York City
Charlie Parker's Reboppers—Parker (as), Miles Davis (tpt), D. Gillespie (p-tpt), Curly Russell (b), Max Roach (d), Argonne Thornton (p).

Billie's Bounce—Take 1	Savoy 12079
Billie's Bounce—Take 2	Savoy 12079
Billie's Bounce—Take 3	Savoy 12079
Warming Up A. Riff—Take 1	Savoy 12079, 12014
Billie's Bounce—Take 4	Savoy 12079
Billie's Bounce—Take 5—orig.	Savoy 12079, 12009
Now's The Time—Take 1	Savoy 12079
Now's The Time—Take 2	Savoy 12079
Now's The Time—Take 3	Savoy 12079
Now's The Time—Take 4—orig.	Savoy 12079, 12001
Thriving On A Riff—Take 1	Savoy 12079
Thriving On A Riff—Take 2	Savoy 12079
Thriving On A Riff—Take 3—orig.	Savoy 12079, 12009
Meandering—Take 1	Savoy 12079
Ko Ko—Take 1	Savoy 12079
Ko Ko—Take 2—orig.	Savoy 12079, 12014

Billie's Bounce and *Now's The Time* are both blues in key of F, but are much different in conception. *Now's The Time* is riff-based throughout (the riff was later stolen and made into the *Hucklebuck*), but *Billie's Bounce* begins with a short riff, expands into a linear flow and echoes the beginning riff at the end of the tune. The rhythmic motif of the beginning and ending riff is the *Moose The Mooche* rhythm "signature." Billy Shaw again is honored with the *Billie's Bounce* title.

Ex. 24 *Now's The Time* Opening Riff

Ex. 25 *Billie's Bounce*—Opening Bars

Diz's piano introduction on *Billie's Bounce*, seemingly constructed from the theme, is reminiscent of Bud Powell's later "little-dab-il-do-ya" lick on *All God's Children*. Perhaps this is why Mehegan insisted in referring to the pianist as Powell on the Savoy LP issue of this complete date. This is the only thing that remotely resembles Powell's playing on the date.

The first take of *Billie's Bounce* runs two theme choruses, after which Bird begins his solo well, but seems disgusted with a squeaky reed, and becomes lethargic. On the recording one can hear Diz's "Yeah" during Bird's solo and can also notice Parker's turning away from the mike. *Billie's* line begins in perfect unison, but breaks into harmony on the beginning and ending riff and at the final two beats of the fourth bar. Bars six to ten are played in octave unison. Miles also plays a fairly good chorus, idea-wise, on the first take, but has some intonation problems. The line is not performed too badly but Bird is a bit squeaky. The second take ends with a Bird squeak, although he sounds good as to ideas. The line is good on Take 3, and Bird plays some good sequences, but is still squeaky; he launches a "Blues In The Night" quote at one point. Miles begins to show his originality on this take.

Bird, with a different horn and reed, next blew through the chords of *Cherokee (Warmin' Up A Riff)* as a warm-up. The take cuts in on his first chorus and fades out after his third. There is poor intonation and poor recording, although there are some good ideas; on one particular "Cocktails For Two" quote in sequence, one can hear Gillespie's guffaw.

Takes 4 and 5 of *Billie's Bounce* are the best of the lot, and Take 4 contains a cleaner theme. There are three fine Parker choruses on Take 4, and Take 5 finds him in magnificent form. Miles makes excellent use of altered tones in his solo on Take 5, although he still has some problems staying in tune. Take 4 is incomplete due to another squeak, but it may have been better in the long run than Take 5 if left run through. Bird's opening chorus contains a beginning motif that would be used by many other improvisors from this time on and by Parker himself in a later rendition of *Now's The Time* (August 1953). The unison theme on the final take is not clean.

Ex. 26 *Billie's*—Bar 4—Harmony

Ex. 26A *Billie's Bounce* Solo Phrase

Gillespie plays a Bartokian tone-clustered introduction over the bass for all takes of *Now's The Time*. The first take is cut during the theme, and the second ends at beginning of the first chorus. On each of the final two takes, however, Parker plays three choruses that go to the depths of the blues without losing the complexity of his rhythmic concept. Miles, although uncertain at times, puts together some spare choruses that abound in ingenious usages of the flatted fifth and other dissonances. Gillespie's piano chords move exactly with the altered melody lines! Davis had intonation problems and difficulties in executing the thematic lines throughout the date, but his improvisations on both blues are indicative of the spare style for which he was to become famous in the late Fifties and early Sixties. There is also a nice example of Russell's "walking" bass on both of the final two takes of *Now' The Time*.

Thrivin' On A Riff is based on the *I Got Rhythm* chord pattern and was later recorded by various groups under the title *Anthropology*.

Ex. 27 *Thrivin' On A Riff*—Opening

The tune is generally credited to both Parker and Gillespie and some interesting comparisons of the theme can be made with Parker's later *Ornithology* (March 28, 1946). The phrase which opens the bridge to *Thrivin'* is melodically comparable to the opening phrase of *Ornithology*. Bird first played this phrase, of course, in his *Jumpin' Blues* solo with McShann.

Ex. 28 *Thrivin*—Opening Bar-Bridge

Ex. 29 *Ornithology*—Opening Bar-Theme

The ending of the bridge of *Thrivin'* compares exactly melodically with the seventh and eighth bars of *Ornithology*.

Ex. 30 *Thrivin'* End of Bridge

Ex. 31 *Ornithology* Bars seven and eight

(NOTE: The examples have been left in the original key and not transposed for examination because of the difference in harmonic function.)

One can also notice the "Moose the Mooche" rhythmic motif in the second bar of the opening *Thrivin'* theme as indicated above.

The first take of *Thrivin'* opens with a weird introduction by Thornton, and on the theme, Miles blows softer than Parker in a "following" manner. Miles has often stated that he did this in his early days with Bird: "I used to play under Bird all the time. When Bird would play a melody, I'd play just under him and let him swing the note. The only thing that I'd add would be a larger sound."[3] Davis is very unsure of the theme on both the first and third takes. (The second take consists of a wild piano introduction and sixteen bars of muted trumpet improvisation.) On the third take, Miles's falling in and out of the theme is noticeable; in fact, Mehegan states in the liner notes to the Savoy LP: "Parker alone on the head." The first take contains excellent solo work by both Bird and Miles. Miles quotes "Honey" and "Shave and a Haircut" in the solo. There is more fine muted Miles on the second take, and Bird constructs two magnificent choruses on Take 3. Miles also plays well on the final take and Thornton (or Hakim) plays a strange "limping" piano solo. Notated below are the opening two bars of each of Parker's choruses on the final take for ease of identification.

Ex. 32 *Thrivin'*—opening bars—Chorus I Take 3

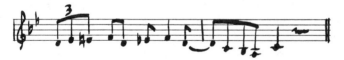

Ex. 33 *Thrivin'*—opening bars—Chorus II Take 3

Meandering is another "warm-up"—on the chords of *Embraceable You*—that was later issued. This is our first look at the motif that Parker would use so successfully in *Embraceable You* through the years.

Ex. 34 *Meanderin'* motif

There is fine Parker on this recording, and Gillespie plays a pensive piano solo that he cuts off at the fourteenth bar.

Roach's exciting drumming opens *Ko Ko* and it is still a thrill to hear. This is Parker's first recording with a drummer compatible with the new music. After the drum introduction, however, the opening chorus is very difficult to analyze. An eight-bar written or memorized theme is played in unison, but the tonality, almost minor sounding, is vague. There is no harmonic accompaniment, only the wild Roach drum background. Gillespie is the trumpet player on this first chorus, as the line proved a bit much for young Miles. Following the first section comes an improvised eight-bar trumpet solo which seems to hint at dominant "suspended" type harmonies; the alto follows with eight bars of the same. Mehegan, in the liner notes, describes these sections as "...seemingly based on a Bb ostinato." This could certainly be true, for on a 1947 radio broadcast, where these sections are being used to introduce all the performers with each one soloing, bassist Ray Brown centers his solo completely around the Bb tonic. There is a final written (or memorized) eight-bar line before launching into the improvisation section proper, which is based on *Cherokee*. The final written section also gives an impression of changing, suspended harmonies, sometimes feeling and sounding like F-minor, or even modal, in nature.

The octave jump on "F" before the "lead-in" section of the final eight bars seems to shout "Ko Ko!" On Take 1, Gillespie bounds back to the piano after the introductory section; Parker starts to blow on the *Cherokee* chords, and Davis intones the melody to *Cherokee* underneath the improvisation. Parker quickly cuts off the take (the melody probably could not be used because of royalties).

On the second take, Davis lays out completely and Parker plays one of the greatest solos in the history of jazz. Bird's two choruses present the ultimate in flowing ideas, flawless execution, and cohesion of thoughts. The ideas seem to explode from his mind and through his fingers with rapid-fire precision. This is the one Parker record that must be present in any jazz collection. A comparison of this solo with the tape recorded one of 1942 at Monroe's should be an inspiration to any young improvisor. The advancement that had been made in Parker's conception, both melodic and rhythmic, in only three years is truly phenomenal. From this time forward, *Cherokee* became a "testing" tune at musicians' sessions. It's notorious bridge, moving rapidly through different keys, could not be negotiated unless a musician had done his "homework."

The bridge, however, was based entirely on ii7—V7—I patterns in different keys, and a musician who "woodsheded" his chords and scales, as Bird had done in the Ozarks, would be able to find his way through this labyrinth without too much trouble, even if he was not able to come near the brilliant flash of invention that Parker had set as a standard.

* * *

The Gillespie entourage—Bird, Levey, Ray Brown, Milt Jackson—was now ready for their West Coast excursion. The final arrangements for the booking at Billy Berg's had been completed by Billy Shaw and the group was looking forward to the Los Angeles train trip. Al Haig, slated to be the group's pianist, was already in Hollywood with the Charlie Barnet band.

Miles Davis, leaving Julliard when Bird left The Street, joined the Benny Carter band which was also headed for the coast. Joe Albany, out west with Georgie Auld, later joined Boyd Raeburn, who at that time only maintained a "rehearsal band." Raeburn's group included, at various times, pianists George Handy and Dodo Marmarosa. These men were all to figure heavily in Parker's West Coast activities as was Howard McGhee, who worked on the coast during 1945 with Coleman Hawkins until summer, when he began leading his own groups. Roy Porter, drums, and Bob Kesterson, bass, were two of McGhee's frequent sidemen. Lucky Thompson, coming off the Basie band in the fall, was becoming one of the busiest sidemen on the coast because of his extreme adaptability. Thompson had also worked in the Eckstine band with Bird and Diz and would later become Parker's "back-up" replacement with Gillespie.

The scene was therefore set for the Gillespie quintet to open on Monday, December 10, 1945, at Billy Berg's on Vine Street in Hollywood.

CHAPTER VI

SO WHAT, HORACE GREELEY
The Western Venture
(December 1945-February 1946)

When I was at home, I was in a better place; but travelers must be content.

William Shakespeare—As You Like It.
Act II

The young men did go west, but the effect on almost everyone was disastrous. The beginning audiences at Berg's were fairly good, because of curiosity, but the nightly clientele soon came to be only musicians and "hipsters", the meager following of the new music. Parker, in a *Metronome* interview, later told Leonard Feather: "...What made it worst of all was that nobody understood our music out on the coast. They hated it, Leonard. I can't begin to tell you how I yearned for New York."

Furthermore, the heroin squeeze also made Parker yearn for New York; prices were high on the coast, and he was addicted to the drug. On the train to the coast, he suffered withdrawal symptoms, and his twenty-five-year-old body was beginning to show the effects of ten years of abuse. His friend, Benedetti, who had followed the Gillespie group to the coast, found Bird a "connection" in Hollywood. A man named Emry Byrd, called "Moose the Mooche" by the hip, ran a Central Avenue shoe shine stand that trafficked in drugs. "Moose" moved about Central Avenue (the Los Angeles equivalent to The Street) on crutches because of polio. Parker became a prime customer of "The Mooche" and also became adept at conning doctors into writing morphine prescriptions for faked kidney pains and other invented diseases. His behavior remained erratic, and most of his time was spent trying to procure drugs for his ever growing habit, or drinking when no drugs were available. At Berg's, he was constantly late or missed the complete set, and Gillespie, through Berg's suggestion, hired Lucky Thompson to be the stand-in replacement for Parker. Gillespie recounts:

...I had a five man contract. But I took six [Milt Jackson] so that I'd have five men on the bandstand all the time. And then Billy Berg said we weren't heavy enough and hired Lucky Thompson to play with us.[1]

The repertoire of the Gillespie group at Berg's consisted of tunes that Parker and Gillespie had recorded during 1945 (*Groovin' High, Hot House, Dizzy Atmosphere, Shaw 'Nuff, Salt Peanuts, KoKo, Thrivin' On A Riff*) and some standard ballads that they were famous for playing together (*All The Things You Are, Loverman, I Can't Get Started*, and others). According to the records the Gillespie group made without Parker before leaving the coast, the repertoire also included *Confirmation*, a Parker tune; *'Round Midnight*, a Thelonious Monk ballad; and *When I Grow To Old To*, a Gillespie comedy vocal spoof. One can make an educated guess that tunes such as *Blue and Boogie, Night In Tunisa*, and *BeBop* were also in the "book." Parker played these tunes on the coast later on and therefore was familiar with their themes. Whether Parker's *Yardbird Suite* and *Ornithology* were being used as themes is also speculative, but it is a possibility since they were already "composed" by this time and ready for use. Moreover, Parker recorded them a month and a half after the Berg engagement. In the few times that Gillespie and Parker were to play together after the stay in California, they generally reverted to the material they had worked out during 1945 and early 1946.

Slim Gaillard, a comedic guitarist, was the co-attraction at Berg's during the stay of the Gillespie group. At the time, Dodo Marmarosa was working with him, and Lucky Thompson had done some recording with him during December. Gaillard formerly had a very successful duo with Slam Stewart (*Slim and Slam*) that was very popular along Fifty-Second Street. The big hit was *Flat Foot Floogie* from 1938, and the duo capitalized on it until they separated at the beginning of World War II. Three days before the new year, Gaillard used Bird and Diz on a record date that he had contracted for Beltone, a small independent label.

* * *

Recording—December 29, 1945—Los Angeles
Slim Gaillard and His Orchestra—C. Parker (as), D. Gillespie (tp) Jack McVea (ts), Dodo Marmarosa (p), Slim Gaillard (gtr-vcl), Bam Brown (b), Zutty Singleton (dr).

Dizzy Boogie—Take 1	BYG (Fr) 529130
Dizzy Boogie—Take 2—orig.	BYG (Fr) 529130, Savoy 12014
Flat Foot Floogie—Take 1	BYG (Fr) 529130
Flat Foot Floogie—Take 2—orig.	BYG (Fr) 529130, Savoy 12014
Poppity Pop—Take 2	BYG (Fr) 529130, Savoy 12014
Slim's Jam	BYG (Fr) 529130, Savoy 12014

Dizzy Boogie is a boogie blues with the first chorus in the traditional eight-to-the-bar style by Marmarosa, who is then joined by Gaillard, banging out licks in the high treble of the piano, a la Lionel Hampton, for the succeeding two choruses. The blowing choruses are all preceded by a standard four-bar boogie style "lead-in" and the solo order is McVea, Diz, Bird. Bird and Diz solo well, if one considers the trite material, and McVea is boisterous, if nothing else. The final chorus is a riff with a typical boogie ending. The initial take has Gaillard wrongly anticipating the first lead-in, and a Parker solo that is inferior to the one on the second take. There is also the annoyance of Gaillard continuing his treble banging behind the soloists. On the final take, however, Gaillard lays out behind the soloists, and the saxes provide variety with a riff behind Diz. On the French label part of the opening piano chorus is cut from the original take.

Flat Foot was an attempt to remake the old hit as a selling point for the small label. The first take is acoustically bad—disturbingly "echo-y"—and is incomplete. Both takes, however, do contain Bird solos, and the first one has the better Parker. The theme is an *I Got Rhythm* derivative in F, with the *Honeysuckle Rose* bridge, and begins with a guitar introduction before moving to a group vocal, with Gaillard singing alone at the bridge. The second chorus is a nonsense vocal riff until the bridge, which McVea blows, and Diz comes in for the last eight. Bird plays a sixteen-bar solo over old-fashioned rhythm; then Gaillard has the bridge and the group vocal takes it out. There is a tag ending, with first a piano break and then bass, and a "flat-five", "be-bop" ending. The first take is cut off before the final group vocal.

Poppity is another nonsense ditty with the harmonic base being *I Got Rhythm* in B-flat. There is a humorous piano intro by Dodo before the inevitable group vocal. McVea and Diz (cup muted) split a chorus, and so do Bird and Gaillard. A full chorus vocal follows, and Dodo plays sixteen before the vocal takes it out. Again, the choruses are enjoyable, in spite of the nonsensical nature of the music, and it is interesting to hear the "flat-five's" against the secondary dominants in Marmarosa's bridge harmonization. On this cut, however, as well as on some of the others, it is evident that Bird is having reed trouble.

Slim's Jam is a "hip talk" ruse by Gaillard over a piano vamp of "We-want-Can-tor" in A-flat. Gaillard talks to each soloist as they appear, and the tune has, therefore, a rare recorded example of Bird speaking; he mentions the reed problem. During Gillespie's conversation, moreover, there is reference to the Armed Forces Radio Services recording (Jubilee) that Parker and Gillespie were to do later in the day, and Diz's final solo transforms the relaxed ruse into a swinging send-off.

The material is humorous, historically interesting, and a clear example of Parker and Gillespie's adaptability, but it certainly is not essential Parker.

Recording—December 29—AFRS Jubilee—Los Angeles
Dizzy Gillespie Sextet—Gillespie (tp); Parker (as); Milt Jackson (vbs); Al Haig (p); Stan Levey (dr); Ray Brown (b).

    Dizzy Atmosphere   Richelieu AX-120

Unlike the previous recording, this is a great example of what the Gillespie-Parker group sounded like in California. The recording "fades in" during the bass and drum introduction but clears as the trumpet and alto state their eight bars apiece in the introductory section. The theme is played in unison by Bird, Diz, and Jackson; and the solos are fabulous. Bird begins with a rousing, idea-packed two-chorus solo and quotes *In the Gloaming* at the beginning of the second eight-bar section of the second chorus. Jackson follows with a fine solo and Diz comes on like "Gangbusters." One of Gillespie's technical "signature" licks can be heard in the second eight of the first chorus, and at the beginning of the second chorus, Diz quotes *Over There* (a good indication that this recording is dated correctly). The piano player seems to play with a bit stronger touch than Haig usually did, but this is debatable. At any rate there is a tremendous piano chorus and a clean ending line. During the alto answer at the coda, Dizzy good-naturedly chides Bird by repeating Parker's lead-in figure (a favorite Bird lick) twice behind the solo.

There is also a *Salt Peanuts* done at this session, but it is very difficult to come by.

Recording—Circa 1945
Gillespie (tp), Parker (as), Rest Unknown
    Groovin' High   Main Man 617
The major thing to look for in identifying this recording is the occurrence of the modulation back to the original key *after* Gillespie's solo, and not before as on the "studio" recording. The tune begins the same as the "studio" recording, however, and there is a bass break that seems to be bowed and hummed in the introduction. This indicates that the bassist *might* be Stewart. Furthermore, the bass is also bowed during the downward modulation to D-flat for Parker's chorus. Bird and Diz both play excellent choruses, and the comping is done by someone knowledgeable about the new music and not a transitionary figure. If the recording was done in New York during Parker's and Diz's early days on The Street, it could be Haig or Joe Albany. If it is later, at Berg's, perhaps Jackson is playing piano, for there is no vibes player on the side. All this is speculation, however, and the only thing we can reasonably be sure of is that the recording was done in 1945 in a club. The improvisations are wonderful statements and the modulation back to E-flat occurs between Dizzy's solo and the piano. It is an interesting recording, but most versions are found only on "bootleg" issues.

The original "studio" recording had a bass chorus by Stewart, then the modulation back to E-flat, then Gillespie; therefore, it is strange that Stewart would not solo, if it was he on bass. The recording, moreover, seems to have a more modern aspect than one which would have been done too early in 1945.

* * *

During the bleak January of 1946, two customers at Berg's—Norman Granz and Ross Russell—were later to figure prominently in Parker's recording career. Granz was a West Coast jazz "promoter" who had been organizing concerts and tours since 1942; and in 1944, he had begun a series of "on the spot" recordings and completed a movie short entitled "Jammin' the Blues". Granz immediately contracted Parker and Gillespie to appear on one of his all star bills at Philharmonic Hall; the concert was scheduled for Tuesday, January 29, and was also to include Lester Young. The "Jazz at the Philharmonic" (JATP) concerts were usually of a "jam session" nature with sometimes both soloists and audience going beyond the limits of good musical taste. Raucous shouts of encouragement inspired bleating, one-note, repetitive solos (or vice-versa), and Granz was known to encourage such proceedings. The inclusion of Parker and Gillespie seems to have been an attempt to attract some of the followers of the new music, along with the standard jazz followers, to the concert.

* * *

Recording—January 29, 1946—Los Angeles
JATP—Al Killian, D. Gillespie (tp), C. Parker, W. Smith (as), Charlie Ventura, Lester Young (ts), Mel Powell (p), Bill Hadnott (b), Lee Young (dr).

Sweet Georgia Brown   Dot DLP 3444

The other tunes from this concert are *The Man I Love* and *Crazy Rhythm*, but Parker is only present on *Sweet Georgia Brown*, where he presents a fine solo. One can easily note the difference in conception between him and the other soloists on the program. Moreover, it is interesting to hear Parker work with this particular piece of material: the rhythm section chugs along in a 1930-like groove, but Bird blows long sinuous lines that are spellbinding; the contrast is at times amusing.

On the original 78 rpm, the performance was too long for one side of the record and was therefore listed as *Sweet Georgia Brown I* and *Sweet Georgia Brown II*. This is just one continuous performance, of course, and not a second version. This is true of many Granz concert recordings and also of other "concert" records of the period. Many times the titles appear in this same manner on LP's, and it is misleading, especially to the novice listener.

* * *

Ross Russell, the owner of the Tempo Music Shop on Hollywood Boulevard, was then starting a small, obscure record label named Dial. Russell had been a champion of traditional jazz, but had decided to try recording some of the "new jazz" since not many labels were doing anything along this line. George Handy, who was doing "rehearsal" charts for the Boyd Raeburn band, was contracted by Russell to form a group that could perform the new music. Handy chose to use Gillespie's Berg's unit with Lester Young added and Handy himself replacing Haig. A session was scheduled for Tuesday, January 22, but Young was out of town and could not make the date. On the following Tuesday (the off night at Berg's), Parker, Gillespie, and Young were involved in the JATP concert. Finally, February 5th was arrived at as a suitable date. This was the day after the closing date at Billy Berg's.

When Handy went about assembling his group for the forthcoming date, however, Lester Young could not be found, and no one had seen Milt Jackson since the night before. To fill in for the missing men, Lucky Thompson and guitarist Arv Garrison were asked to make the session. The entourage, complete with "groupies" as they are known in today's jargon (then known as "hippies"—a derogatory term to musicians meaning pseudo-hip) then made the northeast trek to the Glendale section, near Forest Lawn Cemetery, where Electro Broadcast Studios were located. Because of the presence of the many non-musicians, however, the session dissolved into chaos and Handy only managed to rehearse the group and do one short pressing on *Diggin' Diz*, his original on the chords of *Lover*.

* * *

Recording—February 5, 1946—Electro Broadcast Studios, Glendale, California.
Tempo Jazzmen—D. Gillespie (tp), C. Parker (as), Lucky Thompson (ts), George Handy (p), Arv Garrison (g), Ray Brown (b), Stan Levey (dr).

Diggin' Diz   Spotlite (Eng.) 101

The triplet figure that opens the line is echoed on a secondary dominant a half-step down and ends on the flat-five of the chord. The chords continue downward in half-steps, and the line continues in the same fashion as the opening phrase.

Ex. 35 *Diggin' Diz* Opening Phrase

The sections of the tune are in sixteens instead of the usual eights (A16—A16—B16—A16) and the "line" is only on the "A" section; the bridge is always improvised.

The first chorus is ragged, but Handy plays a beautiful improvisation on the bridge section, starting his solo with the "flat-five" leaps that are bounced around by Diz and Bird at the end of the theme and working this motif into the new tonal area.

Ex. 36 Diggin' Diz Ending Motif

Parker plays the final "A" section of the first chorus and sounds very melodic, almost as if he is purposely avoiding the flat-five sound. This is especially evident when compared with Gillespie's sixteen which directly follows. A statement by Gillespie in an interview with Maitland Edey, Jr. that is quoted in Ira Gitler's *Jazz Masters of The Forties* illustrates the point: "...I was more for chord variation and he was more for melody, I think. But when we got together each influenced the other." On this particular tune, Bird's thinking is horizontal—creating a continuous melody over a set of chords, even though the individual notes make sense with each chord. Diz, however, is thinking vertically—reaching for the intervals related to each individual chord and deriving melody from these intervals. If for no other reason this track is interesting for this striking illustration.

Thompson and Garrison are melodic but undistinguished on the second "A" section and the bridge respectively, and Handy again comes through with a fine solo (both Handy solos are played with right hand alone). The tune ends with the line and an extremely ragged ending.

* * *

Handy tried to organize the group for another, calmer session on February 7, but Young was still missing and Bird had lost Handy, who had stayed with him all through the night of the 6th in an effort to get him to the studio. Exhausted, Handy told Russell he could not go through with the date, but Gillespie, always ready in an emergency, took his regular group, with Haig on piano and Lucky

Thompson replacing Bird, to Glendale and completed five tunes, one of which was *Diggin' Diz*. The tune is done at a crisper tempo than the one with Parker, and, of course, there is no alto chorus on it (although at times this version is listed as the earlier one). The tune is played cleanly and is fitted with better ending sections on the theme chorus and a coda which includes a bass solo. At sometime between the first date and the second, rehearsals were held on this tune; any comparison of the two sides easily substantiates that. The question is: When? Who wrote the better ending sections (or "worked them out")? Haig and Jackson seem familiar with the tune and play well on it. Perhaps some "run-throughs" in a sober atmosphere accomplished this, but—whatever—the contrast is great.

The other tunes recorded were *Confirmation, Dizzy Atmosphere, When I Grow Too Old To,* and *'Round Midnight.* There are some title mix-ups, and on a Jazztone issue, *Confirmation* and *Diggin' Diz* have reversed titles. *Dizzy Atmosphere* was released in two takes as *Dynamo "A"* and *Dynamo "B",* but it is possible that the *Dynamo* title was intended for *Diggin' Diz* since almost a decade later Parker announces on a radio broadcast the title of *Dynamo* and plays the line generally called *Diggin' Diz*; he even argues with Leonard Feather on the point! It is worth hearing the Gillespie-sans-Parker sides to gain an insight into the period, the group's repertoire, and the previous recording. An added attraction is Thompson's fine playing on *Dynamo (Dizzy Atmosphere).*

* * *

Following the February recording session, the Gillespie group was ready to return to New York by plane, but Parker, naturally, could not be found. Stan Levey recounts:

> ...I had all the plane tickets for the guys.... For two hours that night, I took cabs all over town looking for him. Not a trace.... Finally, I gave up, rode out to Burbank Airport, and took off for New York. Bird never made that plane.[2]

Parker is quoted as telling Art Farmer a month or so later; "Diz got away while the getting was good, and I'm catching everything"[3] He implied, of course, that Diz deserted him and left him stranded in California. Hereafter, the relationship between the two innovaters was never the same. Dizzy returned to Fifty-Second Street to the Spotlite and went on to form a big band that brought some public acclaim. Parker, however, remained in the West, became emotionally embittered and physically depleted, and experienced a complete breakdown in late July. The men were reunited in later years on several concerts and on one "studio" recording date. The actual animosity faded with time but strained communications prevailed.

In summation, the impact of the Gillespie-Parker group was probably best assessed by Diz himself:

> Our association—Charlie and me—wasn't a very long association, but it was deep, real deep. It was quick and, you know, like you could draw an analogy—like Hitler. Like Hitler's thing didn't last long, but it was so dynamic and it left such a mark. It's like in music. You don't necessarily play a hundred choruses to make a statement. It's the intensity that counts.[4]

CHAPTER VII

ON THE COAST
A Purgatorial Period
(February 1946-March 1947)

I am the very slave of circumstance and impulse—borne away with every breath.

Byron—Sardanapalus. Act IV

A Bellevue Hospital report on Parker from 1954 states: "There was a history given that the patient was treated in 1945, in Los Angeles, for lues [syphilis] with penicillin, bismuth and arsenic."[1] Parker, however, was in Los Angeles for only part of December during 1945. The treatment could have been during 1946, even after his final collapse. This period of his life, however, can be better understood if one realizes that his central nervous system was battling syphilis and possibly the effects of the drugs used for it. These effects coupled with his own dependence on narcotics and the artistic frustration of not being accepted by the public heaped an unimaginable burden upon the man.

The burden, however, did not cool his enthusiasm for playing. During the Berg's engagement, for instance, Parker had found his way into the Central Avenue clubs for frequent sessions. Lovejoy's and The Club Alabam were two famous spots, and Bird also frequented the Finale Club, an after-hours place in the "Little Tokyo" section west of Central Avenue near First Street. About two weeks after Gillespie's departure, moreover, Parker showed up at Russell's Tempo Music Shop. He spoke apologetically to Russell about the Handy recording date and discussed grandiose plans for future recordings. Russell, therefore, signed Parker to an exclusive contract (even though he had already signed with Savoy before leaving New York). A date was set up for late March, and Bird went about finding work.

Miles Davis arrived in town with Benny Carter's big band, and he and Parker formed the front line of the group at the Finale. The job was from 1:00 A.M. to 4:00 A.M., and Davis was working with Carter at the Orpheum Theatre and making Parker's gig later. Davis ran into some union problems, however, and he soon left Carter and stayed exclusively with Bird. The rhythm section consisted of Joe Albany, piano; Addison Farmer, bass; and Chuck Thompson on drums.

* * *

76   Yardbird Suite

Recording—Probably March 1946— Finale Club.
C. Parker (as), Miles Davis (tpt), Joe Albany (p), prob. Addison Farmer (b), prob.
Chuck Thompson (d).

Blue 'n' Boogie	Phoenix 17
Billie's Bounce	Phoenix 17
Anthropology	Phoenix 17
Ornithology	Phoenix 17
All The Things You Are	Phoenix 17

The Gillespie composition *Blue 'n' Boogie* has a sixteen-bar introduction which
can be diagrammed as follows:

1	2	3	4	
trumpet.	....	....	....	

5	6	7	8	
alto [echo of trumpet four]	....	....	....	

9	10	11	12	
trumpet [echo of last 2]	....	alto [echo of trumpet]	....	

13	14	15	16	
trumpet	....	....alto lead-in	....	

The rhythm section plays an accented "sock" on an anticipated third beat
at the end of the trumpet four, and two "socks" on anticipated beats three and
four of the alto echo. The rhythmic "sock" pattern is repeated after the two-bar
echoes in the same manner. The material in the final four bars of the intro is
in the nature of a free improvisational lead-in.

The opening riff blues is stated in unison by the horns and repeated in octave
unison. Albany plays three exciting choruses, and then a four-bar riff which sounds
like *Now's The Time* launches Bird's improvisation. The riff is repeated at the
beginning of the next chorus after which Bird again blows. He continues through
two more choruses, starting the first with "Happy Birthday." Miles follows with
two choruses and anticipates the "launching" riff that is used following his solo.
The riff appears in the next two choruses—a melody taken from *Opus X*, done
by the Eckstine band, and which later inspired Horace Silver's *Opus De Funk*—
and Miles is the featured soloist on the final eight of each of the partial-riff choruses.
A two-chorus bass solo with inventive comping by Albany leads to a circle-ish
sounding riff which is repeated in octave unison. The next riff (the fifth used in
this version) makes comical use of "stop-time" and is repeated in octave unison
at a lower dynamic level. For a conclusion, the opening theme returns in unison
and is repeated in octave unison.

The *original* version of *Boogie*, done by Gillespie in 1945, (Savoy 12020), is much simpler in conception. The reason for this, one may speculate, is probably because it was done with Dexter Gordon instead of Bird, and Gordon was probably not familiar with all the riffs worked out by Parker and Gillespie together. The only "launching" riff used is the one which suggests the rhythm of the *Now's The Time* riff, and in the intro there is no "echoing"—Gillespie states the first eight by himself and the next four are by both horns in octave unison. The "lead-in" bars are nearly the same as this version. A version done by both Parker and Gillespie in 1951, however, uses all five riffs in the same order as this recording, and the introduction is identical.

The opening phrase of Parker's solo on *Billie's Bounce* is the same as the one used on Take 4 of the November 26, 1945 recording and the *Now's The Time* solo of August 1953. There are four Bird choruses, two of Miles, and five wailing Albany choruses.

Anthropology shows Miles's improvement since the previous year, especially on the theme choruses, and Albany's inventive comping—sometimes using linear single-note phrases—is unbelievable for the time.

The triplet figure that would cause much trouble in Bird's "studio" recording is not used on *Ornithology* (theme), and Albany leads the group in strongly at the close of each sixteen. One can see that this tune would have been more effective on the March Dial recording date if Albany had been the pianist. During Bird's first chorus (of two), however, he does play an improvisational triplet figure that roughly corresponds to the triplet figure used in the theme of the later recording. After Miles's two choruses, Albany plays two excellent developmental-type choruses that abound in inventive left hand work. An eight-bar riff is used on each sixteen-bar section of the next chorus with Bird blowing the latter half of each section. The theme fades out after the first sixteen of the final chorus.

All The Things You are is notable for the extreme melodic invention of Parker and the contrast of lyricism and multi-notedness by Davis. In addition, Albany is almost "Baroque-ish." The intro and coda is the same as the Parker-Gillespie version of 1945 and the format is generally the same—trumpet on "A" section with alto behind, alto solo on bridge. The coda enters immediately after Albany's choruses with no return of the theme.

Albany's playing throughout this set is beautiful and should be heard. In fact, the whole set makes for valuable listening despite the poor fidelity.

* * *

Various musicians would frequent the Finale Club, and from these, Bird got together personnel for the upcoming Dial date. The musicians were familiar with the material from frequent jamming and rehearsing with Bird, and repertoire, therefore, was not a problem. As the date approached, however, Albany and Parker had a disagreement, and Albany left the group. He described it in *Down Beat* (October 24, 1963) in an interview with Ira Gitler:

Bird was singing to me like I wasn't comping right, so I did it every which way, and finally I did what I thought was backwards comping out of time, and I still didn't please him, so I turned around and said "_____You, Bird" and that was the end. He fired me. We made up after that and laughed about it.

On the night before the session, Red Callender, scheduled to be the bassist, also quit; Parker had scheduled a rehearsal, and then had let the musicians sit, as he scurried around for two hours looking for "Moose." The recording did take place, however, with some last minute replacements, and produced some fine Parker.

* * *

Recording—March 28, 1946—Radio Recorders, Santa Monica Boulevard, Los Angeles
*Charlie Parker Septet—*C. Parker (as), Miles Davis (tp), Lucky Thompson (ts), Dodo Marmarosa (p), Arv Garrison (gtr), Vic McMillan (b), Roy Porter (d).

Moose The Mooche—Take 1	Spotlite (Eng) 101
Moose The Mooche—Take 2	Spotlite (Eng) 101
Moose The Mooche—Take 3	Spotlite (Eng) 101
Yardbird Suite—Take 1	Spotlite (Eng) 101
Yardbird Suite—Take 4	Spotlite (Eng) 101
Ornithology—Take 1	Spotlite (Eng) 101
Ornithology—Take 3	Spotlite (Eng) 101
Ornithology—Take 4	Spotlite (Eng) 101
Famous Alto Break—Take 1 (Part of Tunisa)	Spotlite (Eng) 101
Night In Tunisa—Take 4	Spotlite (Eng) 101
Night In Tunisa—Take 5	Spotlite (Eng) 101

Finally, we hear the germ motif that Bird had been using for at least a year in his solos made into a composition—*Moose The Mooche.*

Ex. 37—*Moose The Mooche* Beginning of Theme

The tune is, of course, named for the infamous heroin pusher and is based on the *I Got Rhythm* structure. Dodo plays an introduction based on the theme on all three takes, and the solo order is Parker for a full chorus, Davis and Thompson splitting one, and Dodo going back to the bridge for his sixteen bars. The unison theme follows, with a tag using the "Moose" motif played by alto, then tenor, then piano. The ending is a "ka-boom" drum lick. Miles plays open horn on the first take, then uses a cup mute on the others. His solos are well constructed, and on the hard to find and poorly recorded third take, he develops elements of the theme in his solo. The second take is the one originally issued, although the first one also contains good Parker. Bird probably preferred the muted version. The Parker solo on Take 2 is one of those beauties that contains separate elements hanging strangely together. Notated below is the beginning phrase of his solo and also the phrase that begins the final eight. The latter is an easy one by which to identify the take.

Ex. 38 *Moose* Beginning of Parker's Chorus

Ex. 39 *Moose* Beginning of Last Eight—Parker Chorus

Marmarosa does some comping on the first take at times (rest-2-3-4) that is interesting, especially since Garrison does not play on this tune. The first piano solo contains some two-handed unison playing, and the second one is lighter, but also with one spot of octave unison. The third Dodo solo begins with "whole tone" elements against the bridge chords and moves into a pleasant lead-in to the theme. Thompson plays well, but is rather rough-toned on the original (second) take.

The third take can only be found on Spotlite, but it is worth hearing, for Parker uses elements from both of his previous solos and Dodo does some wild comping behind the theme. The sound (from a poorly preserved master) is bad, but tolerable.

A piano introduction of flippant runs suspended over the thumping dominant pedal tone of the bass begins *Yardbird*. Parker is "cool" on his solos on this tune, especially the first take—much different from his fiery solos. The theme is the tune that was played with McShann as *What Price Love*, and in his solo on the fourth take, Parker plays the phrase that would become *Cool Blues* a year later.

Ex. 40 *Yardbird Suite* Opening of Theme

Ex. 41 *Yardbird Suite* "Cool Blues" Phrase—Take 4 Parker Solo—Bars 7-8

The only takes available are 1 and 4 and the solo order is a bit different on each. On Take 1, Miles and Thompson split the chorus that follows Bird; then Dodo plays half of the next; Garrison takes the bridge, and the ensemble plays the last eight out with the theme. On the fourth take, Davis has the beginning sixteen and final eight, spelled by Thompson on the bridge; then Thompson splits the next one with Garrison. Dodo goes back and improvises on the bridge and the ensemble takes the theme out. Both Parker solos are masterful, and Miles is again muted, using back and forth alternating eighths quite frequently. Thompson is making a transition toward the modern in his solos, and Garrison is pleasant, but repetitive.

Ornithology, a *How High The Moon* derivative based melodically on Parker's opening phrase of *The Jumpin' Blues* solo with McShann, opens with a drum introduction. Porter uses brushes until the final and fastest take, on which he switches to sticks. The second take is lost, but it can be assumed that he also used brushes, as he did on the third. The difficulty in this tune stems from the triplet figure found at the end of each sixteen-bar section.

Ex. 42 Ornithology Theme Figure

Ex. 43 *Ornithology* Triplet Figure

At the end of the first sixteen, the theme contains the triplet figure in the twelfth bar and the pianist is expected to pick up the figure and launch a four-bar improvised solo section back to the theme. Dodo does it differently each time, of course—the cleanest probably being the first chorus of the final take. On the "end" sixteen of the tune, the figure is passed from trumpet (starting in the twelfth bar) to alto to tenor (octave lower) to guitar to piano, ending on the first beat of the next chorus. Dodo does not make the triplet figure cleanly on the first take and uses it as a point of departure into an improvisation. This first chorus was to have been Parker's, but because of the mix-up, Bird does no solo at all on this take. The take was later released on a Dial LP, containing sides made by a Marmarosa trio.

The third take, released as *Bird Lore*, has a good triplet lead-in and a fine Parker "cool" chorus. Miles also sounds good, and Thompson is emotional.

The final take contains a Parker masterpiece of improvisation, and Dodo solves the lead-in problem at the "flying" tempo by playing three "on-the-beat" chords at his "triplet break," leading to a final tonic on the first beat of the next chorus. This kicks Bird off into his flight.

Ex. 44 *Ornithology* Lead-in and Opening to Parker Chorus-Take 4

The Gillespie chestnut, *Tunisa*, has a theme based on Neopolitan harmony ("flatted-fifth" substitute for the dominant) resolving to the tonic; the introduction is also based on the same harmony. The piano, bass, and guitar state broken chord figures in two-bar patterns for eight measures; the saxes then play an accented, swaying, two-bar phrase twice, over the rhythm sections pattern, and then the theme enters on trumpet, with the other patterns continuing underneath.

Ex. 45 *Night in Tunisa* Piano-Bass-Guitar Figure

Ex. 46 *Tunisa* Saxophone Figure

Ex. 47 *Tunisa* Trumpet Melody

The bridge melody moves to the subdominant area and then to the relative major area, employing supertonic-dominant-tonic cadences in both areas. Following the standard thirty-two-bar chorus, there is a sixteen-bar interlude leading to the improvisation section (probably the reason for the old title of *Interlude*). This interlude is based on a two-bar phrase based on three different notes. The top note stays the same, but the others change with the harmony. It gives a "common-tone" effect.

Harmonic Interlude:/Em7/Em7/Eb7/Eb7/Dm7/Dm7/G7/G7/C7(13+11)/C7(13+11)/Gb7+9/ Gb7+9/F/area/A7/area/

⌞___ break ___⌟

Ex. 48 *Tunisa* Rhythmic Phrase in Interlude

The final four bars of the interlude are a showcase break for Parker, and he certainly fills the bill. The first take, rejected for some reason, was issued by Dial as *Famous Alto Break*; it contains the interlude, Bird's break and his sixteen-bar solo. Parker is often quoted as saying after this take "Man, I'll never make that break again." But he does, and the notes are close to the same, if not as keenly placed rhythmically. Miles's best solo is on Take 4 where he is "Dizzy-ish," but Parker's best is the final take. It is interesting to note that Parker ends all of the breaks on the same note (flat two). The format is Bird—16; Miles—16; Thompson—

16; Garrison—bridge, and then eight bars of the theme. The tune ends with a fade-out on the piano-bass-drums figure.

These sides are wonderful examples of Parker's music; the ensemble sounds fine, the solos are varied in style, and the tunes are extremely interesting. In the ensemble, however, this writer cannot detect guitarist Garrison playing chords, perhaps he is only present as a melodic voice. Nevertheless, first rate jazz is played on *all* the tunes on this date.

*   *   *

Dial records was to publish the original Parker tunes used on the March date. According to Russell, however, Parker never prepared the copyright forms and lead sheets to be sent to the Library of Congress; therefore, the tunes remained uncopyrighted.[2] Parker's contract with Dial called for two cents per record sold on his originals.

April proved a fateful month for Parker, The Finale was closing because of the lack of business and money got tighter and tighter. In order to obtain the drugs he desperately needed, Parker signed over half of his royalties from all Dial recordings to Emry Byrd, "The Mooche." Russell reproduces the contract documents—both Parker's handwritten agreement (dated April 3rd) and the later typed and witnessed document (dated May 3rd)—in his book, *Bird Lives*. "Moose" was arrested soon after and sent to San Quentin prison, and from there communicated with Russell.

Parker did two concerts with a Granz JATP group during April and also organized a group of his own to play a concert at the Carver Club at UCLA. The latter group included Davis, Lucky Thompson, Trombonist Britt Woodman, Dodo Marmarosa, and Arv Garrison. He also sat in on some Sunday sessions at Berg's.

*   *   *

Recording—April 1946—Los Angeles Philharmonic Auditorium
Jazz At The Philharmonic—Al Killian, Howard McGhee (tp), C. Parker, Willie Smith (as), Lester Young (ts), Arnold Ross (p), Billy Hadnott (b), Lee Young (d).

Blues for Norman	Mercury MG 35003
I Can't Get Started	Mercury MG 35003
Lady Be Good	Verve MGV 8002
After You've Gone	Verve (Eng) VLP 9089

The two-chorus solo by Bird on *Lady Be Good* is a rough-hewn masterpiece. This is a different Bird from the studio session of March 28. Parker is coarse-toned and squeaky, but the solo is brilliant in conception, technique, and emotional content. He begins with rugged grass-root phrases, turning them masterfully throughout the first chorus. Then, in the fifth measure of the second chorus, he launches sixteenth-note phrases, builds them to a climax, and smoothly recedes back to a grass-root phrase he used in the beginning of the solo. He ends with afterthoughts. Listeners will notice that Parker did not think in terms of thirty-two bar choruses, but conceived his solo in terms of the whole.

Ex. 49 *Lady Be Good* Beginning "Grass Roots" Phrase

Ex. 50 *Lady Be Good* Sixteenths—Fifth Bar— Second Chorus

Ex. 51 *Lady Be Good* Ending "Grass Roots" Phrase—Bars 24, 25, 26—Second Chorus

His reading of *I Can't Get Started* is packed with unusual curving contours and has a whimsical quality, while *Blues For Norman* is rough-edged and blatant. *After You've Gone* combines qutsy, swirling lines with a great amount of drive. The riffing backgrounds of these recordings, characteristic of JATP, may bother the listener, but they certainly did not hamper Bird in his conception of solo choruses.

Recording—April 22, 1946—Embassy Auditorium, Los Angeles, California
Jazz At The Philharmonic—Buck Clayton (tp), C. Parker, Willie Smith (as), Lester Young, Coleman Hawkins (ts), Ken Kersey (p), Irving Ashby (g), Billy Hadnott (b), Buddy Rich (d).

JATP Blues	VSP-23
I Got Rhythm	Mercury MG 35014

This concert at the Embassy also featured Billie Holiday backed by some of the members of the JATP group. Although Bird was not in the backing group, the sides are worth hearing; there is a fine version of *Strange Fruit* (Verve 8098).

JATP Blues begins with piano, and then come two choruses of riffing horns. Bird solos first and plays three beautiful choruses. There is a direct quote of the opening phrase of *Moose The Mooche* near the end of his second chorus; his tone is much cleaner and bigger than the previous JATP date. The tenors wind up doing the "JATP-thing"—Young is honking and Hawkins is fuzz-toning. Smith uses the high register to good effect, and Clayton plays some driving blues over riffling saxes. Near the end, following solos by Ashby and Kersey, Rich plays some stop-time between two-note riffs. The track ends, naturally, with two all-out blowing choruses.

The *I Got Rhythm* take is quite difficult to find on LP, and sometimes only Parker's solo is available. The solo has Bird racing through the chords of the familiar improvisational vehicle in his usual mercurial manner.

* * *

A poignant letter from Chan Richardson to Ross Russell reveals that she had come to the coast in February and stayed until May 1946. During this period, she announced to Bird that she was pregnant from her former husband. Parker was greatly distraught by this and suggested an abortion which Chan refused. She described the period. "...at the Finale he was trying to be real straight.... When that fell through I dug how much it hurt him.... Then at one of Granz's gigs, Bird was juiced and they asked him to get off stage. That was another blow."[4] She also mentions that Parker became so upset that he refused to see her.

Furthermore, after "Moose's" arrest, Parker had no contact through whom to procure heroin. His famous "disappearance" during the late spring was probably because of a number of factors. He was broke; he was trying to stop using heroin since none was available; and he was drinking prodigiously to lessen the withdrawal symptoms. Howard McGhee found Parker living in a converted garage on McKinley Street in "Little Toyko," and attempted to get him back on his feet.

McGhee had re-opened the after-hours Finale Club during May, and he generally used Dodo Marmarosa, Roy Porter, and Red Callender as a rhythm section. Parker was added to the after-hours group, which split the "take" of a charged admission. McGhee has also stated that he was working the Streets of Paris Club during this period,[5] so it is probable that the Finale was strictly "after-hours."

Parker soon moved into the Civic Hotel around the corner from the Finale. He continued to drink heavily, however, and his appearances at the Finale became irregular. He was experiencing strange tics and jerks, and his execution was suffering. In desperation, he tried to "hit" Russell for an advance against future recordings (according to his contract, one date was supposed to have taken place within sixty days after the March 28th session). Finally, Russell and his partner, Marvin Freeman, a lawyer, agreed to try another session even though the company was in dire straits and Bird's condition even worse.

McGhee succeeded in gathering a group for the session (all men who had worked and recorded with him previously that year), and on July 29th, managed to steer Parker to C.P. MacGregor Studios on the southern part of Western Avenue

* * *

Recording—July 29, 1946—Hollywood.
Charlie Parker Quintet—Parker (as), Howard McGhee (tp), Jimmy Bunn (p), Bob Kesterson (b), Roy Porter (d).

Max Is Makin' Wax	Spotlite 101
Lover Man	Spotlite 101
The Gypsy	Spotlite 101
BeBop (originally released by Howard	Spotlite 101
McGhee Quintet)	

Parker, arriving late for the session, looked haggard and in a semi-trance. He later stated that he had to consume "a quart of whiskey" to be able to play at all. Russell, Freeman, and Freeman's brother (a psychiatrist) were present at the studio. Bird sat down; he fiddled with his reed, stared into space, and played short phrases for about an hour. Finally, McGhee organized things enough for the group to try *Max Is Makin' Wax*, an *I Got Rhythm* derivative in the key of C with an altered bridge. The tune was written by Oscar Pettiford and recorded by him in 1945; the arrangement had featured Max Roach and was originally titled *Something For You*. The following sequence is the construction of the bridge:/D7+11/D7+11/Eb7+11/Eb7+11/E7+11/Eb7+11/D7+11/Db7+11/.

There is an eight-bar piano introduction, and then the theme begins. Parker forgets the line and keeps falling back on the same riff; McGhee tactfully waits to see what the next move will be. On the final eight, McGhee is alone until Bird flies in for the final phrase. The theme can be basically described as extremely erratic. All the same, McGhee plays two fine choruses. And then Bird begins. He starts well enough, but in the second eight, he begins to stall and then slows more in the bridge. He does, however, manage some wild interval skips in the bridge! The last eight is very rocky. Bunn plays a nice chorus, and then comes another sloppy theme rendition. Parker only enters after the first four measures, and in the bridge, he is either playing out of tune, or wrong notes, or just lagging so far behind that the effect is like the other two. On the final eight, his reflexes are so far behind that the effect is surrealistic.

Richard Freeman, the M.D., then gave Parker six phenobarbital tablets, according to Russell.[6] Just what this was supposed to accomplish is unclear. What was Parker suffering from? Was it withdrawal symptoms, alcoholism, medicinal treatment for venereal disease? No one seems to know. The more accounts that are written, the more confusion arises. Questions abound. Parker was known to take benzedrine as a "drug substitute," and in Ira Gitler's *Jazz Masters of the '40's*, Gitler states that "an eye witness...says that Parker had been taking the stimulant...for several days." Perhaps the alteration of stimulant and depressant (alcohol) produced the trance-like state or a combination of all symptoms mentioned. It is reasonable to assume, however, that the phenobarbital did not help. Elliott Grennard, a *Billboard* correspondent, was present at the session and wrote a short story, *Sparrow's Last Jump*, that appeared in *Harper's* Magazine in May 1947. Grennard felt that the symptoms were due to addiction withdrawal.[7] We know that Parker's condition was at the breaking point from all types of excesses and emotional disturbances, but as to specifics, we can only speculate from all the facts given.

Beyond speculation, however, is the fact that the second tune, *Lover Man*, is the most famous of the "collapse" date, because of it's pathetic overtones. To begin, Bunn states a lovely intro and then, after striking the opening chord and realizing that Bird has not entered, plays the opening notes of the melody. Bird enters in the second bar, on the last half of the first beat, and knows exactly where he is! A great sadness enters the listener on this tune and becomes a part of him; the effect is indescribable. Parker was turning in circles and moving away from the mike, and a most obvious movement can be heard at the end of the second bar of the second eight where Bird tries one of the few flurries of notes on this tune. The key is D-flat, not a usual one for this tune. Why? The only answer can be that it is the same key in which Bird first played the tune with Sarah Vaughan in 1945 (female vocal keys are usually lower than the original keys; *Lover Man*, copyrighted in 1942, is originally written in F). After the release of the Bird recording, however, many musicians began playing the tune in D-flat.

Pianist Bunn also states the lead-in chords to the bridge that were used on the Vaughan recording by the ensemble.

Lead-Ins:/Db DbMaj7 Ebm7 Em7/Fm7 etc.

Although more than commonplace now, in 1946 the exact sequence was not common.

Bunn's chord sequence in the seventh bar of the "A" section has also become classic and is used to this day. The seventh of one chord to the third of the next forms a melodic accompanying sequence.

Ex. 52—*Lover Man* Melodic-Harmonic Sequence Bar 7

In the last eight bars, Parker's solo contains a great paraphrase of the melodic thought, the rest is close to the melody. Bunn goes back to the bridge following Bird and plays a nice chorus, with clever uses of "flat-fives" and "whole-tone scales." The closing eight is McGhee on top with Bird backing, and except for Bird's pathetic sound at times, it is not bad.

The *Gypsy* is more pathos, again in D-flat, with mournful overtones. Bird starts haltingly, with two notes, corrects, and then launches into a straight melody chorus. The tones resemble human sobbing, and the torture of the man, both physical and mental, is evident in his playing. The performance reminds one of a hopeless cry for help.

A ten-bar unison intro opens *BeBop*, a Gillespie tune, but Bird enters late. The theme is in the minor and is based on thirds leaping upward in the scale, culminating in a leap from the fifth to the tonic that seems to shout "BeBop."

Ex. 53 *BeBop* opening Phrase

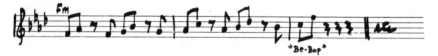

The bridge is basically:/Bb7/Bb7/Eb/Eb/Ab7/Ab7/G7/C7-5/. Some substitutes used by Bunn, in the last four bars are:/Eb7/D7/G7-5/C7-5/.

The line is again marred by Parker's slow reflexes, and he drops out at the beginning of the bridge and then returns. Bird's solo is jerky, but not bad. Bunn plays well, and McGhee crackles on two choruses. The final theme is again ragged, with Bird entering only after the first four bars, and the coda has McGhee beginning it alone. Parker finally enters and there is a "spacey" ending, with Bird giving a final bleat to end the session.

The ballads, while not being idea-packed creations, are certainly heart-rending emotionally, and, except for the false starts, they are technically acceptable. In fact, even the false starts correct themselves and do not lose time. The up-tempo solos are also acceptable, if not among Bird's best efforts. It is on the ensemble themes that Bird's reflexes will not allow him the discipline of up-tempo unison playing. The themes are badly performed and are the worst part of the session.

Russell, anxious about the monetary aspects of both this recording project and his company in general, ordered the mikes kept open. In hindsight, one can say that perhaps trying Bird on ballads or having him just improvise on familiar lines with only the rhythm section may have turned out better. McGhee could have used the remainder of the time for quartet sides (he did record two tracks, *Trumpet At Tempo* and *Thermodynamics* after Bird left the studio). Of course, hindsight means nothing.

The description of *The Gypsy* in Russell's *Bird Lives* (p. 223-224) is inconsistent with what happens on the record: "Phrases came in swoops and gasps, with a lot of air space between. Too much space. Roy Porter yelled 'Blow, man, blow Bird.' Charlie faltered. The trumpet stormed in. Howard McHee tried to pull the music together. The take ended in a fumbled coda." This description applies more to *BeBop*, for on *The Gypsy*, McGhee only plays two soft background notes! The "Blow" comes in *BeBop*, which does have a fumbled coda.

Parker's later hatred of these sides and his embitterment at Russell for releasing them can be easily understood in terms of the artist. Anyone who has created anything—from a Christmas decoration to an amateur painting—wants the world to see the best of his work. If one is not happy with one's own creation, the natural reaction is to not want others to view (or hear) it. Parker, moreover, was respectful of technical musicians, having had the section training of big bands, and probably was ashamed of the ensemble sound on these recordings. He also may have been bothered by his lack of ideas (or inability to execute them).

Russell, however, faced with the reality of a failing venture needed to find ways out of his bind. The release of these sides coincided with the Grennard short story in an attempt to capitalize on the publicity. The records subsequently became valuable, not because they were Bird's best, but because they were his worst! In retrospect, we may say that perhaps hearing a great artist at his worst makes us more intensely aware of the things he feels at his best.

* * *

After the fatal recording, a young man known only as "Slim" escorted Parker to his room at the Civic Hotel. "Slim" worked occasionally as a janitor at the Finale Club and was acting as "band boy" for the session.

Upon "Slim's" departure from the hotel, Parker wandered down to the lobby and tried to use the phone. The Chinese manager quickly had him escorted back to his room for Bird was stark naked except for his socks! After two more clotheless attempts at phoning and much commotion and foul language, Parker was locked inside his room on the fourth (top) floor. Soon after, his mattress was set ablaze, and the confused manager sent for the fire department and the police. How the fire started has never been established. In Parker's state, anything was possible, and because of the many different tales which are tossed about pertaining to this incident, we probably will never know the real truth. In the ensuing confusion, however, Parker was handcuffed, blackjacked, rolled in a blanket and carried away by the police.

Russell, attempting to check on Parker, arrived at the hotel too late and could not find Parker for the next ten days. Russell claims he "lost" Parker's trail at the Lincoln Heights division of the city jail where Charlie had first been taken and "booked."[8] It seems that immediate investigation should have yielded more information. Nevertheless, Russell made strenuous efforts to find Parker, including investigations and queries by Richard Freeman (the psychiatrist). Freeman finally found out through the professional grapevine that Parker was in the psychiatric ward. Upon finding him there, in eastern Los Angeles, Russell was appalled to see him straightjacketed and handcuffed to the cot. He immediately set to work on Bird's case with his lawyer-partner, Marvin Freeman.

There were originally criminal charges—indecent exposure, resisting arrest, and arson—against Parker, but because of Freeman's efforts, the case was transferred to the Superior Court where the decision was to have Parker confined for a six-month period at Camarillo State Hospital and to have the criminal charges held in continuance. The case was to be reviewed after the recommended period of confinement. It is sad, when one looks at the exploits of today's "superstars" to think that Parker, under such physical and emotional stress, was subject to nothing but circumstances. Not that his behavior should have been excused, but rather tolerated, with a view toward helping him. Here, for certain, his blackness was against him. The hospital was located northwest of the city proper and was about twenty miles directly west of the Burbank section, midway between this suburb and the coastal city of Verona. Russell visited Parker frequently, as did Dean Benedetti, the "wily recorder." Furthermore, Doris Sydnor came to the coast when she learned of Parker's trouble; she worked as a waitress and tried to improve his general attitude. Soon after, to be sure, his attitude did improve as he withdrew from heroin. He also began gaining weight and doing some gardening and bricklaying.

No official diagnosis was arrived at by the examiners at Camarillo, however, although schizophrenia was mentioned. Not being a state resident, Parker faced deportation to a hospital in the state where he was considered a resident. But through much legal digging, Russell's lawyer found that an out-of-state patient *could* be released in the custody of a state resident. Russell decided to chance it.

After an unsuccessful attempt in December, Russell finally succeeded in obtaining Bird's release at the end of January 1947. The Dial contract was about to run out with only a few saleable sides created by Parker. Russell claims he told Parker that in view of the circumstances, he felt Parker *should* renew the option. Bird stated later, however, that he felt Russell used the option as blackmail. It was Parker's feeling that Charlie Emge, the *Down Beat* West Coast editor, did much to help him and would have gotten him out eventually.

Russell became sole owner of Dial during the fall of 1946, and both he and Emge were instrumental in staging a concert-benefit for Parker during December. The event raised between $600.00 and $900.00 which was saved for Parker's expected release. After the release finally came, Bird and Doris once again found themselves a "pad," and Bird was truly back on the scene.

During Bird's six-month stay in Camarillo, Gillespie had formed a big band, using the Berg's group as a nucleus. Gil Fuller became the arranger, and the band worked at the Spotlite on The Street, and at the Apollo theatre. The band also embarked on a theatre tour.

Miles Davis had worked with Lucky Thompson during August, 1946 at the Elks Ballroom on Central Avenue. Thompson had leased the ballroom for three nights a week. In September, Miles joined the Eckstine band in Los Angeles and returned East with them. After the collapse of the Eckstine group in early 1947, he worked in Chicago for a brief period. Tommy Potter, later to become Parker's regular bass player, was the bassist on the Eckstine band of this period.

Max Roach, Bud Powell, J.J. Johnson, and Duke Jordan were also all working on Fifty-Second Street. In June of 1946, Roach, Powell and Johnson recorded together under Johnson's name. This was the date that produced *Jay-Bird, Mad BeBop, Jay Jay* and *Coppin' The Bop.* Jordon, for a time was the pianist with the Roy Eldridge big band.

All of the above mentioned men, in one way or another, would color Parker's career during 1947, and it is interesting to note where their respective careers were going during Parker's absence from the music scene.

* * *

Recording—February 1, 1947—"Chuck Kopely's"—Hollywood
Parker (as), Russ Freeman (p), Arnold Fishkind (b), Jimmy Pratt (d).

Home Cookin' I	Spotlite (Eng) 103
Home Cookin' II	Spotlite (Eng) 103
Home Cookin' III	Spotlite (Eng) 103
Yardbird Suite	Spotlite (Eng) 107
Lullaby In Rhythm	Spotlite (Eng) 107

As Bird got back into the Hollywood music circle, he began looking for sessions. These recordings were made at the home of a musician friend very soon after Bird's release from Camarillo. Howard McGhee and one of his students, Melvyn Broiles, were present at the session, as was Shorty Rogers. On all tunes except *Yardbird Suite,* however, nothing remains but the Parker solos. Trumpet playing, however, can be heard on the theme to *Yardbird,* and the liner notes to the Spotlite LP state that it is Broiles.

Home Cooking' I is based on *S' Wonderful* with the *Honeysuckle Rose* bridge, but *Home Cookin' II* is an improvisation of *Cherokee;* the final serving has an *I Got Rhythm* base. There was also a blues recorded at this session that has never been found.

The records were made with a single mike, and on Parker's solos someone managed to hold the mike next to his saxophone bell. Bird is not fiery on these solos, but his connective ideas flow wonderfully into one another. Furthermore, he is much more relaxed and his ideas are less complex than they were in his pre-Camarillo days. He creates simple and sparkly melodies in an offhand manner. The *Cherokee (Home Cookin' II)* improvisation is a bit more intense then the others. These home-made recordings were issued on Dial originally and the quality is passable except for *Yardbird Suite.*

* * *

The next two months proved fruitful for Parker. He was hired by McGhee as co-leader of a group at the Hi De Ho Club, a small jazz club on the southern part of Western Avenue and he agreed to do a "farewell" record session for Dial. Moreover, he did jamming at the Central Avenue jazz bistros, especially the Bird-In-The-Basket.

On one of Bird's all-night jaunts, he heard singer Earl Coleman and was favorably impressed—so much so that he wanted Coleman on the "farewell" date. Russell, however, finally talked Parker into backing Coleman on a separate date and doing the "farewell" session as a strict jazz date. Erroll Garner and his trio were contracted as the rhythm section behind Coleman, and Russell figured on getting several instrumental tracks out of the trio and perhaps some by Bird and the trio. This unlikely-looking combination turned out better than expected for everyone concerned.

* * *

Recording—February 19, 1947—MacGregor Studios, Los Angeles.
Earl Coleman (vcl), Charlie Parker (as), Erroll Garner (p), Red Callender (b), Doc West (d).

This Is Always—Take 3	Spotlite (Eng) 102
This Is Always—Take 4 (Orig.)	Spotlite (Eng) 102
Dark Shadows—Take 1	Spotlite (Eng) 102
Dark Shadows—Take 2	Spotlite (Eng) 102
Dark Shadows—Take 3 (Orig.)	Spotlite (Eng) 102
Dark Shadows—Take 4	Spotlite (Eng) 102
Bird's Nest—Take 1	Spotlite (Eng) 102
Bird's Nest—Take 2	Spotlite (Eng) 102
Bird's Nest—Take 3 (Orig.)	Spotlite (Eng) 102
Cool Blues—Take 1	Spotlite (Eng) 102
Cool Blues—Take 2	Spotlite (Eng) 102
Cool Blues—Take 3	Spotlite (Eng) 102
Cool Blues—Take 4 (Orig.)	Spotlite (Eng) 102

Coleman, an Eckstine imitator, sings well, if not always technically correct. On the opening tune, the first two takes have been lost and will probably never be issued, but Coleman sounds good on both Takes 3 and 4. On Take 3, the lead-in to Parker's solo loses a beat, and this is apparently why the take was rejected, for otherwise it is much the same as the original issue. The tune has the unusual construction of AAB, and the bass interlude following the vocal starts on the last bar of the tune and continues for three more measures. Garner, who is striking the chord on the first beat of each measure, misplaces the final one, early, and this is the cause of the rhythmic confusion. Solo-wise, Parker stays to the melody on both versions; in fact, they are very similar in embellishment. He can also be heard backing Coleman on the first sixteen bars of both takes. On the final take, Bird blows a short lead-in after Garner's piano intro that is not on Take 3; this is one way of telling these similar versions apart (the other obviously being the rhythmic fluff, but many novices may not notice this). After the first chorus vocal, it is Bird for eight, Garner for eight, then Coleman sings out the "B" section with light backing by Parker. Parker ends both takes with a skip from the fifth to the ninth (2nd) of the scale at the tail end of a rubato ending. This particular record sold well, proving Parker's point to Russell.

Dark Shadows, although blues-sounding, is a standard thirty-two bar construction written by trumpeter "Shifty" Henry. It is the chord pattern in the first four measures that bears a strong resemblance to the blues: /I7/IV7/I7/I7/ . The format on all takes is basically the same. Bird plays the intro and Coleman sings the theme, backed, at various times, by either Garner or Parker. Parker plays a half chorus; Garner continues with the bridge, and Coleman takes the tune out. The Parker solos are all excellent. On Take 1 he uses part of the phrase from the fourth bar of his *Hootie Blues* solo with McShann; Takes 2 and 3 begin alike but develop differently, and the long-missing Take 4 has Bird condensing and repeating many ideas used in Take 3—most notably at bar seven. The fourth take is scratchy, having been made from an acetate dubbing, and was not issued until the Spotlite LP. The fine Parker solo on the original Take 3 was later orchestrated for a sax chorus in Woody Herman's *I've Got News For You*. The background accompaniment is a bit different on each take and can be useful in identifying the different versions:

	1st 8	2nd 8	Bridge	Final 8
First Chorus—Take 1	Bird and Garner	Garner	Garner	Bird
First Chorus—Take 2	Bird	Bird	Garner	Garner
First Chorus—Take 3	.....All Garner.....			
First Chorus—Take 4	Bird	Garner	Garner	Garner

The "out-section" of the tune is backed by Parker on all takes; his endings are all similar seqsequences of the later famous *Embraceable You* motif in a slightly changed form.

The *I Got Rhythm* chord pattern appears as the base for *Bird's Nest*, and the bridge is harmonically similar to the one used on *Dark Shadows*. Since the instrumentals were invented on the spot, we can speculate that one bridge inspired the other. The tune has no apparent theme, although Parker does start each take with the same general phrase, and there are some repeated phrases in what would be usually called the theme chorus, but the repeats seem to be at different places on each take!

Ex. 54 *Birds Nest* Opening Phrase

The format has an intro by West—first some "knocks" then a "hi-hat" beat. Parker and Garner play two choruses apiece, and then alternate eight-bar sections for a chorus. The final chorus is Bird, spelled by Callender at the bridge. Takes 1 and 3 contain the most fluid Bird; his tone is fine and his ideas flow endlessly.

On Take 2, there are a few technical fumbles—in the first chorus and in the last (leading to the bridge)—but the ideas are fine.

The melody of *Cool Blues* is completely based on the phrase which Parker played in his solo on the final take of *Yardbird Suite* recorded a year earlier.

Ex. 55 *Cool Blues* Opening Phrase

After a piano intro, Bird and Garner play two blues choruses apiece, then Callender solos before alto and piano come back for one apiece. The theme follows and ends abruptly, with no coda of any kind. Callender plays two choruses on all but the first track.

Garner felt uncomfortable at the fast tempos of the first two takes and asked to have the tempo slowed down. The third take is much too slow for the theme, however, and Parker is not as inspired as on the other three. The fourth is probably the best compromise for both men, although Take 1 is exciting and Take 2 has Garner not too uncomfortable.

The titles of the instrumentals were Russell's, not Bird's, and the first two (faster) takes of *Cool Blues* were later released as *Hot Blues* and *Blowtop Blues*.

The collaboration of such varying stylists as Parker and Garner would seem to be unthinkable, but these sides prove differently. They are a tribute to the innate musicianship of both men. Furthermore, later in his life, Parker listed these recordings among the few of his own efforts that he himself liked, and the original release won the Grand Prix de Disque in France for this year.

Recording—February 26, 1947—MacGregor Studios, Los Angeles
Charlie Parker's New Stars—Parker (as), H. McGhee (tpt), Wardell Gray (ts), Dodo Marmarosa (p), Barney Kessel (g), Red Callander (b), Don Lamond (dr).

Relaxin' At Camarillo—Take 1	Spotlite (Eng) 103
Relaxin' At Camarillo—Take 3	Spotlite (Eng) 103
Relaxin' At Camarillo—Take 4	Spotlite (Eng) 103
Relaxing At Camarillo—Take 5 (Orig.)	Spotlite (Eng) 103
Cheers—Take 1	Spotlite (Eng) 103
Cheers—Take 2	Spotlite (Eng) 103
Cheers—Take 3	Spotlite (Eng) 103
Cheers—Take 4 (Orig.)	Spotlite (Eng) 103
Stupendous—Take 1	Spotlite (Eng) 103
Stupendous—Take 2 (Orig.)	Spotlite (Eng) 103
Carvin' The Bird—Take 1	Spotlite (Eng) 103
Carvin' The Bird—Take 2 (Orig.)	Spotlite (Eng) 103

The "New Stars" label came from the young jazzmen on the date: Marmarosa had recently won the *Esquire* New Star award; Kessel and Gray had done their first recordings as leaders during the past year; and Lamond had made a name for himself as Woody Herman's drummer. The men were also familiar with each other from various groups and recordings. Kessel and Dodo had worked together in Artie Shaw's Gramercy Five during part of 1944-1945 and Marmarosa had also been the pianist on Kessel's Atomic recordings under his own name. Gray, Dodo, and Red Callender were together on a date under Gray's leadership in November of 1946, and Callender, of course, had been with Parker on and off during the West Coast stay and was also the bassist on the previous recording. All of the aforementioned men were frequent "jammers" at the Central Avenue afterhours joints. At this time, Lamond was based in Los Angeles with Herman, who was in the midst of reforming a new band (the "Four Brothers" band) and recording with small groups. Lamond recorded with one of the small groups early in the month, and one can surmise that he also was among the Central Avenue swingers.

Camarillo is a blues with an ingenious melodic and rhythmic construction. The line is difficult to remember in the first three measures, and this writer has seen experienced musicians and advanced students of music have difficulty singing it back on first hearing. The unusual accents typify Parker's music and set it apart from the rest of the music generally lumped under "BeBop." Except for the first note and the last of these three measures, the rhythmic figure is built on only three notes and seems simple, but the rhythmic order of them makes it extremely complex.

Ex. 56 *Relaxin at Camarillo* Opening 3 Bars

On Take 1, a cough is heard; then Lamond begins with two measures of hi-hat followed by six measures of "chunky" piano chords, and then back to two hi-hat measures. McGhee has some trouble with notes on the theme, but the saxes cut it cleanly. Parker plays two fine choruses, and Gray and Kessel follow with two apiece. On this and all subsequent takes, McGhee plays one chorus muted, and Dodo finishes the solos with a solitary chorus; the ensemble has some difficulty entering after the piano solo. After the final theme, Marmarosa gets into a coda with poly-rhythmic accents which he cannot end! He finally gets out of it and someone responds with "Yeah." This coda is used as the intro and coda on the rest of the takes, and whether it is Marmarosa's invention or Parker's is not known, but it sounds pianistic in conception.

Ex. 57 *Camarillo* Intro/Coda

At times there seems to be difficulties stemming from the way Kessel and Marmarosa are placing their respective chords. Therefore, there is a "two-beat" feel at times on this first take against the four of the bass. It is unfortunate that the second take remains missing for it might offer some insight into how the problem was solved.

Take 3 begins with the figure notated above, as an eight-bar piano intro; after the theme, Bird plays two excellent choruses—perhaps the best of the date. The other solos follow the same order except Callender plays a chorus that is part solo and part "walked" before the theme chorus. (Marmarosa's beautiful use of the Neopolitan chord—bII7—at bar two of the blues, behind the bass, has always intrigued this writer). The lead-in to the theme is smoother with the bass, and Dodo finds a better ending for the coda.

Take 4, however, has a fluffed idea on Parker's chorus, and Callender plays ideas for the whole bass chorus. Dodo comes up with another wild ending!

On Take 5, the intro and lead-in are very clean, and the theme is well-stated. Bird's choruses are good, but not as good as Take 3. This take is obviously the cleanest all-around version, but Take 3, perhaps, contains better Parker choruses.

Bird was to have written some originals for this date, but as usual, he was lax in this department and almost didn't make the session. McGhee found him asleep in his hotel room bathtub and quickly hurried him to the studio. Camarillo, therefore, was Bird's only compositional contribution to the session; McGhee provided *Cheers* and *Carvin' The Bird* (although the latter is sometimes credited to Kessel), and Broiles, his student, composed *Stupendous*. Bird's blues line is said to have been written at the last minute in a cab, but this is probably a "factoid" (although *anything* is possible with Bird).

Cheers is an *I Got Rhythm* derivative with chromatic chords in the final half of the "A" section and the *Honeysuckle Rose* bridge. The chords to the "A" section are: /Bb/Cm7 F7/Bb/Ebm7 Ab7/Dm7 Db7/Cm7 B7/Bb/Bb/.

Ex. 58 *Cheers* Opening Line

The intro has piano octave leaps on the tonic over a series of sustained guitar chords; the final two bars are a break, with tasty drum kicks. All bridges are improvised by Parker on each theme chorus and these are little gems in themselves. Solos are: Bird for a full chorus; Gray and Dodo splitting; Kessel and McGhee splitting. On Take 1, Lamond takes a drum break before the final theme, but the ensemble does not enter well; this break is eliminated on the other takes. Kessel's development of a quote from *I Can't Get Started* is notable.

Take 2 is a faster version with good Bird, but the ensemble is still sloppy entering the closing theme. Take 3, moreover, is even worse in this respect, as McGhee begins the first few bars of the closing theme by himself. These two middle takes were only issued on the Spotlite LP, from the acetate dubbings. The final take, however, is certainly the best; it has good Bird and the best entrance to the closing theme (only Gray seems to lay back), and Kessel develops his *I Can't Get Started* quote in a completely different manner.

The blues offering, *Carvin' The Bird*, has an opening theme that is based upon three notes; the line then ascends to the scale fourth and descends to the flat seventh in the traditional place (fourth bar). Kessel fills the rest of the fourth bar with a rhythmic figure based on the I9+11 chord.

Ex. 59 *Carvin' The Bird* Opening Measures

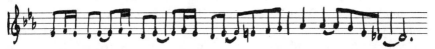

The next three bars contain a beautiful chordal figure based on the IV9+11. This figure is the high point of the line and culminates with the opening three-note figure.

Ex. 60 *Carvin'* Bars 5-6-7

After one chorus of the theme, the solo order is as follows: Bird—two choruses; McGhee, Kessel, and Dodo—one apiece; Callender, Kessel, and Dodo splitting one— four bars apiece; Gray, McGhee, and Bird—one apiece; and the latter three then splitting one in four-bar sections. There is good Bird on both tracks, although at times, he is squeaky. Kessel quotes *Fascinatin' Rhythm* on Take 1.

Both takes are similar, with Gray starting his solo the same both times. He begins with a rhythmic figure on the tonic for two and a half bars, and then leaps to the scale sixth. This whole general section is similar sounding on both takes. Kessel's intros, chordal on both takes, are gems and are both different. The one on Take 2 goes through three different tonal centers before the lead-in.

Ex. 61 *Carvin'* Kessel's Intro—Take 2

Stupendous is based on Gershwin's *'S Wonderful* with the bridge being open for melodic improvisation. The opening phrase contains a sequence in which the second figure is based on a whole-tone scale.

Ex. 62 *Stupendous* Opening Phrase

Bird plays the only full chorus; McGhee and Dodo split, as do Gray and Kessel. On Take 1, Bird plays the opening bridge and also the closing one, but he is hesitant on the latter. Kessel, however, plays the closing bridge on Take 2. The Bird choruses are excellent on both takes, and Marmarosa plays his best solo of the date on Take 1, where he stays away from arpeggiated playing. Both takes are good, and it is probably only because of the slight mix-up at the bridge mentioned above that a re-make was necessary.

Kessel supplies some beautiful accompaniments behind Bird on the last two tunes. Interestingly, it seems as if he and Dodo were alternating backings near the end of the session.

Good examples of Bird are contained in these recordings, and *Camarillo* is a "must" for every collection.

Recording—March 9, 1947—Hi-De-Ho Club—Los Angeles
*Howard McGhee Quintet—*McGhee (tp), Parker (as), Hampton Hawes (p), Addison Farmer (b), Roy Porter (d).

Dee Dee's Dance   Spotlite 107

This is reportedly taken from one of Benedetti's discs (although this has never been substantiated) but contains more of the other solos and theme choruses than he usually recorded. He was usually only interested in Bird's solos (to save space).

The "A" section of this tune is almost identical with *Cheers* (harmonically) and the bridge is based on chromatic chords, using octaves against a "flat five" leap melodically. The same figure moves down chromatically as the chords change. The bridge chords are:

/G7⁶/G7⁶/G7⁶/G7⁶/Gb7⁶/Gb7⁶/F7⁶/F7⁶/.

The introductory figure is the same as the bridge, and Bird states it; then McGhee echoes it. Bird restates it a half step down, and McGhee uses a whole-tone scale figure against the F7 chord.

Ex. 63 *Dee Dee's Dance* Intro and Bridge Figure

Parker leads into the theme, and McGhee begins it; then Parker joins again. It is done very smoothly. The next two sections (second "A" and bridge) are in unison throughout, and on the final eight, the format is like the first. Bird begins to blow, forgetting there is a secondary theme on the "A" section, but quickly recovers and jumps in with McGhee. This secondary theme is sloppily done.

The two Parker choruses are unspectacular, but there are some interesting study points. The scalar motif that is used at the end of the first eight of his first chorus became one of his "stamps", and on the second chorus bridge, he develops a "Latin-sounding" figure (or at least the beginning of it) that he used in his 1945 *Salt Peanuts* solo.

The issue preserves all of McGhee's solo and part of Hawes's and after a pause, has part of the closing theme (the issue is in two parts). The sound is, of course, horrendous, but it is worth hearing—at least by Parker fans—for nostalgic interest and a glimpse at Hawes's playing during this period.

Recording—Circa 1947—Los Angeles—Broadcast
Parker, Willie Smith, Benny Carter (as), Nat King Cole (p), Oscar Moore (gtr), Johnny Miller (b), Buddy Rich (dr).

Cherokee   Sounds 1206

This "live", sitting-in recording is usually dated here, but there is strong evidence that it may have been done in 1946 as Cole and Rich had recorded with Lester Young early in that year and the Benny Carter band was in town at the Orpheum Theater (from whence Miles Davis joined Bird on the coast).

The nightclub patter of the announcer is a break-up—"...a jazz free-for-all that's free for all of you..."—and the presence of such varying musicians is interesting.

Smith opens the proceedings with a cadenza and then launches *Tea For Two*, playing two excellent choruses in a medium four-beat tempo. Carter follows with *Body and Soul* in a ballad tempo, and Bird moves to up-tempo for the *Cherokee* shot. The three choruses are fine Parker statements, although the rhythm section seems a bit too "busy" at times. The other horns join Parker for a final, riffing eight bars.

From the announcer—"...a Jubilee first..."—it can be assumed that the recording was made for the Armed Forces Radio Service Jubilee label.

* * *

During Easter week of 1947, Parker prepared to move east—back to the sanctity of Fifty-Second Street. The Street was not the bustling beehive of 1945, however, and only the Three Deuces, and the Downbeat were operating with jazz policies. Chan Richardson knew Sammy Kaye (not the bandleader), the owner of the Deuces and had spoken to him about Parker working at the club. Kaye seemed amenable to the idea, and the scene was set for Bird's return.[9]

In viewing Parker's emergence from his partly self-made, partly circumstantial purgatorial exile, however, one cannot help but ponder the fact that the people who helped him when in need—Doris Sydnor, Chan Richardson, Ross Russell, Marvin Freeman (Russell's lawyer), and Charlie Emge—were all from the white middle-class. Moreover, although each of them certainly had personal motives, there was some love evident in all their efforts—either of the man, or of his music, or both. somewhere in the aforementioned facts lies a truth that tells us that both the man and his music were not at all racial, but rather universal. It is a truth to keep in mind as we view Bird's "classic period."

CHAPTER VIII

THE CLASSIC PERIOD—PART ONE
Chasin' the Bird
(April-September 1947)

My hoarse-sounding horn
Invites thee to the chase,
the Sport of Kings.

Wm. Somerville—The Chase

After playing an Easter engagement with Howard McGhee at the Pershing Ballroom in Chicago, Bird returned to New York on April 7, 1947, Easter Monday. His early engagements included a Carnegie Hall JATP concert and an appearance with a Max Roach group at a club in Brooklyn. In the June 18th issue of *Down Beat*, he was reported as having played with Gillespie in a Town Hall concert, but Alan Morrison, a writer who helped promote the Town Hall presentation, claims that Parker was ill and could not play.[1] The concert, in honor of black war veterans, was held on May 31st, and Morrison states that Gillespie performed without Parker and was supported by a rhythm section of Bud Powell, Curly Russell, and Max Roach. Furthermore, Roach reports that on the Brooklyn gig, which was to star Parker, Bird showed up at midnight, played one tune, and demanded his money! When Roach refused, Bird went through a Hollywood production of the preparations for a fight. This broke Max up, and he paid him half salary for the engagement.[2]

In New York, Gillespie, with his beret, goatee, and horn-rimmed glasses, was hailed as the "high priest" of the new music. His big band was catching on, possibly because of the public's interest in the trumpeter's comedic antics and flamboyant mode of dress. Parker, however, was envious of Gillespie's success and felt bitter about being away from the public eye for so long (although he had only himself and circumstances to blame). But even with different circumstances, Parker could not have compromised as Gillespie did; he was not the same type of personality. Diz could have fun banging on a conga drum and then turn around and play a meaningful ballad or a virile, uptempo chorus; the two extremes were never confused in his mind. Bird, however, primarily reserved his wild antics for his life and kept his music pure. Furthermore, when he used humor, it was an integral part of the music, meant to convey a feeling to the listener. Gillespie's humor was more for fun, an entertainment, one might say. Indeed, the "in-goingness" of Parker forced the creation of powerful, deep music, but also led to his problem of using drugs and alcohol as escape mechanisms. Gillespie's "outwardness," on the other hand, kept him relatively free of the vices that were so common during the period.

The cool "inwardness" of Miles Davis, however, was a good match for Bird's emotional "inwardness." The forming of the famous Parker-Davis quintet of 1947-48 took place during the spring. The rhythm section consisted of Tommy Potter and Max Roach on bass and drums respectively, and Bud Powell began as pianist but was later replaced by Duke Jordan. Before joining the quintet, Jordan was working on The Street with a piano trio under the leadership of Teddy Walters, and Powell's erratic behavior and shaky mental condition goaded Parker to hire someone with a more agreeable personality. It is well known that Powell and Parker clashed many times later in their careers—they could not resist needling one another. Nevertheless, Powell was the pianist on the group's first set of recordings.

* * *

Recording—May or June 1947—New York City
Charlie Parker All Stars—Parker (as), M. Davis (tp), B. Powell (p), T. Potter (b), M. Roach (d).

Donna Lee—Take 1	Savoy 12001
Donna Lee—Take 2	Savoy 12001
Donna Lee—Take 3	Savoy 12009
Donna Lee—Take 4 (Orig.)	Savoy 12014
Chasin' the Bird—Take 1	Savoy 12009
Chasin' the Bird—Take 2	Savoy 12009
Chasin' the Bird—Take 3 (Orig.)	Savoy 12014
Cheryl—Take 1	Savoy 12001
Cheryl—Take 2 (Orig.)	Savoy 12001
Buzzy—Take 1	Savoy 12009
Buzzy—Take 2	Savoy 12001
Buzzy—Take 3	Savoy 12001
Buzzy—Take 4	Savoy 12000
Buzzy—Take 5 (Orig.)	Savoy 12000

Donna Lee, a line constructed on the chords to *Back Home Again In Indiana*, is listed as a Parker composition, but the continuous strings of eighth notes make it seem more likely it is Davis's. Parker's compositions were generally more rhythmic in nature (compare *Cheryl* from this date and Davis's compositions from the August 1947 date). Ira Gitler, moreover, in *Jazz Masters of the 40's* states that *Donna Lee* is "...said by Gil Evans to have been written by Davis." The tune is titled after a female bass player who worked on The Street during 1945.

Ex. 64 Opening of *Donna Lee*

Note the lack of the syncopated figures that generally colored *all* of Parker's tunes. The two beat pause at the beginning of the theme is much more characteristic of the "cool" style of Davis than of the blistering Parker thought pattern. If Parker did write this line, it is certainly not in his usual style. The tunes of this period, furthermore, were often confused as to composer credit, and the leader of a given date sometimes emerged with credit for tunes which he did not write.

The opening take also supports the idea that it is Miles's tune: it is Parker that has trouble with the line, sometimes falling into the lower octave as if he is unsure whether to play parts in perfect unison or octave unison. This could suggest that it was Parker's first reading of the tune. Following the theme, Bird plays two choruses that are a bit squeaky, and Miles plays a half-chorus that is buzzy and indistinct. Powell can be heard singing along with his half-chorus, and the horns return with the line; Bird again has a bit of trouble. This take and the following one are listed as "2" and "3" respectively (instead of "1" and "2") on Savoy 12001.

Take 2 is faster, and the line is executed better. Bird develops some of the line in his solo but has trouble with some "wolf" tones (untrue notes) in spots. Miles is still not clean in his half-chorus, but Powell is strong. The closing theme uses only the second sixteen bars on this and all succeeding takes. Also, Parker takes the opening triplet an octave lower on this and all succeeding takes.

The third take has a clean theme execution, and Parker plays a "cool" solo. Near the end of his second chorus, however, untrue notes crop up again on a series of repeated tones, and Parker keeps them going almost in self disgust. Miles's best solo on this tune is found on this take, and although Powell solos well, he seems to forget that only the last sixteen bars are being used in the "out-chorus" and plays chords after the first four bars (identical in both halves of the tune) that suggest the first part of the tune.

The final take, however, sounds alive and bristling on the line, more so than the others, and the recorded sound is also better. The Parker solo is excellent, and Miles and Bud also turn in good performances. The final line is executed cleanly, and one must indeed judge this take to be the best all-around performance of the *Indiana* derivative.

Chasin' the Bird has the *I Got Rhythm* harmonic base, and the line is a contrapuntal excursion by the horns; the "B" section is improvised. On Take 1, Bird is squeaky on the final "A" section of the theme, but then plays a good chorus. Miles and Bud split the next chorus, with Bud playing some wild half-step modulations in the final "A" section. In the "out-chorus," Potter takes the bridge. Potter only solos on this take, however, for Miles plays the "out-chorus" bridge on both other takes.

Take 2 has a little better opening theme, although there are slight goofs on the closing theme. Bird is again "cool," as he was on so many "second takes," and Miles and Bud are excellent.

The final take has a fiery Bird solo, and the theme is played with more ease than the other takes. Again, as on *Donna Lee's* final take, the recorded sound is better.

Ex. 65 *Chasin' The Bird*—Opening 4 Bars

The *Chasin' the Bird* theme was probably conceived linearly and not harmonically, but it has always intrigued this writer that the second (trumpet) line, starting in bar two, seems to state the harmony one bar late, as if the second line is starting at the beginning, but a bar late! Some study of the first four bars will give an intuitive understanding of this. The parts seem to be conceived separately but fit together to form a beautiful whole.

The twelve-bar blues form also crops up in this session in the tunes *Cheryl* and *Buzzy*. These lines, however, are about as different as any two blues can be. *Cheryl* is rhythmically and melodically complex, beginning with a full bar of pick-up notes that suggest an altered dominant chord; there are shifting rhythms and wild melodic skips throughout the line. *Buzzy*, on the other hand, is based completely on one phrase, repeated three times, with only one note melodically altered (in the fifth bar to fall with the change of harmony).

Ex. 66 *Cheryl* Pickups and First Phrase

Ex. 67 *Cheryl* Wild Melodic Skips

Ex. 68 *Cheryl* Final 2 Bars

Ex. 69 *Buzzy* Single "Blues" Phrase

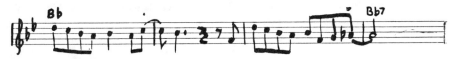

The first take of *Cheryl* lasts only one bar, a quick try at the pickup notes. On the next try, however, the pickups are executed successfully; the difficult line is navigated; and Parker plays three great blues choruses, beginning his solo with a repeat of the last phrase of the theme. He also uses, at the beginning of the third chorus, the phrase that made up *Cool Blues*, which he first played in his solo on the final take of *Yardbird Suite*.

On *Buzzy*, Bird's most exciting solo seems to be the first one, although there is good Parker on Takes 3 and 5. The Parker chorus on the final take contains a slow descent of a diminished chord that later became a jazz cliche. Parker stops Take 2 in the middle of his solo, saying "Piano, Piano!" He may have felt that Powell was rushing behind him. Take 4, however, is cut off by the engineer. There is a slight difference in the solo order on each of the three complete takes. After Bird and Miles play three choruses each on Take 1, Powell plays three; then Potter "walks" one with Bud comping loudly and obnoxiously, and there is one closing theme chorus. On Take 3, there is no bass solo, and the closing theme is repeated pianissimo. The final take has only one Powell chorus, then a bass chorus, then the theme with a pianissimo repeat. Bud again comps loud above the bass. Miles plays better solos on the earlier takes than on the one originally issued.

Roach's drumming is of interest on this date as he plays brushes on the opening theme choruses of all the selections except *Buzzy*. He switches to sticks at the appearance of the first soloist, giving the feeling of lift and drive.

* * *

Parker and Doris Sydnor were living at the Dewey Square Hotel on West 117th Street during the summer of 1947, and The Three Deuces became the "home" of the quintet. Billy Shaw of the Moe Gale agency was beginning to solicit bookings for the quintet at jazz clubs in major Eastern and Midwest cities, and Bird was seemingly healthy and straight. By the fall he would be back on heroin, but when he first resumed the habit is unknown. He had his contract with Savoy to fulfill as well as the one with Russell, who was in the process of moving the Dial headquarters to New York. There were legal tangles over the contracts as the Savoy contract had been signed before Dial's "exclusive" contract, and therefore, Savoy was in the clear. Shaw thought Parker should forget both contracts and bargain with a major label, but when the A.F. of M. negotiations with record companies stalled and another recording ban was threatened at the end of the year, Shaw advised Bird to do any recording that was possible.

Duke Jordan, who became the regular pianist with the quintet describes the atmosphere of this general period:

...The group got on very harmoniously except for slight altercations with Miles...he was tight with John Lewis, and he wanted Bird to substitute John for me in the group. But Bird silenced him by quietly and firmly saying that he chose the guys and Miles could form his own outfit if anything displeased him...[3]

* * *

Recording—August 1947—New York

Miles Davis All Stars—Davis (tp), Parker (ts), John Lewis (p), Nelson Boyd (b), Max Roach (d).

Milestones—Take 1 (Orig.)	Savoy 12009
Milestones—Take 2	Savoy 12001
Little Willie Leaps—Take 1	Savoy 12001
Little Willie Leaps—Take 2	Savoy 12001
Little Willie Leaps—Take 3 (Orig.)	Savoy 12001
Half Nelson—Take 1	Savoy 12001
Half Nelson—Take 2 (Orig.)	Savoy 12009
Sippin' at Bell's—Take 1	Savoy 12009
Sippin' at Bell's—Take 2 (Orig.)	Savoy 12009
Sippin' at Bell's—Take 4	Savoy 12001

Young Miles obviously did have ideas of his own, and when an opportunity came for him to record under his own name, he used Lewis and Nelson Boyd, two of his intellectual compatriots, and had Parker switch to tenor sax. The latter move probably had several motives: (1) to remove the strong image of Parker, whom people identified with the alto, and strengthen Davis' personal identity; (2) to achieve a "cooler" sound by a blend with the lower pitched instrument.

Davis wrote all the material for the date, and his harmonic training at Julliard was coming to the fore. The tunes are liberally sprinkled with key changes, chromatic sequences, and altered seventh chords. Furthermore, the melodic lines contain the strings of eighth notes that were characteristic of Davis's composition and improvisation during this period.

Milestones has an eight-bar composed introduction and a 32-bar (AABA) theme. The figure that begins the theme is a characteristic "bebop" phrase, beginning after the first beat and landing on the flatted ninth of the dominant chord. The identical phrase is used as a "close" to the "A" section with the final note being the third of the tonic. This gives the section a beautiful symmetry.

Ex. 70 *Milestones*—Beginning Phrase

Ex. 71 *Milestones*—Closing Phrase

The bridge begins in a key a half-step below the tonic and moves still another step down before returning through a chromatic harmonic sequence in the final two bars: /Bbm7 Eb7/Bm7 E7/- to "A" section.

Take 1 is excellent both in execution and ideas. Miles is muted (he had been experimenting with mutes since the March 1946 Dial date), but here it is a cup mute and not the stemless Harmon mute he favored during the late Fifties. Roach begins the tune with brushes, and the overall effect is one of "coolness." Miles's chorus and Lewis's half-chorus are beautifully conceived, and Bird's solo on the bridge, although not as "cool" as the others, is a strong statement. The tune ends with the final "A" section. The theme on Take 2 is not quite as clean as the first attempt, and Davis's solo is vague, his ideas not flowing with the changes. Lewis and Bird sound good, however.

Little Willie Leaps is based on *All God's Chillun Got Rhythm* and has both of the horns and Lewis soloing for a full chorus each. The first take is cut after about three quarters of the line, probably for recording balance, but the next two takes are both good. Take 3, however, is noticeably faster than Take 2, and the solos are better. Miles is excellent on the original issue, and Bird sounds like the tenor players of a decade later. Lewis is extremely melodic, but his grunts and mumbles can be heard during his solo.

Half Nelson has the chord base of Tadd Dameron's *Lady Bird*, which Miles probably learned in the Eckstine band. One important substitute chord gives *Half Nelson* its uniqueness from the Dameron harmonic structure, and the unison line breaks into harmony at this point.

Ex. 72 *Lady Bird* Bars 5-8

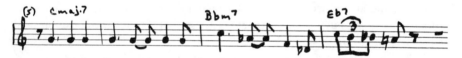

Ex. 73 *Half Nelson* Bars 5-8

The structure is a sixteen-bar theme that is repeated, and the horn solos are 32 bars. Both takes are good, and Bird sounds "cool" on the first take. Boyd plays sixteen bars before the closing theme on both takes, and his soloing possibly inspired the title of the tune (Nelson playing a *half* chorus). Furthermore, Boyd employs some double stops in places on the second take. In fact, the second take has *excellent* solos by all. Boyd's solos, however, are thoughtful, not just "walks," and they are a welcome addition to the date. Lewis does not solo on this tune, possibly because of time limitations on the 78 rpm records.

The twelve-bar blues structure is heavily altered for *Sippin' At Bell's*. A good example is in the fifth and sixth bars, the traditional place for the IV7 chord (Bb7 in this key).

Ex. 74 *Sippin' At Bells* Bars 5-6

This alteration gets away from the traditional "bluesy" sound as does the substitution of F#m7-B7 in the fourth bar, the traditional place for the I7 (F7 in this key). Take 2 is excellent, with all soloists (Bird, Miles, Lewis) playing stimulating two-chorus solos, although Miles and Lewis sound a bit more at home with the altered chords than Bird does. But the fourth take is the worst complete offering of the entire date; Lewis is the only consistent soloist, and the opening theme could be cleaner. Take 1 contains the theme and one and one-half choruses of Bird. The line is fluffed, however, at the beginning of the repeat (the line is repeated on the theme statements), and Bird's solo is fluffed at the entrance. A Take 3 (short take) is listed on Savoy 12001 but is not present; it probably is only an attempt at the line.

The date is the most satisfying example of Miles's early playing, and one can hear the influences that worked upon young trumpeters, such as Chet Baker, in Miles's solos. The group sounds "together" and the compositions are interesting and effective. Moreover, there is ample evidence here that Davis was the first "cool" player (just as Parker was the culmination of the "hot" style). If Miles's later sides (the Capitols of 1949-1950) are known as "Birth of the Cool" perhaps this date should be known as "Conception of the Cool."

* * *

The summer of 1947 found many of the famous "boppers" working The Street at different periods. The Gillespie big band worked at the Downbeat during August with Ray Brown, Kenny Clarke, and John Lewis as the rhythm. In late September, Clarke left to work with Tadd Dameron and other small groups, and Brown left to join a JATP unit. Subsequently, Gillespie replaced them with Al McKibbon on bass and Joe Harris on drums. Gillespie's August recordings were *Ow, Two Bass Hit, Oopapada,* and *Stay On It,* the latter written by Dameron. The group had been named Band of the Year by *Metronome* magazine. Dameron led various units on The Street with Fats Navarro as the trumpeter. He employed either Charlie Rouse or Allen Eager on tenor; Ernie Henry on alto; Curly Russell or Nelson Boyd on bass; and drummers Art Blakey, Shadow Wilson, or Kenny Clarke. It was usually a six piece group: trumpet, alto, tenor, and rhythm. Lennie Tristano, the blind genius pianist, occasionally worked at the Deuces opposite Parker, but the extreme experimental nature and advanced harmonic freedom of his music made work rather sparse. Tristano had been on the scene for about a year and had established himself as a teacher. His usual group was a trio with Billy Bauer, guitar; and Arnold Fishkind, bass; although sometimes one of his students such as John LaPorta, the clarinetist, could be found sitting in. Tristano and Bauer could indulge in simultaneous improvisations that would astound even the most musically astute listeners.

For every action there is a reaction, however, and the revolutionary music of the 1940s was challenged by a renewed interest in early jazz. Young men formed traditional "dixieland" groups and researched old records in order to sound "authentic." A search went out to find New Orleans jazzmen and interview them.

Many leading critics supported the movement, and the frenzy spread throughout the country. The "boppers," however, having difficulty finding receptive audiences for their music, reacted with cynicism and coined the term "Moldy Figs" for the people that were interested in traditional jazz. Indeed, this puerile attitude on both sides certainly solved nothing and only succeeded in tearing a hole in the lines of a music (jazz) that was fast becoming a minority interest.

This type of atmosphere led to a musical confrontation on the Mutual Radio Network between a group of "traditionalists" and a group of "modernists." The series of broadcasts was conceived by Barry Ulanov, then editor of *Metronome* magazine, who supported the modern movement. Ulanov enlisted the help of Rudi Blesh, who ran a weekly jazz show featuring a traditional group, and Larry Dorn, who was doing a series of special Saturday afternoon broadcasts called "Bands for Bonds" in support of the Treasury Department's promotion of its savings bond program. The three men arranged for a "Battle of Bands" series on the Saturday show.

* * *

Recording—Saturday, September 13, 1947—WOR Studios—New York City
Barry Ulanov's All Star Modern Jazz Musicians—Parker (as), D. Gillespie (tp), John LaPorta (clt), Lennie Tristano (p), Billy Bauer (g), Ray Brown (b), Max Roach (d).

Ko Ko (opening theme)	Spotlite (Eng) 107
Hot House	Spotlite (Eng) 107
I Surrender Dear (p, b, g only)	Spotlite (Eng) 107
Fine and Dandy	Spotlite (Eng) 107

As the group awaited "air time," Tristano was experimenting with some strange progressions on a standard tune, and Parker began playing with him. Tristano described the incident. "He wasn't used to the chords I played.... I don't remember the tune, but whatever I did, he was right on top of the chords."[4] Tristano added that he felt Bird was limited in his harmonic thinking because of the sameness of approach by his normal pianists. Indeed, in the few existing examples of Bird and Tristano together (the Ulanov broadcasts and the Metronome All Star session of 1949), Tristano does seem to stimulate Bird's mind. There are times, however on this broadcast when Tristano's chords suggest "outside" melodic lines and Bird's ideas stay within the usual harmony; still, both approaches seem to fit together.

Ko Ko served as the opening theme to the entire broadcast, but only the first section is used; there is no blowing on the *Cherokee* chords. Bird and Diz state the opening eight, and then every player blows eight in a free style over the drums as his name is introduced. Diz and Bird play the final eight.

The Blesh All Star Stompers came next (they are not on the record) and played *Sensation, Save It, Pretty Mama,* and *That's A Plenty.* The group was made of Wild Bill Davison (cornet), Edmond Hall (clarinet), Jimmy Archey (trombone), Ralph Sutton (piano), Danny Barker (guitar), and Baby Dodds (drums).

Hot House is performed excellently by the "modernists," with LaPorta laying out on the theme. Both Bird and Diz structure fine solos, and LaPorta is "spacey." Bauer plays a good chorus with some answers by Tristano, and then the pianist launches a wild solo that begins with crazy block chordal passages and contains the development of a single figure over changing harmony during the bridge. Max plays a fine solo on the bridge section of the closing theme chorus. Throughout the tune, the inventive comping of Bauer and Tristano is a joy to hear.

I Surrender Dear is only Tristano and Bauer, accompanied by bass. The beginning sixteen bars are filled with simultaneous passages; then Tristano assumes the leading role to the end of the tune. Bauer becomes the prime voice as the group returns to the bridge and goes out with a wild running ending by Tristano and Brown. Although Brown probably never played with the other two men before, he does a great job in following the procedure on this tune. Tristano and Bauer had recorded this tune a year before, however, on Keynote, and Brown was probably familiar with the recording.

Fine and Dandy is very free and unorganized. The choice of this tune may have been because of Tristano; it was one of his favorite vehicles, and his *Blue Boy*, recorded in May of this same year, is based upon the same chord structure. The tune starts with a drum intro, and Diz enters; then Bird falls in; they seem unsure about who is to take the lead. Finally, Bird settles into the role of melodicist and Dizzy plays behind him, with LaPorta adding a few licks in the last sixteen. Bird and Diz again come on strong, but LaPorta is not quite up to them. The announcer, Bruce Elliot, begins his closing spiel during Bauer's solo and continues through Tristano's. The final chorus is an "everybody blow" thing, a bit chaotic and noisy and, ironically, is very reminiscent of a "dixieland" treatment! Perhaps this final tune shows that some things, at a given time, are not as far apart as they seem at that moment.

Recording—Saturday, September 20, 1947—WOR Studios, New York City
Barry Ulanov's All Star Modern Jazz Musicians—Parker (as), D. Gillespie (tp), John LaPorta (clt), Lennie Tristano (p), Billy Bauer (g), Ray Brown (b), Max Roach (d)

Ko Ko (Opening theme)	Spotlite (Eng.) 107
Sunnyside Of The Street	Spotlite (Eng.) 107
How Deep Is The Ocean	Spotlite (Eng.) 107
Tiger Ray	Spotlite (Eng.) 107
52nd Street Theme (Closing theme)	Spotlite (Eng.) 107

This date is unbelievable and *must* be heard by anyone interested in the music of this period. The "traditionalists" called the tunes and the "modernists" played them! There must have been some prior knowledge, however—a "You-guys-can-pick-the-tunes-if-you-let-us-know-beforehand-what-they-are" agreement—because the modernists are extremely well prepared. They even have "worked-out" intros and endings.

Ko Ko receives much the same treatment as the preceding broadcast, but Max and Tristano get confused as to which one should play first and so does the announcer. Brown quotes *All God's Chillun* in his solo spot.

Sunnyside, however, is an *amazing* performance. The worked-out intro is in double time and alternates short ensemble phrases with improvisations of trumpet and alto. Diz starts the theme, and the other horns play in a "semi-dixie" fashion (backed of course by modern rhythm), and Bird has the bridge, with wild comping by Tristano and Bauer. In the second chorus, Diz and Bird alternate four bars apiece during the first sixteen, and from the bridge on, they blow *one* bar apiece. Next, Tristano enters with some wild block-chords and later is joined by Bauer. LaPorta plays the second half of the third chorus with adequate ideas. The next chorus opens with Bauer for eight, then Brown for four, and Max for four; the bridge and final eight are borrowed from *52nd Street Theme*.

Tristano opens *How Deep Is The Ocean*, and Diz and Bird alternate the lead every eight bars on the theme; Diz's first entrance is quiet, although the second is loud and abandoned. Tristano follows with a beautiful chorus that has inventive comping by Bauer. Next is a low-key shot by LaPorta, followed by an "everybody blow" theme chorus.

Surely, the next offering, *Tiger Rag*, is the real gem. Diz and Bird use the intro to *Shaw 'Nuff* and then do a traditional treatment (traditional, that is, with tongue in cheek), of the first section with Diz blowing lead. Bird takes the lead in the second section, and the third section (*Hold That Tiger*) is used for free improvisation without four-beat bass. Tristano goes into tempo with the bass, and then Bird and Diz tear into the riffs and bridge from *Dizzy Atmosphere* before going out with *Hold That Tiger*.

52nd is just the theme under the closing announcement.

Most of the sections inserted in the "arrangements" were passages that Bird and Diz had played together before, but there still was probably a "talk-over," at least, on the methods of inserting these passages into the tunes. Furthermore, the passages chosen were from the lines which were in the same keys as the tunes for the broadcast: *Sunnyside* was coupled with *52nd*—key of C; *Shaw Nuff* with the B-flat section of *Tiger Rag*; and *Dizzy Atmosphere* with the A-flat section. It was therefore possible to play the sections exactly as Bird and Diz played them originally, but, still, some thought was necessary. The chords would have not been a problem on the inserted sections since the patterns were familiar to all rhythm musicians. The fact that the rhythm section seems to know exactly what is happening, however, does suggest some preparation.

The listeners were invited to write in and vote for their favorite group—a ridiculous artistic premise, but one that is effective promotionally. The "modernists" emerged victorious after a month of voting and were scheduled for a "victory" appearance in early November.

* * *

Much has been written about the animosity which existed between Parker and Gillespie after the California excursion, but little attempt has ever been made to get to the core of it. Jealousy, of course, was the core, and Parker was a jealous man. Doris Sydnor, speaking of her marriage to Parker, said, "...I really had no strong desire for marriage, but Charlie was going through a jealousy period, a romantically insecure stage with me; so I said 'Yes'."[5] His bass player for the zenith of his career, Tommy Potter reported, "He craved attention, lots of it; but then, he needed a lot of everything."[6] Gillespie himself said of his relationship with Parker, "We were always friends. Sometimes I would beat his brains out in chess, but there was never any real ill feeling between us. . . . People want to believe there was animosity. The press likes it; it makes good copy."[7]

If we examine Gillespie's statement we see that the statement about chess is extremely important. Chess is a highly competitive game from the individual standpoint, and it is not for the faint-hearted. Gillespie, therefore, probably brought this subject into the conversation to show the type of competitiveness that existed in his mind. To Diz, a person with a strong self-image, competitiveness was a game, an intellectual duel that was fun. Bird's ego, however, was not strong and needed constant feeding; he therefore was envious of Gillespie's musical success, although highly respectful of his musical talents and abilities. The animosity, if one must use the term, however, was much different from the feelings which emerged between Bird and Ross Russell. Bird had little respect for Russell, as is the case with most creative artists in their attitude toward non-creative people who fashion their lives. He became extremely upset with Russell's issuance of the different "takes" of his recordings and abhorred the lack of taste with which it was done. Indeed, Bird's animosity in this case was far deeper than his combativeness with Gillespie. In Diz's case, Bird, because of his own insecure feelings, simply resented a thing, another person's success, but where Russell was concerned, Bird harbored a personal grudge. All the same "Symphony Sid" Torin relates an incident (later in Bird's career) in which Parker and Gillespie ruined each other's European souvenirs during a radio interview—Parker first tramping on Diz's pipe and Diz reacting by brandishing a blade and cutting up Parker's Paris beret.[8] Here again, we find Bird as the tormented aggressor, confusing his hatred of the thing with his hatred of a person and acting violently. Gillespie merely reacted in rage.

If all these facts are viewed together one finds a picture of the relationship that is probably close to the truth: Gillespie, a highly competitive, success-oriented individual who did not hold grudges, versus Parker, an insecure, equally competitive individual with inwardly directed drives that resulted in self-destructiveness and an inner confusion of motives.

* * *

Recording—Monday—September 29, 1947—Carnegie Hall, New York City
Dizzy Gillespie (tp), Parker (as), John Lewis (p), Al McKibbon (b), Joe Harris (d).

Night in Tunisia—Part I	Roost 2234
Night in Tunisia—Part II	Roost 2234
Dizzy Atmosphere	Roost 2234
Groovin' High—Part I	Roost 2234
Groovin' High—Part II	Roost 2234
Confirmation	Roost 2234

This concert, promoted by Gillespie and critic Leonard Feather, was Bop's first large promotional venture. It had the Gillespie big band, Ella Fitzgerald and her scat singing, and a twenty-minute set featuring Bird and Diz with the rhythm section of the big band.

Gillespie was the feature artist with his big band, and Bird the guest. This did not sit well with Bird, and he went to the performance with an "I'll show them" attitude. Diz tried to make light of it, but did not back down musically. In fact, Parker's arrogance resulted in Diz's coming back with glib musical jabs, and one must view the performance as a sparring match.

The recordings were originally made by the Carnegie Hall recording service, which functioned only for the convenience of the performing artists, but they were pirated and released on a label called Black Deuce. Soon after, because of much protest by the recording industry, they were removed from public circulation and not released legally until 1960. *Night In Tunisia* and *Groovin' High*, because of their length, were divided into two parts which were issued back to back on the bootleg 78's. This is why they are both listed today in Parts I and II. The piano is almost inaudible throughout the recording.

Tunisia opens with McKibbon playing the opening figure, and Bird blowing the original sax figure with a wild variation on the repeat. Diz then blows the theme, with Parker continuing the background, and as Bird comes in on the bridge, one can hear the applause from his front row claque that came to support him. Gillespie plays the final "A" section, and the horns merge on the interlude. Parker's break is good, and his chorus is extremely exciting, drawing more applause from the claque at certain points. In the bridge, he makes use of the first part of the figure that he used in *Hot House* during 1945 (Ex. 18). Part I ends after Parker's two choruses, and Part II cuts in during the Diz solo. Diz seemingly plays 1½ choruses, wanting Lewis to take the bridge before the "out" section, but when Lewis enters he plays on the "A" section and the bass is right with him (the writer could be mistaken, as the chords during the solo are extremely difficult, if not impossible, to hear, and the record starts in the middle of Gillespie's solo). The horns take the tune out with a final "A" section after Lewis's solo, and they finish with a wild coda.

The speed of *Atmosphere* is shattering, sounding at times like a record played one speed too fast, but the unison line is performed wonderfully. Bird is flying, but there again seems to be a loss of the exact place in the tune by the rhythm section. This may be because of Bird's shifting accents, but again it is the inaudible piano that is confusing to anyone trying an analysis. Bird quotes Gillespie's *BeBop* at one point, probably chiding him for his "BeBop inventor" public image. Dizzy retaliates with a virile two choruses that take no back seat to Bird. Unfortunately, the recording fades after Gillespie's chorus; it would be an experience to hear— at this tempo—the wonderful unison riffs that follow the solos in the 1945 version.

On *Groovin'*, McKibbon plays wrong notes at the modulatory section following the first chorus. Bird's chorus is a fantastic one. He uses the upper reaches of the horn and creates unbelievable sequences; liquid ideas flowing from one to the other; and fiery excitement. Below is a typical example of his use of the upper register on this tune.

Ex. 75 *Groovin High* (Sept. 19, 1947) Bars 6-9 *Alto Key*

The three Parker choruses are the highpoint of this recording and are worth study by all improvisors.

Part I ends at the modulation back to E-flat for Gillespie's chorus and Part II begins in the modulation. The listener, however is aware of where the tune is on this cut as opposed to *Tunisia*. Diz comes on strong, quoting from his original coda on this tune at the end of his first sixteen, but not quite equaling Bird's offering. Lewis follows and seems to be playing well—where one can hear him. The ending offers a new view of the original coda, with Bird straining to equal Diz instead of complementing him.

Confirmation begins with a drum intro followed by an "impossible" theme chorus, with even the most subtle nuances being interpreted together. Bird is excellent on his own vehicle, quoting the "Irish Washerwoman" in the second chorus. This is the earliest available recording of this tune with Bird on it, although it was a standard part of the Gillespie group's repertoire during 1945. Diz, however, recorded it during Parker's "absentee" period on the coast. The concert cut stops after Bird, but one can guess that Dizzy's chorus was a beauty, as usual. For some reason the piano can be heard a bit better on this tune than on the others.

Some of the tunes featured on the Gillespie portion of the program were *Toccata For Trumpet* by John Lewis, *Nearness* and *Soulphony* by Tadd Dameron, and *Salt Peanuts* and *One Bass Hit* from Gillespie's usual repertoire. One of the highlights of the evening was the performance of George Russell's *Afro-Cubano* Suite in two parts—*Cubana Be* and *Cubana Bop*—with Chano Pozo creating exhilarating excitement on congo drums during the second movement. This jazz composition, furthermore, was an echo of the interest in Latin music that was sweeping the country, even at the commercial level.

Gillespie was criticized in the October *Down Beat* for his bumps and grinds, dance steps behind Ella, and general showboating. Indeed, Mike Levin, the reviewer, was really put off by Diz's antics, but to Diz, it was just fun.

* * *

The early "classic period" of Parker can be characterized by two words—the chase. Parker chased Gillespie; Miles chased Parker; Gillespie chased success; Parker chased sensation; and the "pushers" chased Parker. But most important, young musicians, in all corners of the country were hearing Parker's music with open and questioning minds and were becoming completely obsessed with chasing "The Bird."

CHAPTER IX

THE CLASSIC PERIOD—PART TWO
Bird Feathers
(October-December 1947)

That eagle's fate and mine are one
Which, on the shaft that made him die,
Espied a feather of his own,
Wherewith he wont to soar so high.

Edmund Waller—To a lady singing a
song of his composing.

As one views the New York scene in the autumn of 1947 from several perspectives, one finds quite a slice of life. To begin with, on the music scene, Parker's career was approaching its height and his music was creating a stir. Indeed, bop had truly invaded the big bands. For instance, Claude Thornhill was recording many of the bop lines and featuring soloists such as altoist Lee Konitz with Gil Evans arrangements; in fact, the Thornhill "book" included *Anthropology, Yardbird Suite,* and *Donna Lee.* The Woody Herman band also showed the current influence with *Keen and Peachy* (based on *Fine and Dandy*), *The Goof and I* (based on *I Got Rhythm*), and the boppish Jimmy Giuffre sax section feature that gave the 1947 edition of the Herman band its nickname—*Four Brothers.* Even Gene Krupa, always alert to new trends, jumped on the bandwagon and recorded *Disc Jockey Jump,* a Gerry Mulligan opus with a bop-type sax-oriented line. Bop, surely, was the prevailing jazz style.

At the same time the popular music of the day was producing such inane hits as *The Woody Woodpecker Song* (theme from the Walter Lantz movie cartoon). Jule Styne's *High Button Shoes* opened on Broadway, and, coincidentally, the women's fashion industry decried the "New Look"—full skirts reaching almost to ankle length.

New York teams had dominated the 1947 baseball season, and for the world championship, the Yankees, led by Joe DiMaggio, bested the Brooklyn Dodgers in a "subway" World Series that featured the first pinch-hit home run in World Series history—hit by none other than Lawrence Peter "Yogi" Berra, the Yankee catcher, in Game 3. Furthermore, Bill Bevan, also of the Yankees, pitched no-hit ball for eight and two-thirds innings in the fourth game before finally losing the no-hitter and the game! The Dodgers, although losers, were sparked by the play of Jackie Robinson, the first black major-leaguer, who was then finishing his first season.

As to the political picture, people buzzed pro and con about the proposed "Marshall Plan" which would provide foreign aid to European nations for war reconstruction. In addition, the "cold war" between the United States and Russia was about to begin in earnest.

In movies, one of Hollywood's better "B" pictures, *Night Song*, told the story of a frustrated, blind pianist-composer, and used Hoagy Carmichael in a supporting role. The stars were Dana Andrews and Merle Oberon.

Against this diverse backdrop, Parker continued to record his classic performances. For the desire to beat the recording deadline of the AFM was felt by all parts of the music industry. The artists needed recordings to keep their public image high and the companies needed new material in order to exist. Parker and Ross Russell, being no exceptions, planned three final Dial sessions for the end of the year. These recordings, moreover, eventually fulfilled Parker's Dial obligations, for his contract was only good until the following spring and the recording ban would stretch into the following fall.

Since returning from the coast, however, Bird had reacquired his heroin habit, and Russell states that Parker brought his connection with him to the first date and...''said he needed fifty dollars.'' Russell gave him the money and Parker, after a trip to the men's room, played the date without problems.[1]

* * *

Recording—October 28, 1947—WOR Studios—48th and Broadway New York City
Charlie Parker Quintet—Parker (as), Miles Davis (tp), Duke Jordan (p), Tommy Potter (b), Max Roach (d).

Dexterity—Take 1	Spotlite (Eng) 104
Dexterity—Take 2	Spotlite (Eng) 104
Bongo Bop—Take 1	Spotlite (Eng) 104
Bongo Bop—Take 2	Spotlite (Eng) 104
Dewey Square—Take 1	Spotlite (Eng) 104
Dewey Square—Take 2	Spotlite (Eng) 104
Dewey Square—Take 3	Spotlite (Eng) 104
The Hymn—Take 1	Spotlite (Eng) 104
The Hymn—Take 2	Spotlite (Eng) 104
Bird of Paradise—Take 1	Spotlite (Eng) 104
Bird of Paradise—Take 2	Spotlite (Eng) 104
Bird of Paradise—Take 3	Spotlite (Eng) 104
Embraceable You—Take 1	Spotlite (Eng) 104
Embraceable You—Take 2	Spotlite (Eng) 104

Dexterity, a Parker line (as are the other originals on this date), has the *I Got Rhythm* chord base with a chromatic alteration in the seventh bar: /Dm7 Dbm7/ Cm7 F7/. The bridge section is composed, and Parker's melody implies secondary supertonics preceding the secondary dominants that usually harmonize this section (Am7-D7 instead of merely D7).

Ex. 76 *Dexterity* Beginning of Bridge

The solo order is Bird (32), Miles (32), Jordan (24), and Roach (8). Parker's chorus on Take 1 has a continuous flow to the phrases—extending over sectional lines; this is most apparent in the phrase that begins before the bridge and ends several bars into it. Miles also sounds very good; he predates what would later (about 1953) be called a "West Coast" trumpet style. On the final theme chorus, there is a hitch at the end of the first eight where the rhythm stops, possibly anticipating an ending.

Take 2, a faster version, has a better recorded sound, and Parker is more multi-noted than before. This take could be called the "hot" version and the other the "cool" version. The bridge on the closing unison theme could be cleaner, but otherwise it is an excellent take.

A third take was done on *Dexterity* but was lost, and Russell, on LP, erroneously issued *Bongo Bop* instead. The latter tune became confused with *Bongo Beep* done in December! To clarify: Miles plays open horn on *Dexterity*, but on *Bongo Bop*, he is muted. *Bongo Beep* contains J.J. Johnson on trombone. The novice can simply look for the open horn to identify *Dexterity*, but the more musically astute can look for the *I Got Rhythm* form; the other tunes are both blues (*Bongo Bop*, in fact, was also issued on European labels as *Charlie's Blues*). Notated below are the opening phrases of *Dexterity* and *Bongo Bop*.

Ex. 77 *Dexterity* Opening Phrase

Ex. 78 *Bongo Bop* Opening Phrase

The theme of *Bongo Bop* is played in octave unison, and the rhythm is unique: the first, fifth, and ninth bar (or the beginning of each four bar phrase of the blues) are in "Latin" rhythm with Roach using "rim taps," and the rest of each phrase is played straight. Bird and Miles play two choruses apiece followed by Jordan for a singleton, and Potter "walks" a chorus before the final theme. Miles's tone is not good on the first take, and he ventures too many multi-noted passages. On Take 2, Bird begins his solo with the same figure as Take 1 but develops it differently; he appears more relaxed on Take 2. Miles's first chorus (Take 2) is very melodic, but the second is all a multi-noted flurry—a fine contrast. The final figure of the theme (a *Moose The Mooche* rhythmic signature) is in unison on Take 2, but on Take 1, it is harmonized in "flat-five" intervals.

The "A" section of *Dewey Square* is somewhat related to *Yardbird Suite* harmonically. The bridge pattern (improvised melodically) is a common one: / IV / iv /I/ VI7 / II7 / II7 / ii7 / V7 /. Take 1 begins with a rim shot and the theme enters on the second half of the first beat. On the other two takes, however, Jordan begins the proceedings with an eight-bar intro comprised mainly of two phrases of quarter note triplets followed by breaks. The solo order is as usual— Bird (32) (64 on Take 1), Miles (32), Jordan (24), and Roach (8). The ensemble plays a final "A" section.

Dewey Square's first take was issued without the theme under the titles *Prezology* and *Air Conditioning* on various Dial issues and as *Bird Feathers* on some European reissues. On this earliest version, Parker is cool and relaxed, much different from the last two takes. On Take 2, however, Parker is much more driving in his approach, and on Take 3, he synthesizes some of the ideas used in the earlier takes. Jordan begins his chorus on each of the last two takes with the same "Parkerian" phrase— one which begins the second eight bars of Parker's *Moose The Mooche* solo (Take 2) from 1946. Miles's playing on this tune is not his best.

The Hymn begins with four brilliant Parker blues choruses, and the hymn-like theme first recorded by McShann in *Wichita Blues* is then stated by both horns in harmony. The theme is repeated softly an octave lower.

Ex. 79 *The Hymn* Opening Theme

Parker is flying on both takes. He uses the superimposition of a series of diminished chords (a favorite device) during his second chorus on Take 1 and during his fourth chorus on Take 2. Miles's better solo is on the second take as is Jordan's. Jordan, moreover, develops a single figure during the second chorus of his two chorus solo and shows extreme sensitivity. Potter "walks" two choruses on both takes before the closing theme and is extremely effective on Take 2, both in his "walk" and the continuance of it behind the elongated theme. His choice of notes is excellent. Take 2 has better overall sound and was sometimes issued under the title of *Superman*.

Bird of Paradise is *All The Things You Are*, and is fitted with the intro and coda that Gillespie and Parker recorded in 1945. On Take 1, Bird plays a theme chorus and stays fairly close to the melody of the Kern standard until the final eight bars; Roach goes to beguine rhythm at the bridge. Miles plays a half-chorus, and Jordan is again developmental at the bridge. In the final eight, Miles plays the melody with Parker offering gentle obligators. Neither Take 2 nor Take 3 contains a melody statement—Bird launches directly into improvisations after the intro. The chorus on Take 3, however, is probably his best; although the one on Take 2, beginning with a development of the introductory figure, is close behind. Jordan takes his developmental bridge figure from Take 1 and plays it on both Take 2 and Take 3, condensing it on the final one! On each of the two takes, Miles and Bird use simultaneous improvisation for the "out" eight.

The reading of *Embraceable You* on Take 1 of this tune is one of the finest ballad solos in the history of jazz. Jordan's intro is exquisite (he uses the same one on both takes), and Parker builds his chorus from a single germ motif and fills it with sad, beautiful emotion. The solo will be analyzed in depth in the latter portion of this work (see Analysis Section). On both takes, Miles returns to the second eight (portion beginning in relative minor) and plays the tune out; the last few bars are done with Bird in "worked-out" harmony. Parker lightly plays behind Miles on Take 1 but stays out until the final harmonized bars on Take 2. No actual thematic material outside of the final few measures is heard on either take. The Parker chorus on Take 2 is also very good but seems almost anti-climactic against the first which is a masterpiece.

Parker's *Embraceable You* is representative of the jazz ballad playing of the 1940s just as Coleman Hawkins' *Body and Soul* is representative of the 1930s. Both performances were done near the end of their respective decades and serve as cumulative statements for the art of ballad playing. Moreover, both stand up remarkably well in today's world, and both have lessons of lyricism to offer to all young performers.

Recording—Tuesday, November 4, 1947, New York City—Parker Quintet
Miles Davis (tp), Parker (as), Duke Jordan (p), Tommy Potter (b), Max Roach (d).

Bird Feathers	Spotlite 105
Klact-oveeseds-tene—Take 1	Spotlite 105
Klact-oveeseds-tene—Take 2	Spotlite 105
Scrapple From The Apple—Take 2	Spotlite 105
Scrapple From The Apple—Take 3	Spotlite 105
My Old Flame	Spotlite 105
Out of Nowhere—Take 1	Spotlite 105
Out of Nowhere—Take 2	Spotlite 105
Out of Nowhere—Take 3	Spotlite 105
Don't Blame Me	Spotlite 105

The opening blues line is one of those that caused havoc for years because of Dial's indiscriminate titling. It was issued as *Schnourphology* on some European labels; and *some* takes of *Dewey Square* (10/28/47) and *Bongo Beep* (12/17/47) were issued bearing the *Bird Feathers* title. An easy way for the novice to tell the correct titles apart, however, is to listen for a theme (melody) chorus; if it does not have one, it is probably the first take of *Dewey Square* titled wrongly (the musical listener can simply listen for the blues form). If the tune contains a theme that is the blues form, listen for a J.J. Johnson trombone; if there is one present (along with some Latin percussion effects), the tune is *Bongo Beep* titled wrongly. Notated below are the true opening bars of *Bird Feathers*.

Ex. 80 *Bird Feathers* Opening Bars

After the theme, Parker, beginning with a development of the final thematic figure, plays three choruses. The beginning theme figure itself is based rhythmically (as one can see above) on the motif of *Moose The Mooche*. Miles plays two choruses— one lyrical and one multi-noted—and the final improvisationary chorus has Jordan (16), Potter (8-walking), and Roach (8). Roach ends his solo with a series of offbeat rolls, and the horns are a bit unsure at the final theme entrance. The overall feel of the take, in fact, is one of "rushing."

Klact-oveeseds-tene is basically a ii7-V7-I-VI7 tune followed by the II7 chord before the cadence in the "A" section. It is sometimes quoted as being based on *Perdido*, but the presence of the II7 chord makes it a bit different. An example from Parker's improvisation on Take 2 illustrates the point.

Ex. 81 *Klact.* Bars 4-5 Chorus 1—Take 2

The melodically improvised bridge is also a familiar progression: In Bb: / Eb / Ebm / Bb / G7 / C7 / C7 / Cm7 / F7 /.

The quasi-Latin intro and coda (used also by Dexter Gordon and Wardell Gray in their recording of *The Chase* from this period) is in harmony by the horns and is rhythmically interesting by virtue of its off-beat accents. An eight-bar drum interlude precedes the main theme.

Ex. 82 *Klact.* Opening of Intro

Bird's chorus on Take 1 starts with a weird, fragmented phrase and continues on a disjointed path that somehow makes sense as a whole; the fragmentary phrase may have inspired the strange title. Miles plays a very organized chorus, and the rhythm breaks up the final blowing chorus (16-8-8). Miles, however, drops out on the second eight of the final theme, ruining the take. On Take 2, Bird is more organized in his thinking and the final theme is cleaner.

The latter take on *Scrapple* is preferable; Miles plays better, and Bird develops his earlier ideas (from the other take) and plays "outside" at the beginning of the final eight. On the earlier take, Bird is "cooler" and Miles, while full of ideas, has technical problems. The tune has the *Honeysuckle Rose* base with the *I Got Rhythm* bridge, and the format is the same on both takes. Parker improvises the bridge during each take's theme chorus, and the solo order is Bird (32), Miles (32), Jordan (16), Potter (8-bridge-walk). Both takes close with a final "A" section, but on the latter take there is a piano coda. The eight-bar "composed" theme section is one of the most infectious of the Parker lines.

Ex. 83 *Scrapple* Opening Bars

The final three ballads seem strangely related—both in Bird's ideas and in the strange story the consecutive titles tell. Perhaps the titles might remind one of Parker's constant flirtations with heroin. These ballads are the high point of the date and are so emotion-packed that one wants to hear them again and again. Parker breaks up the melodies; that is, he launches into wild improvisation, but comes back and hints at the melody as if to say "Look; here's what I am."

On *My Old Flame* he is sexual and melodic, spurting passion. Davis plays the second half, with Bird backing lightly in the final eight. Bird uses the *Embraceable You* motif (from the last session) as an ending.

Out Of Nowhere—Take 1 is the famous motivic treatment in which Parker develops a fantastic motif starting at Bar 10 (see Analysis Section). The chorus is unbelievable, as are the Parker solos on the other two takes. On Take 2, the motif appears again at slightly different places, but Take 3 does not use it at all. The alternate takes were probably done because of the task of fitting the slow performance on 78's; for the first one contains two full choruses, with Jordan and Davis splitting the second, but the second take eliminates Jordan, and has Davis returning to the second eight and playing out 24 bars. This alternative did not seem to suit either, however, so the final take has Miles returning to the second half of the tune.

Bird is fantastic on *Don't Blame Me*, a performance that is usually underrated. Davis plays a four bar intro and then is not heard until a final "out" eight. The rest is Bird, with breathtaking melodic breakup and an emotional quality that leaves the listener limp. This tune, as are the other two ballads, is a "must" for the collection of every person even remotely interested in Parker.

Recording—Saturday, November 8, 1947—Broadcast-WOR Mutual Studios

Barry Ulanov's BeBop All Stars—Fats Navarro (tp), Parker (as), Allen Eager (ts), Lennie Tristano (p), Billy Bauer (g), Tommy Potter (b), Buddy Rich (d), John LaPorta (clt), Sarah Vaughan (vcl).

52nd Street Theme (Opening Theme)	Spotlite 108
Donna Lee (Parker)	Spotlite 108
Everything I Have Is Yours (Vocal)	Spotlite 108
Fat's Flat (Navarro)	Spotlite 108
Tea For Two (LaPorta)	Spotlite 108
Don't Blame Me (Rhythm Section)	Spotlite 108
Groovin' High (Eager)	Spotlite 108
Ko Ko and Anthropology (Closing Theme)	Spotlite 108

The broadcast was the sequel to the September clash with the traditional jazzmen. The personnel had some changes for this "winners" broadcast, however, because of Gillespie and Ray Brown not being in town. All the same, the addition of Navarro and Eager from Tadd Dameron's group gave another dimension to the group.

After 24 bars, the opening theme has each member of the group improvising eight measures as he is announced. Potter, however, "walks" past his eight-bar section and confuses Rich, who is forced to enter late; this, in turn, causes a shoddy ensemble entrance to the theme restatement.

Bird begins the opening of *Donna Lee* alone—starting with a single note rather than the triplet which caused problems at the May session; then Navarro joins muted after the first eight. Bird plays three wailing choruses, and he and Fats are together on the "out" chorus.

Ex. 84 *Donna Lee* Triplet and Single Note

The vocal on *Everything I Have Is Yours* is well done, and Sarah shows her harmonic knowledge on the "tag" (last eight bars repeated). Tristano, surprisingly, is an effective accompanist; the horns do not play on this track.

Fats is alone on the theme-chorus to *Fat's Flats*, a *What Is This Thing Called Love*-based tune, and he then plays a tremendous two and 3/4 chorus solo. He quotes *Goody Goody* at the first bridge in an especially humorous fashion and *Sing For Your Supper* at the beginning of the third chorus. He and Parker state the last eight bars of *Hot House* as a final signature.

LaPorta plays very "outside" on *Tea For Two*, sometimes pretentiously so, but in contrast, Tristano and Bauer's 1½ chorus version (backed only by Potter) of *Don't Blame Me* is beautiful. Tristano plays to the bridge, using lovely lines and inventive blocks of chords; Bauer takes the bridge, and then there are eight bars of swirling simultaneous improvisation. Tristano returns to the bridge, and he and Bauer both function melodically in the final eight. A fine rendition.

All the horns except LaPorta are in the ensemble for *Groovin' High*, and the original modulation is not present on this version. Eager plays a Young-ish solo, and Bauer plays eight by himself and eight with Tristano (in simultaneous improvisation). Before the closing ensemble chorus, Rich plays sixteen.

Rich opens *Ko Ko* (there is no thematic material), and Bird whacks directly into the *Cherokee* chords for two choruses. Fats, however, follows with two that rival Bird's in invention and possibly surpass them. LaPorta then contrasts nicely in his chorus, breaking into running, fugal improvisation with Bauer and Tristano at the bridge, but Eager sounds very straight-forward following LaPorta. Tristano finishes up the improvisations. His bridge is beautiful. The ensemble (mostly Bird and Fats) plays the last eight of *Anthropology* as an out-chorus and closing theme, and Bird cuts off the broadcast with a flippant phrase from *52nd Street Theme* (on the Spotlite issue, however, the listener can hear the rhythm section continue for awhile in the studio).

Recordings—Late 1947 or 1948 ??

Repetition (Neal Hefti Orchestra—plus strings)	Verve 8001
The Bird (Parker plus a rhythm section)—Hank Jones (p)	
Ray Brown (b), Shelley Manne (d)	Verve 8001

These two recordings were done for Norman Granz (then at Mercury) but cannot be dated exactly. Russell feels they were done in 1947, in violation of Parker's contract, and states that Granz had offered Dial a Lester Young track in return, but it never materialized.[2] The solo stint with the big band is a spur-of-the-moment affair (the arrangement was not written with a soloist in mind), and one therefore must wonder why Granz would risk legal hassles to record just one planned quartet track.

The Hefti original, *Repetition*, opens with four bars of poly-rhythms and then the strings lay down a "vamp" passage. The tune proper is basically a chromatic melody with a ii7-V7-I harmonic pattern in two basic tonalities—F and Db. The sax section states the theme over Latin percussion for the first sixteen then comes the brass (8); and finally the strings enter with the brass backing. From this point, there is a rather elaborate interlude beginning with an eight-bar string passage. The rest of the interlude follows with short sections: sax and string vamp (four bars); string break (2); percussion break (2); brass and percussion break (2); sax-figure (4); string "circular" sounding figure (3)—(actually starts on fourth bar of preceding section); string "vamp" and "lead-in" measure (5). At this point the theme returns in almost the same manner as the opening, but with Parker blowing on top of the melody statements! The chorus is dazzling, starting with a development of the circular sounding figure played by the strings, and it contains a fine cadenza-type retarded ending followed by an "after-thought" cadenza. Bird played this tune with his string group later in his career, and this was probably the performance that inspired him to use the tune—and perhaps the strings.

The Bird has a unique construction that cannot be explained by words:

8 bars   /Cm/ Ab7 G7   /Cm/ Ab7 G7   /Cm/ Ab7 G7   /Cm/ G7/
8 bars   /C7/ C7   /Fm/ Fm   /Fm6/ G7   /Cm/ G7/
8 bars   /C7/ C7   /Fm/ Fm   /Ab7/ Ab7   /G7/ G7/
8 bars   Cm/ Ab7 G7   /Cm/ Ab G7   /Cm/ Ab7 G7   /Cm/ Cm/

It has some elements of *Topsy* and *What Is This Thing Called Love* to its construction, but they are used in an unusual manner.

Bird's playing is fantastic, and the rhythm section is excellent. Indeed, this is only his fourth recorded effort at tunes based in a minor key, the others being *Tunisia, What Is This Thing Called Love* (this tune, in fact, is not really minor, but rather uses minor areas), and *BeBop*. There is no thematic material, but one phrase that is used in Bird's final chorus several times is worthy of mention. It appears during the first and last eight-bar sections.

Ex. 85 *The Bird* Repeated Phrase

Jones begins the tune with a piano intro, and Bird goes immediately into improvisation. He is having reed trouble, but not idea trouble. In his two-chorus solo, the riff that was used to open *Bird's Nest* (Ex. 54) can be heard at one point. Jones and Brown play one chorus apiece, and Bird returns with four wailers, using one of his favorite ideas from *What Is This Thing Called Love* (Ex. 8) and the repeated phrase mentioned above. The final chorus gives the impression of a theme chorus because of the aforementioned phrase, but it is really just a suggestion.

In the numerical listing (Appendix I) at the end of this work, both of these recordings are listed as "circa 1948" and assigned a 1948 number; this is probably the best policy until a more exact date can be placed.

* * *

The quintet spent late November and early December at the Argyle Lounge in Chicago and at the Downbeat Club in Philadelphia. Parker's vices, however, were again beginning to cause lateness and obnoxious behavior. Duke Jordan tells of an incident at the Argyle which could have happened during this tour. Parker was drunk and unable to play, but the four other members worked the engagement. The management, however, docked the group the full amount for the engagement and had the support of the union.[3] It is possible that this incident triggered Parker's scandalous retaliation of urinating in a phone booth at the same club a few months later.

When the group returned to New York in mid-December, Ross Russell suggested a date using J.J. Johnson, the bop trombone voice. Parker agreed, and a rehearsal was set for December 15th with the session scheduled to follow two days later. At the time of the actual recording, however, Russell was ill, and his wife supervised the session. Perhaps this accounts for Russell's confusion of the titles from this session on various Dial issues.

* * *

Recording—December 17, 1947—New York City

Charlie Parker Sextet—Parker (as), M. Davis (tp), J.J. Johnson (tb), Duke Jordan (p), Tommy Potter (b), Max Roach (d).

Driftin' On A Reed—Take 2	Spotlite (Eng) 106
Driftin' On A Reed—Take 4	Spotlite (Eng) 106
Driftin' On A Reed—Take 5	Spotlite (Eng) 106
Quasimado—Take 1	Spotlite (Eng) 106
Quasimado—Take 2	Spotlite (Eng 106
Charlie's Wig—Take 2	Spotlite (Eng) 106
Charlie's Wig—Take 4	Spotlite (Eng) 106
Charlie's Wig—Take 5	Spotlite (Eng) 106
Bongo Beep—Take 2	Spotlite (Eng) 106
Bongo Beep—Take 3	Spotlite (Eng) 106
Crazeology (incomplete)—Take 1	Spotlite (Eng) 106
Crazeology (incomplete)—Take 2	Spotlite (Eng) 106
Crazeology—Take 3	Spotlite (Eng) 106
Crazeology—Take 4	Spotlite (Eng) 106
How Deep Is The Ocean—Take 1	Spotlite (Eng) 106
How Deep Is The Ocean—Take 2	Spotlite (Eng) 106

Johnson is a welcome addition; he and Miles are muted on all the ensemble choruses, and the three-horn blend is very satisfying.

The bouncy blues theme of *Driftin' On A Reed* with its off-beat accents was released under the titles *Air Conditioning* (Take 2) and *Giant Swing* (Take 4) at various times, and Bird was known to refer to it in live performances as *Big Foot*. It is difficult to hear Johnson in the ensemble on the earliest take, but on the other two, the trombone voice is obvious. The solo order is Bird, J.J., Miles, Jordan, and Potter, with Bird playing three choruses and Potter "walking" one before the final theme; the other soloists take two choruses apiece. Miles falls out momentarily in the final theme of the earliest take. Parker solos passionately throughout all takes, however, and Davis develops the beginning theme idea in all his solos. But the final take, as usual, is the masterpiece for both men; it seems to bring together the experiments of the earlier cuts.

Quasimado, Bird's line on *Embraceable You*, begins with one of Jordan's introductory gems that culminates with the three "pick-up" notes to the theme.

Ex. 86 *Quasimado* Opening

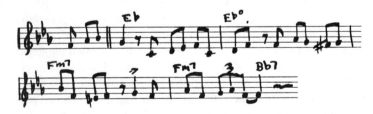

The horn blend is very successful, and Take 1 contains a Parker solo that hints at the motif from his version of October 18. He and Jordan split the first improvisationary chorus, and Johnson and Davis play eight apiece before the theme closes with the second half. The sound on Take 2 is better, but the Parker chorus on Take 1 is probably more valuable. The second take was also issued under the title *Trade Winds*.

Charlie's Wig is an interesting cut. The chord base is *When I Grow Too Old To Dream*—which Parker played in the 1945 Gillespie group—and the theme is preceded by a wild out-of-tempo unison introduction.

Ex. 87 *Charlie's Wig* Intro and Opening

The melody is constructed ABCD with the "B" and "D" chord patterns being similar. The "C" section, however, is always improvised by Parker and the "D" section gives the listener a "tag" effect when it occurs after the improvisation. Parker and Johnson both play full choruses, and Miles plays 24 bars, followed by the "D" section tag by all. All soloists play well throughout the three takes although Johnson is rather repetitive when the three takes are viewed as a whole. The fourth take was issued erroneously as both *Bongo Beep* and *Bongo Bop* and the second take was sometimes issued as *Move*.

Bongo Beep (the actual tune) is a Latin-tinged blues and can easily be identified by listening for the Latin percussion beat throughout the theme. It is the only Parker Dial recording that has this feature (*Bongo Bop* is broken up with straight fours). The tune was also issued under the incorrect titles of *Dexterity* and *Bird Feathers*. All solos are two-chorus statements except Roach's twelve-bar stint before the closing theme. The entrance back to the theme is cleaner on the final take and Parker's earthy statement on the later version is also preferable.

Crazeology has an altered *I Got Rhythm* base; a modulation to the key of the bVI (Gb in the key of Bb) at bars 5 and 6 (/ii7 V7 / I / in the new key) characterizes its harmony. Although Dial was consistent in the use of this title, other recordings exist in which this line is called *Bud's Bubble, Ideology*, and *Little Benny*. The latter title is probably the original given by the composer, trumpeter Benny Harris, who was with Bird in the Earl Hines band. The incomplete takes consist of the theme plus Bird's chorus; and only Bird's chorus, respectively. On the complete takes, the horns play complete choruses, and Jordan splits a chorus with Potter (walking-bridge) and Roach (last eight). Very fine solos abound, and the Parker statements are especially wild. He begins his solo on the final take with a flying triplet phrase that is repeated—acting as a sort of "call" before the string of ideas.

Ex. 88 *Crazeology* Opening Phrase-Solo

There was another chaotic version issued by Dial that came about through an engineering mistake which resulted in a "time-lag," overlapping version of the final take. True to form, Russell issued the side commercially.

How Deep Is The Ocean has Bird stating the theme after a Jordan intro. The theme begins fairly straight with subtle decorations, but in the second half, Bird stretches out a bit. Johnson plays his only open horn of the date as he returns to the second eight after Parker, and Miles enters at the final eight and stays on top for a rather free ending by the group. The sound on the second take is bad, but Bird, using some well-chosen harmonic notes, is a bit more free in his statement. Johnson only returns to the second half of the tune on the later version.

Miles's solos are impressive throughout the entire date and Johnson's trombone adds a new dimension, but the overall recorded sound is not as good as some of the other Dial sessions. Moreover, there is a great deal of difference between successive takes—sound-wise—suggesting some engineering experimentation.

This was the final date that Parker would ever record for the world's most obscure jazz record label.

* * *

The Parker group was booked into the *El Sino* in Detroit for the period of late December 1947-mid-January 1948 and during the stay in the Motor City recorded two blues tunes and two improvisations on standards for an independent label. These tracks were later issued on Savoy.

* * *

Charlie Parker All Stars—Detroit—December (late) 1947
Miles Davis (tp), Parker (as), Duke Jordan (p), Tommy Potter (b), Max Roach (dr).

Another Hairdo—Take 1 (Partial)	Savoy 12000
Another Hairdo—Take 2 (Partial)	Savoy 12000
Another Hairdo—Take 3 (Original)	Savoy 12000
Blue Bird—Take 1	Savoy 12000
Blue Bird —Take 3	Savoy 12014
Klaunstance—Take 1 (Original)	Savoy 12014
Bird Gets The Worm—Take 1	Savoy 12000
Bird Gets The Worm—Take 2 (Original)	Savoy 12014

The first two compositions are blues, but the latter two are based on "standard-tune" chord sequences—*Klaunstance* being derived from *The Way You Look Tonight* and *Bird Gets The Worm* from *Lover Come Back To Me.*

Takes 1 and 2 of *Hairdo* are only theme statements, but careful listening will reveal the rhythmic difficulties inherent in this seemingly simple blues frame. The frame begins with thematic material for three measures, then six measures of improvisation and a return to a final thematic statement of three measures. The

Ex. 89 *Another Hairdo*—Schematic

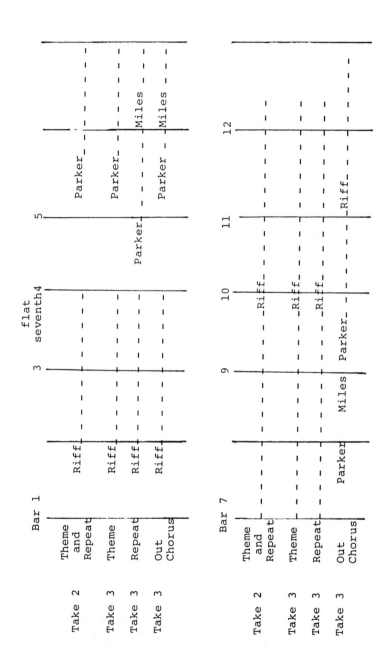

melodic announcement of the flat seventh of the scale in the third measure instead of the more commonplace fourth measure placement makes the improvisor's entrance to the middle six bars extremely difficult to feel.

The original take has some typical Parker blues excursions and an excellent introspective solo by Davis. Moreover, the final theme chorus contains one-bar improvisational exchanges between Parker and Davis in the middle six bars, but Parker extends his last statement for an extra bar, and the final thematic material, therefore, is stated a full bar later than it was in the opening chorus! Whether this is done purposely or not will remain an enigma (see schematic).

Bluebird is an earthy blues theme liberally sprinkled with grace notes. The earlier take has better Parker choruses, but the latter one reveals a more complete introductory statement by Parker and a refinement of Davis's ideas. The theme is based on a simple blues figure.

Ex. 90 *Bluebird* Opening Phrase

The final three tracks are mercurial improvisational showcases in which Parker shines brilliantly. These contain no thematic material except a brief melodic passage in the final section of *Klaunstance*. Jordan's relaxed solos on these up-tempo pieces are a perfect foil for the multi-noted excursions of Parker and Davis, and Roach and Potter are a joy—both in their accompanying roles and their brief solo appearances in *Bird Gets The Worm*.

Klaunstance is in normal AABA form but with sixteen-bar sections and a four-bar "tag" section. The "tag" was used on Jerome Kern's original show version of *The Way You Look Tonight*, but its inclusion in this improvised version can be confusing if the listener is not familiar with it. The format is Bird and Miles with full choruses, then Jordan with a half. The following bridge section has exchanges of "fours" by the horns leading to the "worked-out" eight-bar section. Parker finishes the tune (eight more bars) improvisationally and is joined by Miles for a running coda with shifting rhythmic accents.

Ex. 91 *Klaunstance* Melodic Section

Ex. 92 *Klaunstance* Coda

Although Sigmund Romberg's semi-classical standard *Lover Come Back To Me* (the harmonic base of *Bird Gets The Worm*) is written in eight-bar sections, the note values are doubled when performed at four-beat jazz tempo—therefore making each section sixteen bars long.

Ex. 93 *Lover Come Back* Original Notation

Ex. 94 *Lover Come Back* 4 Beat Jazz Version

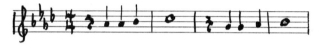

After choruses by Bird, Miles, and Jordan on Take 1 of *Bird Gets The Worm*, Potter and Roach trade fours for sixteen bars and Potter walks the repeated "A" section. Alto and trumpet trade fours in the bridge, and the final section has simultaneous improvisations between the two horns. The track ends with one of Bird's favorite humorous "bluesy" licks with Miles joining him on the repeat of the figure.

Ex. 95 *Bird Gets The Worm* Ending Figure

On Take 2, Jordan begins his solo with slow chordal figures and plays spare inventive lines throughout his chorus—a perfect contrast to the rest of the tune and an example that specifically points out Jordan's value to the Parker Quintet. Potter and Roach return only to the bridge for their fours, and the horns follow immediately with the simultaneous improvisation on the "out" eight.

The freedom of this recording session makes the date an attractive one to own. Parker's virile and inventive statements on *Klaunstance* and both takes of *Bird Gets The Worm* rival *Ko Ko* in their fluency and conception and are often overlooked when Bird's work is viewed as a whole. Miles also sounds very "together" throughout the session. Furthermore, the date acts as a final punctuation for 1947—the year of Bird's return.

* * *

Parker's middle "classic period," which includes the final three Dial dates, presents him at his best. His ballad playing had reached its height and his up-tempo excursions were dramatic statements. Bird was furiously creating, and the feathers were flying; they would be caught and examined by men who would shape the various jazz styles of the 1950s: cool jazz, West Coast jazz, hard bop, and funky jazz. Bird feathers were in the air and on the air, and their presence added a brilliance to an otherwise drab American music scene. Unfortunately, however, one had to look to find them, and to most of the music audience, this was an unthinkable chore. The feathers, therefore, fell to only a few, but they were valued beyond measure.

CHAPTER X

THE CLASSIC PERIOD—PART THREE
Merry-Go-Round
(January-August 1948)

I'm up and down and round about,
Yet all the world can't find me out;
Though hundreds have employed their leisure,
They never yet could find my treasure.

Jonathon Swift—On A Circle

The year 1948 found the recording ban keeping musicians out of the recording studios and the stripteasers squeezing them out of The Street. Indeed, it was again a matter of circumstances that Parker, at the zenith of his career, could not record commercially and was limited in his work opportunities in America's "jazz capital." On The Street, the only clubs hanging on to a jazz policy were the Deuces and the Onyx, and the Parker group worked both of them frequently during the first four months of 1948, sandwiching the engagements between their out-of-town bookings. The original quintet, however, with Jordan on piano, would not record again together in a studio. This is unfortunate; for, as can be seen from the last recording, much of value could have been recorded during the early half of 1948.

In mid-April, the group accompanied Sarah Vaughan on a month-long tour through the Midwest (Sarah, incidently, had solved the recording problem by doing some tunes with only a choir for backing; *Nature Boy*—available on Everest F5-250—is a prime example). Following the Vaughan tour, the quintet became part of a "Bop versus Boogie" tour throughout the same area during the remainder of May.

In spite of the recording ban, the record industry had not been idle. It had been working on a new phenomenon—the long playing record. On June 19th, Columbia presented the first demonstration record—a 12-inch LP, developed by Dr. Peter Goldmark, Director of CBS Research. The LP, however, would not take effect until a year later, but the breakthrough had been made and possibly helped hurry the settlement between the AFM and the recording industry.

129

Meanwhile, Parker had developed a severe peptic ulcer and was warned by his doctor to stop drinking or expect an early death. He drank when he could not obtain drugs, but he also drank with drugs. During his New York stays, he could often be found in one of the small bars on Sixth Avenue, around the corner from The Street, too drunk to complete his engagement for a particular night. He was also involved in disputes and incidents on the road, capped by the "wrong men's room" incident at the Argyle Lounge in Chicago. The extra weight he had acquired in Camarillo had stayed with him, and he looked much older than his twenty-seven years. His immense appetite, of course, only contributed to the weight and the ulcer, and unlike most addicts, he ate continuously.

Indeed, in his need to obtain "advance" money to support his habit, Bird hassled constantly with agent Billy Shaw, who was also having problems with Gillespie's highly-touted European tour. Because of Bird's often outlandish behavior, Shaw was having trouble booking him. Gillespie had met with a "con-man" promoter in Sweden, and a ban on U.S. bands was set up by the British Labor Ministry. The spring of the year, with Gillespie safely home and Bird working on Fifty-Second Street, was probably a great season for Shaw.

* * *

Recording—Spring 1948—Possibly Onyx Club, New York City
Charlie Parker All Stars—Parker (as), M. Davis (tp), D. Jordan (p) Max Roach (d), Tommy Potter (b).

52nd Street Theme	America (Fr) 30AM 6061
Shaw 'Nuff	America (Fr) 30AM 6061
Out Of Nowhere	America (Fr) 30AM 6061
Hot House	America (Fr) 30AM 6061
This Time The Dream's On Me	America (Fr) 30AM 6061
Night In Tunisa	America (Fr) 30AM 6061
My Old Flame	America (Fr) 30AM 6061
52nd Street Theme	America (Fr) 30AM 6061
Way You Look Tonight	America (Fr) 30AM 6061
Out Of Nowhere	America (Fr) 30AM 6061
Chasin' The Bird	America (Fr) 30AM 6061
This Time The Dream's On Me	America (Fr) 30AM 6061
Dizzy Atmosphere	America (Fr) 30AM 6061
How High The Moon	America (Fr) 30AM 6061
52nd Street Theme	America (Fr) 30AM 6061

Although the recorded sound is generally terrible (the trumpet and piano are recorded very poorly), these tunes offer some interesting examples of Parker's playing. Most of them, however, contain only Parker's chorus and the theme. They were probably recorded on two different evenings, with *The Way You Look Tonight* beginning the second night's offerings and the latter group of tunes being slightly better recorded.

The mood is much lighter here than on Bird's "studio" recordings and there is much humor in his playing. There are some "moaning" phrases in the opening *Theme* and the first *Nowhere*; a "shave and haircut" lick and some slap-tongued "chicken" phrases in *Hot House*; a phrase from the *Kerry Dancers* in the second

Nowhere; and a *Jingle Bells* quote in *Chasin' The Bird*. Both versions of *Nowhere* contain the short motif that he used on his "studio" recording of November 4, 1947, but the best solos are on *Tunisa, Dizzy Atmosphere,* and *The Way You Look Tonight*—with Bird really stretching out. Throughout all the tunes, there are honks, groans, squeaks (mostly intentional), humorous quotes, and some tongue-in-cheek "swing" phrases. There are also a few garbled words by Bird on the second *Theme,* during which he announces the set break.

Parker seems to be affected by either drugs or alcohol or both on the first set of tunes; there are strange, lagging entrances on *Tunisa* and *Hot House* (although the home-made recording cuts in and out at strange places), and at times, he seems to have problems keeping his ideas with the chord changes. Nevertheless, Bird achieves a surrealistic effect on *Tunisa* by developing theme phrases in his solo and stretching them out of their original position. He is having intonation problems, however, and at times seems to be doing a giant "put on." Throughout the entire set, the theme choruses (when one can hear them) seem to be very careless. On *My Old Flame* a rarity occurs; he uses the same motif that he used in his versions of *Embraceable You* (October 28, 1947—Take 1); he generally developed this phrase only on *Embraceable You* in different spots in the tune.

The second group of tunes, however, presents a bit better Parker, but he does have reed problems at times. On *The Way You Look Tonight* one can hear the theme chorus and it becomes obvious that the *Klaunstance* recording (based on the same chords) was done with only improvised sections because of Savoy's unwillingness to pay the royalties. On this "live" version, however, Parker wails out phrases from *Can't Help Lovin' That Man Of Mine* at different places in the tune, finding a parallel in both Kern compositions. The second *Nowhere* contains a decent Parker solo, but the contrapuntal theme of *Chasin' The Bird* is wasted because of the poorly recorded trumpet. Harold Arlen's *This Time The Dream's On Me* (from the 1942 movie—*Blues In The Night*) is an interesting vehicle for the quintet and has a swinging "stop-time" theme statement. This tune, furthermore, would have been worthy of a "studio" performance if the ban had not been in effect; on the second version, Potter plays a fine solo that is not "walked" at the bridge of the final theme chorus. Another interesting point of the second set is the Latin treatment of *The Moon.*

This recording gives an idea of the quintet's repertoire and gives us an insight into a typical "Parker night", but it should not be the first Parker that one buys; the effect could be very misleading. It is interesting only if one has heard the previous "studio" version of the tunes.

Recording—1948
Parker (as), unidentified (ts, gtr, p, b, d)

There's A Small Hotel	Savoy MG 12152
These Foolish Things	Savoy MG 12152
Fine And Dandy	Savoy MG 12152
Hot House	Savoy MG 12152

This is a much different Bird than that of the previous recording; the atmosphere is again free, but Parker is on top of everything. Unfortunately, Savoy spoiled most of the tracks by splicing in parts of solos at certain places to lengthen the tracks. This irresponsible act not only mars some tremendous Parker, but at best, tends to confuse the listener. Moreover, although the soloists can be clearly heard, the rhythm section is barely audible. Analytic listening becomes a chore.

On *Small Hotel*, the tenorist states the theme, and Parker, freely using the lower register of the alto, backs him. After four tenor choruses, however, a splice occurs and the tenor solo is repeated! Following a four-chorus guitar offering, Bird plays two fine choruses; the solo is his only recorded improvisation on this tune. The out-chorus has Bird and guitar stating *Crazy Rhythm* behind the tenor's theme statement and Parker improvising the bridge.

Bird offers a beautiful reading of *Foolish Things*, but again at the end of the bridge, the whole previous solo is repeated by means of a splice. The final quarter-chorus, with tenor and guitar behind, follows the splice and the tune ends with the *Country Gardens* coda.

Fine and Dandy causes more confusion, and to understand it, one must start with the final "out-chorus:" The horns and guitar state the Woody Herman band's *Keen and Peachy* riff for eight bars, followed by eight bars of drums. The riff returns and leads to some Parker blowing which is capped by a confused ending. The tenorist jumps in and sustains a note to signal the ending and is joined by the others, with the guitar stating a *You Go To My Head* figure. Indeed, this closing chorus appears to have been spliced in as the opening statement (the extemporized line and drum solo are exactly the same) for 24 bars (riff—drums— riff); then another splice occurs using 14 (!) bars of material from the original solo (which, at this point of the recording, has not yet been heard). This has the effect of either disorienting the listener or giving him the feeling that Parker is playing on the wrong chords (since in effect that is what is happening in relation to the tune). The section played should be the final eight bars of the song, but what happens is that the splice uses the second half of the tune ("When You're Gone...") beginning at the third bar (..."Sugar Candy"). Below is the final idea of this fabricated section.

Ex. 96 *Fine and Dandy* Last Figure of Splice

Following the splice there is great Bird (the actual solo in entirety) and some inventive guitar work. A figure that constantly draws roars and laughs from the crowd during Parker's solo is worth noting.

Ex. 97 *Fine and Dandy* Laughter Figure

Hot House appears to be presented as played and Parker is magnificent. The ideas are fluent and presented with his usual drive.

The Savoy liner notes state that the recording was done at Bird's apartment, but the atmosphere is obviously one of a club (a reissue Savoy 1132, states the recording took place in Chicago; this issue lists personnel).

* * *

The summer of 1948 was the beginning of the end for the Parker-Davis Quintet. Miles was upset with Bird's "impossible" behavior and was interested in rehearsing his own group (the group later referred to as "Birth of the Cool"). His main pursuit was furthering the ideas set forth by himself and Gil Evans, a former Claude Thornhill arranger. Baritonist Gerry Mulligan, altoist Lee Konitz, and pianist John Lewis were also members of Davis's clique, and the central idea was for a tight, arranged group with a light, "cool" sound and space for improvisation. French horn and tuba were being used to enhance the group and to "cool" the sound further.

By the end of the summer, Duke Jordan, who had become another victim of the narcotics plague, was gone from the quintet, and Potter also took a short leave of absence. Parker had been guesting with the Gillespie big band as single attraction and work for the other men was desperately needed. There were also small jealousies within the group. Jordan spoke of Miles: "He and Max sort of formed a little clique. They were both getting $135.00 a week, ten more than me and Tommy."[1]

In August, a Saturday night concert featuring Bird and the Gillespie band at Chicago's Pershing Ballroom drew over 3,000 people, and Bird left the crowd mesmerized. At the end of the month he did two final Savoy recording sessions for which Davis procured John Lewis to play piano and Parker brought in Curly Russell, an old Fifty-Second Street buddy, to handle the bass chores. Lewis had been on Gillespie's European tour, but remained in Paris with Kenny Clarke after the band's departure and returned to New York later in the year. Both Savoy sessions were "undercover" affairs as the recording ban would not end until November. Interestingly, the second tune of the second session (*Marmaduke*) is most likely a tribute to Duke Jordan.

* * *

Recording—August 29, 1948—New York City
Charlie Parker All Stars—Parker (as), Miles Davis (tp), John Lewis, (p), Curly Russell (b), Max Roach (dr).

Barbados—Take 1	Savoy 12000
Barbados—Take 2	Savoy 12009
Barbados—Take 3	Savoy 12009
Barbados—Take 4 (Orig.)	Savoy 12014
Ah-Leu-Cha—Take 1	Savoy 12000
Al-Leu-Cha—Take 2 (Orig.)	Savoy 12000
Constellation—Take 1	Savoy 12000
Constellation—Take 2	Savoy 12000
Constellation—Take 3	Savoy 12009

Constellation—Take 4 (Orig.)   Savoy 12009
Parker's Mood—Take 1   Savoy 12000
Parker's Mood—Take 2   Savoy 12009
Parker's Mood—Take 3 (Orig.)   Savoy 12009

Barbados is one of Parker's best blues lines; it begins with a Latin background and goes to straight four on the repeat. The out-chorus on each take is in straight four until the repeated ending figure, under which the Latin beat returns.

Ex. 98 *Barbados* Opening

Ex. 99 *Barbados* Ending Figure

On Take 1, Bird is having reed trouble (as he is throughout this date), and Miles sounds like he is warming up. But the ideas are good, and the take is worth hearing. Take 2, however, is cut off after the theme. Lewis solos after Davis on Take 3 (he did not on Take 1), and Parker continues to be fluent but squeaky; the beginning theme entrance after the intro is also unsure. The final take has tremendous Bird; two contrasting Davis choruses; and an inventive twelve bars by Lewis—in short, a wonderful performance.

The contrapuntal *Ah-Leu-Cha* is based on *I Got Rhythm* (this writer, however, has often played the line using the *Honeysuckle Rose* "A" section chords with good results, especially when using a more recent modal-type approach in the improvised sections. The group here, however, does improvise on the "Rhythm" chords). The first take ends after Bird's improvised bridge, but the second take is a clean performance. Davis and Lewis split a chorus after Bird, and Bird returns for the final chorus, beginning it with the *Kerry Dancers*. The final bridge has "twos" with bass and drums before the theme returns in the final eight.

Ex. 100 *Ah-Leu-Cha* Opening

Constellation is again *I Got Rhythm,* although this time with the *Honeysuckle Rose* bridge. The theme is just a four-bar syncopated scalar riff followed by four-bar improvisation—first Bird then Miles. Bird takes the bridge plus the last eight, and then the full chorus improvisations begin. The first take is good, with Bird flying and Miles beginning his chorus with *When The Red, Red Robin;* after Lewis solos, however, the group cannot enter on time with the theme. Take 2 goes a bit further; they make it through the final theme chorus up until Max's bridge statement, and then there is another faulty entrance to the last eight. Parker ends Take 3 in mid-first chorus with a squawk, but Take 4 is well done. Bird negotiates the changes at a ridiculously fast tempo and the other soloists are good. Interestingly, Miles ends his solo on this final take with *Red, Red Robin* (a continuing sarcasm at Bird?). The final theme chorus has the four-bar riff played twice in each eight-bar "A" section.

Ex. 101 *Constellation* Riff

Parker's Mood is a classic blues with only Bird and rhythm. To begin, Bird states a two-bar rubato figure and Lewis launches the intro. Parker then proceeds with beautiful improvised blues. Take 1 is slower than the others and has some fine Parker, but the rhythm section misses on the retarding ending. Take 2 is faster and contains more good Bird until he cuts off the take with another squawk. The final take, however, is the beauty. Parker refines elements played on the other takes and colors the whole performance with beautifully bare emotion. Lewis plays a well-conceived solo, and the ending problem is solved by using Bird's rubato phrase (from the beginning) again at the end; the phrase is followed by some feathery Lewis piano chords that lead to a final bass after-thought. This tune is an indispensable Parker item.

The entire date, in fact, is a good cross-section of Bird's music. It contains a modern blues, a traditional blues, a contrapuntal excursion on *I Got Rhythm,* and a mercurial flight through a "combination form" of *I Got Rhythm* and *Honeysuckle Rose.*

Recording—Late August-Early September 1948—New York City
Charlie Parker All Stars—Parker (as), M. Davis (tp), John Lewis (p), Curly Russell (b), Max Roach (dr).

Perhaps—Take 1	Savoy 12014
Perhaps—Take 2	Savoy 12009
Perhaps—Take 3	Savoy 12009
Perhaps—Take 4	Savoy 12000
Perhaps—Take 5	Savoy 12000
Perhaps—Take 6 (Original)	Savoy 12000
Marmaduke—Take 1	Savoy 12000
Marmaduke—Take 2	Savoy 12000

Marmaduke—Take 3	Savoy 12001
Marmaduke—Take 4	Savoy 12001
Marmaduke—Take 5	Savoy 12009
Marmaduke—Take 6 (Orig.)	Savoy 12009
Steeple Chase—Take 1	Savoy 12000
Merry-Go-Round—Take 1	Savoy 12000
Merry-Go-Round—Take 2 (Original)	Savoy 12014

Perhaps is an engaging blues line; *Marmaduke*, a *Honeysuckle Rose* derivative; and *Steeplechase* and *Merry-Go-Round* are both based on *I Got Rhythm*. *Merry-Go-Round*, however, employs the *Honeysuckle* bridge chords and has no thematic material except for a four-bar riff in the "out" chorus. The last three all have improvised bridges (melodically).

Parker is again hampered by reed squeaks, and *Perhaps* proves the point. Take 1 contains good ideas but also many squeaks, and Take 2 is cut off after the theme because of a squeak. Parker wails on Take 3, but the reed problem remains. Davis, however, develops Parker's ending idea at the start of his (Davis's) third take solo, and Lewis works a *Moose The Mooche* development into his. The fourth take is again cut during Bird's first improvised chorus with some purposely self-depreciating figures. The fifth take is a bit faster and has three good Parker choruses; the squeaks, unfortunately, are still there. Furthermore, Miles's 24-bar solo is very good, and Lewis also plays two choruses on this take and the next, whereas before he had been limited to one. Take 6, however, is the best for Bird, and Miles extends his solo to 36 measures as he also is wailing. The ending figure of the line seems to say "Perhaps" three times.

Ex. 102 *Perhaps* Theme Ending

Squeaks also force the cutting off of *Marmaduke's* first take at the bridge of Parker's first improvised chorus. The second take, however, has good choruses by Bird and Miles and a fine half-chorus statement by Lewis. The following bridge is supposed to be "twos" between drums and alto, but Parker enters too soon during the first drum solo and the rest of the bridge plus the entrance to the final theme eight is rather ragged. Take 3 is again cut by Bird in self-depreciation, and there is a quick try at the pickup notes to the theme between Takes 3 and 4 on the Savoy issue. Take 4 goes right through and there are some good moments, but the "twos" on the final bridge are still not clean. There is a ragged entrance to the last eight (following Bird's improvised bridge) of the opening theme on Take 5, and Bird stops this one at the beginning of his solo. On the original issue, however, everything goes fairly well; the final bridge is a bit better, and Bird, Miles and Lewis all sound fine. Miles again develops Bird's final figure.

Ex. 103 *Marmaduke* Opening

Steeplechase is based melodically on a short figure which culminates on the flatted fifth (or augmented eleventh) of the dominant chord.

Ex. 104 *Steeplechase* Figure

After some very good Bird, Miles springs a great solo, stressing his individuality, and Lewis takes a half-chorus in which he tries some rhythmic trickery that confuses the rhythm section. Because of the confusion, there is a mix-up by Roach and Parker going into the final bridge; there appears to be some lost beats.

Merry-Go-Round is lightning fast with stupendous Parker on both takes. Davis seems more at home at this tempo than ever before, and Lewis is melodic, quoting *Move* on Take 1. The final chorus contains a four-bar riff followed by alternate improvisation of Bird and Miles.

Ex. 105 *Merry-Go-Round* Riff

Bird takes the final bridge and the tune ends with the riff (short of the normal 32 bars). The primary difference on Take 2 is that a sixteen-measure drum solo follows Lewis and leads to the out-chorus.

* * *

The final two Savoy dates truly end Bird's "classic period." Within four months, the Parker-Davis Quintet would dissolve and would only be reunited for one other "studio" recording (the four-tune quintet session for Norman Granz in January 1951). Although there were great moments after the "classic period," most of them were either echoes of this period or else they occurred in a format not entirely compatible with Bird's art. Moreover, his health also began declining further after this period, and his physical condition, to some extent, affected his playing. In spite of this, Bird's merry-go-round continued to churn away; unfortunately, the brass rings would be few in number and almost impossible to grasp.

CHAPTER XI

THE ROYAL ROOST
Live Recordings
(September 1948-March 1949)

...O holy tavern!...holy because no carking care's are there, nor weariness, nor pain...

Aretino—quoted by Longfellow in *Hyperion*.

Since the striptease takeover of Fifty-Second Street, Monte Kay (a former Street proprietor) had promoted sessions at Ralph Watkin's Broadway chicken restaurant, the Royal Roost, located at Forty-Seventh Street. Tadd Dameron became the house band-leader, and Parker and his men were frequent "guests." The jazz policy, which began as a one-night-a-week experiment, blossomed into a regular six-night gig and triggered the move of jazz onto New York's main drag. The club, which featured a low (ninety cents) admission charge, a peanut gallery for non-drinkers or adolescents, and a bop primer at every table, became a sensation; and almost every name associated with the bop movement, including Gillespie's big band, appeared on its bandstand. Bird was there during his "home" stays during the summer of 1948.

In early September, Davis's experimental group, using Lewis and Roach in the rhythm section, was booked into the Royal Roost. Parker, however, also worked the club, using both Davis and Roach in his group and any "bop" pianist that was available. Tadd Dameron, the Roost's resident band leader, is known to have doubled with Bird's group, and John Lewis and Al Haig would be other likely pianists. Although Davis and his cohorts were striving for something a bit different than Parker's concepts, their *basic* music came from the ideas pioneered by Bird. Gerry Mulligan recently stated: "With all the great bands that were around then, big and little, it was an exciting time musically....Everybody influenced everybody and Bird was No. 1 influence on us all".[1]

* * *

Recording—September 11, 1948—Royal Roost
Parker (as), M. Davis (tp), Tadd Dameron (p), Curly Russell (b), Max Roach (d).

52nd Street Theme	Savoy 12186
Ko Ko	Savoy 12179, Charlie Parker 701-A

The recording cuts in on Bird's first improvised chorus on *52nd Street Theme,* and he goes through two more with abandon; he ends with a *"Cool Blues"* phrase. Miles is simply over-flowing with ideas as he goes through his three-chorus stint, and Dameron, although hard to hear on the recording, uses some of his famous block-chordal "arranger's piano" and employ many chord alterations. The final theme is stated with a wonderful freedom that is hard to describe. Parker and Davis toss the theme motifs around between each other; they jab the motifs in at random and make the whole closing theme a wonderful collaboration. Bird has the final bridge to himself.

The fast beginning section of *Ko Ko,* which Davis could not cut at the 1945 studio session (November 26), is handled with ease. Bird and Miles exchange phrases going into Parker's first chorus with great effect, and the solo (two choruses) is very good except for a mechanical breakdown at the first bridge. Drums follow Parker for 32 bars; then the "theme" (if it can be called that) returns. Miles quotes *Honey* in the final exchange.

These two tunes are excellent examples of the Parker group's in-person performance during this period. The horns work very well together and the freedom of the performance plus the wealth of melodic ideas make this an attractive "recording" despite the poorly recorded rhythm section.

* * *

At the end of September, Parker did another guest shot with Gillespie in Chicago and then returned to New York before joining a Granz JATP unit. Al Haig, who was becoming Parker's regular pianist, and Tommy Potter also joined the unit for the fall tour.

In late November, when the package was to open at the Shrine Auditorium in Los Angeles, Parker suddenly urged Doris Sydnor, who had accompanied him to the West Coast, to make their relationship an official marriage. The couple eloped to Tia Juana, Mexico, much to the chagrin of Granz, who offered a reward for finding Parker. Subsequently, Bird was located by tenorist Teddy Edwards, and he soon returned—happily married—to the tour. His marriage, however, was really not official after all, since his wife, Gerry, of the Hines period, was never officially divorced. Nevertheless, this fact would not come to light until after Bird's death, and for the moment, therefore, the couple was man and wife.

After returning to The Apple with the package, Parker took his group, with Haig on piano, into the Royal Roost for the month of December; Charlie Ventura's group was working opposite the quintet. Fortunately, there were weekend broadcasts from the club, and many tapes exist that give an accurate picture of the group.

During the subsequent "Roost period," two developments on the 1948 national entertainment scene had some influence on Parker's work. They were the popularity of Frank Loesser's *Slow Boat To China* and the release of the Bob Hope-Jane Russell comedy movie, *The Pale Face.* Bird began playing *Slow Boat* at an uptempo as part of his repertoire, and the opening phrase of *Button and Bows,* a hit tune from the Hope movie, began creeping into his solos. Movies were one of Parker's favorite afternoon activities, and he was quite fond of westerns and gangster flicks.

It is quite possible, therefore, that he saw Hope's western-satire and thoroughly enjoyed it.

* * *

Recording—December 11, 1948—Royal Roost
Parker (as), M. Davis (tpt), Al Haig (p), Tommy Potter (b), Max Roach (d).

Groovin' High	Savoy 12186, Charlie Parker 701-A
Big Foot (Drifting' On A Reed)	Savoy 12186, Charlie Parker 701-B
Ornithology	Savoy 12179, Charlie Parker 701-B
Slow Boat To China	ESP—Bird 1

Miles is muted on the line to *Groovin' High* and there is no modulation to the lower key for Bird's solo as there is on the original Parker-Gillespie version (1945). Bird, however, is exceptionally fluent with long lines of thought extending through normal section endings.

Ex. 106 *Groovin' High* Parker's Solo Bars 15-19

The above example has the phrase starting at the end of the first sixteen-bar section and extending three bars into the second half of the tune with one continuous thought.

Miles is very good; he quotes *Honey* and *There's A Small Hotel* (perhaps an invitation?) and at two points in his solo uses a phrase which is a good Davis "identifier."

Ex. 107 *Davis Identifier*

Miles uses this phrase in other tunes on this session; it was part of his "vocabulary" during this general period.

The closing theme on *Groovin'* is treated with some liberties in the nature of good humor, and the ending is a short poly-tonal sounding phrase built on the higher chord intervals of the tonic.

Ex. 108 *Groovin' High*—Ending

Big Foot is the same theme that was recorded in December 1947 and titled *Driftin' On A Reed*. The opening line is notated in the Analysis Section of this work. There is some wonderful blues playing on this track, and even Haig's solo comes through clearly on the home-made recording. Miles develops the *Jumpin' With Symphony Sid* figure, and in the wild exchanges of fours between the horns, Parker states "I Wanna Go Where You Go...", a phrase from a pop tune of the day titled *Then I'll Be Happy*. The fours precede the final theme.

The theme to *Ornithology* is altered from the original 1946 version by having the triplet figure eliminated (see Ex. 43) at the end of each sixteen bars and replaced with more modern (and more musical) phrases.

Ex. 109 *Ornithology* New Figure Bars 13-16

Ex. 110 *Ornithology* New Figure Bars 29-32

Parker plays three fantastic choruses, and at the beginning of the third one, he develops *I'll Remember April* in his line. Furthermore, Miles and Haig both turn in sterling performances. This tune, however, is wrongly titled *Thrivin' From A Riff* on the Savoy issue listed above.

Davis plays a running obligato behind Parker's theme statement on *Slow Boat To China* and shows his new-found extended range in his solo. Parker goes through the rapidly moving chord changes as if they were melted butter, and Haig plays well but is badly recorded. There is a short "tag" on the final theme. This is a good set for getting the "feel" of the 1948 group.

Recording—December 12, 1948—Royal Roost, New York City
Charlie Parker's All Stars—C. Parker (as), M. Davis (tpt), Al Haig (p), Tommy Potter (b), Max Roach (dr).

Hot House	Savoy 12186, Charlie Parker 701-C
Salt Peanuts	Charlie Parker 701-B

There's great Parker and Miles on these tunes. Miles states the *Salt Peanuts* theme superbly, and his range in his solo is excellent; he develops the *Country Gardens* phrase. Bird sings the *Salt Peanuts* phrase and uses an intentional squeak effect in the beginning of his solo; this effect comes about through a "beep beep" exchange (inspired by Broadway traffic?) that develops between the two horns during the first eight bars of Bird's solo. The rest of the solo features wild development of some of the interlude themes.

Hot House has Bird building a fine chorus and Miles picking up Parker's two closing eighth-notes and developing them exquisitely. It is obvious that young Miles was prepared to embark on his own.

The playing of Al Haig adds some excellent dessert to the tasty playing of both horns. He uses the phrase given as the Miles identifier (Ex. 107) at one point in his fine *Hot House* solo and plays an exciting role as the first soloist (after the theme) on *Salt Peanuts*. Roach is also exciting on the final bridge to *Hot House* and his full chorus of *Salt Peanuts*.

Miles is muted on the theme to *Hot House*, but plays outstanding open horn on *Salt Peanuts*, both lines, moreover, are cleanly executed except for one spot in *Hot House*. On the Charlie Parker label, however, the trumpeter is listed erroneously as Kenny Dorham for this version of *Salt Peanuts*.

* * *

As the end of the year drew near, Davis and Parker squabbled more and more. Miles's maturation gave him added confidence and Parker's habits were not easy to cope with on a night after night basis. Davis, therefore, recommended Kenny Dorham to Bird as his replacement, and Parker took the suggestion. Dorham joined the group on Christmas Eve at the Roost, but many taped recordings of the group's standard repertoire made between December 1948 and February 1949 confuse the two trumpeters in the personnel listing. Two characteristic phrases (along with Ex. 107) might help to identify the correct trumpet player.

Ex. 111 *Davis* Characteristic Phrase

Ex. 112 *Dorham* Characteristic Phrase

The phrases are not meant to be exact pitch examples, but rather to show certain characteristics. Davis used the two repeated tones in eighth notes—back and forth—and then usually descended. Dorham at times over-used the descending triplet figure.

* * *

Recording—December 18, 1948—Royal Roost—New York City
Charlie Parker's All Stars—Parker (as), M. Davis (tp), Al Haig (p), Tommy Potter (b), Max Roach (d).

Out Of Nowhere	Charlie Parker 701-B
How High The Moon	Charlie Parker 701-B

This is the first Parker up-tempo version of *Nowhere* and he states the theme freely, with Davis blowing an obligato behind him. Miles solos first and turns in a good performance. Bird's first half-chorus, however, sounds like a condensation of his studio recording (November 1947), but soon he breaks the mood with a *Kerry Dancers* quote. Haig plays a beautiful half-chorus; then Bird takes it out, with Miles behind again. The horns state the *Country Gardens* ending.

The Moon is taken at a fast Latin tempo, much like the Spring 1948 "live" recording (only this time it is audible), until the final eight bars; the group then breaks into straight four and uses the new *Ornithology* ending (Ex. 110). Miles states the theme this time, with Bird backing, and both horns plus Haig play extremely effective solos, with Miles being rather introspective.

The characteristic Davis phrase can be found in both trumpet solos on this recording, Miles's last at the Roost with Parker, but the Charlie Parker label again lists Dorham as the trumpeter.

* * *

Parker began his recording relationship with Norman Granz at the end of 1948; it would last for the rest of his life, for better or worse. Indeed, the Granz contract opened new economic possibilities for Bird, but there are those who feel it hurt him artistically. Granz had grandiose plans for recording Parker in a variety of settings other than a small group, and Parker, being a "ham" at heart, was very receptive toward them. The first attempt at a different setting was Bird with Machito's large Latin band.

* * *

Recording—December 20, 1948—New York
Charlie Parker with Machito's Orchestra—Parker (as), 3 trumpets, 4 saxes (as, as, ts, bars), piano bass, Latin percussion.

Mango Mangue	Verve MG 8000

The full band opens the first introductory section, which ends with sustained notes in the saxes for a two bar extension; the saxes then state another introductory figure with the brass answering. Parker is alone with rhythm for the first eight-bars of the theme; the saxes have the next section; and the theme then returns to full band. Preceding Parker, there is an eight-bar section of trumpet and saxophone exchanges with the saxes again sustaining a four-bar extension. Bird then really goes to it; he flies through the F-minor tonality with ease for 40 bars while the band states melodic material beneath him (the last eight of this section is really a static-type "extension"). Next is another "exchange" section between trumpets and saxes, with Parker wailing the first sax figure an octave above. More Bird follows for sixteen bars; then the saxes lead to pyramiding trumpets. The full band enters with some of the beginning thematic material harmonized interestingly, and Bird soars above it. A "Mangue" chant follows for 32 bars with Bird again blowing on top. He keeps wailing as the full band enters with thematic material to take the tune out with a typical Latin ending.

Indeed, this is not Parker's best recording, nor perhaps the ideal setting, but it is interesting to hear him in this context.

* * *

Parker's new trumpet player was a veteran of both the Eckstine and Gillespie big bands and was a member of Art Blakey's Jazz Messengers (the first edition) in 1947. His first name went from McKinley to Kinny to Kenny during his formative years in the field, and the last nickname stayed for the balance of his career. Dorham had a quick-thinking style, like Davis, but was not as "cool" in conception. He, again like Davis, was really only developing during his stay with Parker. Bird seems to have had the magic touch for helping young musicians come into their own.

* * *

Recording—December 25, 1948—Royal Roost
Charlie Parker Quintet—Parker (as), Kenny Dorham (tp), Al Haig (p), Tommy Potter (b), Max Roach (d).

Half Nelson	ESP Bird 1, Okie Doke (Amalgamated Labels)
White Christmas	ESP Bird 1, Charlie Parker 701-A
Little Willie Leaps	ESP Bird 1, Okie Doke (Amalgamated Labels)

Dorham cuts most of the lines cleanly, although the blend between the horns is not good. He also has intonation problems, and his solos are ridden with the triplet figure given earlier as an identifying factor.

White Christmas is, of course, humorous, and trumpet and alto state the theme in harmony. Bird cunningly injects a *Jingle Bells* quote into his solo and also a suggestion of the *Irish Washerwoman*. Dorham's solo leaves much to be desired in the way of intonation, and he is repetitive in ideas.

On the other two tunes, however, Dorham does a bit better solo-wise, and Haig also gets to play. As usual Haig is inventive. Bird quotes *Why Was I Born* and *Happy Birthday* in his solo on *Little Willie* and he is dramatically cool on *Half Nelson*. It is noticeable that almost all the lines in Parker's repertoire that were previously recorded are done much faster on the "live" performances than on the original record. It could be that in this case familiarity bred speed.

There is good Bird on this date, but the horns are not quite as tight, naturally, as when the Bird and Miles group was at its height.

* * *

During late December Parker also continued his "guesting" single policy; he appeared with Dizzy at the McKinley Ballroom in the Bronx and traveled to Philadelphia to do a short stint at the Blue Note with a local rhythm section that included Ray Bryant on piano. Gillespie spoke of his guest appearances:

He used to come and play with my big band. He'd never heard the arrangements before, but you'd think he'd written them. The brass would play something and bang! Charlie Parker was there, coming in right where he was supposed to.[2]

Perhaps in his mind—in his dreams—he had written those arrangements.

The Royal Roost held over both the Parker Quintet and the Ventura group for January 1949. Ventura's band, with its large "front-line" of trumpet, trombone, tenor sax, and baritone sax, and featuring the bop vocals of pianist Roy Kral and his wife, Jackie Cain, was being billed as "Bop for the People."

Within a short time, the "Cool" would be born with the Capitol recordings of Miles's group, and a new, soft, semi-commercial sound pioneered by George Shearing would sweep the jazz community. The "Shearing Sound," with the pianist-leader playing melodic block-chords doubled on top by vibes and on the bottom by guitar, was only commercial in the sense that the melody presentation was very evident. On the improvised sections, Shearing could, and did, play impeccable, first-rate jazz. In another direction, Lennie Tristano and his pupils Lee Konitz and Warne Marsh would soon make the first records featuring "free" improvisation (yes—in 1949!). Representative recorded performances might be Davis's *Boplicity;* Shearing's *September In The Rain;* and Tristano's *Intuition.*

Meanwhile, Parker continued to have sideman problems; Miles was gone, Max Roach wanted to leave, and at the beginning of the year, he did, only to return three weeks later. Roach was working with Davis's group which had become mainly a "rehearsal band," and he was the drummer on Davis's January recordings. To fill the gap, Bird brought in Joe Harris, a drummer who had worked with Gillespie's big band.

* * *

Recording—January 1, 1949—Royal Roost
Parker (as), K. Dorham (tp), Al Haig (p), Tommy Potter (b), Joe Harris (d).
    Slow Boat To China   Charlie Parker 701-C
    On this version, Bird states the theme alone; there is no trumpet obligato. Parker sounds very good on his two-chorus solo; he runs strings of ideas effortlessly and quotes *Why Was I Born* at the beginning of the second chorus. Dorham, however, is again plagued by the triplet figure, although he stays with the changes quite well. The piano chorus is another Haig masterpiece, and at one point, he develops an idea of continuous triplets much like the troublesome *Ornithology* phrase (Ex. 43). Bird is again alone with rhythm on the out-chorus until the short coda.

* * *

Metronome magazine was founded as a general music magazine in 1884, but in 1935, George Simon made it the major jazz voice; it remained powerful until its demise in the late fifties. Each year, beginning in 1938, the magazine ran a popularity poll for its readers and the results were published in January of the following year. The winners were often recorded in an all-star session by one of the major labels, but membership in the recording group depended, obviously, on availability and willingness to participate. In 1949, for instance, Ernie Caceres was the baritone saxist in the recording group, but was not even among the top three in the poll, and Bill Harris, who won the trombone poll, was not in the recording group. Parker, however, was the winning 1949 altoist, having bested Johnny Hodges and Willie Smith, and was slated for the recording group which included many old friends.

* * *

Recording—January 3, 1949
Metronome All-Stars—D. Gillespie, M. Davis, Fats Navarro (tpt), J.J. Johnson, Kai Winding (trb), Buddy DeFranco (cl), Parker (as), C. Ventura (ts), E. Caceres (bar), L. Tristano (p), Billy Bauer (g), Ed Safranski (b), Shelly Manne (d).

Overtime—Take 1	RCA LPV 519
Overtime—Take 2	Unavailable on LP
Victory Ball—Take 1	RCA LPV 519
Victory Ball—Take 2	Unavailable on LP

The second take of each tune was the original 78 rpm issue, while the earlier, longer takes contained more blowing space per man and gave room for more soloists. The original 78 takes may be available on some obscure LP, but they would be difficult to obtain.

Overtime starts with two bars apiece by Bird, Diz, Ventura, and probably Johnson. DeFranco breaks for four measures over a sustained chord, and Safranski "walks" two bars leading to the theme, which is basically saxes in octave unison with brass accents in the background; at the bridge, the melody is tossed back and forth between saxes and brass (two bars apiece). Parker blows first and whistles through the familiar chords (*Love Me Or Leave Me*) with ease. Winding and Johnson split a chorus, and DeFranco takes a break into the next chorus followed by Tristano at the bridge; next is eight-bars of simultaneous Bauer-Tristano improvisation. The full band wails for four bars; then Safranski does the same; the pattern is repeated with Manne before Bauer and Tristano again engage in simultaneous wailing to complete the fourth chorus. The full band again opens the next chorus with four, and Ventura answers; he continues throughout the chorus with the band shouting accents. The high point of the tune, however, is the series of four-bar exchanges (two choruses) between Navarro and Gillespie before the final theme chorus; indeed, pyrotechnics in the sky abound, and the duel is surely a tie. To conclude, Bird and Bauer play a humorous polytonal ending.

Tristano's *Victory Ball* has the chord base of *S'Wonderful*, and the beautifully conceived line is played in running harmony by Parker and Bauer. Bird sounds very much at home with the line—as if he had been playing with Tristano and his disciples for some time. Even his sound seems to fit perfectly. In fact, it is worth hearing the side just for the theme execution. Parker solos on the bridge of the opening theme chorus and the full chorus directly after. The chorus is excellent; it contains cohesive ideas and extremely clean execution. The rest of the choruses are split, with the exception of Tristano's; the order is: Davis-DeFranco; Johnson-Ventura; Winding-Navarro; Tristano; Caceres-Gillespie (the trumpet and trombone judgements were done entirely by ear and this writer will welcome any constructive criticism or disagreements). Take 2 is three choruses shorter; only a half chorus is allowed to Bird and Tristano, and cut from the bill are Gillespie, Caceres, Navarro and Winding. The apparent order is: Bird-DeFranco; Johnson-Ventura; Tristano-Miles. DeFranco takes the bridge of the final theme. Johnson's solo is notable for his coupling of *Country Gardens* and *Driftin' On A Reed* in his quotes.

These are very rewarding tracks to hear, and they give a good picture of some of the brightest stars of the era: Winding, Safranski, and Manne were all alumni of the Kenton band, where they gained their reputation. In addition, Winding was with both Ventura and Tadd Dameron and also had his own small group. Manne did time with Ventura and, at the time of the recording, had been touring with JATP. Along with the above mentioned men, DeFranco was a frequent sitter-in at The Roost and had been working with George Shearing during the last of 1948; he had finished second in the poll to Benny Goodman. Navarro's records with Howard McGhee and Tadd Dameron had deservedly brought him to the public's eye, and Ernie Caceres, the lone "traditional" maverick, was well-known to long-time jazz followers (Serge Chaloff, the Herman Herd's anchor, was the actual winner of the baritone poll). Interestingly, Miles Davis and Navarro were, at this point, both working with Oscar Pettiford at the new Clique (the Broadway club which would become Birdland later in the year). Pete Rugolo, of Kenton fame, arranged *Overtime* and directed this group of all-stars.

Recording—January 8, 1949—Royal Roost, New York City
Parker (as), K. Dorham (tp), Al Haig (p), Tommy Potter (b), Joe Harris (d)
    Cheryl   Charlie Parker 701-B
The horns are not together on the line, the tempo being a bit fast for Dorham at this stage. Some masterful Parker blues playing comes through in his five choruses, however: In the second chorus, he develops syncopated figures related to the end of the theme; the third chorus has a notable *High Society* quote; and a "scream" is used to good effect in chorus four. Dorham is a bit more confident in his solo than he was on the last date, but he still has intonation problems and the "triplet plague" invades at times. Following Dorham's solo, Bird and he exchange fours for two choruses, with Bird quoting *The Man On The Flying Trapeze* at the end of the first chorus. On the final theme, Bird breaks away from the unison at the final two-bar syncopated figure and plays a simple descending scale figure (do-ti-la) in contrary motion to the rising melody (do-re-fa) that gives an added dimension to the ending.

Recording—January 1949
Charlie Parker with Machito's Orchestra—3 trumpets, 4 saxes (as, as, ts, bs), piano bass, Latin percussion, Parker (as).

Okie Doke   Verve 8000

This rumba's "A" section is harmonically constructed like *Perdido* and *Satin Doll* (ii⁷-V⁷-iii⁷-VI⁷), and the bridge goes to several distant keys (using ii⁷-V⁷-I) before returning.

The introduction begins with saxes performing rhythmic octave leaps on G; the trumpets enter with a series of descending dissonant diminished chords (with major seventh) until the cadence into Eb.

The theme chorus has staccato trumpets with sax counter-melody at A¹; saxes in broken chord patterns backed by punching brass at A²; Parker improvising the bridge over held sax chords; and a return to staccato trumpets for the final eight.

Octave leaps on Eb between brass and saxes lead to two pyramided, modern (13th) chords which act as a modulation to the key of G.

From this point on, there is all Parker, three wailing choruses-full. Bird is thoroughly familiar with the chord changes and blows very creatively the band seems to stimulate him. The trumpet and sax figures which back him at various places do not seem obnoxious (a purist might disagree), and Bird stays fluent until the final, short, swirling cadenza over another ultra-modern (13th) chord.

This tune seems a bit more successful than the earlier *Mango Mangue*, perhaps because of Machito's experience working most of December 1948 at the Clique with Dexter Gordon as the soloist.

Recording—Circa 1949—New York City
Charlie Parker with Machito and his Orchestra—Parker (as), Flip Phillips (ts), Buddy Rich (d).
Note: This recording is often dated December 1950 but discographical research has indicated that it was done during the period of the last two Machito "recordings". Moreover, Flip Phillips was at the Roost during January 1949—this could further support this earlier dating.

Mambo—Part 1   VSP 19
6/8   VSP 19
Jazz   VSP 19

These selections are part of arranger Chico O'Farrell's *Afro-Jazz Suite*, and Machito's usual personnel of the period is augmented by two trumpets and one alto sax. The added men are all solid "studio-type" musicians—Harry Edison and Al Stewart (trumpet), Sol Marowitz (alto sax)—and their addition may have been for the reason of sight-reading the difficult arrangements.

The main portion of *Mambo, Part 1* is what many working musicians term a "C⁷-mambo"—a section based on a single chord, sometimes using repeated rhythmic figures. The full band begins the introduction with sixteen bars followed by a section of rhythmic "stop-time" chords. Saxes begin a repetitive figure over percussion, and the brass enters, building and building over the single chord. There is a "lead-in" section over two chords (four bars apiece), and then Bird is turned loose with a break. He plays two screaming sections (eight bars apiece) on the single C⁷ chord, and at the bridge section, the band states four followed by Parker's answering four; Bird continues through a final, single-chord, eight-bar section. The band moves to F-minor and is again answered by Bird; then the band moves to the dominant (Eb7) of the relative major (Ab) and Parker answers on the tonic. Parker's improvisations continue through a modulatory section back to the minor and the band answers. The ending sections include a climactic, punching brass portion; a fine "Latin-type" piano chorus by Rene Hernandez on a "C7" section; and an out-chorus with the band on top and the percussion wailing. Flip Phillips is heard on a short cadenza at the very end. *Mambo, Part II* features Phillips at a slow Latin tempo; he uses the cadenza phrase at the beginning of his feature.

A fast and slow section are contained in *6/8*, and Phillips and Bird blow only a few bars in the slow section.

The *Jazz* portion of the suite is the most rewarding it contains a fantastic chorus and fiery exchanges between Bird and Phillips. The construction is a sort of *I Got Rhythm* in D-minor, with a bridge of secondary dominants. Phillips begins the tune with two choruses of improvisation, and Bird follows with a beauty; then the fun begins. Phillips is the challenger on the exchanges of fours and Parker the defender—and what defense! The beginning exchanges are serious with Parker turning around Phillips's ideas. On the final eight bars of the chorus, Phillips goes into one of his typical, JATP, one-note "honking" phrases, and Bird mocks him with sarcastic honks and then a flurry of ideas—as if to say "If you've gotta do that to swing, okay, but here's a better way to use your brain." The wailing full band leads to Rich's solo which is technically creative, but not exactly inspired. The saxes state a full-blown figure and the brass comes in swirling above; the tune ends with a few staccato sax blasts.

This is again not classic Parker, but the exchanges are a break-up, and his playing is excellent throughout.

Machito, whose real name is Frank Grillo, continued the policy of occasionally recording with jazz soloists until the late fifties.

Recording—January 15, 1949—Royal Roost, New York City
Parker (as), Dorham (tp), A. Haig (p), T. Potter (b), Joe Harris (d)

Scrapple From The Apple	Charlie Parker 701-C
BeBop	Charlie Parker 701-C
Hot House	Charlie Parker 701-C

The group sounds good here; Dorham cuts the themes technically, but the horns do not seem quite together. This session has some of the best Parker solos on record however, and should not be missed. *Hot House* is the masterpiece; the Parker solo not only abounds in unbelievable (and unplayable) ideas, but, in the second eight bars of his second chorus, he runs an idea up through harmonics (false fingerings) that culminates on a high C (A on the alto). This note is a third above the normal range of the instrument (concert Ab) and has been done by other players, but the fluency with which Parker plays it at the fast tempo and as an extemporaneous idea is unbelievable; his intonation on the false note is also excellent. Parker's first chorus bridge, furthermore, incorporates *Pop Goes The Weasel*. Dorham uses Bird's idea from the original recording (Ex. 18) to start his chorus and shows his first jaunt of real inventiveness with the Parker Quintet. Haig is sophisticated and Harris plays with much verve in his four-bar exchanges with

Bird in the next to last chorus. At the final bridge Potter takes a pleasant (not "walked") solo.

Parker is creative on the other tunes also; his ideas are beyond description. In addition, Dorham shows much improvement and is more melodic than ever before. Contrary to popular opinion, Harris sounds good with the group. He plays a full chorus on *BeBop* and the final bridge on *Scrapple*, which tune also contains the intro and coda by Haig (originally done in 1947 by Jordan). Haig's best solo is also on *Scrapple* in which he constantly develops the theme motif.

Recording—January 22, 1949—Royal Roost, New York City
Max Roach replaces Joe Harris (d), Others are the same as January 15.

Oop Bop Sh'Bam   Charlie Parker 701-C

The tune is a typical Gillespie nonsense ditty based on the *I Got Rhythm* "A" section and the *Honeysuckle Rose* bridge. The "A" section is two bars of singing—"Oop Bop Sh'Bam, a Klook-a-mop"—followed by an instrumental answer. Bird begins his solo with the complete statement of the *Buttons and Bows* line, extending it into the second eight, and on his second chorus he develops the "Oop Bop Sh'Bam" phrase. Dorham is melodic again (one can hear *Bonaparte's Retreat*, an insipid popular ditty, and *Goody Goody*), and Haig is intellectually cool. Bird and Dorham trade fours on the next to last chorus, and at the bridge, Parker comically quotes *Charmaine*. The performance is basically well done. *Oop Bop Sh'Bam* was probably brought to the quintet by Dorham who had recorded it in 1946 with Kenny Clarke.

* * *

During February, Billy Shaw broke from the Moe Gale Agency and formed his own agency. He took many of the artists, including Parker, with him. Shaw had great plans for promoting Parker as a jazz attraction. He felt the Granz contract could be helpful in bringing Bird before the public, and he was anxious to try such new things as the use of a vocalist with the combo. Indeed, bop vocals had become quite the rage with the popularity of Ventura's group and the recordings of Dave Lambert and Buddy Stewart. Moreover, Al Haig had recorded with Lambert and Stewart at the end of 1948 and had also done a date under his own name featuring Jimmy Raney (the guitarist) and Terry Swope on wordless vocalese. Lambert and Stewart were also featured at various times with the Parker group at The Roost during late February and early March.

* * *

Recording—February 5, 1949—Royal Roost, New York City
Parker (as), Dorham (tp), Haig (p), Potter (b), Roach (d).

Barbados   Charlie Parker 701-C
Salt Peanuts   Charlie Parker 701-B

The themes sound clean and together on this date; Dorham plays very well on the opening statements.

The Bird solo on *Salt Peanuts* is great; it's a long-lined creation that is almost non-stop connected ideas from beginning to end. Dorham and Roach are also very good, and the trumpeter develops *High Society* during his spot. This version is often confused with the December version with Miles, but the laymen can simply listen for a muted trumpet on the theme if it is present, it is this version.

Barbados (erroneously dated January on the *Charlie Parker* LP) has more clean-cut ideas by Bird; he gets into one of the riffs from*Blue and Boogie* on his third chorus (of five). Dorham and Haig also play some exquisite modern blues, and there are two choruses of excellent exchanges between trumpet and alto.

On this date the Parker-Dorham group seems to have jelled completely for the first time; it presents a sound of its own, different from the Bird-Miles alliance. The difference stems mainly from a certain "grittiness" added by Dorham (although he had many "Milesian" qualities), and from his use of a slightly higher volume level than Davis.

Recording—February 12, 1949—Royal Roost, New York City
Personal same as last date.

    Barbados   Savoy 12179

This is a slower version than the preceding one, with Max using tom-tom effects behind the improvisations. On both these later versions Roach uses Latin rhythm on the theme chorus and the repeat; whereas the studio version had the first chorus Latin and the repeat in straight four.

Parker has a bit of reed trouble on this tune, but the solo has very wild moments; each chorus is presented in a different manner. Choruses 1 and 3 are straight-forward Bird, but the second one has night-marish phrases—originally intended for humor but turning to surrealism. Quotes abound near the end of the solo as *Buttons and Bows* takes up most of the fourth chorus, and *Why Was I Born* opens the fifth.

Dorham sounds good solo-wise but he seems to lag behind Parker on the theme statements; this gives a"ragged-edge" presentation to the opening and ending. There are no four-bar exchanges on this version.

Recording—February 19, 1949—Royal Roost, New York City
Personnel same as last date.

    Groovin' High   Charlie Parker 701-C

Dorham is muted on the theme, and there is no modulation for Bird's solo, which is beautifully conceived. The solo does, however, contain some repetition involving a leap upward from the scale fifth to the third (Bb to G); this seems to cement the ideas together. At the end of the first chorus, Bird plays a "bluesy" phrase reminiscent of *My Kind Of Love*; it connects in his mind and he plays the next phrase of that tune! Dorham also moves well but still has intonation problems at times, and Haig centers much of his solo around developing an *Ornithology*-type phrase. Following the solos, the exchanges between the two horns are exciting and humorous, with Dorham finishing up with a reference to *Symphony Sid*. The break into Parker's solo, interestingly, is very similar to the one used on December 11, 1948, and the closing theme is treated freely by Bird as it was on that same date.

When comparing this Parker solo with earlier versions (1945-47-48), one finds similar phrases but they are put together in different ways. It is as if *Groovin' High* represented certain things in Parker's mind for development, but he would use these differently each time he played the tune—variations upon the variations, one might say. Lennie Tristano, speaking of bop in general, illustrated this point:

This may be compared to a jigsaw puzzle which can be put together in hundreds of ways, each time showing a definite picture which, in its general character, differs from all the other possible pictures.[3]

* * *

In early February, Parker participated in the Granz JATP presentation at Carnegie Hall, and later in the month, two of his old comrades from the Gillespie days (1945), Milt Jackson and Lucky Thompson, joined the combo at The Roost. Along with Stewart and Lambert on vocals, the men remained with Parker for a two-week stint.

This personnel change brings to mind the marvelously free atmosphere and the abundance of good musicians that abounded during the "Roost Period" of late 1948-early 1949. Jackson was around the scene (with Howard McGhee and Navarro), often doubling on piano; the Dameron group, with Allen Eager and Dexter Gordon on tenors, Kenny Clarke on drums, and Curly Russell on bass, was performing "house band" chores; and hordes of "sitters-in" such as DeFranco, Thompson, Budd Johnson, Chuck Wayne, Cecil Payne, and J.J. Johnson were always waiting in the wings. The weekend remotes done by "Symphony" Sid Torin were bringing the new music to thousands of casual listeners, and a variety of modern jazz groups could be found on the bill during a single week.

It had been less than four years since the Parker-Gillespie recordings, but the music scene had come alive with ideas set forth by these two giants. Bird, still not 29 years of age, was showing the effects of his pioneering efforts; his habits were locking him in and his physical condition was worsening. He used the habits to lessen his physical pain, but the habits worsened the causes of the pain, and so the circle continued.

The changing circle of New York jazz clubs also continued. The Roost would exist for only two months past Bird's winter stay. It then moved to another Broadway location, the Brill Building at Forty-Ninth Street, and was re-christened Bop City.

* * *

Recording—February 26, 1949—Royal Roost, New York City
Parker All Stars—Parker (as), Dorham (tpt), Haig (p), L. Thompson (ts), Milt Jackson (vbs), T. Potter (b), Max Roach (d), Buddy Stewart and Dave Lambert (bop vocals).

Half Nelson	Blue Parrot AR703, Savoy 12179
Night In Tunisa	Blue Parrot AR703, Savoy 12186
Scrapple From The Apple	Blue Parrot AR703, Savoy 12179
Deedle (Vocal)	Blue Parrot AR703
What's This (Vocal)	Blue Parrot AR703

This recording is not very satisfying; Bird is not up to form, and the group does not jell. The proceedings seem very confused; Bird is having reed trouble, and most of the themes and solos contain squeaks and other discordant sounds. None of the soloists are particularly outstanding on *Half Nelson*, although Jackson is a bit more intellectual than the others. The closing theme begins well, but at one point it is lost, and only Dorham continues playing.

There is confusion regarding the entrance of the horns on *Tunisa*; Bird blows some weird figures over the piano, and finally the horn introduction starts. Dorham has intonation problems on the theme, and the group in general fails to blend. Parker's break after the interlude is lackadaisical and bland, and his chorus, while perking a bit, does not do him justice. Bags, however, turns in a nice solo. Potter plays a melodic eight bars leading to a different interlude that launches Dorham's solo with a four-bar break. Dorham is good—probably the best soloist on the tune; he plays a fine 1½ choruses followed by Haig at the bridge. The final eight bars is the full group taking the theme out.

Thompson does not play the theme chorus on *Scrapple From The Apple*, and Bird improvises the opening bridge; Roach has the closing one. Parker's solo on this tune is the best of the lot, but he still sounds as if he is "strung out." Thompson is virile, but rather arpeggiated, and Bags and Dorham turn in adequate choruses. The final line is unclear, and Bird butts in on Haig's coda with a bleat that does not enhance the performance. The rest of the group falls in on the ending.

Lambert and Stewart had been performing wordless vocals since the mid-1940s when they both were with Gene Krupa; in fact, *What's This*, a piece with chromatic harmonic movement in the main section and the *Honeysuckle Rose* bridge chords, is a remnant of the Krupa days. The vocals themselves go well, but the horns— which seem to be transposing from a "lead sheet"—sound flustered on *Deedle*. Bird's lone solo excursion on the vocal tracks, a half-chorus statement on *Deedle*, is spent in search of the correct chords, rather than in search of creative ideas. The piece, although based on the cycle of fifths, is difficult to hear because of the presence of the flatted fifth on each minor-seventh chord. In the key of G: / C#m7-5 / F#7 / Bm7-5 / E7 / Am7-5 / D7 / G / G //.

Not even the Parker solos can save this date from disaster. It is just not good Parker. The new format was probably being tried for the first or second time and the group sounds very uncomfortable. As evidenced by his playing, however, Parker was in no condition to lead, and this certainly added further tension. These tracks can only be recommended to die-hard Parker collectors.

Recording—March 5, 1949—Waldorf Astoria
Parker All Stars—Personnel (omit vocalists) as last date.

Barbados	Jazz Showcase 5003
Anthropology	Jazz Showcase 5003

Potter begins *Barbados* with a charming rhythmic bass solo. Only Parker and Dorham are heard on the line—here again Roach keeps the Latin beat through all theme statements. The solos are at a much higher level than the previous set, although there are only four on each tune (Jackson does not solo on *Barbados*, and Haig does not solo on *Anthropology*).

There is a great Bird chorus on *Anthropology*, which tune is performed by the full complement on the theme statement; the tempo is unbelievably fast. There is a small hitch getting back to the theme after Thompson's chorus, but otherwise the performance is well done. Roach takes the final bridge.

Dorham uses a lick suggesting Morton Gould's *Pavanne* at the beginning of his third chorus in *Barbados*. It is worth noting because he uses this idea in early performances with Parker, and it can be helpful for identification:

Ex. 113 *Dorham's Lick*

Dorham often used this phrase at the beginning of a chorus, and one can find it in some of the previous recordings.

This set was part of a *Herald Tribune* two-session concert for young people of various countries. Along with Bird's group, the afternoon concert also included Sidney Bechet's Dixielanders; and composer Virgil Thompson had presented some Metropolitan Opera performers during the morning session.

Recording—March 5, 1979—Royal Roost
Parker All Stars—Personnel as before

| Cheryl | Blue Parrot AR703 (English) |
| Anthropology | Blue Parrot AR703 (English) |

Symphony Sid's introduction to this set on his Saturday WMGM radio show is interesting. He makes reference to both the ninety-cent admission charge and the pending move to Bop City. The flavor of the patter transports one immediately back to 1949. In fact, the patter is one of the features that makes the complete *Blue Parrot* issue (containing Roost 1949 dates of February 26—March 5—March 12) an attractive buy.

The absence of Al Haig for most of this set (he returns during Thompson's *Anthropology* solo), however, hurts the group, especially on *Cheryl* where the lack of harmonic support causes confusion. After Parker, Dorham carries his final phrase (Bud Powell's lick that became "Brylcream; a little dab'll do ya") into the next chorus; but Jackson hears it as an end of a chorus; he therefore begins his solo at the wrong place in the form (he is at the beginning while the bass player's chord sequence is well into the form). When Jackson ends (well into the form), Parker completes the blues chorus by stating the "signature" motif of Ellington's *Main Stem* and leads Thompson into his chorus. Things then are righted for one chorus of fours between Bird and Dorham before the final theme chorus. One must wonder why Jackson did not play piano for at least part of the performance; he plays adequate "comping" piano and the tune was in the familiar blues form. But—whatever—there still is an interesting Parker solo. It is a study in contrast and subconscious organization. The first chorus has extremely long phrases, but the second reverts to conventional phrases—almost riff-like; on the third, however, there is a magnificent blending of both previous elements into a summation. Roach's drumming sounds unconventional at times, but he is actually striving to fill the rhythmic void left by Haig's absence by using bass drum and tom-tom punctuations. These "bombs," however, do not really detract as much from the piece as do the poor performances on the "head" (theme); the opening line has Bird dropping out and the close is extremely ragged (these theme choruses have only Bird and Dorham on the melody). On the whole, therefore, this tune has little besides the Parker chorus to its credit (although Dorham and Thompson turn in good solos).

Anthropology is much better. The line has the complete ensemble as in the previous recordings and all solos are excellent. Parker's offering is original in thought; he avoids the commonplace, and graceful phrases slither from his horn like charmed serpents; it must be regarded as one of his best solos on the *I Got Rhythm* form. Dorham is fluent, Bags intellectual, and Thompson virile. A humorous moment occurs during Thompson's solo as Haig slips back to the piano. As the tenorist hears the chords start behind him, he blows the *Main Stem* phrase that Parker used, to right the form, on *Cheryl!* Max's accents on the theme choruses enhance the line and create a wonderful rhythmic feel. Indeed, the whole tune stands up very well except for the missing piano punctuations, which leave a *rhythmic* void as well as a harmonic one.

The group ends the set with *Jumpin' With Symphony Sid.*

Recording—March 12, 1949—Royal Roost
Charlie Parker All Stars—Personnel as before

Cheryl	Savoy 12179
Slow Boat To China	Savoy 12186
Chasin' The Bird	Savoy 12179

This is the best Roost date of those containing an augmented personnel. The added men were becoming familiar with the material, and their solos are much looser.

On *Cheryl*, however, Thompson does not play on the theme at all, and Jackson plays only on the closing syncopated scale figure. Nevertheless, the soloists (all horns, plus Haig and Jackson) are very good with two choruses apiece, and all goes well until the end of the first closing theme chorus. Parker wants to end, but Dorham continues to the repeat; Bird then falls back in. On the final theme, Jackson does not play at all.

Bird is alone on the *Slow Boat* theme, and again there are fine solos. Thompson, however, does not play at all on this tune. The closing theme has Dorham playing some mild obligatos at times as Davis did on the first version of this tune.

Chasin' The Bird is the lengthiest and most satisfying of these tracks, although the theme has that peculiar un-togetherness to which Parker and Dorham were often prone (the added men are not on the theme statements). All soloists blow two full choruses, and Dorham ends up with the "little-dab'll-do-ya" phrase later made famous by Bud Powell and then exploited by Madison Avenue's "Bryl-cream" ad. Haig quotes *Let's Fall In Love* near the end of his solo, and Max is driving in his spotlight at the bridge of the closing theme. If one considers the added men, the final title is apropos for the end of Parker's Roost recordings.

＊ ＊ ＊

In 1949, as Parker repaired at The Roost, the recording industry stood at the brink of revolution; the long-playing record was ready for public consumption. Important questions rattled the industry. What form should the record take—large or small? What speed should the record be—45 rpm or 33-1/3 rpm? RCA developed the seven inch 45 rpm record with a large center hole, and Columbia tried a seven-incher at the 33-1/3 speed with the normal (small) center hole. Even when it became apparent that the best market value was for a smaller, large-holed record at the fast speed and for a large, normal-holed record at the slow speed, the industry squabbled over the size of the large 33-1/3. Twelve-inch records were tried first, but it appeared that the public would more readily accept a ten-inch (the size of the 78's) record and the whole industry swung in that direction for awhile. Appearances can be deceiving, however, and obviously the success of the ten-incher was short-lived; extended jazz performances, symphonies, operas, and album "packages" made the large record more practical. For less expensive shorter offerings the 45 rpm was ideal.

Dial records issued the first jazz 12-inch LP in July of 1949. Entitled *Bird Blows The Blues (Dial* 901), the album had all original takes (from the 78's) on the "A" side and other alternate takes on side "B". The other twelve-inch LP's featuring Parker material were 903, 904 and 905. Dial 200 series were ten-inch LP's issued after the non-too-successful 900 series. Records 201, 202, 203 and 207 dealt entirely with Parker and there were some single Bird tracks on later numbered records. The Parker 78's on Dial began with record number 1002 (*Ornithology* and *Night In Tunisia*—final takes), issued in April 1947, and continued (not always consecutively, of course) through to 1058 (*Bird Feathers* and *My Old Flame*). The infamous *Lover Man/BeBop* record, which Parker hated, was 1007, and the "New York" recordings began at 1015 with *Quasimado*. Russell also obtained and issued the Red Norvo session with Bird and Diz from June 1945.

The Savoy Parker 78's (original takes) with the exception of the two 1944 Tiny Grimes vocals, are in the 900 series. The vocals are on Number 613 and also a part of some early releases in the 500's that had Parker 1944-45 material. The original takes also appeared on 45's (45-300 series); extended play (two track to a side) 45 (XP-8000 series, 7 albums); and ten-inch 33-1/3's (9000 series—4 albums). The alternate takes were not issued until the 12000 series (33-1/3's) listed in this work.

Beginning in 1949, Parker's association with Norman Granz's Clef Division of Mercury Records produced 78's in the 11000 series. Granz later became sole head of Clef and Norgran and issued a variety of EPs (extended play 45's) and LPs. Only the original takes were first issued until the formation of Granz's Verve label which issued most of the Parker material, including some alternate takes, in the 8000 series cited in this work.

As to the "live" recordings of the "Roost" period, the labels of Savoy, Charlie Parker, and ESP contain most of the available tracks, and there is much to be seen from them: the ragged beginnings of the Parker-Dorham quintet; the difference in style between Dorham and Davis (much confused in personnel listings); the fallacy of adding *too many* good musicians to a group led by a free spirit such as Bird; and, most important, a glimpse at the thrill of hearing Parker in a night-club atmosphere.

CHAPTER XII

A EUROPEAN JAUNT
The Paris Festival
(April-May 1949)

That sweet enemy, France.
Sir Philip Sidney—Astrophel and Stella, No. 41

In the early spring of 1949, Parker was on a Granz presentation at Carnegie Hall, and consequently, trombonist Tommy Turk, a JATP stalwart, was recruited as an added starter for a Parker record date in April. During the second week of April, a few days after the record date, the Parker-Dorham Quintet (without guest stars) hit the road for Chicago where they had a two-week gig at the Music Bowl. Meanwhile, The Roost had begun the shift to Bop City at 49th and Broadway, and within a month, the move would be completed. Upon the Quintet's return to New York, Granz had more recording activities planned, after which Bird would be ready for his first European adventure—the International Jazz Festival in Paris.

* * *

Recording—April 1949—New York City
Charlie Parker and his Orchestra—Parker (as), K. Dorham (tp), Al Haig (p), Tommy Potter (b), Max Roach (dr), Carlos Vydal (bongos), Tommy Turk (trb).

Cardboard	Verve 8009
Visa	Verve 8000

The trombone that is added for these two tunes would be a welcome addition were the voice a less raucous one. Turk could have been palatable had he used a mute as J.J. Johnson did on the 1947 session. As it is, he sounds like an intruder at times.

Cardboard seems to be based on *Don't Take Your Love From Me* (there are other possibilities), with a strikingly altered chord in the first eight bars (see Analysis Section). The form is ABAC, and the theme breaks into three-part harmony at times and has two bars of three-part counterpoint at the beginning of the "C" section.

158

Ex. 114 *Cardboard*—2 bars of Counterpoint

Visa, a twelve-bar blues that has a fourth bar suggestive of the same spot in *Relaxing At Camarillo*, also breaks into harmony at times; it seems if Parker was trying to expand his compositional efforts at this time. The tune, moreover, was apparently named in honor of Bird's preparation to leave for the International Jazz Festival in Paris.

In examining *Visa*, there are some interesting building patterns and comparisons: The tune is built from a favorite Parker rhythm pattern which occurs seven times in twelve measures. This pattern is coupled with other favorite devices and also with short strings of eighth notes.

Ex. 115 Rhythm Pattern

Ex. 116 *Visa* notated rhythmically with pattern bracketed

Examples like the *Visa* rhythm pattern are not easily heard until pointed out, and it is a credit to Parker's intuitive craftsmanship that a single rhythmic figure could provide the cohesiveness for an apparently complex modern blues.

Below is a comparison between *Visa*'s fourth bar and the fourth bar of *Camarillo*. The phrases eventually end on the same note, but the first example approaches the sixteenth note figure from below, using no altered tones in the second half of the measure; whereas in *Visa*, the figure is approached from above, with altered tones on the sixteenth notes.

Ex. 117 *Camarillo* and *Visa* Fourth-bars

The "fourth bar" example can be used to see another element of Bird's genius—the interchangeability of many of his lines. If one hums the beginning four bars of *Camarillo*, for instance, one can go directly to the fifth bar of *Visa* and come up with a "new" blues. This is another good example of Tristano's "jigsaw puzzle of many pictures" analogy (See Recording—February 19, 1949).

In the same direction, the eleventh bar of *Driftin' On A Reed* breaks into harmony as does the second bar of *Visa*, and in comparison, it can be seen that the harmonized passages are similar (*Driftin'* is transposed from Bb to C for ease of examination).

Ex. 118 *Driftin'* Bar 11 and *Visa* Bar 2

The melodies are, of course, slightly different in relation to the rhythm, but the important tones (using only the final four in the *Visa* example) are exactly the same and resolve to the same place (think of a repeated note as being the same note for purposes of analysis). The comparison shows the identical over-all rhythm but with the melody notes in different places—or, another way—the same notes arranged differently in the same over-all rhythmic figure (more "jigsaw puzzle").

Suffice it to say that this writer feels that *Visa* is a fine example of Parker's "composed" blues that is often lost in the shuffle; it is really an outgrowth, as has been shown, of successful elements that were used in his earlier blues tunes. In addition, *Cardboard*, because of the harmony and counterpoint—as well as the form itself—is also worthy of compositional study.

The blowing on this date goes well (except for Turk's blattiness), and Dorham's solo on the blues shows the beginning of the "funky" style that he later developed with Art Blakey's Jazz Messengers. The presence of Vydal on bongos, however, adds little to the performances, except perhaps during Haig's solo on *Visa*; other times the bongos are practically inaudible, although it is true that they can be "felt" at certain places.

Recording—May 5, 1949—New York City
Charlie Parker and his Orchestra—Parker (as), K. Dorham (tp), Max Roach (dr), Tommy Potter (b), Al Haig (p)

Segment	Verve (Ger.) 511033
Passport—Two Takes Listed	Verve (Ger.) 511033
Diverse	Verve (Ger.) 511033

A great deal of confusion exists over the titles on this date, and the complete mystery may never be solved. This work will, however, attempt to look at the existing evidence:

1. Three tunes were recorded with the above titles, and two takes were issued from one of the tunes.
2. The master numbers were 294-3; 295-2; and 296.
E. One tune is minor; one is a blues; and the other an *I Got Rhythm* derivative.
4. The two takes are on the minor tune (usually called *Segment*); and obviously, the titles and the master numbers were confused; for on Verve 8009, the tune titled *Diverse* is really a second take of the minor tune, and the blues does not appear. On the German Verve version cited above, however, the two takes of the minor tune are both listed as *Segment*, but the blues and the *I Got Rhythm* based-tune are both called *Passport!* The minor tune (of which there are two takes) is noted below:

Ex. 119 Opening Phrase of *Segment*

Most probably the title *Passport* (the only one listed with two takes issued) should be assigned to the minor theme (the only theme of which there are two takes), and the other tunes listed as *Segment* and *Diverse* (although there is no way of telling which tune goes with which title). The minor tune, however, is listed on so many issues as *Segment* that the only *practical* approach is to *keep* that title for the minor opus and assign the other two titles arbitrarily. This writer's suggestion is to assign the *Passport* title to the blues since it never appeared on an *American* 33-1/3 twelve-inch LP (it did appear on a ten-incher), but came out first in Europe. Let us review these suggestions:

1. *Segment*—minor; two takes; should be called *Passport*; title retained because of many issues under same.
2. *Passport*—blues; title arbitrarily assigned; never appeared on American 33-1/3 twelve-inch LP
3. *Diverse*—*I Got Rhythm* form; title arbitrarily assigned.

The minor tune has a Latin-rhythm introduction and has a well-played unison by Dorham and Bird on the theme (on the better take—on the other take Dorham, who is cup-muted, is out of balance and cannot be heard too well). Bird has the bridges (improvised) on the theme choruses, and there is a fine Parker improvisation on the better take. Bird is squeaky, however, on the lesser take.

The blues, an exciting line that was later recorded by Charles McPherson, features exact unison for eight measures and then octave unison for four. The line is done very well, and all the soloists are cooking.

Ex. 120 Opening of *Blues*

On the "Rhythm" theme, the opposite of the normal Parker-Dorham problem happens; the line is phrased well together, but one or the other (mostly Bird) drops out of the line at various times. Bird has a strange cool aloofness to his solo on this tune; his breath accents, moreover, are an important part of solo. The attractive theme is done in octave unison.

Ex. 121 Opening of *Rhythm* Line

This date is a good recording of the Parker-Dorham combo, and since no later "studio" sessions exist (in fact, this recording is the *only* "studio" quintet session), it is a good example for any collection. Dorham plays well; he predicts his mature playing of the Fifties. Further, the sound of the rhythm section is very driving and alive and adds to the appeal of the session.

* * *

The International Jazz Festival was to be held at the Salle Pleyel (Pleyel's Hall) for the week beginning Sunday, May 8, 1949. The festival was the dream of Charles Delauney, French critic and discographer, who had worked tirelessly to promote it. Besides the Parker Quintet, the bill included Sidney Bechet's Dixieland group; a Miles Davis-Tadd Dameron group; "Hot Lips" Page's Kansas City-styled group; and a variety of French musicians. Don Byas, who had been living in Europe, and James Moody were also to be heard in a variety of contexts.

The American entourage left the States on Friday, and immediately upon arriving in France, Parker split from the group; he was not to be found for the Saturday rehearsal. Parker was the toast of Paris; he jammed with French musicians, attended parties in record shops and, unfortunately, had ample access to the Parisian "pushers."

The French audience was not pleased with Parker's on-stage attitude. They felt he should have acknowledged their applause more graciously. But in reality, the habit of turning away and kicking off the next tune during the applause was merely Parker's style it was not, to be sure, intended as arrogance, but rather as modesty. There are, however, the incidents of Parker eating a rose that was given to him at a performance and answering all questions posed to him by an English critic with quotes from the *Rubiayat*. These were probably reactions of Bird under the influence of drugs or alcohol.

The Quintet appeared on the Sunday and Monday evening concerts, booked a short tour of cities and universities for the rest of the week, and returned for the Saturday night performance and a matinee and final evening concert on Sunday. There were recordings made on home equipment during the five concerts, but it is impossible to tell at which concert or concerts the recordings were done.

* * *

Recording—International Jazz Festival—May 1949

Scrapple From The Apple	Yard CP 3
Out Of Nowhere (1)	Yard CP 3
Out Of Nowhere (2)	Yard CP 3
Barbados	Yard CP 3
52nd Street Theme (1)	Yard CP 3
52nd Street Theme (2)	Yard CP 3
Salt Peanuts (1)	Yard CP 3
Salt Peanuts (2)	Yard CP 3
Allen's Alley	Yard CP 3
Final Jam Blues (Most of Festival Personnel)	Yard CP 3

The atmosphere is very loose on these sides, and the recorded sound is bad; one cannot think of these as prime example of the Quintet of this period. Bird is strangely inventive, however, even though he seems at times to be bored with the material and to be poking fun at himself. There is a strange, dream-like quality coupled with faulty (purposely?) intonation on some of the Parker solos. These tunes may have been recorded during the same set; they are: *Scrapple, Nowhere No. 1, Barbados, Salt Peanuts No. 2*. Throughout the whole performance most of the lines have some ragged spots, and the most consistent soloist seems to be Haig; he is relaxed and inventive on all the tunes.

Scrapple is very fast, and the opening line is poor, but the ending theme is improved. In Bird's solo, there is *Buttons and Bows* at the beginning of the second chorus and *Woody Woodpecker* in the third chorus. After a sloppy beginning, the fours between Bird and Dorham are fairly well done, but the tune cuts off soon after Roach's bridge on the out-chorus.

Nowhere No. 1 is done at a faster ballad speed than normal (*everything* seems to be faster on these takes) and the Parker solo is not really very good. Dorham starts unevenly but pulls himself out and plays a fairly good solo. Potter takes a "melody-type" solo for sixteen bars following Haig, but Bird butts in with "*Happy Birthday*" on the end (supposedly meant for someone in the audience). Bird takes the tune out with Dorham behind and the *Country Gardens* ending with an extra-long trill ends the piece.

Parker is better on *Nowhere No. 2*, although he does use some of his original ideas from the studio date, including the famous motif. Dorham, however, plays a very nice solo and finishes with a development of *Country Gardens*. The take cuts off during Haig's solo.

Only the last two bars of the opening theme chorus are heard on *Barbados*, and here again Bird brings in *Happy Birthday* during the second chorus. He then proceeds to play a repeated phrase which seemingly pokes fun at himself. Dorham sounds very good—Dizzy-ish—and there are some wild fours between Bird and Max following Haig. During the second chorus of fours, Bird plays a strange, minor-sounding *Woodpecker* lick (against IV⁷—bars five and six) and keeps repeating it. In addition, the final theme has Potter playing a wierd bass line on the repeat just before the take cuts off.

52nd No. 1 has good solos, with Haig playing wild pedal-type octaves during the "A" sections of his chorus. The closing chorus has the "introduction riff" for the first half of the tune; then Max at the bridge; and then the actual theme figure.

52nd No. 2 cuts right in on Bird's solo, without theme. Haig, however, *develops* the theme on this second version.

Unlike most of the other tunes, *Salt Peanuts No. 1* has a clean line, but there is a ragged entry to the singing section. During the vocal section itself, Bird humorously does the final singing octave-jump in French. Bird is very weird on *No. 1* and even weirder on *Salt Peanuts No. 2* in which he uses the pathetic intonation mentioned before. Moreover, the theme is out of sync on *No. 2*.

Bird is playing other intervals rather than unison on the theme to *Allen's Alley*. All the choruses, however, are at a high level on this tune, and there are some interesting alto-drums four-bar exchanges. The final theme is cut.

The final *Jam Session Blues* is from May 15—a grand finale with most of the men on stage. This has become the rule at jazz concerts ever since (unfortunately) and generally proves very little; this recording is no exception. The writer's listing of the solo order was again done by ear, so one should not take it as law. The take cuts in on a tenor—probably Byas—and then goes to a mainstream trumpeter—probably Page—with saxes riffing underneath. Bechet is next, and he screams over the build-up of brass and saxes. The riffs continue after Bechet into a modern trumpet solo—probably Miles (with much technique). Bird follows, using two favorite blues motifs in the first four bars of each of his choruses and sounding very "off-hand."

On this final Festival weekend, Max Roach led the quintet (with James Moody replacing Parker) on a "studio" record date that produced, among other tunes, *Prince Albert* (based on *All The Things You Are* and written by Dorham and Roach) and *Ham 'n Haig*.

* * *

Musically, the European jaunt proved little except that Bird needed new material to hold his interest. The Paris Festival recordings are certainly not good examples of Bird, and the French "pushers" only contributed to his dependence on drugs.

CHAPTER XIII

THE STRING GROUP
Lullabies of Birdland
(June-December 1949)

Longing not so much to change things as to overturn them.
Cicero—De Officiis

After returning from France, the Quintet made arrangements for a summer road trip through the Midwest. The trip consisted of some stationary gigs (a week or more), but mostly it was made up of one-nighters. One must remember that ballrooms, a product of the "big band" days, were still in vogue (a sort of a "cultural lag"). It is hard to imagine the Parker combo, with only the small hard-core of local hipsters to support it, working in this type of atmosphere.

The New York scene, however, was rapidly changing: The Roost management had officially moved its bop policy to Bop City, and plans were laid for a swank new Broadway jazz club just above Fifty-Second Street. The club was to be christened Birdland in honor of Parker and would feature an admission policy similar to the Roost's; it would also have—as a "gimmick"—live birds in cages hanging from the ceiling. Symphony Sid ran a weekend all-night remote from Bop City during the summer of 1949 which helped the new music slowly seep into all corners of American life. On Fifty-second Street, however, the Three Deuces (newly reopened) kept a jazz policy, and the old Onyx was soon to be reopened as the Orchid Room, but other than that, The Street was dead.

Parker's Quintet returned from the road in August and worked the Clique (the original name of the club slated to become Birdland) and Bop City. Leonard Feather was running all-star sessions every Tuesday at the Deuces, and Parker was a sometime participant. It has always seemed to this writer that Parker's recordings with Fats Navarro and Bud Powell, usually listed as May 1950 at the Cafe Society, probably date from somewhere around this period. Navarro was working The Street with J.J. Johnson's Boptet during the late summer and fall and Powell was at the Orchid with a trio. Later, Miles Davis, Wardell Gray, and Sonny Stitt joined the Powell combo, and Parker's group often worked across the street at the Deuces. Roy Haynes was working with Powell and Davis, but was urged by Max Roach to switch to Bird's group because Roach had plans for forming his own combo.

Dorham left the Quintet in September and was replaced by Red Rodney. These events give us a general picture of the scene from August to December.

The September 9th issue of *Down Beat* carried an interview of Bird by Mike Levin and John S. Wilson in which Parker gave many of his now-famous quotes along with most of the biographical material which is common knowledge today. He spoke of his interest in Paul Hindemith, the modern classicist, and mentioned the early jam session humiliations and the discoveries (1939) at the chili parlor. He spoke of the freedom of the small group compared to the tyranny of the big band and gave Gillespie as an example of an artist who had succumbed to the tyranny.

Bird's definitions of bop, however—"Bop is no love-child of jazz...Bop is something entirely separate and apart.... It's just music.... It's trying to play clean and looking for the pretty notes.... It has no continuity of beat, no steady chug-chug. Jazz has and that's why Bop is more flexible"—were disagreed with by Gillespie in a later interview. Gillespie felt that Bop was just a different way of interpreting jazz.

Parker also spoke with disgust of Dial's *Lover Man* release and of the general commercialization of Bop. In spite of his statement on commercialization, however, he mentioned that strings could soften and color a performance better than a large group of the standard jazz instrumentation. He obviously had high ideals in this direction. Unfortunately, the group never quite fulfilled them.

In the week following the *Down Beat* interview, as he waited for his string group to materialize, Bird appeared on a Granz JATP presentation at Carnegie Hall.

* * *

Recording—September 18, 1949—Carnegie Hall
Parker (as), Lester Young (ts), Flip Phillips (ts), Roy Eldridge (tpt), Ray Brown (b), Hank Jones (p), Buddy Rich (d).

The Opener	Barclay (Eng) 6912
Lester Leaps In	VSP 23
Embraceable You	VSP 23
The Closer	VSP 23

Embraceable You is a classic performance; it contains a beautiful heart-rending first chorus by Eldridge, a lovely Young solo, some classic Parker with the use of the motif, and a big-toned Phillips statement. Turk starts with a lovely pianissimo tone and sounds very nice until he trys a contrasting climax in the second half of the theme. The contrast is too much too soon, and coupled with some poor choices of notes (*wrong* notes with the harmony, if you will), it ruins the solo. Parker develops the motif along with other material from the 1947 record and at one point quotes *On The Trail*. Moreover, Hank Jones is extremely sensitive to the different needs of each soloist, and the success of this performance owes much to his perceptiveness; at bars 15-16 of the Parker solo, for instance, he and Bird collaborate on a beautiful substitute progression: /Am⁷ Ab⁷/ Dbmaj⁷ Gb9+11/ (this progression has now become well-known and was probably originally a product of Lennie Tristano). It is interesting to compare Young's opening figure to Parker's famous motif; they are very similar in conception and use almost identical notes (in different places, of course).

Ex. 122 Young's Opening to *Embraceable*

(Parker's motif is found in the analysis portion of this work.)

This exquisite jazz version of the Gershwin tune is rarely written about, but it certainly should be. Bird is a bit squeaky, but the overall performance is an emotional experience.

Lester Leaps In mainly features Young, but Parker and Eldridge play well on their chances. Turk is really raucous on this one, however, especially after the inevitable background riffs enter.

Parker has a good solo on the opening blues, although he is a bit rough-house. He quotes *Blues In The Night* and hints at *Why Was I Born*. This track is the hardest for a collector to find; it has not been re-issued in the United States (at this writing).

The closing blues begins with a short, swinging riff for two choruses; then Phillips moves in and after awhile resorts to the good old JATP "honks." Turk begins with *Here Comes The Bride*; then there is more blattiness, and Young succumbs to the raunchiness with a "dirty" interpolation of *Bye Bye Blackbird*. Eldridge and Rich exchange screams and bangs in four-bar patterns, and after the pandemonium subsides, Rich sets tempo for Parker's solo. Here again Jones and Parker run a series of substitute "cycle of fifths" chords; this time on the first four bars of the blues.

Except for *Embraceable You*, the concert is typical JATP.

* * *

In the fall of 1949, Parker finally achieved his ambition of playing with a string section. Granz is often blamed for coming up with the idea as a commercial gimmick, but Doris Parker claims differently:

Norman Granz did not conceive the idea of Charlie working with strings. This was Charlie's dream, and perhaps it bugged him later. But Norman did it only to please Charlie.[1]

Granz, however, by his own admission, tried various ideas (most surely with sales in view) of his own:

Charlie, I think, understood my love for what he did and went along with my various experiments...he was willing to try anything. As a result, I was able to record Charlie with strings, Charlie with a big band; and I insisted that Charlie play pretty tunes by good song writers instead of just the blues...[2]

* * *

Recording—November 30, 1949—New York City
Charlie Parker with Strings—Parker (as), Stan Freeman (p), Ray Brown (b), Buddy rich (dr), Mitch Miller (ob), Meyer Rosen (harp), Jimmy Carroll (arr-cond), strings.

Just Friends	Verve (Ger) 511033
Everything Happens To Me	Verve (Ger) 511033
April In Paris	Verve (Ger) 511033
Summertime	Verve (Ger) 511033
I Didn't Know What Time It Was	Verve (Ger) 511033
If I Should Lose You	Verve (Ger) 511033

Parker, at this time in his time in his life, did need new material and different ways of expressing himself. He was getting tired of using the same themes and formats, as is evidenced by his sometimes self-mocking playing on the recordings done at the International Jazz Festival. Indeed, this session fulfills the need for new materials and format, but does not always allow him the freedom of expression he desperately needed.

The string sound is lush, and Parker plays with a beautiful singing sound, staying exactly near the melody on most of the selections. On *Just Friends*, however, he shows what could have been by rearing back and playing one of his greatest solos. He later cited this performance as one of the pieces of his own work that he himself liked.

Don Heckman in his *Bird In Flight* article (*Down Beat*, March 11, 1965) states the following of the second chorus of *Just Friends*:

This chorus opens with a declamatory phrase, immediately answered by a similar phrase up a minor third—a splendid example of Parker's talent for improvising melodic paraphrases that far excelled the sources from which they were drawn. The first and third eight-bar segments are based on similar melodic and harmonic material, are less ornate and use fewer sixteenth-note figures. The opening phrase of the first eight bars is balanced by a contrasting melodic phrase in Bars 3-6 of the second eight.

The total solo sounds like a confusing succession of random 16th-note embellishments, but it includes many repeated patterns. Notice the similarities between the 16th-note figures in Bars 5, 8, and 29. These 16th-note figures are also similar to the 16th-note ran in Bar 9. Bars 13 and 29 are almost identical, suggesting that Parker's response to the chords in that location was repetitious. The same is true of Bars 6 and 28—in both cases the phrase occurs on the second, third, and fourth beat. Finally, the last beat of Bars 14 and 30 and most of Bars 15 and 31 are closely related.

Parker's lines in *Just Friends* are motivated by the chord changes, but one should also consider them in the context of the overall rhythmic flow. Although the second and fourth eight-bar groups consist mostly of 16th-note patterns, Parker obviously conceived them as more melodic than ornamental. The opening eight-bars, for example, include first a declamatory pattern, then two bars of 16th-notes and then a rising, almost impossible-to-notate, rhythmic line. The second eight bars provide immediate contrast with a bursting series of 16th-notes made more complex by the inclusion of two 16th-note triplet fragments. The second bar allows a brief pause; then Parker begins a 16th-note line that continues almost without rest until the 18th bar. Notice especially its continuing up and down shape; one of the consistent aspects of Parker's fast playing is the tendency towards rising and falling patterns, sometimes connected by wide interval leaps—4ths, 5ths, 7ths—but more often running diatonically or up and down arpeggiated 7th chords.

Ex. 123 *Just Friends*—Alto Key Solo

The third eight bars begin with a rapid-fire 16th-note sequence, the final spurt from the previous phrase. In the second bar, a long phrase of placid, but strongly rhythmic, dotted-eighth notes begin. They reveal Parker's exceptional lyricism; his simple blues line is far more appealing than the original melody of *Just Friends*. At the end of the phrase, Parker plays a double-time, 16th-note pattern in which tied notes produce a tantalizing hesitation in the rhythmic flow.

The last eight bars, like the second, consist almost exclusively of 16th-note phrases. The first two have a typical rise and fall. Nearly all the phrases in the last four or five bars duplicate previous lines, appropriately summing up the choruses.

The *Friends* arrangement begins with cascading harp over the strings, then a viola solo moves to Parker improvisations as a theme lead-in. Bird has the first half-chorus; then the strings for 8; then Bird returns—this is all in Ab. An oboe solo is used as a modulation to a key one step higher for the classic chorus. Next, two bars of strings enter beneath, and Bird takes the tune out. He plays improvised phrases over short accented string chords as a coda.

Everything Happens To Me has pizzicato strings in the intro dissolving back into *arco* before the theme. Bird is very melodic, and the strings alternate lush and pizzicato sounds beneath him. The strings take six bars of the bridge; then Parker enters and plays half of the next section; the strings answer. An oboe solo leads back to Bird at the bridge, and he plays prettily till the end. There is almost no improvisation, but it is a beautiful reading of the tune.

After the string intro on *April In Paris*, Parker carries the theme until the last eight where the strings take over. He improvises behind the string melody. An eight-bar modulation, featuring oboe and pizzicato cello and bass, moves the tune from the key of Bb to C for a block-chord piano solo. Bird enters for the second half with some improvisation, and ritards before starting the final section. The strings have the coda, with the piano echoing the theme in block-chords at the very end.

There are three Parker choruses on *Summertime* after an intro by the low strings. Parker, however, only slightly embellishes the melody on all three, and here, for sure, boredom can set in. One wonders why this tune, the simplest in construction and harmony, was played so straight; it should easily lend itself to improvisation. Evidently Parker felt differently.

Strings, followed by oboe, open *I Didn't Know What Time It Was*, and Bird goes three-fourths of the first chorus; the strings and oboe (solo) finish. The oboe then answers the strings in a short modulatory section—G to Ab—and Bird launches some good improvisations. The oboe again enters for half of the bridge, and Bird returns, playing melodically until the end.

The beautiful *If I Should Lose You* is performed simply but poignantly. Bird takes the first half of the tune; then oboe with "two-beat" background; then Bird again. The modulation (from Bb) goes up a step to C, and Parker improvises a half-chorus. The cello has the third eight of this chorus with the other strings behind, and Parker takes the theme home. An attractive, cadenza-like cello solo based on the main theme is featured in the coda before the harp plucks the final notes.

Some of the tunes do not contain Bird's most inventive improvisations, but they do make enjoyable listening. Bird was a master of melodic interpretation and *Just Friends* is one of his crowning achievements.

* * *

Birdland opened on December 15th at 1678 Broadway. The new club was located below street level, a few doors north of 52nd and Broadway on the east side of the street. It was hailed as the "Jazz Corner of the World" for almost two decades. The gala opening featured Parker, Tristano, Lester Young and others, including some traditional stars. The club combined the atmosphere of a Broadway "Theatre-

Club" with that of a "blowing" room such as the Fifty-Second Street clubs. In fact, Monday nights became session time—no organized groups would be booked (early 1950 is another possibility for Parker's recordings with Navarro and Powell— both were known to be at the Monday night sessions). "Pee Wee" Marquette, a diminutive ex-band singer became the emcee, and Symphony Sid Torin left Bop City within the next year and began doing nightly broadcasts from a special studio built into Birdland by WJZ. Indeed, "Birdland" would become a household name.

The Parker quintet that opened Birdland (and remained until January 1950) featured Red Rodney (nee Robert Chudnick) on trumpet. Rodney was a veteran of the big bands, including Jimmy Dorsey, Gene Krupa (his 1946 solo on *How High The Moon* is a break-up—it incorporates *Deep Purple* into the solo line), Claude Thornhill, and Woody Herman. He was a Dizzy disciple and had technique and tone to prove it, plus a brash, out-going attitude. Unfortunately, he also fell victim to the "monkey."

* * *

Recording—December 24, 1949—Carnegie Hall
Charlie Parker Quintet—Parker (as), Rodney (tp), Al Haig (p), Tommy Potter (b), Roy Haynes (d)

Ornithology	S.C.A.M. (Eng) JPG 1
Cheryl	S.C.A.M. (Eng) JPG 1
Ko Ko	S.C.A.M. (Eng) JPG 1
Bird of Paradise	S.C.A.M. (Eng) JPG 1
Now's The Time	S.C.A.M. (Eng) JPG 1

This is a tremendous all-around performance; it contains some of Parker's best work and is well recorded for a "live" recording of this period.

Symphony Sid introduces the group and wishes Bird a "Merry Christmas," and after four foot taps, *Ornithology* is launched with good unison horns. Bird is eloquent; his technique is flowing and his tone is round and full. His ideas, moreover, are fresh and the long lines hold the listener hypnotized. Rodney also comes on beautifully; at one point he develops a four-note motif on the same pitch.

On *Cheryl*, Parker gets into Louis Armstrong's *West End Blues* solo, and Symphony Sid announces this fact on the spot. Rodney displays his technique, goes "outside" at times, and develops *Country Gardens*. Haig is more "bluesy" than usual, also developing *Country Gardens*. The theme choruses are again very clean.

Ko Ko is well done, with Rodney sounding excellent on the introductory section. The choruses are very good, and Bird's one short stumble is in the act of inventive seeking, not in technical haste. Parker actually paraphrases some of his ideas from earlier recordings of this vehicle based on the *Cherokee* chords.

The masterpiece, however, is *Bird of Paradise*, with its second chorus containing an actually endless flow of ideas that incorporates a *Moose The Mooche* quote, *The Kerry Dancers,* and Bird's own *Embraceable You* motif. The intro (and coda) is treated rather freely, and Parker's first chorus is also improvised. This first statement has a beguine tempo at the bridge. Rodney (muted) and Haig follow Bird's classic, but they are anti-climactic. Rodney's intonation is not as good with the mute as it is without. Potter plays a sinewy melodic solo for sixteen bars after which Bird enters with two blasts of the *Woodpecker Song* and takes the tune out.

On the repeat of the opening statement on *Now's The Time,* Parker treats the line with humorous freedom. His choruses are good. He uses a few of his favorite blues phrases at the "first-four-bar" sections of some choruses. Rodney climaxes his chorus with a fantastically clean display of inventive ideas in mercurial double-time, and Haig works in *Jumpin' With Symphony Sid.* Bird can be heard telling the group that "Salt Peanuts is next" during Haig's solo. The closing theme is again treated with humor. Bird plays the "flat-five" of the scale instead of the natural five of the original melody in order to cross up Rodney at the end of the first chorus, and on the repeat he plays some free-flowing phrases against the theme.

This group of tunes is a good collection of classic Parker. The label listed, however, is an English one and the abbreviation stands for Specially Collected American Music (a later issue is on Blue Parrot).

Recording—Circa 1949—New York City
Parker (as), unknown (p), Don Lamond (d), Ed Safranski (b)

Cool Blues	S.C.A.M. JPG 1

The piano is recorded too poorly to make any identification by listening, and no information exists on the true date of this recording. At one point, however, Bird alludes to his *Confirmation* chords in the first four bars of a chorus, which he was prone to do on some blues around 1952; this could suggest a later date.

The performance is extended Parker blues-playing, with Bird and Lamond exchanging fours near the end. Bird is loose and free-flowing; he quotes *There's A Small Hotel* and the *Habanera* from *Carmen.* Lamond, however, seems a bit heavy-footed both on the "fours" and the closing theme. There is a need for further research on this date.

* * *

The Fats Navarro-Bud Powell recordings with Bird will be listed here since evidence seems to suggest that they were done in the fall of 1949 or Spring of 1950. Ira Gitler, speaking of Navarro, states, "...I question the May 1950 dating of records made of his broadcasts from Cafe Society.... His playing seems too vibrant.... too alive for man who would be dead of tuberculosis on July 7."[3] These recordings could have been made on Fifty-second Street during the fall of 1949, or possibly Monday nights at Birdland (Navarro and Powell were in the house band) early in 1950. It is also possible that they were done at an earlier date at Cafe Society. The usual listing (during May 1950) of each tune will be listed behind it (U.L.) but the tunes will be reviewed in bulk here.

* * *

Recording—Circa 1950
Parker (as), Navarro (tp), Powell (p), Curly Russell (?) (b), Art Blakey (?) (d).

Perdido (Wahoo)	U.L. May 8	Charlie Parker 701-B
Round About Midnight	U.L. May 8	Charlie Parker 701-A
Move	U.L. May 8	Charlie Parker 701-A

This Time The Dream's On Me	U.L. May 8	Columbia JG 34808
Dizzy Atmosphere	U.L. May 8	Columbia JG 34808
Out Of Nowhere	U.L. May 15	Columbia JG 34808
Night In Tunisa	U.L. May 15	Columbia JG 34808
Street Beat (Rifftide)	U.L. May 15	Charlie Parker 701-B
Cool Blues	U.L. May 15	Charlie Parker 701-A
52nd Street Theme (3 Bird Choruses)	U.L. May 15	Charlie Parker 701-A
Little Willie Leaps	U.L. May 22	Columbia JG 34808
52nd Street Theme (no choruses)	U.L. May 22	Columbia JG 34808
Ornithology	U.L. May 22	Charlie Parker 701-A
I'll Remember April	U.L. May 29	Columbia JG 34808
52nd Street Theme (2 Bird choruses)	U.L. May 29	Columbia JG 34808
Embraceable You	U.L. ?	Columbia JG 34808

The Columbia issue (which contains *all* of the above tunes) gives a recording date of June 30, 1950, at Birdland for all tunes. This seems questionable as there is simply too much music to be taken from a half-hour (or even an hour) radio show (from which the recordings, made by Boris Rose, were taken). Furthermore, this date comes even closer to Navarro's death.

The *Embraceable You* take has an embarrassing vocal by black entertainer Chubby Newsome (a female singer-dancer) and the trumpeter sounds more like Red Rodney than Navarro (the fact that the tune contains a *Country Gardens* ending might also suggest a Parker-Rodney alliance). The Bird solo is well done and highly emotional.

There are three versions of *52nd Street Theme*, the Parker "set-ender" of this period and two of them contain Parker statements. The longest (three-chorus) take has long been available on the older (Charlie Parker 701-A) release. Both "blowing" versions are screaming, uptempo excursions. Each of the three versions follows, as a "chaser," the tune listed directly before it in the above list.

Navarro is featured alone on *Tunisa* (played without the "interlude" section) and also plays the theme to *Move* alone as Parker had probably left the stand during the feature for a "taste" at the bar.

Denzil's Best's *Move* has the *Honeysuckle Rose* bridge and an "A" section with common chords: /Bb/Cm⁷F⁷/Bb/G⁷/Cm⁷/F⁷/Bb/Bb/. It is often described as having an *I Got Rhythm* base, but the chords indicate a progression that is a bit different (hear Powell's quote of Monk's *Rhythmning*, however). Although, as mentioned earlier, Parker can not be heard on the opening theme; he plays the closing statement in harmony. This tune, moreover, has excellent solos and four-bar exchanges by Bird and Fats, and Bird uses several "out-of-key" statements of the opening theme motif throughout his solo.

Perdido does not quite measure up as well on the whole, although Powell solos beautifully on this tune and also on *Round Midnight*. The theme to *Perdido* is not used; instead the group plays a riff based on its changes. This riff, known as *Wahoo*, was written by Bennie Harris and recorded by Red Rodney's group (including Buddy Stewart and Dave Lambert on vocals) in 1946.

On *Midnight*, Bird stays fairly close to the melody. This is, incidently, his first recorded version of the Monk classic. Powell, however, plays an impassioned chorus that is brilliant in the use of "double-timing;" he seems inspired by Monk's difficult chord changes. The recording cuts off before the tune ends.

Two tracks, *This Time The Dream's On Me* and *I'll Remember April* contain only Bird and rhythm. The latter track is a sterling performance. The exchanges of "fours" with drums are superb, and Bird launches some "scherzo" atmosphere with some humorous doings such as a quote from *The Peanut Vendor*.

The abstract Bird can be heard on *Out Of Nowhere* (on which Fats is again solo on the introductory chorus) and *Little Willie Leaps*. On the former, he develops his motif from the original Dial recording in an abstract fashion, and on *Willie*, he shows jagged abstractions over a furious tempo.

Dizzy Atmosphere moves at its usual lightning-fast pace with wild drum "bombs" (perhaps too many) and a thrilling Powell piano solo. Fats quotes *All Of Me*, perhaps ominously, if one considers his soon-to-come demise; and the unisons, although sometimes ragged, carry an excitement that sends chills through the listener. A good example of live be-bop.

The *Street Beat* (mistitled *Rifftide* on some issues), is the Sir Charles Thompson original based on *I Got Rhythm* that Bird and Thompson recorded in 1945; however, here the theme is treated more freely (see Example 23—Chapter V). The solos are wild and humor-filled, and Powell, being bugged by Bird's flippant background blasts during his solo, sarcastically interpolates the *Clap Hands, Here Comes Charlie* phrase into his solo and ends the statement with more sarcasm by repeating Bird's "ool-ya-koo" motif over and over. Parker again does not play on the opening theme.

Cool Blues has good blowing by all (on the Charlie Parker issue the piano solo is removed), although the trumpet again sounds like Red Rodney. It is also interesting to hear the pianist imitate Erroll Garner's chording style from the 1947 recording of this tune in his backing of the "out" chorus. (Columbia lists Walter Bishop as the pianist on this and *Embraceable You*, and careful listening reveals some phrases that seem to substantiate this, especially a hint at *Le Secret*, a favorite Bishop quote. The presence of Bishop and Rodney, however, would suggest a later date for these tracks.)

Ornithology, an item not to be missed, is the highpoint of this group of recordings. The rhythm section drives like mad, and the solos are unbelievable— especially Powell's; his work on this recording is a further example of his genius. Moreover, words are inadequate to describe the intense feeling found in all of the solos on this piece. The performance stands (except for the recorded sound) as a great example of the jazz of the period and how it sounded in person.

Indeed, Parker chooses some humorous quotes throughout these tunes; the *Carmen Habanera* in *Move*, and *High Society* during the fours on the same tune; the "Whose that knocking at my door?" phrase from *Barnacle Bill* to start the "fours" on *Perdido*; the *Moose The Mooche* phrase in his solo and more *Habanera*, plus the *Prisoner's song* ("I wish I had someone to love me" phrase) during the fours on *Street Beat*; *Poinciana* during the solo and again (!) *Habanera* during the fours on *Ornithology*. The recurrence of the *Carmen* theme *might* suggest that the tunes were done on the same night, although this phrase was a favorite Parker quote.

There are also moments of looseness in the spirit of spontaneous expression. On the closing theme to the *Street Beat*, for instance, no one enters for a few bars, and the rhythm section chugs along by itself. Bird takes many liberties on the theme choruses to most of the tunes. For instance, there is an interesting treatment with contrasting sets of ideas on the end of *Ornithology's* first theme (Ex. 110) which works out well; it sounds like free, wild counterpoint.

As to the personnel, the driving "backbeat" on drums suggests that the drummer might be Blakey (Roy Haynes is another possibility), and his bombastic style is at times overbearing (especially on *Perdido* and *Dizzy Atmosphere*), but the hard-driving swing he gives the group more than makes up for the more obnoxious moments. On the Charlie Parker release, Max Roach is listed as the drummer, and *52nd Street Theme* (three Parker choruses) is listed as by the Bird-Miles group, September 1948.

The crowd noise and other distractions are annoying, but two interesting comments can be heard: On *Ornithology*, as Parker begins his solo, a voice which sounds like Pee Wee Marquette shouts "Go, Bay-bee", and "Go, Girl" (Navarro was affectionately known as "Fat Girl") and can be heard during Fats' solo on *Street Beat*.

For pure "session atmosphere" of the "Bebop period," these sides are some of the best ever made.

* * *

In viewing the end of the Forties decade, one sees that in less than ten years Parker rose from a little-known sideman in a Midwest-based band to an international celebrity with a New York night-club named after him. One also sees a man who was dismissed from many bands because of his undisciplined behavior becoming the leader of a group that contained some of the most respected string players in New York City. One can not speak of Parker's trials and hard times without mentioning that he was, by many standards, a successful person. Unfortunately, he did not handle it well.

CHAPTER XIV

INTO THE FIFTIES
Reunion With Diz
(January-June 1950)

The present contains nothing more than the past, and what is found in the effect was already in the cause.
Henri Bergson—Creative Evolution

The saxophone voice of the late Forties was the alto, made by Parker into a searing temptress with a shrieking, shrewish sound. The early 1950s, however, was the time of the tenor; in the hands of Stan Getz the temptress became "cool" and seductive with only occasional sexual screams. Was this a racial thing—a black and white difference? It seems not, for Getz's main influence was Lester Young, and Parker, as has been shown, also partially came from Young. Perhaps it was just different ways of hearing the same thing. Moreover, Getz was also influenced by Parker himself (as was everybody) and coupled Parker's quickness with the cool, melodic style of Young.

Getz, a Philadelphian, had been with the big bands of Jack Teagarden, Bob Chester, Stan Kenton, Jimmy Dorsey, and Benny Goodman; he was also one of the "Four Brothers" of the Herman Band of the late Forties. Furthermore, through his solos with Herman, he was becoming *the* tenor saxophonist and, beginning in 1950, was the consistent winner of the Metronome Poll.

Al Haig was allied with Getz on many recording dates during 1948-1949, and through this mutual alliance, Parker and Getz, using the same rhythm section, sometimes appeared on the same bill during 1950; this was especially true during some of the "Bird With Strings" bookings. Indeed, as the Parker Quintet closed at Birdland during the first week of January and prepared for a jaunt to Philadelphia's 421 Club, Getz and the Parker rhythm section (Haynes-Potter-Haig) cut a group of standards. These tunes (*Small Hotel, What's New, I've Got You Under My Skin,* and *Too Marvelous For Words*) are available on *Prestige*.

The "Bird With Strings" album was released in late January as the Quintet returned to New York for a stay at the Club 845 in the Bronx. In addition to this quintet booking, Parker also worked as a single with a local rhythm section at the Latin Quarter in Fall River, Massachusetts, and fulfilled some "one-nighters" in and around New York City during February.

176

* * *

Recording—February 18, 1950—St. Nicholas Arena, New York City
Parker Quintet—Parker (as), R. Rodney (tp), Al Haig (p), Tommy Potter (b), Roy
Haynes (dr).

I Didn't Know What Time It Was	America (Fr.) 30AM6062
Ornithology	America (Fr.) 30AM6062
Embraceable You	America (Fr.) 30AM6062
Visa	America (Fr.) 30AM6062
I Cover The Waterfront	America (Fr.) 30AM6062
Scrapple From The Apple	America (Fr.) 30AM6062
Star Eyes	America (Fr.) 30AM6062
52nd Street Theme	America (Fr.) 30AM6062
Confirmation	America (Fr.) 30AM6062
Out Of Nowhere	America (Fr.) 30AM6062
Hot House	America (Fr.) 30AM6062
What's New	America (Fr.) 30AM6062
Now's The Time	America (Fr.) 30AM6062
Smoke Gets In Your Eyes	America (Fr.) 30AM6062
52nd Street Theme	America (Fr.) 30AM6062

St. Nick's Arena was famous as a boxing auditorium, but this occasion was
a concert-dance featuring the Quintet. The recorded sound is bad, and there is
a lot of noise, but the recording is still worth hearing; there is a different Parker
here than on any other recording. He is *extremely* inventive and free and there
is much humor and abandon in his playing. Unfortunately, on most takes there
are "cuts" to different places in the tune (for the most part, only Parker and the
themes are present on these sides) which tend to disorient the listener. This spoils
some of the glamour of the performance, although it is still an essential item.

From the tune *Out Of Nowhere* until the end of the recording there is a different
recorded sound—as if the bass was turned up and the treble turned off. The piano
chords and the string bass can be heard a bit better on these tunes although the
sound is "boxy." It also seems as if the crowd is "thinned out" a bit on these
tunes, although the bassy sound could have cut down on the noise.

I Didn't Know What Time It Was, Embraceable You, Out Of Nowhere, and
Smoke Gets In Your Eyes all use the *Country Gardens* phrase as a coda. It is
interesting, therefore, that a *Down Beat* review (November 18, 1949) of the quintet
in live performance mentioned that the horns were "...fascinated by the English-
round type coda." This recording certainly supports the statement as do other Parker-
Rodney alliances.

Parker freely states the theme to *I Didn't Know*; he uses glissandos, suggests
the harmony through embellishing phrases, and uses a "broken-record" effect
coupled with a suggestion of *On The Trail* at the bridge. Chorus two is a beautiful
improvisation by Bird, and then a cut occurs (probably Rodney's solo) and the
tune returns to the bridge (Parker improvising). Rodney enters with the melody
on the final eight while Bird continues to blow, and the tune goes out.

Ornithology contains a complete theme chorus but also has annoying cuts in the solo. Parker quotes *Why Was I Born* and *Poinciana,* and he and Rodney play some exciting "fours," with Rodney quoting *Deep Purple.*

The famous motif is used at the opening of *Embraceable You* and coupled with a staccato descending scale phrase which culminates in an upward burst towards the answer to the motif (see Analysis Section—Motif). After the first chorus, the tune "cuts" to the second half, which has Bird developing *Jingle Bells* coupled with the staccato, descending phrase.

Visa is bit raucous compared to the studio version, and Haynes does not help the situation with his tom-tom accents on the theme. There's fine Parker blues-blowing, however, and then a sudden cut to four-bar exchanges with Rodney occurs.

The recording of *I Cover The Waterfront* starts in the bridge, finishes a chorus, and then "cuts" back to the bridge where Parker develops *Woody Woodpecker.* The last "eight" is done in harmony (trumpet lead).

Bird has three good choruses on *Scrapple*; indeed, he is very "outside" at the end of the first one. The recording then cuts to the bridge, and Parker plays a half-chorus and another full one before the recording again cuts to the fours. Haynes improvises the bridge to the closing theme. Interestingly, there is a similarity between Parker's improvised bridge of the opening theme chorus and the opening improvised bridge to the final take of *Chasin' The Bird* (June 1947), both of which have the same harmonic base.

Star Eyes has Bird on a complete theme; then an improvised chorus; then another "cut" to the theme; Rodney joins at the end. Directly after the ending, the "signature" phrase of *52nd Street Theme* is used as a "chaser."

The two Parker choruses on *Confirmation* have ideas flying everywhere, and *Woody Woodpecker* again appears in the second improvised chorus. Again, however, there is a "cut" before the exchanges. Haynes's tom-toms, as on *Visa*, are annoying; it is not the accents that are out of place—they would be fine on snare—but rather the choice of using tom-toms.

Nowhere is done at a driving tempo, and the "cut" goes to the second half. Rodney again joins at the end of the tune.

Hot House contains a full theme, three Parker choruses (excellent excursions), four-bar exchanges between the horns, and a Haynes solo on the final bridge. The "cut" goes from Bird's solo to the exchanges.

The renditions of *What's New* and *Smoke Gets In Your Eyes* are the only ones available by Parker and make interesting listening. *What's New* has Bird on the theme and then a "cut" back to bridge; the final section is done in free harmony. The first chorus of *Smoke* has Bird suggesting interesting harmony to help Haig at the bridge, but after this opening statement, the "cuts" make the tune confusing. It moves this way from that point on: ABA (all Bird), A (out chorus—Rodney melody—Parker counter-melody).

Haynes tom-toms are again a bit out of place on *Now's The Time,* but the recording contains seven wailing Bird choruses. The theme is treated freely and humorously by Bird (differently each time), and *Woody Woodpecker* and an outside version of *Louise* appear in his "fours" with Rodney.

The final *Theme* has some blowing space for Bird over some more Haynes tom-toms.

The obnoxious "cuts" and poor recording do destroy some continuity of thought for the listener, but Bird does some fantastic things here, and it is worth wading through the swamp. Indeed, this writer hopes that the above observations will be a helpful guide for the journey.

* * *

A JATP tour embarked from Buffalo in the spring of the year, and the Parker group was part of the westward-moving package. A Kansas City stop-over gave Parker a chance to look up some old acquaintances and to visit his mother who had recently (1949) graduated from nursing school and was working in a Kansas City hospital. Charlie and his four cohorts visited her at home and took their meals there during the short stay. After two days, however, the rhythm section took the train (they had sent their luggage ahead) to St. Louis, the site of the next JATP concert. Bird and Rodney remained in Kansas City to attend an all-night session at the Playhouse Club; a jazz fan who owned a private plane had been persuaded to pilot them to St. Louis after the session.[1] Enroute to St. Louis, however, Parker's penchant for dangerous fun almost became a disaster. Tommy Potter states:

> Red told me that Bird asked if he could take the controls;...suddenly, Bird leans left, and the plane banks to the right. The guy grabs the controls real fast. Red was shaking with fright. Bird said he just wanted to hear the motor when he banked the plane.[2]

During this period (probably directly after the tour's return to New York), Parker recorded with a Granz-selected rhythm section. Most probably the rhythm section also had been on the JATP tour as part of the "all-star" group.

* * *

Charlie Parker Quartet—March-April 1950, New York City
Parker (as), Hank Jones (p), Ray Brown (b), Buddy Rich (d).

Star Eyes	Verve 8009
Blues (Fast)	Verve 8009
I'm In The Mood For Love	Verve 8009

The two standards offer excellent examples of the Parker ballad style. On the seldom-heard *Star Eyes*, he offers an introduction (also used as a coda) that beautifully states the mood of the piece. Jones's piano chords, which provide the rhythmic accents to this introduction, seem to state the words "Star Eyes" over and over in anticipation of the first bar of the theme. Parker's introduction is notated below:

Ex. 124 Introduction to *Star Eyes*

On *Mood For Love,* Parker plays one of his personalized melody statements that is somewhat reminiscent (at least in feeling) of *Don't Blame Me* recorded in 1947. Once again, he takes an overworked standard and makes it into a thing of personal beauty. Jones's concerto-like introduction (and coda) is in beguine rhythm.

Blues hints at a theme in the first 12 bars but sounds like one of Parker's "on-the-spot" creations and is not heard again.

Ex. 125a 1st phrase of *Blues* (fast)

The above phrase opens the blues after Rich's drums and occurs twice more (in each four-bar segment of the blues) but with a different ending each time. After this extemporaneous riff, Bird constructs four singing blues choruses, and Jones follows with an exquisite three-chorus solo that ends with a *Moose The Mooche* phrase. Rich plays twelve measures and Parker returns for another fluent-sounding three choruses. The ending section consists of "free" (without rhythm) "dixie-type" solo breaks of four bars apiece (Rich-Jones-Brown-Parker). Bird moves into tempo after his break and goes through some traditional eight-bar "tag" chords—/Eb/ Ebm/Bb/G7/C7/F7/Bb/Bb/—to the end. The final two bar ending (the Bb section of the above chords) comes from nowhere, surprise-like, and Rich is right on top of it rhythmically.

Ex. 125b ending of *Blues* (fast) Bars 7-8 or "tag"

Jones plays a beautiful 24-bar solo on *Star Eyes,* and he and Brown contribute eight-bar solos on *Mood For Love* (the bridge and final eight respectively). Both ballads contain sensitive theme readings by Parker, and *Star Eyes* has a full improvised chorus. Parker plays a half-chorus improvisation on *Mood For Love* and returns to the bridge after the piano and bass for the concluding statement. A humorous phrase in the bridge is reminiscent of *Happy Birthday,* in spite of the fact that the notes are completely different from the birthday standard.

* * *

The period from late April to June presents some problems in documentation, but the quintet was at the Hi-Hat in Boston for two weeks and at the Metropolitan Opera House in Philadelphia for a one-nighter. The group also did a long stint at the new Village club, Cafe Society (Downtown), supposedly during May and

June. Rodney was hospitalized for an appendectomy in May, and the famous recordings with Navarro and Powell (listed in Chapter XIII) are usually listed as being done at the Cafe Society during May. Art Tatum and his trio were playing opposite the Parker Quintet during the Cafe Society stay.

* * *

Recording—May 23, 1950—Cafe Society (Downtown)
*Parker Quintet—*Parker (as), Kenny Dorham (tpt)
Rhythm unknown
> Summertime   Okie Doke Records

The trumpet player is obviously Dorham, who is known to have worked this club with Bird during this period. The rest of the men are difficult to place, however, although the pianist seems to have a lighter touch than is characteristic of Bud Powell, who is sometimes given in the personnel for this date. It is possible that it is Haig and that Haynes and Potter (the regular rhythm section) are also present.

Bird and Dorham are the only soloists and although Parker is a bit freer than the "studio" session of November 1949, he still does not really "stretch out." Dorham does fairly well, however, especially on his second chorus, and Bird joins for a few bars of theme at the end.

Available only on various "boot-leg" labels, this and other tracks from this session are difficult to find.

* * *

The Cafe Society (Downtown) was owned by Barney Josephson and had a sister club, The Cafe Society (Uptown). The downtown club, in Greenwich Village, was located in Sheridan Square where West Fourth merges with Washington Place. Tony Scott lived in an apartment above the club during this period and was a composition student of Stefan Wolpe, a contemporary, classical composer. According to Scott, Wolpe loved Bird's playing and when the two men met in Scott's pad, the traditional behavior patterns of classicist and jazzman were reversed; Wolpe reacted with jubilant jumps of joy and Parker professorially told Wolpe that he "would like to commission him to do a work."[3]

* * *

Recording—Cafe Society (Downtown), New York City, Probably Early June 1950
*Charlie Parker Quintet—*Parker (as), Kenny Dorham (tpt), Al Haig (p), Roy Haynes (d), Tommy Potter (b), Tony Scott (clt—sitting-in on *Moose The Mooche*).
> Just Friends ("Pop Goes The Weasel" quote)   Blue Parrot AR704
> April In Paris ("Irish Washerwoman" quote)   Blue Parrot AR704
> Just Friends   Blue Parrot AR704
> April In Paris   Blue Parrot AR704
> Moose The Mooche   Blue Parrot AR704

Both sets of the two standard tunes are probably from the same week—and possibly from the same night, as Bird precedes the second version of *Just Friends* with the opening announcement of the "second show." Furthermore, *Moose* because of the unmistakable presence of Kenny Dorham also seems to be from the same general period. Exact dating, however, has never been established and further research proved futile. Therefore, for identification purposes, the quotes listed behind the titles of the one set of standard tunes will act as easy, "by ear" guides for the novice listener.

Because no other "combo" versions are known to exist, the standards are interesting items. The Parker improvisations on both versions of *Just Friends* are much different from the studio version with strings; this is probably because of the improvisations being done in Ab (the *opening* key of the string version) rather than Bb as on the string version. Neither version of *April In Paris*, however, has much true improvisation; one must be satisfied with Bird's technique of sandwiching improvisational phrases between melody phrases.

The *Friends* format has Parker with a freely-rendered version of the theme, followed by full-chorus improvisations by Bird and Dorham (muted); then Haig and Bird (mostly improvisation) split the last chorus; the trumpet joins for the ending. The second version, however, seems almost a refinement of the first (although both versions are excellent); for instance, there is more "push" to the rhythm, and the performance, therefore, has a more driving, alive feeling. Furthermore, Haig's solo on the second version is absolutely brilliant in conception and has a Bud Powell-like drive to its rhythmic feel. The Parker solos on both versions, however, are beautiful creations and essential items for the Parker collector.

The versions of *April In Paris*, are not in the same class. Although the format is essentially the same as *Friends*, there is no improvised chorus by Bird; and both versions are similar—down to the use of an *On The Trail* phrase by Dorham and the use of the same opening (in thirds) by Haig on his solo (on the second version, however, Haig continues this "thirds" phrase beautifully, rather than continuing in block chords as he did on the first version). Dorham plays open horn, and after beginning with the melody (both versions), is fairly adventurous. He returns at times to melody, however, perhaps to keep his place. *Country Gardens* serves as an ending for the two versions.

The slower-than-usual *Moose* has Dorham alone on the theme (with some able help by Haig) but he does not perform it well; in fact, he does not know the bridge. His solo is a different story, however, it is done in a self-confident, "funky" manner—really an early example of Fifties trumpet style. After Dorham's three choruses, Haig plays a short (one chorus) solo that is very satisfying despite its brevity (the piano comes through rather well here for a live recording), and Scott's icy-toned clarinet then takes over for four well-played choruses. Next, there is a "fours" chorus between Dorham, Haynes, and Scott. A second "fours" chorus begins to unfold, but Bird jumps in after Scott at the last four of the second "A" section and continues solo from there on through another chorus. The solo contains some phrases which are similar to phrases in the *Bloomdido* solo (see *Recording* June 6). The rather ragged ending theme is performed by all three horns, although Bird is alone on the bridge.

Recording—Probably June 1, 1950—Cafe Society (Downtown)—Session
Parker (as), Tony Scott (clt), Brew Moore (ts), Dick Hyman (p), Chuck Wayne or Mundell Lowe (gtr), Leonard Gaskin (b), Ed Shaughnessy (d)

Lover Come Back To Me   Blue Parrot AR704, Parktec 4627

52nd Street Theme Blue Parrot AR704, Parktec 4627

The drums lead in to *Lover Come Back*, and Scott sneakily begins the theme statement in the chalameau register. Clarinet has the full theme with Bird adding a bit of humor, and the solo order is alto-piano-guitar-tenor-clarinet, followed by fours between drums and Bird. Parker, as he did on *Moose* in the preceding recording, again uses a phrase that he also employed in the *Bloomdido* improvisation, and he quotes *Habanera* during the fours; he sounds very inspired. Hyman's solo is also well done; it has a full single-line chorus, packed with sequential ideas, plus a chorus that is mainly fast passages of block chords spelled by a single-line bridge. The guitar solo does not quite measure up to the rest of the company, but the tenorist makes a fine statement. Scott's solo features the high register coupled with some Pee-Wee Russell "whiskey tone" effects. The final "everybody blow" chorus is a joyful thing to hear.

The set-break theme (*52nd Street Theme*) is unbelievably fast and Bird is the only soloist. He plays fantastically, and the ensemble is again thrilling on the free-for-all out-chorus. The original introductory figure is used at the beginning of the out-chorus; then Shaughnessy takes the bridge, and the actual theme figure is used during the last eight in a swirling, surrealistic fashion.

This set is highly recommended for the "session" atmosphere and for the high level of the solos.

* * *

Around the time of the Cafe Society booking, Bird attended several sessions at the William Henry apartment building at 136th Street and Broadway; the sessions were recorded by some of the other participants. The six-story building, terraced with fire escapes and housing a storefront, contained a sub-basement, one-room apartment that was sought after by musicians because of its sound-proof location; it was sometimes sub-let to other musicians if the tenant or tenants were on the road. Recently, tenorists Gers Yowell (who lived in the one-room pad with trombonist Jimmy Knepper and altoist Joe Maini during 1950) and Don Lanphere found their copies of the session tapes and Art Zimmerman produced them commercially.

* * *

Recording—Circa 1950—Wm. Henry Apartment Building—New York City
Lanphere Tape—Parker (as), Jon Nielson (tp), Frank Isola (d), Al Haig (p), Unknown (b); other horns present but mostly not heard: Don Lanphere (ts), Joe Maini (as), Jimmy Knepper (tb).

Half Nelson	Zim 1006
Cherokee	Zim 1006
Scrapple From The Apple	Zim 1006
Star Eyes	Zim 1006

Although no bass is listed on the Zim release, this writer can hear—or at least feel—one on all tunes except *Half Nelson*. Further, the extra horns are only in evidence on the opening theme of *Half Nelson* and the closing one to *Star Eyes* (some do sneak in at the end of *Cherokee* also).

Parker sounds good throughout, but not his best; he has strange lapses of attention which cause some long spaces without playing. On *Scrapple*, however, the best of these recordings, this does not happen. He keeps a constant flow of ideas and springs many original turns, such as the abstraction of the theme at one point.

Star Eyes also has some good moments, and one can again (as in some of the Cafe Society cuts) hear the *Bloomdido* ending phrase (theme).

Cherokee begins just before the bridge and contains some good Bird except for the lapses mentioned above. The final eight is where some of the added horns join.

Throughout all the tunes, there are many annoying cuts, since the musicians had only enough tape to record Bird's solo spots, but the rewards, especially on *Scrapple* make the annoyance worthwhile.

Recording—probably early June 1950—Wm. Henry Apartments—New York City Yowell Tape—Parker (as), John Williams (p), Buddy Jones (b), drummers as listed below; horns present on some themes: Jon Eardley and Norma Carson (tp), Jimmy Knepper (tb), Gers Yowell and Bob Newman (ts).

Bernie's Tune (Buzzy Bridgeford-d)	Zim 1006
Donna Lee (Phil Brown-d)	Zim 1006
Out Of Nowhere (Frank Isola-d)	Zim 1006
Half Nelson (Phil Brown-d)	Zim 1006
Fine and Dandy (Phil Brown-d)	Zim 1006
Little Willie Leaps (Phil Brown-d)	im 1006
All The Things You Are (Frank Isola-d)	Zim 1006

This session seems more organized than the one on the Lanphere tape, and the Bird solos are truly classic masterpieces. Parker is at his best here, even with (or because of) the loose format. Moreover, when theme choruses can be heard, he is usually wailing a wild obligato on top of the ensemble.

The best tracks are probably *Donna Lee, Fine and Dandy*, and *All The Things You Are*, which contain endless strings of exciting, original thoughts performed flawlessly. In fact, one can *feel* the excitement as one marvels at the virtuosity and invention.

Bernie's Tune, which starts in mid-piano solo, is an interesting vehicle for Parker, but there are so many "cuts" in it that it does not make easy listening. There are, however, some interesting inter-polations that are easily discernible: the use of a phrase that he used in his *Bloomdido* solo (one which starts the third improvised chorus on that tune and the same one he used on some Cafe Society improvisations) at two different places; and the use of the *I Wanna Go Where You Go* phrase from the pop tune, *Then I'll Be Happy*.

Before the start of *Nowhere*, Parker humorously (but fluently) plays some saxophone runs and mentions the name of Rudy Weidoeft, the saxophonist of the Twenties whose syncopated, highly technical, but "corny" solos were played by most aspiring young saxophonists in their high school days (this writer can remember performing Weidoeft's *Sax-o-phobia* in a high school concert during this period). The amazing thing about the Weidoeft-type runs that Parker played, however, is that he next *used* them at various places in the *Nowhere* solo (a similar use of a Weidoeft phrase can be heard on the February 12, 1948 recording of *Barbados*—2nd chorus). On *Nowhere*, there is also abstraction of the *Country Gardens* phrase by Bird and the ensemble at the end of the tune.

Although the other two tunes, *Half Nelson* and *Little Willie*, have excellent, cerebral Bird; Parker and Williams do not seem to get the essence of the *Little Willie* chord changes across (Is it Williams' "feeds" or Parker's conception?); and *Half Nelson* is not as driving as the other tracks.

No listener should pass up this set because of sound (which is really not that bad); the solos are a monument to Bird's invention.

* * *

A large (27-piece) Kenton-styled group had been organized during the spring by arranger Gene Roland: the band was to feature Parker improvisations with screaming brass and sax backgrounds. The band's two-month existence proved unfruitful, however, and its only scheduled engagement, at the Adams Theatre in Newark, was canceled before the opening date. Many top New York professionals were members of the experimental group, and Bird, who was to rehearse the band, dug into his supervisory capacity with relish. The men, however, were amused one day to find that his professional-looking arrangement case contained nothing but a bottle of gin![4]

Charlie Ventura also had a short-lived big band during the first half of the year which included at various times multiple-reed man Tommy Mace on alto-sax and Swedish trumpeter Rolf Ericson. Mace later became the oboist with the Parker string ensemble, and Ericson later played with Bird on a Swedish tour. In addition, Red Rodney was on the Ventura band's first recording in late December 1949.

Dizzy Gillespie, meanwhile, had disbanded his big band; he was working with a small group and formulating plans for some string and woodwind recordings *ala Parker*. Norman Granz, therefore, decided to try a recording reunion of the two pioneers.

* * *

Recording—June 6, 1950—New York City
Gillespie (tp), Parker (as), Thelonious Monk (p), Curly Russell (b), Buddy Rich (dr) (All tunes also issued on German Verve 711049.)

Bloomdido	Verve 8006, 8409
An Oscar For Treadwell—Take 3	Verve 8006
An Oscar For Treadwell—Take 4 (original)	Verve 8006
Mohawk—Take 3	Verve 8006
Mohawk—Take 6 (original)	Verve 8006
Melancholy Baby	Verve 8006
Leap Frog—Take 4	Verve 8006
Leap Frog—Take 6 (probable original)	Verve 8006
Relaxin' With Lee—Take 2	Verve 8006
Relaxin' With Lee—Take 3 (original)	Verve 8006

Parker had not recorded with Gillespie in a studio setting since 1945. Therefore, these recordings are a wonderful example of the growth of the two giants, and the presence of Monk is an added attraction.

Bloomdido, named for Teddy Blume, a New York violinist who was in the process of becoming Bird's manager, is a blues in B-flat with an ingenious harmonic twist at bar eight and an ending that is rhythmically complex because of its changing accents.

Ex. 126 *Bloomdido* Bars 7-8

Ex. 127 *Bloomdido* Ending

It is interesting to note that this blues ends on the fourth note of the scale, which is harmonized with the dominant chord. This *should* give a feeling of incompleteness, but it does not! The two horns end in a descending glissando starting with this fourth scale tone, and the theme sounds finalized and exact!

Treadwell has an *I Got Rhythm* base with a typical Parker theme for the "A" sections and a melodically improvised bridge. Parker solos wonderfully on both takes, but Gillespie seems to have problems with the chords on the earlier take. This earlier take is also marred by a faltering ending, but all is remedied on the later take on which Diz gives his old friend a running battle for solo honors. Monk's rhythmic imitation of the first bar of the theme in his introduction is humorous and original.

Ex. 128 *Treadwell—Monk's Intro figure*

Ex. 129 *Treadwell* Opening Phrase

The themes to *Bloomdido* and *Treadwell* are both done in octave unison with Gillespie using a cup mute. Diz's solo on the latter tune, however, is performed on open horn, and he comes through with some flashy high note antics on the original take.

Mohawk is another angular blues line with typical Parkerian harmonic implications in its melodic line (see Analysis Section).

Ex. 130 *Mohawk* Opening

There is a rhythmic similarity between its seventh and eighth bars and the identical place in *Bloomdido*.

Ex. 131 *Mohawk* Bars 7-8

Monk's introduction to *Mohawk* is also similar to the one he invented for Bloomdido; it makes use of a major 2nd (Bb and Ab—the root note of the key plus the "blue" 7th) to achieve a Bartokian effect. On *Mohawk*, he also plays weird moving intervals behind the octave-unison line and uses some dissonances (not altogether fitting) behind Parker's earthy solo. Gillespie is again muted throughout the second blues, and Russell has a pleasant solo following Monk's statement. The later take of *Mohawk* is much more fiery and has a clean closing theme, whereas the final statement on the earlier take is bothersome.

Melancholy Baby is a worthwhile offering; it is one of those tragi-comic performance that makes it difficult to know where the line is drawn. There is a wild Monk intro; then Parker plays a theme statement, broken by strings of ideas. He finishes with a reference to the *Embraceable You* motif in sequence. Gillespie is funky—almost dirty—and Monk plays a surrealistic half-chorus before Bird returns to the second half for the close. There is a ritarded, rubato ending moving into the *Country Gardens* coda with an extremely long trill before the final two notes.

Leap Frog is all improvisations—a chorus apiece for the horns and then exchanges of "fours." The horns exchange for two choruses starting with Parker, then Rich begins the next chorus and the order continues (Rich-Bird-Rich-Diz) for 64 bars. Rich takes the tune out with a drum coda culminating in "Shave-and-a-haircut-two-bits." The fourth take has a confusion in the solo order; Bird enters after Gillespie in the horn and drum alternations and the take ends abruptly.

(There is a strong possibility that the take numbers are confused on the German LP since the "cutoff" take is assigned the later number. Furthermore, the album lists yet another take, but it is only a repeat of the complete [probably 6th] take. The original American LP [Verve 8006] has no take designations and lists only two takes.) Rich has a different concept of time than the "boppers" and at times the fours with drums seem severely strained. This strain, moreover, can also be felt in some of his backings. In regards to structure, *Leap Frog's* "A" section has a chord pattern like *Exactly Like You* or *Take The "A" Train*, and the bridge has a familiar pattern also—Key of F:/A7/A7/Dm/Dm/G7/G7/C7/C7/.

The only melodic statement in *Relaxin' With Lee*, a *Stompin' At The Savoy* derivative, is a riff-like theme played in unison for the final eight bars of the piece, the rest is pure improvisation.

Ex. 132 Riff *Relaxin' With Lee*

The riff repeats with the ending note on the "flat-five" (G). Russell begins the tune with walking bass, and Parker plays a stunning chorus, using the *Carmen* idea at one point. Gillespie suddenly jumps up a key (to D) for his chorus and plays marvelously. Monk waits for the walking bass to come back to Db and then plays a spare solo. Following the piano, Bird returns with a development of *County Gardens* in an inventive turn of phrase, and another phrase that centers around the major-seventh of the scale, reminiscent of *The Gypsy*. Gillespie takes a half-chorus; then Rich enters with a bombastic bridge; then comes the final riff. The later take is much shorter, and there is no key change on Gillespie's solo; Rich enters directly after Monk, and then the ensemble states the closing riff. The tune is probably named for Billy Shaw's wife, Lee.

Here again, new material *does* make a difference, and it is always a thrill to hear Bird and Diz perform together. If Monk and Rich are not the most appropriate accompanists at least they are interesting, and Monk's inventive introductions certainly lend the date a specific character. Furthermore, this date offers the only opportunity to hear Monk work with Bird—moreover, with Diz and Bird together.

* * *

Indeed, the reunion of the two innovators of the 1940s was a fitting way to go into the 1950s, a decade that would have the "children" of Bird and Diz as the dominant jazz force. For the 1950s was really a decade of refiners and synthesizers rather than innovators; in other words, the young musicians spawned by the "boppers" used this period to find discriminating new ways to use the knowledge they had gained. They found ways to arrange and harmonize Bop-type lines for an ensemble; they found obscure tunes for "blowing frames" and used discreet substitute harmonies that were further developments of Parker's and Gillespie's ideas; and, possibly most important, they became carriers of tradition, a necessary ingredient for the survival of any art. At the end of the decade, of course, there were the experiments of Miles Davis and Ornette Coleman—Davis with modal thinking and Coleman with free playing—but these really came to fruition during the 1960s. Both men, moreover, were originally shaped by the "Boppers"—Davis (who, of course, was one) in conception and Coleman in sound. The jazz of the 1950s, therefore, although containing subtleties for which the innovators had no time, was truly a reflection of the music of Bird and Diz.

CHAPTER XV

MORE STRINGS
Granz Productions
(July-October 1950)

Sooth'd with the sound, the king grew vain:
Fought all his battles o'er again;
And thrice he routed all his foes, and thrice
he slew the slain.
John Dryden—Alexander's Feast

At the end of June 1950, as America entered the Korean conflict as a "police action," the economic scene was not attuned to large jazz ventures; even Count Basie was working with a small group. Parker, however, was readying himself for a forthcoming engagement at Birdland with the full string group and also working on material for another string album which would include a French horn among the "color" instruments.

The group that was slated for bookings included a normal "quartet" string group: two 1st violins, a 2nd violin, a viola, and a cello. Oboe and harp were the "color" instruments and the arrangements were mainly from Parker's record dates. The group totaled eleven men counting Parker and the rhythm section.

In the beginning of the string project, Al Haig's level head helped keep things together, but later Teddy Blume became Parker's personal manager and helped with the conducting and payroll problems. Blume was a violinist who was familiar with the "classical" musicians in the group and in the fall of the year, he, himself, became a playing member of the group.

* * *

Recording—July 5, 1950—New York City
Charlie Parker with Strings—Parker (as), Joe Singer (French Horn), Edwin Brown (oboe), Verley Mills (harp), Ray Brown (b), Buddy Rich (d), Bernie Leighton (p), Joe Lippman (arr-cond), Strings.

Dancing In The Dark	Verve 8003
Out Of Nowhere	Verve 8004
Laura	Verve 8003
East Of The Sun	Verve 8004

They Can't Take That Away From Me	Verve 8004
Easy To Love	Verve 8004
I'm In The Mood For Love	Verve 8004
I'll Remember April	Verve 8004

There seems to be a freer atmosphere on these recordings than there was on the earlier string session, although Bird still stays relatively close to the melody on most of the tunes. There are some improvisations, however, but nothing extended. Bird uses his pet phrases as embellishments to the original melody rather than as new melodic material.

The harp kicks off shimmering strings over a recurrent horn note in the introduction to *Dancing In The Dark*. Parker enters with the melody (the horn is playing lovely countermelodies) at a driving ballad tempo for half of the first chorus and then yields to the strings for an eight bar section in "two-beat" tempo; Bird returns for the final eight. The oboe plays an eight-bar modulatory section from Eb to F, and Parker plays some improvisations (slightly adventuresome) in the new key. The horn line at the end of Parker's chorus moves the tune back to the lower key, and Leighton's piano returns to the second half of the tune for an eight bar solo. Parker has the ending eight plus a "tag."

Out Of Nowhere, however, does contain some good improvisations and is usually an over-looked item. The strings open out of tempo, then the oboe enters in rhythm. Parker again has the first half-chorus; then come the strings with horn counter-melody for eight; then Bird blows again; he develops the *Nowhere* motif in the last eight of the exposition chorus. There is a short two-bar modulation by the oboe from the key of G to F, and Leighton starts the next chorus with some delicate piano. Bird moves in for a fine eight bars of improvisation and Leighton comes back with a block-chordal solo section; an oboe solo ends the second chorus. Parker moves the tune into Bb and plays the second half of the tune and a beautiful coda in which he alludes to the opening melody statement coupled with a phrase from the 1949 *Just Friends* solo.

The arrangement on *Laura* is lovely, but there is almost no improvisation by Parker. Hand-muted horn and oboe alternate over strings, and the harp shimmers into Bird's melody statement. He plays eight measures, and then there is a serene horn solo for eight. Parker finishes out the first chorus (eight without strings— eight with) with more beautiful horn counter-melody permeating the final eight. The oboe immediately enters in Ab (the opening was in C) and states the melody over pizzicato strings. Parker enters in beguine tempo for the next eight-bar section and leads back to the key of C for the second half of the tune (the strings move the harmony underneath him, and Parker merely moves up a half step in the melody). The last eight begins at a driving tempo but relaxes at the end, and the oboe and horn add a coda which echoes the introduction.

East Of The Sun begins with oboe over pizzicato strings; then the strings enter melodically, and the horn moves to Bird's exposition of the melody. The horn has an eight-bar melody statement at the second half, with the oboe playing counter melody, and Parker finishes the opening statement. The tune moves from F to Eb in a four bar modulation and English horn (the oboe player is doubling) opens the second chorus with eight measures. Strings have the next section followed by

Bird's improvisations, and the final section of the second chorus is split by oboe and strings. Parker enters at the very end over the strings and moves the tune back to the key of F for a final statement on the second half of the tune (some good improvisation). The coda is strings and harp with a horn call on the end.

Block-chord piano over strings alternates with alto breaks in the intro to *Can't Take That Away From Me*, and Bird (yielding to oboe at the bridge) plays a swinging melody statement. He plays a "bla-bla-bla" effect at the beginning of the second eight which is reminiscent of his exchange with Flip Phillips on the Machito *Jazz* recording. The oboe is used to modulate from Eb to F, and Leighton plays a good half-chorus, beginning with block-chords and moving to single lines. Parker plays fine improvisations at the bridge, and the final "A" section is divided between horn-oboe exchanges and Bird. Parker then moves back to Eb for a statement of the "A" section and answers the oboe in the short coda.

On *Easy To Love*, Parker has some out of tempo improvisations following the strings and oboe. This leads to the exposition chorus which lines up as follows: Bird (16)—Strings (8)—Bird (8). A four-bar modulation by the oboe moves the piece from G to F, and the French horn opens the second chorus with oboe counter-melody. Bird takes the next sixteen with some improvisations, first over strings and then over block-chord piano, and the strings finish the chorus with oboe entering on the end. The tune moves back to G, and Parker plays half—improvised; then the strings move in and Parker returns for the closing section.

Mood For Love has Bird leading into the Db theme, after the strings and oboe, to state the first half-chorus. Cello and string tutti divide the exposition bridge, four bars apiece, and Parker has the final eight. The oboe and horn move the tune to Bb for an all block-chord piano half-chorus, followed by Bird at the bridge. The final eight of the second chorus is split between English horn and strings, and the French horn moves the tune back to Db for Bird's closing statement on the second half of the tune. In the coda, Bird answers the horn figure.

The final offering has no modulations and will be used as an example to show Parker's general improvisational approach to the "string" recordings. *I'll Remember April's* structure is a bit unusual, and it is worth mentioning before any examples are given: A(16)—B(16)—A(16). The format after the string introduction is: Alto(A); Oboe-Strings(B); Alto(A); Piano-Alto(B); Alto(A). The coda has Parker moving sixteenths notes over fragmentary strings and woodwinds.

A look at Parker's statement at the final "A" section of the opening chorus shows very clearly how Bird would only gently embellish the melody (although playing it rhythmically free) and then break into a short burst of invention before returning to the melody.

Ex. 133—*I'll Remember April* Bars 33-39

This approach is, in general, the way Parker worked most of his ideas into the string format. One wonders why. Did Parker want a more saleable sound? Was Granz suggesting that Bird "take it easy" on the improvising? Or was Bird's impressionable mind bowled over by the "legitimacy" of the format? It is also possible that Parker simply played this way because it felt right and sounded good to him. Another consideration that one must look into is the arrangements; the key changes would make concentration a very necessary element, and it is possible that Parker became a bit enmeshed in the technical aspects and therefore let creativity slide a bit in favor of perfection. Whatever the reason, the tunes make pleasant, if unexciting, listening.

Recording—Circa 1950—New York City
Parker (as), Bernie Leighton (p), Ray Brown (b), Buddy Rich (d)

I Can't Get Started   S.C.A.M. (Eng.) JPG 1

This tune was probably done sometime near the July 5th string session, for the rhythm section is the same on both recordings. There is marvelous Parker, and in bars 3 and 4 of the "A" section, Leighton uses a lovely progression that was originally devised by Lennie Tristano: Key of C:/Bm7 to 6 Bbm7 to 6/Am7 to 6 Abm7 to 6/(with bass notes, the progression can be considered Bm7-E7, etc.— the cycle of fifths). The inner voices of the progression (7 to 6) have the effect of "chain suspension", and Parker plays beautifully on top of them.

Leighton has a pleasant, tasty introduction over Brown's punctuating bass, and then Parker plays a theme statement and an improvised chorus; in the solo, there is a hint at *Moose The Mooche* at the end of the second eight. Leighton sounds like a cross between Erroll Garner and Teddy Wilson in his half-chorus and is sometimes listed as one or the other on various issues of this tune. Bird takes the tune out from the bridge.

The rhythm section sounds excellent on this tune and the recording is good for a "live" session. It is one of those recordings in which one finds new delights with each playing.

Recording—C. Summer 1950—New York City
Unknown Latin Band—Trumpets, Saxes, Latin Percussion, Piano, Bass, Drums, Parker (as)

Bongo Ballad   Jazz Showcase 5003

Bird's Mambo   Jazz Showcase 5003

The titles are obviously reversed on the record label for the first tune is a fast mambo, and the second a slow Latin tune. On bootleg labels, however, the more logical titles of *Mambo Fortunado* for the fast offering, and *Lament For The Congo* for the slower one, have appeared. The band *could* be Luis del Campo. He was hiring some jazz musicians, including Red Rodney, during this period (note review of balladic tune below). However, there is really too little information to be positive.

The fast mambo is based on the common Latin device of two repeated chords (F-Eb) a whole-step apart, much like the late-Fifties semi-rock standard, *Tequila*. Bird comes in after the band statement and a piano improvisation, and plays very well, not sounding out of place at all; the underpinnings are bothersome to the listener, however. Here one hears the quality of playing over the chords (horizontally) and not up and down them. In other words, Parker does not let the simple repeated pattern regulate his thoughts; he constructs a line which moves with them, but not necessarily *within* them.

The balladic tune has the chord pattern of /Cm/Bb/Ab/G7/with the root notes serving as unison melodic material. There is again a piano solo, and a trumpet improvisation that sounds as if it is a "bebopper" sitting in. In contrast to Bird, however, the trumpeter's self-conscious "bop licks" and "outside" playing make him sound out of place at times. Parker's solo again is perfectly placed within the style without sacrificing any individuality.

* * *

The engagement at Birdland with the string group was not accepted too readily by the trade reviewers; an August issue of *Down Beat* said, "Bird has allowed his playing to degenerate into a tasteless, raucous hullabaloo." When one considers the cautiousness of the string recordings, however, it is difficult to imagine Bird being "tasteless and raucous," although certainly *anything* was possible with Bird.

Indeed, Parker had placed much hope on the string venture as a mark toward success, and his shaky ego did not withstand the criticisms very well. Here again we have the case of Bird trying to live up to society's definition of success and then being condemned as a whore by the hip community. Is it any wonder—not even considering his blackness—that escape mechanisms were necessary?

Furthermore, the marital relationship between Doris and Charlie had been strained for some time. Bird had been seeing Chan Richardson on a regular basis and finally, during July, he ended his alliance with Doris and moved in with Chan on a common-law basis.

The Quintet, with Rodney healthy and back in the groove, left the city for a 2½-week tour of the South during mid-summer. Rodney masqueraded as a Black (Parker referred to him as Albino Red) and Kenny Drew is believed to have replaced Haig because of the touchy racial situation. The tour basically consisted of two-night engagements in major southern cities and often included two separate concert-dances, a black and a white. The pace and the strained relations made the tour grueling, and Parker vowed never to go south again; the terrible living accommodations and racial barriers had rallied the hate in his bones. The money, however, was good, and Bird returned to the city with some "real gold."

In late August, the string group worked the Apollo Theatre, sharing the bill with the Stan Getz big band. One tune, a *new* arrangement of *Easy To Love* (see the next recording) is preserved (Columbia JC34832) from this concert. This booking was one of Teddy Blume's first experiences as the complete manager of Bird's activities, and he was immediately initiated to the confusion. Bird slept as Blume tried to pay the men backstage after Blume locked himself inside a dressing room to restore order, the men constantly rapped on the door, demanding their "bread." Blume almost gave up in disgust, but after he opened the door and threw the money on the floor, the men came to their senses and allowed him to finish his business calculations.

The string group's September activities included bookings at the Club Harlem in Philadelphia, a midnight concert at Carnegie Hall, and two weeks at the Blue Note in Chicago. Parker also participated in a JATP film during this month which included a performance of *Body and Soul*. Also in the film were Harry Edison, Coleman Hawkins, Ella Fitzgerald, Flip Phillips, and a standard JATP rhythm section—Hank Jones, Buddy Rich and Ray Brown.

* * *

Recording—September 16, 1950—Carnegie Hall, New York City
Charlie Parker with Strings—Parker (as), Tommy Mace (ab), Wallace McManas (harp), Al Haig (p), Tommy Potter (b), Roy Haynes (dr), Strings.

Repetition	Verve 8001
What Is This Thing Called Love	Verve 8001
April In Paris	Verve 8001
Easy To Love	Verve 8001
Rocker	Verve 8001

Parker does some fine playing on these tunes, a group of selections that is often overlooked because of the limited availability. They were first issued on a Granz LP titled *Midnight Jazz at Carnegie Hall* and reissued on UMV 2562 (Jap. Verve).

Neal Hefti's *Repetition* begins with strings over a beguine rhythm and Parker blows the beginning of the theme over the rhythm section—sans strings. The oboe and strings play the second eight, and Bird finishes the theme; he plays rhythmic phrases with the strings (probably extemporaneous) in the interlude that follows. Violins and percussion alternate breaks, and the ensemble moves to a long interlude as the Hefti band did on the earlier recording. Parker follows with some excellent improvisations before the close.

A short string figure opens *What Is This Thing Called Love*. The exposition chorus is Bird (16), strings (bridge), and oboe (final eight). Parker plays a swinging chorus—really stretching out; he sounds unhampered. The next chorus is an interlude: strings (16) with trilling oboe in the background; piano at the bridge; strings for the final eight. Bird plays a full closing statement using some improvisations with the line and there is an oboe coda. This is the first time that one encounters the string arrangement of this tune on record; therefore it was probably done especially for this date (or for the Apollo theater engagement mentioned earlier).

The *April In Paris* arrangement is the same as the 1949 studio arrangement and is generally done the same way. Parker does not offer any extended improvisations.

Easy To Love, however, is the new arrangement (same as the Apollo Theater performance mentioned before), not the one done in the studio in early July 1950. This probably was due to the slightly different instrumentation (no French horn) used with the touring group. The introduction is oboe over shimmering strings, and Parker plays the first half of the opening chorus. The rhythm begins in a vigorous beguine, but gradually moves to straight rhythm. The oboe begins the second half, and Parker plays the last eight bar section. There is a string interlude, but no modulation, and on the second chorus Parker improvises behind the string melody for the first half. Oboe enters with the strings playing running pizzicato figures underneath, and Bird returns to close the tune. This selection has a good "feel" to it, mostly due to the Jimmy Mundy arrangement.

This version of Gerry Mulligan's *Rocker* is often listed as *I'll Remember April* (it is on the source cited) because Parker starts his improvisation with the beginning phrase from this tune. Probably, when it was listed, the opening theme was thought to be an "arrangement" of *I'll Remember April*. The tune itself consists of a repeated rhythm on single notes being underlined by moving harmony; these figures are approached by running lines. There is a wild modulation to the mediant key at the center of the tune, and the repeated figure is used as a basis for return. The oboe states the opening theme until the middle section where Parker enters. After completing the exposition, Parker plays two choruses of improvisation, but not on the intricate moving chords of the piece; he uses the *I Got Rhythm* form in C instead. This section is done with only the rhythm section and Bird wails; he uses *Reuben and Rachel* in a humorous way at one point. The closing statement is the same as the opening. This tune was recorded by Miles Davis' "Birth of the Cool" group later and the arrangement—done by Mulligan himself—uses a similar improvisational format; the bridge, however, uses a 16-bar section that stays close to the original harmonization. This bridge would cause problems in Bird's only other recording of this tune (see March 1951—Chapter XVII).

Recording—October 1950—New York City
Parker (as), Coleman Hawkins (ts on *Ballade*), Hank Jones (p), Ray Brown (b), Buddy Rich (d).

Celerity	Verve 8002
Ballade	Verve 8002

The first tune is sometimes listed as *Celebrity*, but the real title is obviously the one given above which means quickness of motion; the tune is a fleet improvisation on *I Got Rhythm*. It begins with a Rich drum blast, and then Parker blows like wildfire; the ideas flow clearly and rapidly. Rich has a bombastic 32-bar solo, and Parker takes a full chorus for the close. Rich's "time-feeling" again does not fit with Parker's, but there is a credit to his professionalism contained in this tune. Parker plays a short phrase at the beginning of the final eight bars (Bars 25-26) of the closing chorus, and Rich "picks up" the rhythm perfectly and plays it exactly *with* Bird when the phrase is repeated two bars later as an ending.

Ex. 134—*Celerity*—Closing Phrase

Ballade is improvised by Hawkins and Parker on a familiar set of chords that this writer has never been able to associate with a particular tune (Harold Arlen's *As Long As I Live* is one improbable guess). It most assuredly is based on some tune, however, and some of the musical-minded readers might have some fun with this.

Ex. 135—*Ballade Chord Pattern*

A Section   /F/Em7 A7/D7/D7/G7/Gm7 C7/F/Gm7 C7/
B Section   /F7/Bb/Bbm/F/Dm DmMaj7/Dm7 G7/Gm7/C7/

Hawkins plays beautifully here; he has the opening sixteen and is spurred on by Jones's tasty chording. Bird plays the second half and has some reed trouble plus a hitch at the first chord of the "B" section. He gets going, however, and turns in a soulful statement. Hawkins goes to the bridge and takes it out with more big-toned, breathy blowing.

Hawkins and this rhythm section were on the same midnight concert at Carnegie as the Parker string group (September 16—previous "Recording").

* * *

In reviewing the total recorded output of the period July-October 1950, one concludes that the string pieces are most representative of Parker's work during this time and that from these, the essentials would be the *Out Of Nowhere* from the July 5th "studio" date, the *Easy To Love* from the August 23rd Apollo Theatre concert, and the entire Carnegie Hall concert of September 16th. The small group recording of *I Can't Get Started* certainly must also be included in a list of essentials, however, although it cannot be dated exactly.

CHAPTER XVI

SWEDISH SCHNAPPS
Alone Abroad
(November-December 1950)

Rings put upon his fingers,
A most delicious banquet by his bed,
And brave attendants near him when he wakes,
Would not the beggar then forget himself?
Wm. Shakespeare—The Taming of the Shrew

In late November 1950, Billy Shaw set up a week's tour of Sweden for Parker. Bird was to go as single and would use some of the modern Swedish musicians as accompanists. Shaw also contacted Roy Eldridge, who was in Paris, and persuaded him to share the bill with Bird. As an advertising venture, a Swedish jazz publication called *Estrad*, published by Nils Hellstrom, sponsored the tour. The booking arrangements between Shaw and Hellstrom, however, were done quickly and haphazardly and there was little time for advance publicity. Moreover, some of the bookings were done even after Parker and Eldridge arrived in Sweden.

The concert tour began in the Swedish capital on Monday, November 20, and then crossed to Gothenburg on the west coast. From Wednesday through Friday, however, the itinerary was completely in southern-most Sweden with one jaunt across the Sound to Denmark's capital. After an appearance at the Admiralen Dance Hall in Malmo, Parker did some jamming at the University of Lund and then was on a bill in Copenhagen that featured Eldridge, Rowland Greenberg (a Norwegian trumpeter), and special guest Benny Goodman. The next day the entourage returned to Sweden for a concert at a dance hall in "Folkets Park" in Helsingborg. After the concert, a group of jazz buffs, critics, and musicians gathered in the Park's restaurant for "rapping and jamming."

* * *

Recording—Admiralen Dance Hall, Malmo, Sweden—November 22, 1950
Charlie Parker and his Swedish All-Stars—Parker (as), Rolf Ericson (tp), Gösta Theselius (p), Thore Jederby (b), Jack Noren (d).

Cheers	Spotlite 124/125
Anthropology	Spotlite 124/125

Lover Man   Spotlite 124/125
Cool Blues   Spotlite 124/125

There is a liquidness to Parker's flow of ideas and to his saxophone sound on these four tunes. The better moments offer a wonderful look at the mature Bird—perhaps past his peak as an innovator, but growing as an artist. The way his ideas flow into one another is absolutely incredible (note the section beginning at the bridge of the second improvised chorus on *Cheers*); he seems to be in complete control of himself. Furthermore, he was not on hard drugs at this time (although he drank heavily to relieve his pangs), and perhaps this made a difference in his motor control. There are no jerky, disjointed ideas (which are used with ingenuity in many other recordings) but rather a smooth, cerebral flow. Even in his use of some favorite quotes (for instance, *High Society* in the third improvised chorus of *Anthropology*), he answers them (the quotes) with an "outside" version immediately following the quote itself.

Cheers is harmonized with "straight" *I Got Rhythm* chords; it does not use the altered version (not even on the theme choruses) of the original (1947) recordings (see Chapter VII). Ericson picks up Bird's final phrase of his three-chorus solo and plays a sharp solo of his own. Bird returns before the final theme chorus for another improvised chorus, but his entrance phrase ("In and Out the Window") and the space following give evidence that he was anticipating an exchange of fours.

On *Anthropology* the "fours" *do* come about—beautifully! Parker jumps into the "fours" section a bit early (from the preceding chorus), however, and makes everyone hold their own. He injects a humorous quote of *Stumbling* at one point (perhaps reflecting on some of the rhythmic tension of the early entrance) and generally keeps a running duel with Ericson. Theselius's piano touch is much like Billy Taylor's and this track contains an excellent example (preceding the fours) of his fluid drive.

The *Lover Man* is a simple 1½ chorus (all Bird) version—more "up" and driving than Parker's other renditions, although nothing really tremendous happens. In fact, it sometimes seems as if Bird is being a bit flippant—perhaps trying to forget the painful version of 1946. The tune is well played however.

The "fours" again are the prime interest on *Cool Blues*, which contains no Bird solo and opens in mid-trumpet-solo. Here again, Bird and Ericson answer, jibe, mock, and humour each other in a beautiful "fun" joust. This type of "ping pong" exchange between the two horn-men would continue throughout the tour.

The Spotlite issue listed above contains all the tunes taped on the Swedish tour and is the best issue to have for complete coverage.

Recording—November 24, 1950—Helsingborg, Sweden
Charlie Parker and the Swedish All-Stars—Parker (as), Rolf Ericson (tp), Gösta Theselius (p), Thore Jederby (b), Jack Noren (dr).
Session: Theselius (p-ts), Lennart Nilsson (p), Rowland Greenberg (tpt on Body and Soul), others probably the same as before.

Anthropology   XTRA (Eng.) 1010
Scrapple From The Apple   XTRA (Eng.) 1010

Embraceable You	XTRA (Eng.) 1010
Cool Blues	XTRA (Eng.) 1010
Star Eyes	XTRA (Eng.) 1010
All The Things You Are	XTRA (Eng.) 1010
Body and Soul (Session)	XTRA (Eng.) 1010
Fine and Dandy (Session)	XTRA (Eng.) 1010
Strike Up The Band (Session)	XTRA (Eng.) 1010
How High The Moon (Session)	XTRA (Eng.) 1010

The praise which Bird later lavished on the Swedish musicians was merited, according to this recording—at least by Ericson, the trumpeter. Ericson, in many ways, sounds like a combination of all of Parker's trumpeters: he has the virility of Gillespie; the linear ideas of Davis; the "funkiness" of Dorham; and the brash confidence of Rodney. He uses all of these traits in an original fashion and is a joy to hear. The exchanges between him and Bird on *Anthropology, Scrapple, Cool Blues,* and *Fine and Dandy* are real "fun" battles of wit; the listener wonders what will happen next. For instance, on *Fine and Dandy,* Bird plays and develops a "Country Gardens" phrase, and Ericson counters in his four bars by beginning with the ending phrase of this cliché. On *Anthropology,* the exchanges seem to run together, at times, in the same line of thought.

There are numerous moments of exciting Bird on these tunes: excellent solos on *Embraceable* and *All The Things You Are;* development of a single phrase by repetition in *Cool Blues;* and intense, inspired playing on *Scrapple.*

During the *Scrapple* exchanges, Bird develops the theme phrase and Ericson answers with an *Ornithology* figure. Indeed, this version of *Scrapple* is completely based on *Honeysuckle Rose* rather than combining the "A" section of this tune with an *I Got Rhythm* bridge as usual. The piano player strikes the first chord of the bridge going to Parker's improvisation during the exposition chorus, and Bird hesitates for a moment—listening—and then dives right into the *Honeysuckle* "B" section. The intro-coda which had become standard on *Scrapple* is not used on this version.

On *Embraceable You,* Parker uses the motif in an off-hand manner at the start of the second half of the exposition chorus and again at the very end. He plays another very inspired chorus containing a bit of *Memories Of You* in the last half (a tribute to Goodman's appearance the day before?). To close, he plays a cadenza, capping it with the *Country Gardens* coda in unison with the trumpet.

The "fours" on *Cool Blues* begin with Bird's phrase (a *Country Gardens* relative) that broke up the crowd on the 1948 "live" version of *Fine and Dandy* (he also begins the fours on *this* version of *Fine and Dandy* with a derivative of the same phrase—see Example 97, Chapter XI). *Cool Blues* also contains the "A-Hunting-We-Will-Go" call during the exchanges.

All The Things You Are begins with Bird only hinting at melody during the exposition chorus and has a fine second chorus by him, with some nice sequential development of a familiar sounding phrase at the bridge. Ericson solos on this ballad (he does not on *Star Eyes, Embraceable You,* or *Body and Soul*) and develops *Country Gardens* at one point. At the bridge of the closing chorus, Bird uses the *Kerry Dancers* quote, and he ends the tune (as usual) with the *Bird Of Paradise* coda.

Star Eyes, although abbreviated, contains two sinewy Bird choruses—a theme statement and an improvisation.

The final four tunes were taped at the post-concert session and, of course, the atmosphere is much looser. *Body and Soul* is double-timed, but on the recording it sounds chaotic because of the inaudibility of the bass and the indiscriminate drumming. Bird interpolates *When The Red, Red Robin* into his *Fine and Dandy* solo and plays the opening bars of *Crazeology* behind the trumpet player during the bridge of *Strike Up The Band*. In the same manner, Parker plays a bit of *Little Willie Leaps* behind Ericson during the final, freely-rendered theme of *Fine and Dandy*.

The "double-time" on *Body and Soul* is of the type mentioned earlier in this work; the melody note-values are twice as long in relation to the fast rhythm (see recording—Detroit—Late December 1947—*Bird Gets The Worm*).

Ex. 136 *Body and Soul*—Double Time

This tune cuts in on the end of the second eight and has a free style ending, with the trumpeter sounding a bit like Eldridge; Bird's solo is wild (a more complete version is available on Spotlite 124/125; it includes some four bar exchanges, a tenor solo by Theselius, and a trumpet solo).

Writers Ira Gitler (*Jazz Masters of the Forties*) and Mark Gardner (Liner Notes—Spotlite LP 124/125) have made mention of a phrase from the Wichita version (1940) of this tune that appears in the Parker solo. This phrase appears as a lead-in to the bridge in both versions and can be viewed in two ways. It is a "connective" phrase—a "throw-away", in other words—not one that is used for creative invention; but the fact that Bird remembered it for ten years after the original use is remarkable (although *all* improvisors have pet phrases on some tunes that help the flow of ideas). More intriguing, perhaps, is Bird's interpolation of *Clair de Lune* behind the trumpet on the closing theme (or at least more humorous).

Strike Up The Band (which could possibly be from the concert—it has a less "echo-y" sound than the other session tunes) is an interesting vehicle for both horns, although it is cut off before the piano chorus. This is Bird's lone version of the Gershwin classic.

Parker begins *How High The Moon* unaccompanied, until the rhythm section joins, and then he plays some extended improvisations; the tune ends with the *Ornithology* theme.

Rowland Greenberg on trumpet and Lennart Nilsson on piano are known to have been at the session, and Theselius—on *Body and Soul*—doubled on tenor sax; Nilsson then moved to the piano. The Eldridge-like trumpet on *Body and Soul* is certainly Greenberg rather than Ericson, but the "concert" group seems to be intact on the other "session" tunes.

* * *

On the Sunday following the end of the tour, Parker decided to take a short holiday in Paris. French jazz critic Charles Delauney was promoting a concert for the following week-end and scheduled Parker for a special guest appearance. Bird, of course, drew an advance and renewed acquaintances made the preceding year at the International Jazz Festival. He was constantly on the go—day and night—jamming, visiting friend's houses, listening to French jazz groups, and drinking all the time. He sat in on radio broadcasts, did promotional interviews at record shops, and attended gala parties. The whirlwind pace soon took its toll on Parker's ulcers, however, and he left Paris suddenly, without notifying Delauney that he would not participate in the concert.

* * *

Recording—Broadcast—ORTF Studios, Paris
Maurice Moufflard Orchestra—Parker (as), 3 trumpets, 3 trombones, 5 saxes (2 soprano; alto; tenor; baritone), piano, bass, drums, several guest Latin percussionists.

Ladybird   Yard (Eng.) CP3

Parker arrived at this broadcast with the Latin percussionists as his guests. The announcer (in French, of course) introduces the tune while the percussionists beat out a persuasive Latin beat beneath the patter. The recording is very badly distorted, but there are some interesting moments. The band, sounding like a "theater orchestra" opens the tune (full band-16; saxes-8; full band-8) and then Bird flies with just the rhythm section and the added percussionists for three full choruses. The band uses a semi-riff half-chorus for the closing statement with a format like the opening (cut in half, of course).

The Latin percussion is distracting to the listener and was, no doubt, one of Bird's fanciful whims. The orchestra is entirely out of context with Parker's playing and the recorded sound further detracts from the performance. Nothing seems to bother Parker. He plays well throughout his solo.

* * *

Back in the States, Leonard Feather persuaded Parker to appear on his internationally-heard radio show, and Delauney, when he learned of the scheduled event, arranged to have the broadcast heard during his concert so that Parker could offer an apology to the audience. Bird childishly apologized and told Feather that he was in Paris for a vacation and did not want the pressure of a concert appearance. He never brought up the subject of Delauney's advance, however, and with this in mind it is very hard to justify his behavior.

During December, Parker was hospitalized with a severe attack of his ulcers and responded well to treatment, although he was again warned to change his life-style or risk death. Liquor, the heroin plague, lack of sleep, artistic frustration, racial tensions, and other less serious pressures had taken their toll on Bird's thirty-year-old body. But change was difficult for a man who had known no other way of life since adolescence; he was on a road of no return.

CHAPTER XVII

AU PRIVAVE
Alone At Home
(1951)

Chaos of thought and passion, all confused;
Still by himself abused and disabused....
Alexander Pope—Essay on Man

After his release from the New York Medical Arts Hospital, Parker found himself
groupless; the rhythm section and Rodney had been forced to look elsewhere for
work. Consequently, pianist Walter Bishop and bassist Teddy Kotick joined Parker
and were fairly regular members of Bird's various groups until his death. The trumpet
spot, however, was a large problem, for many of Parker's gigs were with the large
string group and therefore did not provide steady work for a trumpet player. Benny
Harris, Parker's buddy from the Hines days; and his former trumpet men from
other years, Dorham and Rodney, all filled the spot at various times during 1951
and throughout the period 1952-1955. The usual drummers were also alumni—
Roy Haynes and Max Roach—although later, in the final years, Kenny Clarke
was often the time-keeper.

During 1951, Chan Richardson and Bird lived in the "East Village" section
at 422 East 11th Street, about six blocks from the East River. Later they moved
three blocks closer to the River—to 151 Avenue "B", in the immediate vicinity
of Tomkins Square. As a "family man" Parker had a warm relationship with Chan's
five year old daughter, Kim, and treated her as if she were his own. This is, of
course, the same child whose conception caused the first jealous tiff between Charlie
and Chan in the California period of 1946. Another eruptive relationship, however,
that of Bird and Billie Shaw, finally came to a head, and the two men parted
company for the time being; although within two years they would renew the alliance.

Meanwhile, Norman Granz, who was Bird's only promotional hope after the
break with Shaw, had set a recording date for mid-January and Parker contacted
Miles Davis, who had just returned from the West Coast, to play on the date. Davis
agreed, and on the same day he also recorded his first sides for Prestige (with Sonny
Rollins, John Lewis, Percy Heath, and Roy Haynes).

* * *

Recording—January 17, 1951—New York City
Charlie Parker and His Orchestra—Parker (as), Miles Davis (tp), Walter Bishop (p), Teddy Kotick (b), Max Roach (d).

Au Privave—Take 2	Verve 8010
Au Privave—Take 3	Verve 8010
She Rote—Take 3	Verve 8010
She Rote—Take 5	Verve 8010
K.C. Blues	Verve 8010
Star Eyes	Verve 8010

These tunes are excellent examples of Parker and Davis; Miles shows his growth since 1948 and Parker sounds inspired. The rhythm team is a driving one, and they spur the soloists to greater heights.

Au Privave, however, gives Miles some trouble on theme, but the solos (hear Roach) are enthusiastic and individually creative. The line is very "catchy" melodically, especially in the first four bars and is one of the most engaging of Bird's blues compositions.

Ex. 137 *Au Privave* Opening

There is a "back-beat" introduction and coda to *She Rote* but no other thematic material. The chord base is often referred to as an *Out Of Nowhere* derivative, but in reality it is more like a combination of that tune and *Slow Boat To China* (Nowhere-8[1]; Slow Boat-8[2]; Nowhere-8[3]; Slow Boat-8[4]).

Ex. 138 *She Rote* Chord Pattern

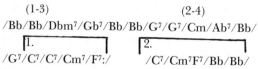

Ex. 139 *She Rote*—Intro and Coda Opening

The liner notes to the Verve issue are enlightening and give the solo format in detail, but the additional takes are only listed as "alternate." One assumes that the other take is the original. Two short phrases may help future identification. On the take listed as "alternate" (probably Take 2) of *Au Privave*, there is an *Ornithology*—derived lick at the beginning of Bird's second chorus, and on *She Rote*, Bird plays an "Over There" phrase on the take not marked "alternate."

K.C. Blues is a "down-home" blues with a single repeated figure (stated alone by Bird) in the first four bars serving as its theme; the rest is pure improvisation. Parker is "gutsy" with Kansas City overtones as suggested by the title, and Miles, although more sophisticated, plays some good blues; funky block chords make up Bishop's offering. Bird is again alone for the out-chorus (alluding to the *Bluebird* riff done in December 1947).

Ex. 140 *K.C. Blues* Opening Phrase

Bishop is very masculine, thoughtful, and forceful until the final offering, *Star Eyes*, where he seems "hung-up" on his solo and inadequate in his comping for Davis. Bishop stated in the Reisner book:

> Sometimes we got to a record session without any rehearsal. Bird would have some little bits of marks on scraps of paper. "Here, Miles, this is how it goes." We did a number, *Star Eyes*. I didn't know how the tune went, but Bird knew I had big ears. He just ran it down once or twice and I got it.[1]

It is quite possible that this session is the one to which Bishop had reference since he and Davis were not with Bird at any other recording date. If this is so, Bishop's performance is certainly creditable.

All the same, *Star Eyes*, because of the pianist's problems is the least successful cut. Miles, however, probably due to Bishop's chords, is also unsure of himself on the ballad solo; moreover, he doesn't play the theme choruses, although he adds an attractive muted line to the Latin intro and coda. But in truth, some of the "happenings" (Miles on intro, Bird on theme—Bird improvising the opening and closing of *K.C.*) tend to add variety when the session is viewed as a whole. Regardless of its haphazard nature, therefore, the date must be considered essential Bird. The session was engineered well and the overall sound of the group is fine.

* * *

On his occasional small-group jobs around the city during the winter, Parker sometimes substituted guitar for trumpet in the Quintet's instrumentation. His most frequent work, however, was done with the string group, which appeared at the Paradise Theater in Detroit during the first week in March and was booked into Birdland for the end of the month. During the engagement at Birdland, Parker appeared on a Saturday evening broadcast that featured an all-star group including Gillespie and Powell. His only "studio" recording of the period is a group of Latin-based tunes with only the alto as a front line and Latin percussion added to the rhythm section.

* * *

Recording—March 12, 1951, New York City
Charlie Parker Jazzers—Parker (as), Walter Bishop (p), Teddy Kotick (b), Roy Haynes (dr), Jose Maguel (bgo), Luis Miranda (cga).

My Little Suede Shoes	Verve 8008
Poquito de tu Amor	Verve 8008
Tico Tico	Verve 8008
Fiesta	Verve 8008
Why Do I Love You—Take 2	Verve 8008
Why Do I Love You—Take 6	Verve 8008
Why Do I Love You—Take 7 (orig.?)	Verve 8008

These tunes contain some typical Parker harmonic frames, although they may not be obvious at first hearing. *Poquito* and *Fiesta*, for instance, both have the *Honeysuckle Rose* bridge; it is a bit more harmonically sophisticated than usual, but it definitely has the same basic chordal roots. Moreover, *Poquito's* "A" section is based on ii^7-V^7-I progression as is the whole tune of *My Little Suede Shoes*.

Ex. 141 *My Little Suede Shoes* Opening Figure

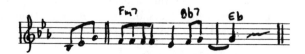

All the tunes except *Why Do I Love You* begin with a Latin percussion introduction and the format is generally: Bird—theme chorus, then blowing chorus; Bishop and Latin percussion—improvisations; Bird—close. All of the tunes fade out over Latin percussion except *Fiesta*.

On *Poquito* the percussion follows Bird's improvisation with a half-chorus; Bishop takes the bridge, and Bird closes. *Suede Shoes*, however, gives Bishop three-quarters of a chorus before the alto closes. *Tico Tico*, probably because of the unadaptability of the fast Latin tempo to piano solo work, contains no Bishop solo. Instead, it has a full chorus of percussion followed by more Parker improvisation (full chorus) before the recapitulation.

The opening of *Fiesta* is based on a chromatic chord progression and the melody is a haunting one.

Ex. 142a *Fiesta* Opening Figure

The bridge of the exposition chorus is taken at a "straight four" tempo (contrasting with the Latin tempo) as are Bird's (full chorus) and Bishop's (half chorus) solos. The Latin tempo returns, however, during the percussion feature at the bridge, preceding Parker's closing eight. Bishop strikes a single, pianissimo Ab-augmented triad for an ending.

It is impossible to tell which "take" of *Why Do I Love You* is 2, 6, or 7. A reasonable assumption is that the one not marked "alternate" is the original (probably Take 7), but the others would be pure guesses. On all, Bishop has a full chorus after Parker; then the percussion takes a half chorus before the close. The take not marked alternate begins with a Bishop intro over only a cymbal beat, but the other two takes have the bass playing time underneath. Further, on this supposed original take, the blowing is all done over the Latin rhythm. One of the "alternates", however, has rhythmic confusion at the start of Parker's improvisation. The rhythm does not seem to know whether they should stay Latin or go to "straight four." After a few bars, however, Kotick finally settles on a "straight four" and all goes well. The other "alternate" has a clean entrance into the "straight four" and two hints at the *Embraceable You* motif in Bird's improvised chorus (the motif is only used for phrase endings, but the usage is poetic; for the listener tends to remember the first reference at the moment of the second—rhythm-like).

Although not among Parker's best, the date certainly has its rewarding moments. Parker's improvisations are sharp, especially on *Tico Tico* and *Fiesta*, and his charmingly simple *Little Suede Shoes* is so "catchy" that it later became a "musicians standard." Moreover, the "straight four" sections on *Why Do I Love You* also have a good feel, and Bishop's strong, Bud Powell-type piano is pleasureable to hear.

Recording—March 1951—Rockland Palace, New York City
Charlie Parker Quintet—Parker (as), Walter Bishop (p), prob. Mundell Lowe (g), Teddy Kotick (b), prob. Roy Haynes (dr).

The Sly Mongoose	Charlie Parker 401
Moose the Mooche	Charlie Parker 401
Star Eyes	Charlie Parker 401
This Time The Dream's On Me	Charlie Parker 401
Cool Blues	Charlie Parker 401
Little Suede Shoes	Charlie Parker 401
Lester Leaps In	Charlie Parker 401

The Sly Mongoose is a simple Latin riff, repetitious but fun to hear; it has the form of ABAB for the purpose of improvisation. The "A" section has two four-bar phrases based on the harmony /I/I/V/I/ and sounds like a verse, whereas the "B" section has two /I/V/V/I/ phrases and sounds like a chorus. Bird plays the calypso-like melody and stops to chat with someone as Bishop plays a 64-bar solo—half block-chordal and half single line. Parker returns—one can hear his friend say "Take care of yourself"—and plays 64-bars, interspersing the melody with improvisation. The tune fades out with rhythm.

   Moose is a fine version; Parker begins with *Humoresque* and literally flies through four choruses, but after the guitar plays two nice choruses, the take suddenly stops.

   The Latin intro used on the January 17th version of *Star Eyes* is used on this version also, with Bird joining the rhythm section on the figure. Parker plays the theme and a blowing chorus, with Bishop comping very well (he must have "woodsheded" the tune since the first try of January 17). The guitar player begins, but then the take "cuts" to Bird at the final bridge.

   The bridge progression to *This Time The Dream's On Me* is just another sophisticated version of the *I Got Rhythm* bridge, and the "A" section is also a common pattern. Bishop's substitutes, however, are very tasty, especially during his own solo.

Ex. 142b This Time The Dreams On Me Substitutes—"A" Section

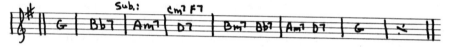

   The tune cuts in on the end of the second eight of the exposition chorus, and alto, guitar, and piano all have extremely exciting solos. Bishop develops the theme in an unusual manner and plays very strong ideas. Bird, however, is wailing like a wild auk; he sends ideas flying crazily, both on his solo and in a set of two-chorus exchanges with Haynes (in the solo, the *Embraceable You* motif appears as phrase-ending material again). The recapitulation chorus has Bird improvising the bridge.

   Cool Blues cuts in at the last four bars of the theme and tends to confuse the listener because Parker carries the theme phrase over to the next chorus as part of his improvisation. The chords used for improvisation on the first four bars of the blues form are the same as the chords to the beginning of Bird's *Confirmation* (/I/vii⁷III⁷/vi⁷II⁷/v⁷ I⁷/), and this same progression was used in two of Parker's later blues compositions. Another substitution (see *Ex. 126—Bloomdido—*June 6, 1950) occurs at bar eight of the blues. Parker is inspired and plays excellently, and Bishop and the guitarist cooperate with some nice interplay at the start of the guitar chorus. The take cuts off after the guitar.

   The *Little Suede Shoes* cut is very confusing because of the similarity of the "A" and "B" sections and also because of Bishop's substitute chords, which are also similar in both sections during the improvisations. The tune *seems* to cut in at the end of the first eight-bar section and Parker plays the melody until the bridge—from there on he improvises. He and Bishop, however, are not always in agreement on the substitute chords (again of the "half-step" variety) and when Parker ends there is an eight-bar section left in the tune (if the writer's diagnosis of the starting point is correct). The guitarist waits as Bishop comps out the section, but Parker seems to re-enter too early—thinking of the "comping" section as part of the guitar solo. Realistically, none of this makes much difference since the harmony on both sections is so similar that it is like improvising on a single section; but the format is confusing to the listener who listens to form as a whole.

Lester Leaps In is an exciting, lightning-fast flight through the *Rhythm* chords; it generates energy and emotion as it rolls along, and the crowd is caught up in the excitement. Parker at one point develops the melody in sequence in an unrelated key with good effect, and his relentless drive bowls over the listener. This is a very worthwhile cut. The crowd noise on these tracks is bad and the sound is poor, but most of the important things are audible—one can hear the rhythm section readily—and the excitement is worth the low fidelity.

Recording—March (?), 1951—Birdland (?), New York City
Charlie Parker with Strings—Parker (as), W. Bishop (p), Strings, Oboe, Harp, prob. Kotick (b), prob. Haynes (d).

Laura	Charlie Parker 401
Rocker	Charlie Parker 401

The arrangement on *Laura* is the same as the July, 1950 studio date, but the horn is absent. Parker himself fills the void; on the intro, for instance, he plays the phrases originally scored for the horn, and he also plays a full exposition chorus instead of being spelled by the horn. There is very little improvisation, except as embellishment.

Rocker can cause confusion to the listener because of the poor sound quality and a series of spur-of-the-moment occurrences. First of all, the strings are almost inaudible, but the piano can be heard very well. This leads the listener to think it is a quartet date until close listening reveals that Bird is doubling the melody with the oboe (this is the same arrangement as September 16, 1950) on the theme statement. Moreover, Bishop, who is obviously playing the arrangement for the first time, uses a chord frame in the improvisational section that relates to Mulligan's original arrangement for Miles Davis's group; this was AABA, but with an important difference. The "B" section was sixteen bars instead of eight. Parker, however, was accustomed to playing the improvised section over the 32-bar *I Got Rhythm* chord frame (see September 15, 1950—Chapter XV), and although he realized that some minor adjustments must be made—the "A" section is only slightly different from the "Rhythm" form and the bridge begins in the mediant key area instead of going through the standard cycle of fifths (beginning with the III7)—he does not reckon on a sixteen bar bridge. Furthermore, the second half of the bridge section that Bishop is using contains chords that lead back to the tonic and, therefore, fit passably with Parker's "A" section ideas. Consequently, it is well into the second improvised chorus that Parker discovers the clash. To further complicate things, a guitarist arrives during the beginning of Bird's second chorus (just before he discovers the clash) and is ready to "sit-in" at the beginning of the second eight (a chord is heard). The clash is discovered in the third eight of the second chorus—Bird attempts to enter "B" while Bishop remains on "A"—and Parker's solution—a stroke of genius—should be a lesson to all musicians as well as a source of humor. He quickly plays crazy, anything-goes phrases to "blur" the tonality and moves back to the tonic; then, when he realizes Bishop has entered another clashing section, he repeats the "blurring" procedure. In the third chorus, he finally rights things by implying the "Honeysuckle Rose" bridge at the "B" section and outlining the next to last chord with one of his favorite figures (see Analysis Section—Approach to II7 Chord). Bishop, however, also must be credited for his "ear" musicianship, as he immediately catches the hint and plays softly—while listening—through the next chorus; in improvised chorus 5, however, Bishop is right on the chords and loudly states the "Honeysuckle" chords during the "B" section; he also uses that bridge during his subsequent solo. The following chart shows the relationship between Bird's concept of the improvisational frame and the one actually played by Bishop:

	PARKER	BISHOP
CHORUS 1	A	A
	A	A
	B	B
	A	B cont.
CHORUS 2	A	A
	A	A CHORUS 2-guitarist arrives
Parker blur	B clash	A
Parker blur	A clash	B
CHORUS 3	A semi-clash	B cont.
	A	A
"Honeysuckle"	B	A-B SWITCH
	A	A
	CHORUS 4-Bishop plays softly-listens.	

CHORUS 5-Together-Bishop states Honeysuckle chords loudly at "B"

Bird's first improvised chorus has an interesting development of one phrase through the first twenty-four bars; it implies a different tonality in each 8-bar section—first the tonic and then upward in minor thirds.

Ex. 143 *Rocker* Development Phrase—First Eight

Ex. 144 *Rocker* Development Phrases—Second and Third Eights

The figure notated below begins Parker's second improvised chorus, and he also begins the fourth solo chorus with the same phrase (probably to assure that everyone is together).

Ex. 145 *Rocker* Opening of Second Improvised Chorus

The recorded sound on these tracks is horrendous, but *Rocker* is interesting because of the amusing on-the-job incident and Parker's method of solving the problem. Moreover, although sometimes listed as part of the following "recording," these tunes seem entirely different in recorded sound and also in Parker's concept. *Laura*, for instance, contains a "scream" phrase leading to the final eight here, but has a staccato phrase in the same place on the next version.

Recording—March 24, 1951—Birdland, New York City
Parker (as), Strings, Oboe, Harp, Rhythm (Bishop, Kotick, Haynes).

Jumping With Symphony Sid (Theme-Parker and Rhythm)	Columbia JC34832
Just Friends	Columbia JC34832
Everything Happens To Me	Columbia JC34832
East Of The Sun	Columbia JC34832
Laura	Columbia JC34832
Dancing In The Dark	Columbia JC34832
Jumpin With Symphony Sid (Theme)	Columbia JC34832

Just Friends and *Everything Happens To Me* are arrangements from the original string date (November 1949), and although Bird treats the latter much the same as before, he turns in an interesting performance on *Friends*. His opening improvised figure from the "studio" version is used merely as a jumping off point into different interpolations. In other words, it almost seems as if the new improvisations are related more to the original solo than to the theme! Judging from the evidence presented by various "takes" on other tunes, this would seem to be a logical conclusion. His mind merely concocted variations upon former variations, forming a "building" effect.

The other three string pieces are arrangements originally recorded in July, 1950. A French horn was used on the original recordings and at times there are obvious "holes" in these "live" versions (the worst being the second half of the exposition chorus to *East Of The Sun*, which was originally a horn solo). Bird and the oboe player manage to fill most of the other spaces nicely, however, and it probably was an oversight (Bird forgetting who had the solo) that made that particular spot so glaring. *East Of The Sun*, however, has good Parker improvisation with some humorous quotes (*Kerry Dancers, National Emblem March*), and *Dancing In The Dark* is funkier than the "studio" version; but, *Laura*, as usual, is a straight, lyrical performance. Interestingly, the ending of *Dancing In The Dark* contains a Parker figure with the "flatted fifth" resolving upward. He was using this at various string performances of the period (see also *Easy To Love*-April 7, 1951).

The "Themes" are merely accompaniment to symphony Sid's patter for the opening and closing of his radio show, although Bird's use of a "cornball" ending on the final "Theme" (do-re-mi-re/mi-do) is a "fun" way to end the set.

Recording—March 31, 1951—Birdland, New York City
Dizzy Gillespie Band—Parker (as), Gillespie (tp), Bud Powell (p), Tommy Potter (b), Max Roach (dr).

Blue 'n' Boogie	Saga (Eng) 8035, Columbia 34831
Anthropology	Saga (Eng) 8035
'Round Midnight	Saga (Eng) 8035
A Night In Tunisa	Saga (Eng) 8035
Jumpin' With Symphony Sid (Theme)	Sage (Eng) 8035

This all-star group was featured on Symphony Sid's Saturday night broadcast and the complete radio shot—conversation, friendly jibing, and all—is contained on the English issue. Torin mentions the "one-dollar admission charge" in his come-on patter for the club and also alludes to the rivalry between Bird and Diz: "...I don't know who's getting top billing; so Dizzy Gillespie, Charlie Parker—Charlie Parker, Dizzy Gillespie...."

The *Blue and Boogie* format is identical with the one described in the "recording" at the Finale Club in Los Angeles during 1946. All five riffs are used in the same order and one can surmise that this tune, as well as the rest of the material on this date, was part of the regular "book" of 1945-46 Gillespie Quintet. Parker quotes *I Dream Of Jeanie* and *Ladybird* in his solo spot and Gillespie uses *A-Hunting We Will Go*. Powell, asserting his own ego against the other two giants, plays a phrase from Thelonious Monk's *In Walked Bud* during his lengthy excursion.

Parker's quotes on *Anthropology* tell a little story in themselves. They are, in succession: *Honey, Tenderly, High Society,* and *Temptation!* One can only guess that someone in the audience had made a strong impression upon him. The execution of the line is clean, although the fast tempo sometimes give one the impression of glibness. Following the solo choruses, there are two choruses of "fours" (Bird-drums-Diz-drums) which add to the excitement. Haynes plays a "Salt Peanuts" lick in one of the exchanges.

Gillespie plays the introduction to *'Round Midnight* as Parker backs him. Next, Parker plays the "theme" until the bridge and then backs Diz once again; the final eight goes to Powell (possibly the best solo on this tune). Bird has the melody on the coda, with Gillespie backing, and the familiar ending figure is performed in harmony. Powell's off-beat humor can be heard in his "oom-pah" double time under Parker's second eight bars.

The infectious, off-beat background riff that Parker used on the 1948 Royal Roost version of *Night In Tunisa* is the one employed here, rather than the original backing figure. Also identical with the earlier live version are the eight-bar bass section and the second interlude that follow Parker's improvisations and lead to the trumpet break. Bird and Diz both use a familiar figure (Ex. 18) in their solos, and Powell's 1½ chorus excursion is full of surprises, including a long pause during the second eight. Bird follows Powell at the bridge, and Gillespie takes the tune out with a cadenza following the final eight.

Jumpin' With Symphony Sid is the usual sign-off theme under Torin's "hip" conversation.

This date is possibly the best recorded of all the Parker "live" performances, although there are, at times, some level changes.

Recording—April 7, 1951—Birdland, New York City
Parker (as), Strings, Oboe, Harp, Rhythm (Bishop, Kotick, Haynes).

What Is This Thing Called Love	Columbia JC34832
Laura	Columbia JC34832
Repetition	Columbia JC34832
They Can't Take That Away From Me	Columbia JC34832
Easy To Love	Columbia JC34832

Laura is once again pretty, but lacking in improvisation; indeed the only distinguishing factor is a quick turn of the "Cool Blues" phrase which can act as an easy identifier of the "take" (this take is found on many "bootleg" LP's). *They Can't Take That Away* (also originally from July 1950), however, has an exciting feel with Bird answering the oboist several times.

The other three pieces were arranged for the string group in the late summer of 1950 in preparation for concerts at the Apollo Theater and Carnegie Hall. Ironically, although these arrangements have the best jazz feel of all the string writing and give Parker plenty of room to "stretch out" (which he did), they were never featured in a studio session!

Some features on this session, however, other than Parker's stellar improvisations are: his conversation with Symphony Sid; the *Barnacle Bill* quote in *What Is This Thing*; and the flatted fifth ending (see *Dancing In The Dark*, March 24, 1951) on *Easy To Love*.

* * *

The string group opened at the Apollo Theater during the first week in April for a two-week stay, and Bird was also on a Symphony Sid concert presentation in Uline's Arena in Washington, D.C. The Washington bill also included June Christy and Johnny Hodges. At the end of the month, Parker took some single quintet engagements in New England.

Indeed, Christy's Restaurant, outside of Boston, was famed as a "session place" and when Parker worked there, as he did during April, the prospective "jammers" came in droves. The restaurant was located twenty miles west of the city in a small town called Framingham on Route 9. Howard McGhee recalled: "It overlooked a lake, and Bird played his most relaxed horn in a separate little wing, while the rest of the band was in the next room."[2]

* * *

Recording—April 1951—Christy's Restaurant, Framingham, Mass.
Charlie Parker Quintet—Parker (as), prob. Benny Harris (tpt), Teddy Kotick (b), prob. Roy Haynes (d), Walter Bishop (p), Plus "sitters-in": Wardell Gray (ts), Charles Mingus (b), Dick Twardizik (p).

Happy Bird Blues	Charlie Parker 404
Scrapple From The Apple	Charlie Parker 404

I'll Remember April	Charlie Parker 404
Lullaby In Rhythm	Charlie Parker 404

A session atmosphere prevails and the music is punctuated with many shouts of "Go!" Gray sits in on all the tunes except the blues (he may have been present on this tune at the session, but since the recording only presents Parker's solo it is impossible to tell). The other men (including the trumpeter) only play on *I'll Remember April.*

Bird does sound happy on the blues, and he plays quotes from *Cross My Heart* and *Star Eyes* along with some favorite blues phrases (Ex. 27). The solo is pleasant, but certainly not his most creative, and the take fades out after the solo.

I'll Remember April has free rendering of the theme; the trumpet begins with the melody, but Bird jumps in at one point and then goes back to background. The Parker solo is fair; and the piano, although difficult to hear, sounds rather ultra-modern. Mingus plays a wonderful bass solo in which he quotes *All God's Children Got Rhythm* and the "You and Me We Sweat and Strain" phrase from *Old Man River*; this solo is the highlight of the tune. The recapitulation chorus is again very free, with Bird in the middle and a Latin treatment of the final eight. Parker plays a Latin background riff during this final section.

On the Charlie Parker issue, *Lullaby In Rhythm* is erroneously titled *I May Be Wrong.* After the free, relaxed theme Gray blows some extended improvisations which include several quotes of *Louise*; Bird follows with a solo spot—rather mediocre for him; and Gray returns with more blowing. Gray sneaks into the theme, and soon Bird joins him for another free "out-chorus."

Scrapple must have been done late at night for both Parker and Gray sound as if they are "out of it;" the performance is not a credit to either man. The opening theme is extremely unorganized, with Bird dropping out at various times, and the intonation of both horns is very bad. Gray becomes hesitant in the middle of his solo and Bird's intonation remains poor throughout his. The Parker solo contains an out-of-key rendition of the theme; a *Buttons and Bows* phrase; and a development of the *Au Privave* opening figure; but Bird is very repetitious and sounds as if his embouchure is loose. The excellent piano solo does not sound like Bishop, but comes across well on the record; whereas the two-chorus "walked" bass solo (also well done) that follows is very poorly recorded. There are four-bar exchanges between the horns and drums (tenor-drums-alto-drums) before the final chorus in which Bird has the bridge. On the final line, Parker sometimes stops and bleats behind Gray.

Although the atmosphere makes the recording exciting, it is really a poor example of Parker's playing.

* * *

In May, Parker took the string group to Lindsay's in Cleveland for a week and worked in Philadelphia later in the month with the Quintet. On the Philadelphia gig, Bird and Benny Harris, who had recently become his regular trumpet player, had a hassle and Parker suddenly fired Harris and hired Clifford Brown, the young trumpeter who would become the definitive brass voice of the decade. Harris describes the incident:

He had come in two hours late....I had let some guys sit in and there was one on the stand who played awful. "Go up and get him off...." Bird said to me. And I answered, "Being you are the leader, you go up there and get him off...." Well then he said, "You are through:"—two months later I was back again, playing with the group.[3]

Parker's 1950 tour of Sweden had set a trend; Stan Getz visited the Scandanavian country during the spring of 1951 and made a group of memorable recordings with Swedish musicians. The American jazz press also began to pay attention to important Swedes such as Bengt Hallberg, pianist on the Getz recordings; Lars Gullin, baritone saxist; and Rolf Ericson, the trumpeter. In mid-June, after returning from Sweden, Getz, with a rhythm section was on the same bill at Birdland that featured Parker as a guest with Machito's big band. Slim Gaillard, doing a comedic single, was an added attraction.

The Quintet (probably with Benny Harris) worked St. Louis in July and Bird guested with the Woody Herman Herd in that city and his home town. While Bird was on the road, a daughter, Pree, was born to Chan and him on July 17.

After arriving back in New York, Parker contacted Red Rodney, who was working in the Catskills, for a forthcoming August record date. Also slated for the date were Kenny Clarke, who had recently returned from Europe, and John Lewis. (If the "plane incident"—see notes Chapter XIV—took place during Bird's Midwest jaunt of this year, Rodney would have had to have rejoined Bird's group a few weeks earlier.) Parker closed the summer with a "string" engagement at Lindsay's in Cleveland during late August.

* * *

Recording—July 1951—St. Louis
Parker "sitting-in" with Woody Herman's Band

You Go To My Head	Main Man 617
Leo The Lion	Main Man 617
Cubop Holiday	Main Man 617
Nearness Of You	Main Man 617
Lemon Drop	Main Man 617
The Goof and I (listed as Sonny Speaks)	Main Man 617
Laura	Main Man 617
Four Brothers	Main Man 617

This "live" performance is recorded poorly, but it is, to say the least, interesting. On the ballads, Bird stays close to the melody although he does stretch out and play a moving solo on *You Go To My Head*. *Nearness Of You*, however, has a modulation to a higher key, and Parker plays in both keys. One wonders whether these ballads were originally vocals or solo vehicles for Herman since the backing seems to fit with a solo instrument.

Leo The Lion is a blues with fine sax section work and a good tenor solo (probably Bill Perkins). Bird plays several wailing blues choruses, at one point interpolating the *Cool Blues* lick. This is probably the most musically satisfying tune in the set.

On *Cubop Holiday*, a Latin-tinged excursion on the *Honeysuckle Rose* base, however, the band and Bird have difficulty getting together on the improvised section, probably because of trying to adapt the arrangement (on the spur of the moment) to feature Parker. A riff sets up the solo opening (after the exposition chorus) and Bird enters, as intended, in the latter half of the "A" section. The brass background accents seem to be with him, but in the middle of the second "A" section, the saxes enter with a background chord that suggests the opening bridge harmony and then quickly drop out. Bird continues through the chorus and at the very end plays a phrase that implies harmony which would lead to the bridge; the saxes, however, begin the "A" section with a background riff of the theme, and Parker quickly changes. Then someone (probably Herman) screams "Bridge!" and the next section is together. The following "A" section contains a brass riff based on the theme and Parker picks it up and blows it with them, but then the brass play a figure that harmonically implies the bridge but which only lasts four bars (!). The trombones then surprise Bird with the entrance (early?) of the melody. This writer, after many hearings, cannot arrive at reason why the mix-up happened or a logical explanation of how it transpired, but the following graph will allow a listener to follow the piece:

4 riff	A	4 Bird
saxes middle	A	wrong sounding chord
	B	
at end	A	suggests he is going to bridge
"A" sax figure	A	Bird changes
	B	someone hollers
	A	riff
riff	B?	only gets 4 bars
trombones	A	melody (early?)

Lemon Drop, the humorous bop vocal, is an *I Got Rhythm* derivative, and Bird plays a wild solo which includes a quote from *Mean To Me. The Goof and I* also has the chord base of the Gershwin standard, but Parker is a bit cooler on this one. In addition, he has horn problems at one point (what saxophone players call a "wolf D") but otherwise plays well. He also engages in exchanges with the brass and quotes the opening riff to Denzil Best's *Move.*

As Bird approaches the bridge to *Four Brothers*, the Herman sax showpiece, he realizes the harmony changes to distant keys and just stops and listens! He then attempts it on subsequent choruses and on the fifth attempt shows evidence that he has the progression in his mind! This should give some insight into both Parker's character and his musicianship. Bird plays the break that the individual saxes did on the 1947 Herman recording of this tune, and it becomes obvious that he was familiar with the recording.

Some interesting developments in Parker's solos on this side are quotes from *Johnny One Note* and the use of his own motif from *Embraceable You* as phrase-ending material.

A note for collectors: On the LP listed, the outer jacket is listed as *Main Man*, but on the inner label is the title *La Mere*, made in France. The issue is a part of the group generally listed as "Amalgamated Labels."

Recording—August 8, 1951—New York City
Charlie Parker Quintet—Parker (as), Red Rodney (tp), John Lewis (p), Ray Brown (b), Kenny Clarke (d).

Blues For Alice	Verve 8010
Si Si	Verve 8010
Swedish Schnapps—Take 3	Verve 8010
Swedish Schnapps—Take 4	Verve 8010
Back Home Blues—Take 1	Verve 8010
Back Home Blues—Take 2	Verve 8010
Lover Man	Verve 8010

The level of musicianship is extremely high on these recordings, and although they are not as highly-touted as some of Bird's more flamboyant efforts, the overall performance should be ranked as one of Parker's best. The unisons are flawless, solos excellent, and the rhythm section tight. Of interest is Parker's penchant for using a "growl" tone more frequently on this date (hear *Swedish Schnapps*—alternate take) than he had at any time in the past.

Alice, Back Home and *Si Si* are all blues, each possessing a different personality; and *Schnapps* is an *I Got Rhythm* derivative with an improvised bridge.

Ex. 146 *Swedish Schnapps* Opening figure

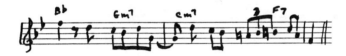

The differences in the three blues stem largely from the harmonic treatment of the first four bars; *Alice,* for instance, employs the chords from Parker's tune *Confirmation* in the first four bars. The germ of this idea can be found on the *Cool Blues* recording from the Rockland Palace in March. It is used there in an extemporaneous fashion. On *Alice,* however, the opening figure has a descending line that indicates the harmony at each strong beat of the first two bars.

Ex. 147 *Blues For Alice* Opening Figure

Ex. 148 *Blues For Alice* Bars 6-8

There is also substitute harmony at measure six (see Ex. 74) and measure eight (see Ex. 126—*Bloomdido*). The tune ends with a short motif which was used in different ways throughout the tune, and is bracketed above in the opening figure (the triplet in the second usage is merely decorative).

Ex. 149 *Blues For Alice* Ending Motif

In *Back Home* a progression is again employed that has the melody outlining the harmony on the first beat of each of the first four bars. The progression is pleasantly "old-fashioned" but this writer cannot recall ever having heard it on the first four bars of the blues.

Ex. 150 *Back Home Blues* Opening Phrase

Ex. 151 *Back Home Blues* Harmonic Implications

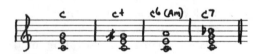

The first take of *Back Home* contains a beautifully constructed Parker blues solo; and *Lover Man* contains no pathos this time, but rather the jealous passion of an enraged lover. Lewis repeats Jimmy Bunn's intro from the infamous 1946 recording of the ballad and plays a lovely solo laced with interplay from Brown. Bird's improvisations on *Lover Man*, however, are reserved mainly for the bridge section of the tune where he bursts forth with double-time passages such as the following:

Ex. 152 *Lover Man* Bar 22 *Alto Key*

The rest is a beautiful reading of the melody, liberally embellished. There is also a fine Parker obligato behind Rodney at the end of the tune, before the "Country Gardens" coda.

Si Si is one of Bird's angular lines. It transfers the *I Got Rhythm* chords to the first four bars of the blues.

Ex. 153 *Si Si* Opening Phrase

On his final improvised chorus on *Si Si*, Bird alludes to the *Confirmation* chords in the first four bars (the sequence used in *Blues For Alice*).

The extra "takes," as on all Verve issues, are listed as "alternates" and some observations may be helpful. (1) On the take not listed as "alternate" on *Back Home*, Rodney begins to *repeat* the theme after the first chorus while Bird moves right into improvisations. This does not sound like a mistake, but rather comes off as a "send-off" for Bird. It is a helpful "identifier," however, (2) Parker's solo on the take of *Swedish Schnapps not* listed as "alternate" begins with the same figure as the original solo on *Moose The Mooche* from 1946 (Take 2).

Ex. 154 *Schnapps* and *Moose The Mooche* Opening 2 Bars

The record label lists Shavers (trumpeter Charlie?) as the composer of *Swedish Schnapps*, but one has only to hear it once to realize it is a Parker original. It is possible that another line had been given the same title and that it was taken for granted that this was the same tune.

Because of the excellence of the recording (due to the rapidly advancing electronic technology during the early 1950s) and the fine musical elements, these tunes must be considered essential Parker for the collector and musician and are perhaps one of the best choices for the casual listener to own.

* * *

After appearing at the Apollo Bar in Harlem at the beginning of September, Parker, along with Rodney, joined a JATP tour that was slated for Germany,

Belgium, Holland, and France. Granz had also scheduled a special Paris concert featuring Bird with a symphony orchestra. Indeed, Parker and Rodney did quite well until they met a legal heroin dealer in Brussells; from then on they missed concerts and rehearsals—even the one for Bird's special feature. Granz finally gave up and sent them home; the rest of the unit, however, continued the tour sans Bird.[4] And so, Parker continued his struggle with the "monkey."

CHAPTER XVIII

NEW SETTINGS
Big Bands and Latin Groups
(January-May 1952)

All things change, nothing perishes.
Ovid-Metamorphoses

The seeds of "West Coast Jazz" were being sown during 1952. This style was based on the "cool" approach pioneered by Miles Davis, but contained a great many individual approaches within the large general designation. Dave Brubeck, a pianist with a classical compositional background, formed a quartet with altoist Paul Desmond that played in a relaxed, free manner and used some classical techniques. Gerry Mulligan and Chet Baker played free contrapuntal lines on baritone sax and trumpet (respectively) and eliminated the piano from the rhythm section; they used only bass and drums. Shorty Rogers had a tightly arranged ensemble with specially designated "blowing spaces" (a "small big band" approach) that featured soloists such as altoist Art Pepper and pianist Hamp Hawes. Indeed, even the Kenton band had a "cooler" sound after Lee Konitz joined during the summer. Records made by these groups would not cause any real furor until the following year when headlines such as "Is there such a thing as West Coast Jazz?" would permeate the trade papers. Viewed today, the style seems merely a lyrical off-shoot of bop with added elements from the mainstream of jazz and some "legitimate" techniques, but during the 1950s it was something to argue about. Strangely enough, Davis, who pioneered in the "cool" direction was in relative obscurity during the early 1950s. He would again emerge as a major voice near the end of the decade.

Elsewhere, Charles Mingus, was forming his own record label, Debut, and readying some experimental recording sessions. Stan Getz did some memorable "mood" recordings with guitarist Johnny Smith and also worked as a studio musician on Kate Smith's afternoon TV show. He and Mingus also worked together at times in small groups.

The changing jazz scene left Parker, Gillespie (who spent part of the year in Paris with a small group), and Bud Powell standing alone as some of the last giants of the "pure" Bop style. Many of the men who had pioneered with them were more mutable, probably because of their less individual styles, and were easily absorbed into the new trend. Others, such as Monk and Tristano, were so individual that they were never really a part of any "school" at any time.

Bird began 1952 with two record dates for Granz: one involving a big band with added strings and harp and the other another "South of the Border" venture with a small group. He also "guested" with Gillespie's all-star group at Birdland for a short period, and he and Diz did a short TV appearance.

* * *

Recording—January 22, 1952—NYC
Charlie Parker and His Orchestra—Chris Griffin, Bernie Privin, Al Porcino (tp), Will Bradley, Bill Harris (tb) Parker, Toots Mondello, Murray Williams (as), Hank Ross, Flip Phillips (ts), Stan Webb (baris), Verley Mills (harp), Lou Stein (p), Art Ryerson (g), Bob Haggart (b), Don Lamond (d), Joe Lippman (arr., cond), strings, woodwinds.

Temptation	Verve 8003
Lover	Verve 8003
Autumn in New York	Verve 8003
Stella by Starlight	Verve 8003

Lover is the only AABA-type of tune in the set; *Temptation* can best be thought of as AABAC and the other two have four different eight-bar sections (the relationships between the sections of the final two "standards" are certainly more complicated, of course, than "four different sections," but they do not merit serious study in this work).

Kenton-like brass opens *Temptation* and then yields to Bartokian strings; the oboe completes the intro over pizzicato strings. Parker plays the theme during the first two sections, being backed by pizzicato strings which are later joined by sustained oboe tones and rumblings from the lower strings. The strings have the "B" section with a trombone obligato behind, and they continue into the next section with brass behind them. At the "C" section the rhythm moves from the beguine tempo to a straight four, and Bird finishes the chorus with some slight embellishments. The saxes have a short modulation from C to Eb. Chorus two uses only one "A" section (ABAC) and that consists of a "swing-style" trumpet solo over the sax section. Parker then re-enters with the brass behind him and plays through to the end. He stays fairly melodic, although he does venture a few scattered improvisations. The beguine tempo returns at the very end, and Parker plays into the final coda which features melodic oboe passages. Flute "tweets" are answered by muted trumpets and the tune fades out with pizzicato strings.

The introduction to *Autumn in New York* begins with the oboe which is then joined by other woodwinds; the strings lead into the tune. Parker plays the first chorus (spelled by one section of string soli) with the rhythm beginning in "two-beat" and moving to four during the second eight; strings and muted brass alternate in the background. There is a modulation from Eb to Db, and the second chorus begins with a trombone solo over woodwinds and continues with cup-muted trumpet over clarinets. Bird immediately moves the tune to the key of F as he enters at the third section, and open brass and he split the final section. The strings lead the tune to a close.

Lover, probably the best track in the set and the only one with extensive Parker improvisations, begins with a "big-band" intro. Bird begins with the theme in the first section and then starts to "blow" with a quote from "Reuben and Rachel." The band is behind him all the way and the brass shouts in at the beginning of the final "A" section. The tune moves from C to Db for a trombone solo over saxes during the first half of the second chorus; an exceptionally clean high-note trumpet solo follows, and Stein's single-line piano completes the chorus. Bird goes back to the lower key and really wails, with strings and brass behind him; he moves to the melody for the final "A" section and improvises into the coda. There is a harp flash and short pause before the brass ending.

The lovely *Stella by Starlight* gets a beautiful reading by Parker even though there is no extensive improvisation. Brass accents and melodic strings begin the tune, and Parker plays the first half over the strings. The brass takes over at the third section with strings and oboe in the background, and Bird re-enters for the last section. There is a modulation from Bb to Eb, and the final section is repeated in the new key with the strings and piano splitting the statement. Bird returns to the second-half of the tune in the original key and plays until the end. There is an allusion to his *Embraceable You* motif at the beginning of the final eight (the chord is functionally the same as the second chord in *Embraceable You*) and some other interlacing of improvisation. It is interesting to hear Parker's reference to the *Embraceable You* figure, as it sounds as if he is quoting himself. This is generally the only way he used the figure other than on the tune itself.

Recording—Early 1952—TV Show C. Parker (as), D. Gillespie (trpt), Dick Hyman (p), Sandy Block (b), Charlie Smith (d).
Hot House   Phoenix LP12

Diz and Bird were the *Down Beat* Poll winners for 1951 on their respective instruments and were presented with their awards on this show (the name of which is not known). There is a mention, however, of Leonard (Feather ?) and Earl (Wilson ?). The rhythm section is probably from the regular band on the show.

There is an unusual treatment of the beginning of the theme in that Diz starts with two bars unaccompanied before the rhythm enters (same effect as *Dizzy Atmosphere*—in feeling). Bird is especially inspired; for the most part, he does not even develop his favorite phrases, but rather looks for new cerebral areas. Diz picks up Bird's ending phrase (in the same manner as the 1945 recording!), however, and blows it back at him. Gillespie continues to chide Parker with the *Habanera* phrase, first low then screamingly high. This is done in the nature of "kidding"— not in animosity. In addition, Hyman has a good solo that is sprinkled with Shearing-like block chords. The drums start the fours and continue in alternation with the horns for three-quarters of chorus before the closing eight bars. The usual two-note ending is omitted on this version and the horns simply sustain a note (the fourth of the scale!!); this gives the effect of hanging in the air.

The recording is lacking in bass, and the balance as a whole is not good, but the solos are excellent.

Charlie Parker Sextet—Recording-January 28, 1952-NYC

Parker (as), Benny Harris (tp), Walter Bishop (p), Teddy Kotick (b), Max Roach
(dr), Ralph Miranda (congo and bongo dr.).

Mama Inez	Verve 8008
La Cucuracha	Verve 8008
Begin the Beguine	Verve 8008
Estrellita	Verve 8008
La Paloma	Verve 8008

These recordings were coupled with the March 12, 1951 date to form an LP
entitled *Fiesta* on Verve. The liner notes list Kenny Dorham as the trumpet player,
but authorities such as discographer Jorgen Jepsen and critic Ira Gitler have stated
that it is Harris. It certainly does not seem to be Dorham, if one compares his
other work of this period.

The presence of the trumpet adds a further detriment to a date already bogged
down because of the trite material. The trumpeter, much of the time, is horribly
out of tune, especially on the lower tones, and seems to be unfamiliar with the
tunes. Harris later stated, "My lip went bad after a year in the Earl Hines band.
They swung so hard and played so much."[1]

Most of the tunes begin with the rhythm section in a Latin vein. *Estrellita*,
however, has a plain piano intro and *La Paloma* has some "authentic" Latin shouts.

Parker plays the "A" sections on *Mama Inez* and the horns are in harmony
on the bridge. Bird has two choruses that are not bad for having to work with
ridiculous material; then Harris plays one (his best of the date) and Bishop follows
with a single-line half chorus. The horns return to the bridge, and Bird closes.
There is a percussion fade-out.

The exposition of *La Cucuracha* is split between the horns—Parker, then Harris
(muted). A bongo roll substitutes for the final note and sends Bird into his one-
chorus solo; Harris follows with a solo that uses "a-little dab'll-do'ya" at the
beginning of the second eight. Next, Bishop takes half of the final chorus and
Bird takes the melody out with the bongo roll again substituting for the final
note.

Bird plays a gorgeous melody statement on *Estrellita* only to have the mood
broken by Harris' worst offering on the date (half-chorus). Bird blows on the second
half of the tune with some nice ideas, and Bishop returns to the bridge for a chordal,
melodic solo. Parker has the close with Bishop playing a coda based on the bridge.

Begin the Beguine is done at a fast Latin tempo that is not a beguine! It
is one of the brighter moments of this quite dismal date. Parker jumps right in
with a full chorus, and Bishop takes the first half of the next; the ending is all
Bird. The absence of Harris makes the tune at least palatable, and Kotick's "walking"
(even though the Latin rhythm continues otherwise) on the improvised sections
gives this tune some added jazz interest.

The chords of *La Paloma* do not lend themselves to good jazz improvisation
(this is true of most of the tunes on the date), but Bird gives it a whirl. He even
manages a *Moose the Mooche* quote. Harris is again hard to listen to and Bishop
plays a "Latin-type" octave solo with more "authentic" hollering behind it. Bird
takes the tune out with a sustained tone.

These tunes are some of the worst of Parker's work and are not recommended listening except for the most die-hard fans. The earlier date, with which this one is coupled, is more satisfactory, both in improvisational content and over-all performance.

* * *

As one views pictures of Parker from the 1952 period, one cannot help but see the sadness in the man. His extra poundage was becoming genuine obesity and his face was turning into a bloated caricature of his former countenance. His ulcers were extremely painful, and yet he ate and drank with the gusto of a sailor. He carried special salt and ulcer pills with him, but would consume spicy foods, quarts of wine, and double orders of full platters (sometimes "going easy" on the bread and butter!).

It is also during this period that his behavior started to become more irrational. Although his earlier days are certainly not model examples of how to live, it seems that the bizarre incidents were more isolated and not quite as constant as was true during these later years. Indeed, he began carrying a pistol with him, probably because of his underworld heroin contacts, and it is from these last three years of his life that most of the fantastic "Bird stories," real or imagined, stem. Parker's ever-shaky ego was at this time trying to battle the effect of becoming a "has-been." It was a role that he would not wear well.

A role he did enjoy, however, was that of "Commandant" of the various large groups that Granz assembled for recording dates; he was especially professional when the group contained a large number of his talented peers, as did the "big band" assembled for a March recording.

* * *

Recording—March 25, 1952—NYC
Charlie Parker and His Orchestra—Jimmy Maxwell, Carl Poole, Bernie Privin, Al Porcino (tp); Bill Harris, Lou McGarity, Bart Varsalona (tb); Parker, Harry Terrill, Murray Williams (as); Flip Phillips, Hank Rois (ts); Danny Banks (bars); Oscar Peterson (p); Freddie Greene (g); Ray Brown (b); Don Lamond (dr); Joe Lippman (arr-cond.).

Night and Day	Verve 8003
Almost Like Being in Love	Verve 8003
I Can't Get Started	Verve 8003
What is This Thing Called Love	Verve 8003

These sides use the conventional "big band" instrumentation and the up-tempo offerings, *Night and Day* and *What is This Thing Called Love*, have ample space for Parker to stretch out.

He plays the melody statement on *Night and Day* for half of the tune, and then the band alternates with a trombone soloist for the rest of the first chorus. For the second chorus the tune modulates from Eb to C and has single-line piano followed by "swingy" trumpet for the first half; the full band kicks off the last half, and Parker wails the rest of the way. The final chorus has the band alternating with Parker and sometimes getting in the way of his train of thought. The saxes back him at the very end and the tune ends with screaming brass.

Almost Like Being in Love is a rather straight ballad performance in which Bird states the "A" sections in the exposition chorus. There is trombone backing at the beginning, and the ending section builds from saxes to trombones to full in the background; the full band has the bridge. A solo trombone plays a modulatory section from F to G and moves directly to the next chorus. Muted trumpets alternate with the trombone on the "A" sections and employ some orchestrated "Bird licks" in their segment of the second eight. Parker moves in for the bridge and suddenly modulates up a half step for the close of the tune.

Vernon Duke's beautiful ballad, *I Can't Get Started*, is also done fairly straight. Bird again has the "A" sections with sustained saxes underneath at times, and the band has the bridge—brass with unison sax obligato and then saxes with brass accents. After a modulation from C to Ab, Peterson returns to the bridge for a pleasant solo (in "two-beat," however) and the full band moves into the final section with Bird taking the final four bars alone. There is a "tag" with Parker participating.

The best performance of the lot is *What is This Thing Called Love*; it has much space for Parker improvisations (in two separate keys) and the arrangement is interesting. The first-chorus format is the same as the ballads—Parker on the "A"'s and band at the bridge, but Bird really blows on this one. He uses a humorous bending of the melody (to the "flat-five") during the final eight bars and there is a driving feeling to his phrasing. The second chorus is all improvisation with only rhythm background, and Bird gets in his *Carmen* quote at the final section. The third chorus, which moves from the original C to Eb, features other soloists; it begins with some high register trumpet followed by a saxophone solo section; trombone has the bridge, and Peterson finishes the chorus. A band-riff in the new key of F opens the beginning of the fourth chorus and launches Bird into a swirling solo; he continues until the closing eight where the pattern is repeated. The coda features Bird's blowing, sandwiched between the full band accents.

These tracks are really not as trite as is usually assumed. They have some good moments, and for a "big-band" lover they are a fine introduction to Parker's work. The musicianship in the band is excellent.

* * *

Kenny Dorham and Stan Levey were with Parker in the spring of the year and one of their engagements was at the Howard Theater in Washington, D.C. Bird also appeared as a single at the Times Square Hotel in Rochester where the local rhythm section provided by the union was especially miserable. Lon Flanigan, Jr., a jazz fan, describes his first hearing:

I thought for a minute it was a novelty record on the juke box, but I saw a disconsolate Bird on the bandstand.... Bird took the manager of the place aside, and, with some help from us, convinced him that his house band did not play an appropriate style for a bebop musician. The next day, Art Taylor and Walter Bishop arrived by plane to salvage the rest of the week.[2]

Even though the new settings and Granz's promotions were giving him the chance to reach a larger audience; understanding did not come with the chance.

Regarding the new settings themselves, however, one does not find all of them to be merely commercial tripe. Indeed, the *Lover* rendition, from January 22nd, is virile, honest jazz, and *What is This Thing Called Love*, from the March "big band" date, is one of the most intellectually stimulating versions of the tune (especially with the change of tonality) that Bird had ever done. Both of the above tunes plus the *Hot House* from the TV show are the essential items from the first half of 1952.

CHAPTER XIX

WEST (AGAIN) AND BACK
Some Sessions
(May-December 1952)

As the old cock crows,
the young one learns.
English Proverb

During the end of May, 1952, Parker left for a string of summer engagements on the West Coast. He disliked the area because of his previous experiences, but the money offer was good, and Chan was six months pregnant. He opened at the Tiffany Club in Los Angeles on Memorial Day eve with a rhythm section of Art Blakey, Curly Russell, and Kenny Drew (Drew had often been the piano player at Christy's in Boston, both as a single and as a member of the sessioneers).

Again there were wild doings in California: Bird was stranded without funds in San Francisco (when he went to session at Bop City) for a few days and he was fired from a club job in Los Angeles for misconduct. The club was the Say When, and Bird, being deeply moved after appearing on the Cerebral Palsy Telethon, took up a collection in the club. The owner refused to contribute, and Parker announced this fact to the audience, whereupon he was promptly fired! Earlier, however, both the Say When and the Tiffany Club were the scenes of some blowing sessions including Chet Baker and altoist Sonny Criss.

* * *

Recording—June 16, 1952—Say When Club—Los Angeles
Parker (as), C. Baker (tpt), S. Criss (as), Donn Trenner (p), Harry Babison (b) Lawrence Marable (d).

The Squirrel	Jazz Showcase 5007
Be Careful It's My Heart (?)	
(listed as "They Didn't Believe Me")	Jazz Showcase 5007
Indiana	Jazz Showcase 5007
Liza	Jazz Showcase 5007

These tracks are well recorded—under the "live" conditions—and the Parker-Baker collaboration is interesting to hear. A striking comparison can be made between Parker and Criss, then a young Bird disciple. Parker's mastery of rhythm in his

228

inventions is not present in Criss's work. Criss mainly alternates strings of eighth-notes with riff-like figures and is often rhythmically repetitive in his phrasing. This same problem was present with many of the "Bird-schooled" alto players of the period; they grasped much of the essential *sound* of Parker's music but failed to assimilate the rhythmic subtleties (which, of course, was a large part of Bird's genius).

Trenner's playing, however, is very strong—reminiscent of Bud Powell—and (unlike Criss) shows a pronounced individuality of approach. (During the early Sixties, Trenner led the band on Steve Allen's West Coast TV show.) In fact, the rhythm section as a whole sounds very "up" and driving, and Babasin has a two-chorus solo (mostly walked) on *Liza*. There are some weird "knocks" at times (especially behind Criss's solo on *Indiana*) that one can mistakenly blame on Marable, but on closer listening they seem to be caused by someone tapping on or near the mike (on beats one and three).

The Squirrel, Tadd Dameron's bop blues, is played free style on the head, and Criss fires off eight wailing—or better, screaming—blues choruses; he sounds clean and sure although repetitive. Baker follows with a Miles-ish solo, but has some intonation and technical difficulties. In spite of this, there are some interesting moments, such as the use of a quote from *Manhattan* during his third chorus. After Trenner, Criss returns with a "Bird" solo-—developing the "Cool Blues" phrase and also *Cocktails for Two* (which Bird used in his 1945 recording of *Warming Up A Riff*, based on *Cherokee*); there are also some "do-wah" effects near the end of his solo. Baker and Parker, respectively, then play extended solos, and this time, Baker is much more sure in both intonation and execution. Parker, however, begins his solo far into the chorus—letting the rhythm drift by for a long period—and builds the latter part of his solo on a favorite Parkerian device: that of playing a favorite phrase at the beginning of each chorus and using this as a springboard for ideas. Thirteen one-chorus solos follow in the order of Baker-Parker-Criss; the series ends with Baker. The short solos are sparklers, and Criss pulls some humorous surprises: *Santa Claus is Coming to Town* (his 2nd solo); an imitation of Parker's (immediately preceding) chorus and some "outside" playing (third solo); *Music Goes 'Round and 'Round* (fourth solo).

The tune listed as *They Didn't Believe Me* is actually *Be Careful, It's My Heart* with a slightly altered second eight: Key of F: /Bbm⁷/Bbm⁷Eb⁷/Abmaj⁷/Abmaj⁷/Abm⁷/Abm⁷Db⁷/Gb maj⁷/Gm⁷C⁷/ The other sections of the tune are basically derived from ii7—V7—I pattern (of the original key) as is *They Didn't Believe Me*. The mistaken identity, therefore, probably comes from Parker's use of phrasing in the melody (which is similar to the Kern tune anyway) that echoes certain spots in *They Didn't Believe Me*. In reality, the tune *Be Careful, It's My Heart* is an Irving Berlin creation written for *Holiday Inn* (1942), and its second eight is vastly improved harmonically by the slight alteration used on this recording. Perhaps there is another tune which would fit these chords, but it seems unlikely to this writer. Indeed, the solos move smoothly (Bird-Baker-Criss-Trenner) and the strong piano solo contains one "outside" moment. On the out-chorus, the bass walks the first eight and then Bird enters; the last sixteen measures are stated by Bird (as was the opening theme statement) with Baker backing with long tones and answering phrases. At the end of the line, Bird plays a series of octave leaps which seem to say, "Be Careful."

The beautiful Bird improvisations on *Indiana* keep the listener on the edge of the seat. This is truly one of his best "blowing" versions of this time. At various places, Parker uses a phrase, and before it's finished, he quickly repeats it (almost an afterthought) and then turns it in another direction. In addition, there are ingenious developmental usages of fragments from *Donna Lee* that must be heard— they cannot be described. Parker plays *Indiana* as the theme for most of the exposition but uses the *Donna Lee* line for the last eight. There are two sets of solos (Bird-Baker-Criss-Trenner), and Baker (first solo) and Criss (second solo) make good attempts at developmental usages of *Donna Lee* phrases. Parker's second solo has a phrase with a large upward leap used in a sequence at one climactic point, and Baker begins his second solo with Bird's last idea. Baker, however, had not achieved his technical excellence of a few years hence and has difficulty fitting his ideas with the tempo. The *Donna Lee* theme is used as a close, but Bird is the only horn who knows the line well; the ensemble, therefore, is rather ragged. The "Shave-and-a-haircut" ending bespeaks of the "session" atmosphere.

Liza is the poorest performance[1] of the lot although it has some lessons for the jazz student. The theme is a disaster, never quite coming together at all; and the solos do not seem to give the characteristic harmonic "feel" of the tune. Bird, in fact, seems to make his own pattern at times. The relation of improvised material to theme is very poor. Trenner is best at this (possibly because of the innate harmonic nature of the piano) on the first set of solos. Parker amazes again, however, for after the bass solo, he does much better on the harmonic lay of his ideas, and on the third solo, he plays a tremendous (especially the bridge) offering! Baker and Criss also improve in this manner; strong examples *do* seem to make a difference. The closing theme is still messy, however, with drums at the bridge and Baker running out the melody (last eight) as Bird blows obligato.

This is a much recommended set if one understands the "session" atmosphere.

Recording—June 1952, Los Angeles
Parker (as), Oscar Peterson (p), Ray Brown (b), J.C. Heard (dr).

Jam Blues	Verve 8002
Dearly Beloved	Verve 8002
Funky Blues	Verve 8002
What Is This Thing Called Love	Verve 8002

The full complement for this session included Johnny Hodges and Benny Carter on alto sax; Flip Phillips and Ben Webster on tenor sax; and Charlie Shavers on trumpet. The issue listed here contains only Parker's solos, but *Funky Blues* was issued in full on Verve's *The Essential Charlie Parker* (8409), and the full session plus some other Parker items was first issued on *Norman Granz Jam Sessions #1 and #2* (Verve 8049 and 8050).

Jam Blues has seven Parker choruses and there are many points of interest. Chorus 1 ends with the development of a favorite "bop lick" that Parker did not use as often as some of his contemporaries (see Davis identifier—end of 1948— Ex. 107) and Chorus 3 has the *Confirmation* chords used in the first four bars.

Peterson is not always with Parker, chordally, on this blues, but at the beginning of Chorus 3 they sound very good together. Choruses 4 and 5 have the inevitable riffs behind the solo alto, and Chorus 6 contains Parker's lazy descent of a diminished chord. Bird was a man of varied sounds in regard to his tone, and the sound he achieves on *Jam Blues* was favored by some "West Coast" altoists of later years, notably Herb Geller.

Dearly Beloved is a semi-obscure Mercer-Kern tune from a 1942 movie entitled *You Were Never Lovelier* and was Bird's choice in a ballad medley. Why he chose this tune is a mystery, for there is no other recorded evidence of his playing it before or after. It is possible, of course, that he had seen the picture, for he loved movies. Whatever the reason one line of the ballad's lyric, out of context, is very poignant at this point in Bird's life: *Nothing could save me; fate gave me a sign.* Although exactly on the melody Bird makes a beautiful jazz piece; he uses two altered melody tones in two places in the tune, and although this seems rather subtle and insignificant, it has a lot to do with the transformation.

Ex. 155a *Dearly Beloved* Original Figure and Alteration

On *Funky Blues*, the Kansas City roots show, although he unleashes some sixteenth-notes to show where he went as well as from whence he came. In fact, the solo seems to evolve from "funky" into "ultra-modern."

There are three choruses on *What Is This Thing Called Love*, and the last two contain background riffs on the "A" sections. The solo is good "down-the-middle" Parker, however, with the *Carmen* quote near the end.

* * *

Chan Richardson gave birth to Bird's second son, Baird, on August 10th 1952 (the first son was Leon from Rebecca). Indeed, Parker's familial obligations were growing, for he now had three children living in his household: Baird, Pree (his daughter from Chan), and Kim (Chan's daughter—at the time aged six—from a previous relationship).

Soon after the birth, Parker returned to New York and made Birdland his scene of operations. He worked there in September with Mingus and Duke Jordan (this could have been on the same bill as Stan Getz for both rhythm men worked with the tenorist around this period) and also in the beginning of November with Milt Jackson's quartet, who would make, a month later, their first Prestige recordings under the name of The Modern Jazz Quartet.

* * *

Recording—September 20, 1952—Birdland, NYC
*Charlie Parker Quartet—*Parker (as), Duke Jordan (p), Charles Mingus (b), Phil
Brown (d)

Ornithology	Mark 101
52nd Street Theme	Mark 101

The dating of this set is a pure guess, as the author has only heard the original
tape and not a commercially issued record (the "bootleg" label listed above has
long been out of circulation). A quote of *The Song is You,* however, that appears
in the middle of the Bird solo, suggested this date, since Bird would record the
semi-classical standard within two and a half months (December 30). This quote,
moreover, serves as an easy "identifier."

Both tunes are taken at break-neck tempos and feature exciting solos by both
Bird and Bishop (although the pianist does fall into a few of his favorite phrases).
The *Ornithology* solo, however, is wonderfully inventive, with a rhythmic intensity
that bowls the listener over. Indeed, the set is worth a listen, even though the recorded
sound is hard to take.

* * *

In mid-November a Carnegie Hall Tribute was given for Duke Ellington's
25th anniversary as a leader. The line-up included the Ellington Band, Parker with
strings, Dizzy Gillespie, Stan Getz Quintet, Billie Holiday, Latin-percussionist
Candido, and Ahmad Jamal. Discographers, moreover, believe there were two
separate concerts with slightly different formats. Bird performed on one of them,
at least, both with the strings and with Gillespie plus rhythm. In addition, Candido
also guested with the Parker group, and Billie Holiday and Diz did solo appearances
with the Ellington Band in the second concert.

* * *

Recording—November 14, 1952—Carnegie Hall, NYC
Parker (as), D. Gillespie (tp), (on final two tunes), strings (only on first three tunes),
Candido (on last three tunes), Walter Bishop (p), Roy Haynes (d), Walter Yost?
(b).

Just Friends	FDC 1005
Easy to Love	FDC 1005
Repetition	FDC 1006
Night in Tunisa	FDC 1006
52nd St. Theme	FDC 1006

The arrangement on *Just Friends* is the same as the original recording, and
Parker plays a solo that begins with the same phrase as his original improvisation.
There are other phrases during the improvisation that are similar to phrases in
the original solo, but the best and most daring ideas are ventured after the piano
solo in the section usually designated as the recapitulation statement. On this last
half of the third chorus, Parker plays completely fresh and is excellent through
to the coda.

Easy to Love is the same arrangement (the "new" version) as September 16,
1950, as is *Repetition* except that there is solo space provided for Candido. The
Porter ballad has good blowing at the first half of the second chorus and the Hefti

tune also provides for a healthy solo following the string interlude; Candido adds little other than excitement to the latter. An added feature is Bird's own verbal introduction to *Repetition*.

Diz and Bird along with Candido collaborate with the rhythm section on *Tunisa*, and it is not a very good version. Candido begins with rhythm, and Bird and the rhythm section enter with background (not the original). Gillespie states the theme and does not sound good. It is one of his rare bad nights. Bird has the theme chorus bridge to himself and takes his usual wild break following the interlude. His solo is good, but it is almost impossible to hear the rhythm section except for Candido. Diz, however, sounds as if he lacks ideas and is having lip trouble. During Candido's lengthy excursion, Bird and Diz try to use the "second" interlude first heard in the Parker repertoire in February 1949, but Candido pays no attention and it does not come off well. The entrance to the closing theme chorus is very sloppy and the whole chorus is not a classic one; Diz screams upward in his ending cadenza.

52nd Street Theme is the real abomination, however. Bird jumps right into it at a ridiculously fast tempo, but Diz cannot get into the line at all. He makes a few futile attempts with wrong notes, but never really works into a unison with Bird. Parker plays two choruses, and because of the extremely fast pace, the rhythm men seem to lose their place during the first. Bird hesitates, however, and plays a slow phrase during the first eight of his second chorus, and then, to establish togetherness, plays the theme riff for eight bars; he improvises from the bridge on. At the end of Diz's lone chorus, Parker, probably being unable to take any more, jumps in with the introductory riff (this riff was originally used as an introduction, but was often later used on the "A" sections) and Diz takes the hint. Bird takes the bridge by himself and Diz, remembering his problems on the exposition chorus, blasts high notes over the closing theme riff. The coda is rather chaotic and bleating. This performance is certainly not a credit to either of the giants.

The pianist with the string group is sometimes listed as Teddy Wilson, but it is most certainly Bishop. The announcer (Symphony Sid?) does introduce Bishop before the "session" tunes, and he also introduces the bass player as Walter Yost—whoever that may be. (There is a bassist named Walter Yoder who was with Woody Herman in the early 1940s).

The FDC (For Discriminate Collectors) label is an Italian product and the translated notes are riotously funny (unintentionally). A great amount of the other material from both concerts is included on the double record set.

Recording—December 30, 1952—NYC—Charlie Parker Quartet
Parker (as), Hank Jones (p), Max Roach (d), Teddy Kotick (b).

The Song is You	Verve 8005
Laird Baird	Verve 8005
Kim—Take 2	Verve 8005
Kim—Take 4	Verve 8005
Cosmic Ray—Take 2	Verve 8005
Cosmic Ray—Take 5	Verve 8005

As on the August 1951 date there is excellent musicianship here. Bird navigates the difficult chords to *Song is You* with extreme ease, and Jones' substitute chords are appealing. As was the case with many tunes, this semi-classic ballad (done as an up-tempo) became a standard jazz vehicle just because he played it.

Laird Baird, named for his new son, and *Cosmic Ray* are both blues—*Ray* being "down-home" and *Baird* being a modern blues frame with the *Confirmation* chords in the first four bars:

Ex. 155b *Laird Baird*—Opening

The two takes of *Kim* (Chan's daughter) are both amazingly fluent travels through the *I Got Rhythm* pattern, and the alternate can be identified (probably Take 2) by the hint at *Johnny One Note* and the *High Society* quote.

On *Cosmic Ray* the original (probably Take 2) ends with a *Temptation* quote and has a *Blues in the Night* quote in the bass solo. Max's solo on each take moves into 3/4 inflections.

Kotick's bass solos on both blues are thoughtful and soulful, and Max uses the tom-toms to great effect. This is perhaps some of the best drum work from a musical standpoint that was done on any group of Parker's recordings. Jones' work can be summed up in one word: tasty. He is not only an excellent accompanist, but his solos bear careful listening; they say more than is evident on first hearing. The piano player is listed as Al Haig and the bass player as Percy Heath on the Verve issue, but it has been well established[2] that the personnel is as listed above.

This set is highly recommended, for it has a wonderful light feel in the rhythm section and it is very well recorded. It is easy to relate the sound to modern times, even for young musicians, and the choice of material (an *I Got Rhythm* improvisation, a "modern" blues, a traditional blues, and a difficult standard) gives an accurate picture of Bird's music—both as a creator and as a craftsman.

* * *

The Say When session allows us to hear Bird alongside some of his "children"— the innovator along with the refiners—and makes us more acutely aware of how much influence Bird was on even the "coolest" of Fifties players. The December "studio" recording, however, is valuable for the opposite effect: the refiners influencing the original innovator. The playing of the rhythm section is light and tasty (even on the mercurial *Kim*) rather than overpowering, and this quality affects Bird by osmosis. Although it does not make him "cool," it allows him a more relaxed frame of mind. Whatever intangible property we are speaking of here lends a decidedly 1950s quality to the December date. This is probably the first time we can hear this quality in a Parker small group date (although the August, 1951 date with Rodney comes close), and it would only come through clearly at one other recording session—August 4th, 1953.

CHAPTER XX

THE SERPENT'S TOOTH
But Little Time
(1953-1954)

At the last it biteth like a serpent, and
stingeth like an adder.
Proverbs 23, 32.

Narcotics addiction, the modern jazz musician's plague, was becoming familiar to police vice squads of the early 1950s. In earlier times the "mainline" problem was not often encountered, and the musician-addict was often over-looked. At the beginning of the decade, however, the police soon learned of known addicts and lay in wait for them. Indeed, Red Rodney was busted and served time both in jail and at the Federal Narcotics Hospital at Lexington, Kentucky; and Bud Powell was also taken into custody for possession of narcotics. He was then placed in the Pilgrim State Hospital for shock treatments to help his unstable mental state.

Parker, although not arrested, soon had his cabaret card revoked. This card is issued by the New York State Liquor Authority and can be revoked at the discretion of the police. Without it, a performer cannot work in a New York City establishment where liquor is served. Forced to work "underground" clubs and out of town bookings, therefore, until his card could be regained (Billy Shaw was instrumental in finally achieving the reinstatement), Bird, fortunately, was able to continue his recording activities. But his erratic behavior and schizophrenic frame of mind continued.

* * *

Recording—January 30, 1953—NYC
Miles Davis and His Orchestra—Davis (tp), Parker, Sonny Rollins (ts), Walter Bishop (p), Percy Heath (b), Philly Joe Jones (d).

Compulsion	Prestige 7004
The Serpent's Tooth—Take 1	Prestige 7004
The Serpent's Tooth—Take 2	Prestige 7004
Round About Midnight	Prestige 7004

Immediately before this recording, as the proceedings were being readied, Parker consumed the better part of a fifth of gin and then fell asleep! He awoke in a trance, and needless to say, the date was a bit shakey, for besides Bird's condition, he was also playing an unfamiliar instrument, the tenor, which he had not played since 1947.

The two Davis originals are very fine lines, however, and they are well written and worth hearing. *Compulsion* is based on *Just You, Just Me*, whereas *The Serpent's Tooth* is an *I Got Rhythm* derivative with the *Honeysuckle Rose* bridge. Both tunes have composed introductions, and the unisons break into harmony at several places to add ensemble interest to the date. *Compulsion*, has a four-bar "launching" riff used during Miles's first chorus and Bird's second (although Bird plays right through) and repeated in place of the theme during the first half of the out-chorus. Parker is the first tenor soloist on *Compulsion* and the second on *The Serpent's Tooth* (all the horns have two-chorus solos on these tunes).

The lead-in from the introduction to theme is ragged on *The Serpent's Tooth* (Take 1), and Bird sounds as if he is having trouble adjusting to the larger horn. Miles, however, plays a fine solo and quotes the *Blacksmith Blues* (Jo Stafford's "pop" hit of the period) and *Heart and Soul*. The ensemble is a bit better on the second take, but Bird is quite slow in starting his solo and is still having horn problems. Miles chides him with *Clap Hands, Here Comes Charlie* and also returns to the *Heart and Soul* quote. Both takes have exchanges of fours with drums, but the first contains only Miles, whereas the second adds Parker and Rollins (in that order). In addition, Miles improvises the bridge section on all theme choruses.

Midnight has Bird and Miles on the theme (Bird backing) and Rollins playing the bridges (the album notes state it is Bird on the bridges, but Ira Gitler, who was A & R man on the session and wrote the notes, later corrected himself in his book *Jazz Masters of the 40's*). Bird sounds a bit better on his improvisation, but he still has some intonation problems. The solo, however, does fill one with pity upon hearing it. Unlike previous recordings (1950, 1951), this version of Monk's *Midnight* gives Bird room for extensive improvisation. The earlier versions had restricted him to theme statements.

Ira Gitler's liner notes on the Prestige issue are complete and concise (except for the *Midnight* mistake mentioned above) as regards the format and make the tunes much easier to follow (Prestige reissued these tunes in their 2400 series). Conversely, the fact that Bird, because of his contract with Granz, was listed on the original recordings as "Charlie Chan" (a pseudonym that he also used on a "live" recording of a concert in Montreal later in the year) can cause confusion for the novice.

* * *

Pree, Bird's 1½ year old daughter from Chan, was never a healthy child, and in early 1953, she was hospitalized with a wracking cold from which she would never recover. In his now-famous February 17th letter to the Liquor Control Board (a plea for the return of his cabaret card), he mentions that his blameless family was suffering most from the punishment being imposed upon him. He mentioned that he had "...made every effort to become a family man..." and that his daughter's health problem was caused by the fact that he "...hadn't the necessary doctor fees." In desperation, he offered to go to prison, but Ross Russell feels this was a ploy to gain sympathy.[1] As he awaited the re-instatement of his card, he sat-in with various groups (illegally, of course) at the Band Box and later worked there with groups of his own. He also went out as a single to the High Hat in Boston and the Beehive in Chicago, and while in the latter city, he participated in a session at Roosevelt College.

* * *

Recording—Feb. 6, 1953—Band Box, NYC
Parker (as), Charlie Mariano (as), Harry Johnson (ts), Sonny Truitt (tp), Bill Harris (tb), Chubby Jackson (b), Morey Feld (d).

Ah, Your Father's Moustache   Queen (It.) 002
The theme of this tune is a repeated, comedic vocal of the title line. It was first recorded by Woody Herman in 1945, and some of the men in this group are Herman alumni. The construction is *I Got Rhythm* with a minor chord as the second change in the bridge.

After a rhythm section intro, there is the vocal for sixteen-bars on the "A" section chords—this is a separate section. The instrumental portion has riffing "A" sections and a written bridge, and is followed by an eight bar launching section that goes into a tenor solo. Johnson's long excursion is raucous and boring and the listener is relieved when someone announces "Here Comes Charlie Parker!" Bird plays well on the familiar chords, although the recorded sound is extremely bad. The tune ends with two riffing "A" sections and an ending that echoes the opening bridge. Bird is not present on the ensemble; he probably just jumped in for his solo.

Recording—February 22, 1953—Washington D.C.
Willis Conover "The Orchestra"—Parker plus big band.

Fine and Dandy	Electra Musician—XEl—60019
These Foolish Things	Electra Musician—XEl—60019
Light Green	Electra Musician—XEl—60019
Thou Swell	Electra Musician—XEl—60019
Willis	Electra Musician—XEl—60019
Don't Blame Me	Electra Musician—XEl—60019
Medley: Something to Remember You	
By/Blue Room	Electra Musician—XEl—60019
Roundhouse	Electra Musician—XEl—60019

"The Orchestra" was the brainchild of drummer-arranger Joe Timer and several other Washington musicians. Conover, however, long associated with the Voice of America jazz broadcasts, provided the "clout" to present the band publicly. In 1953, the group had been in existence for about a year and a half and was soliciting guest soloists such as Gillespie and Stan Getz. But because of Parker's poor reputation for meeting his professional obligations during this period, Conover decided to do no advertising of Parker's guest shot other than word-of-mouth rumors that Bird might appear. All the same, Parker did appear—although not in time for rehearsal—and roared through the complex arrangements done by Al Cohn, Gerry Mulligan, Johnny Mandel and others.

Bill Potts, who contributed the composition/arrangements of *Light Green* and *Willis*, produced this marvelous recording from his personal tapes and wrote the extremely clear, descriptive notes which eliminate the need for any detailed analysis in this book.

Bird is in excellent form, although unfamiliar with the key changes in some of the arrangements. Mulligan's *Roundhouse*, for instance, which has a blowing section based on the *Out of Nowhere* chords, stops abruptly at one point for a solo break into a new key, but Bird, not realizing the new key is coming, takes the break in the same key he is in and continues into the next chorus. Upon hearing the new key, however, he quickly rights himself. The medley was to be three tunes (Potts states in the notes that the second tune written on the arrangement was *Taking A Chance on Love*), but Bird, again not aware, goes right back to *Something to Remember You By*. He is startled when the band begins *Blue Room* (Bird only adds a few flurries of notes in the latter piece and it is not included, therefore, in the detailed listings in Appendix I and Appendix III of this work).

The most satisfactory track is *Willis*, obviously dedicated to Conover. It has the chord frame of *Pennies from Heaven*, perhaps referring to the funding of the project. Bird sounds inventive and fresh (it is his only recorded example on this chord frame), and solos in both keys used in the arrangement. There are also good Bird solos and few hang-ups on *Fine and Dandy*, *These Foolish Things*, and *Light Green* (a blues). *Thou Swell* is certainly adequate, but Bird is too intent on the arrangement and the material to really be inspired. The key on *Don't Blame Me*— a much lower one than usual (could it have been intended for a female vocal?)— is not the most comfortable one for the alto, and, further, Potts had to cut a half chorus because of sound problems; the resultant splice, although excellently done, is not aesthetically pleasing.

This set is highly recommended for the beautiful remastering job, the meticulous notes, and the unusual setting and material for Bird's improvisations. An added attraction is the Red Rodney monologue on Parker that ends the side.

Recording—March 23, 1953—Band Box—Milt Buckner Trio & Charlie Parker
Parker (as), Buckner (organ), Bernie McKay (g), Cornelius Thomas (dr)

　　Groovin High　　　　　　　　　　　　　　　　Columbia 34831
Buckner and Parker sound good together, but the absence of a bass gives a "two-beat" sound at times. Bird plays some interesting ideas—of a different type than he used on other versions of this tune—and his solo is notable for the development of the phrase from the "live" *Fine and Dandy* recording of 1948 (Ex. 97).

The exchanges of fours between Parker and the drummer which follow Bird's solo do not quite come off; the drummer's ideas are puerile and his sense of time is awful. The "fours" consequently have a very nervous feel.

Buckner's presence, however, adds a new sound to the Parker catalogue, although the track is poorly recorded.

Recording—March 30, 1953—Band Box, NYC—Charlie Parker Quartet
Parker (as), W. Bishop (p), Kenny O'Brien (b), Roy Haynes (d)

Star Eyes	Queen (It.) 002
Ornithology	Queen (It.) 002
Diggin' Diz	Queen (It.) 002
Embraceable You	Queen (It.) 002

 Star Eyes opens with the Latin intro that Bishop and Parker used on earlier versions of the tune, but here they are in disagreement on some of the notes.

Ex. 156 *Star Eyes* Latin Introduction

 Parker sounds tired as he plays through a theme chorus and an improvisation, but Bishop's 1½-chorus solo is fine; he uses a block chord approach for his final sixteen measures. After the piano, Bird states the theme from the second half and plays a *Temptation*-type melody over the Latin figure to end the tune.

 In the opening chorus of *Ornithology*, Parker's melody is used, but the recapitulation chorus has the *How High The Moon* melody over Latin rhythm until the final four bars, where the ending of the *Ornithology* theme is employed. Parker gets off a good solo, but Bishop again comes on like a storm; he uses a furious attack and quotes *Bushel and a Peck* (from Frank Loesser's *Guys and Dolls*— 1950) and *Little Spanish Town*. In the four-bar exchange with Haynes, Parker flounders quite noticeably, but Haynes sounds good and contributes some thoughtful ideas.

 Leonard Feather is heard talking to Parker before *Diggin' Diz* and suggests that the tune is really *Dizzy Atmosphere* and not *Dynamo "A"* as Bird had it listed. Both men were wrong, however, as the tune played is the *Lover*-based line (Feb. 5, 1946) and not *Dynamo "A"* which was Ross Russell's incorrect title for *Dizzy Atmosphere*! It is most probable, as mentioned before, however, that the *Dynamo* title was originally intended for the line played here, but was confused at the time of the first issue. Parker's chorus is mediocre; he keeps returning to the melody in an attempt to get a smooth flow going. After Bishop's solo (chorus and a half), Bird blows a half-chorus; uses bridge melody of *Lover*; and takes the tune out with the line.

 There is a very tired Bird on *Embraceable You*; he plays only the melody in the exposition chorus and in the half-chorus recapitulation. Bishop again is very inventive throughout his solo and at one point (end of the first half-chorus) develops the verse of *Tea for Two*—perhaps referring to his and Bird's penchant for marijuana. At the end, Bird starts the *Country Gardens* coda—hesitates—and then seems to think "Ah, What the hell, I'll play it anyway" and proceeds to end the tune in self-disgust.

This set acts as a harbinger of doom and the listener senses for the first time that Bird is faltering; that most of the great moments are behind; that there is little time to create. In fact, *Embraceable You* enables one to see the shadow of the Reaper's waiting arms.

* * *

Late in April of 1953, Bob Reisner, the author of *Bird: The Legend of Charlie Parker*, began producing Sunday night sessions at Sol Jaffe's Open Door in Greenwich Village. Parker soon became a regular featured attraction and drew hordes of "hip" Villagers and "blowing" musicians.

An engagement at Birdland, in early May, preceded Parker's trip to Canada where he was on an all-star concert with Gillespie. The Canadian musicians welcomed Bird with open arms and he was a participant in many local jam sessions in Montreal and Toronto. During this period, he experimented with the newly-invented plastic saxophone as evidenced by a picture taken at the all-star concert.

* * *

Recording—May 9, 1953—Birdland, NYC
Parker (as), John Lewis (p), Curly Russell (b), Kenny Clarke (d), Candido (bongo).

Star Eyes	Columbia 34831
Cool Blues	Columbia 34831
Moose the Mooche	Columbia 34831
Broadway	Columbia 34831

Cool and *Moose* are wonderful performances. This is the Bird of the long flowing ideas, unexpected twists of phrase, wild rhythmic drive, and quick-witted humor. Lewis is also excellent, combining quick drive with intellectuality. Bird's *Moose* solo contains some interesting quotes including *Let's Fall in Love, Over There,* and the *Woodpecker Song.* After the tune ends, the group goes into George Shearing's *Lullaby of Birdland* as a theme.

Broadway is completely given to Candido as far as improvisation is concerned; he plays a long, exciting solo after the opening theme, and unlike many solos of this type, the excursion *does* hold the listeners attention (don't miss the development of the *Salt Peanuts* phrase).

Russell is more venturesome here than on earlier examples. On the opening theme to *Cool Blues* there is an inventive "pedal tone" type of bass, and *Moose's* theme shows some deviations from a straight-four bass at times. On *Star Eyes,* however, Russell begins the "time" one bar after Bird's break to the improvisations, but Lewis seems confused. The rest of the chorus is spent in trying to make the chords match. This is a shame, as Parker's ideas are really hanging together. Russell was doing the tune in Parker's usual manner (as evidenced by 3/30/53), but the spot sounds confusing to someone hearing it for the first time.

On about every other chorus during *Cool Blues,* Bird alludes to the chords that he and Lewis played on *Back Home Blues* (8/8/51). This makes for interesting listening, especially with a tasteful accompanist like Lewis who waits to hear where the soloist is going before stating his chords. Also interesting are the exchanges between Bird and Kenny Clarke (hear Clarke's famous *Oop Bop S'Bam* lick).

The Columbia issue has Symphony Sid's patter intact—complete with the introduction of the group members, and the set is essential "live" Parker despite the problems on *Star Eyes*.

Recording—May 15, 1953—Massey Hall, Toronto—Quintet of the Year
Dizzy Gillespie (tp), Parker (as), Bud Powell (p), Charlie Mingus (b), Max Roach (dr)

Perdido	Fantasy (8) 6003
All The Things You Are	Fantasy (8) 6003
Salt Peanuts	Fantasy (8) 6003
Wee	Fantasy (8) 6003
Hot House	Fantasy (8) 6003
Night in Tunisa	Fantasy (8) 6003

Mingus eventually issued these tracks on his *Debut* label after Granz had turned down Parker's asking price of $100,000! The bassist did some "over-dubbing" of the bass parts and various other rhythm parts, but there is no mention of this on the Fantasy LP. The dubbed-in bass part is obvious at times, especially in *All The Things You Are* where the original bass solo can be heard in the background of the dubbed-in one.

There were again ego battles between Diz and Bird, but they seem to be more in the form of jibing each other. Diz quotes *Laura* in several selections, probably ribbing Bird's string recordings, and Bird introduces Diz as "my worthy constituent," but there seems to be no animosity. Both men play well throughout the concert.

Perdidio cuts in at the last "A" section of the theme chorus and goes right to Bird's inventive improvisation. Diz picks up Parker's final phrase (a favorite Diz trick) for his solo opening and manages to quote *Laura* and his own composition, *Birks Works*. After Powell, the ensemble goes to the Ellington background riff for a half-chorus; then Roach solos on the bridge, and Parker returns to the melody with Diz screaming above. The bass on the end of this tune also seems obviously dubbed.

The "arrangement" of *Salt Peanuts* causes confusion at times between the two men and certainly lacks the sharpness of the studio recording of eight years earlier. There is no transition section after the vocal; Bird jumps right in—not being sure, at first, whether to continue or state the theme again. He continues with a good solo, however. An attempt at the next transition section (the one which usually launched the trumpet solo) also strikes a snafu, and there is an ominous pause before Gillespie's solo gets under way. Diz is again powerful, this time he chides Bird with *Nightingale*. The transition section that originally followed the opening theme launches Powell, and Max follows with some thoughtful thunder. The usual ending is employed.

There is a beautiful Parker improvisation on *All The things You Are* that uses the *Kerry Dancers* quote, and Diz's muted statement contains *On The Trail*. The *Bird of Paradise* intro and coda is used, and the theme choruses have Diz on the melody with Bird behind, except for the bridge, which Parker takes alone. After this tune there is a short version of *52nd Street Theme*—probably to close this particular concert segment.

The tune called *Wee* is the *I Got Rhythm* line generally referred to as *Allen's Alley*. The recording cuts in on the second eight-bar section, and Bird and Diz follow with some simultaneous improvisation at the bridge before returning to the line. Indeed, the soloists are all fluent, especially Powell; and Roach has an exciting drum spot before the recapitulation chorus.

The exactness and extreme unity that Parker and Gillespie achieved in their 1945 recordings is again lacking on the theme to *Hot House*, but the unison is certainly passable. Parker takes a great solo; he starts softly, almost hesitantly, and builds to a stirring climax of sixteenth notes, with quotes from *Please*, and with his old standby, *Carmen's Habanera*, worked into the texture. Gillespie counters with a sequential development of the *Habanera* figure mid-way through his powerful, high-note solo; he also uses *Laura* in a sequential manner. Gillespie's chorus, at the very beginning, seems to have elements of the theme mixed into it, and the flow of his thoughts is at times astounding.

Parker's break on *Tunisa* is not of the blindingly fast variety; he saves the speed for his facile solo. Gillespie, however, plays high throughout his spot and reminds the listener of the Roy Eldridge heritage. There is the usual cadenza-type ending after the closing theme. The "dubbed-in" bass part does not seem to be quite with the horns on the theme choruses.

Throughout the concert the solos by all concerned are very worthwhile, but the ensemble choruses could have been cleaner—without disturbing the good "free" feeling that the group achieved. As on the January 30 recording, Parker was again listed as "Charlie Chan" on the first release because of his commitment with Granz.

Also included on this concert and later issued on Debut was a version of *I've Got You Under My Skin* by the rhythm section along with a solo (*Drum Conversation*) by Roach.

Recording—May 1953—Montreal, Canada—Session
Parker (as), Brew Moore (ts), Paul Bley (p), Dick Garcia (gtr), Neil Michel (b), Ted Pastor (d).

Cool Blues	Jazz Showcase 5003
Bernie's Tune	Jazz Showcase 5003
Don't Blame Me	Jazz Showcase 5003
Wahoo	Jazz Showcase 5003

The rhythm section is excellent on these tracks and the recording is not too bad for "live" taping. On *Cool Blues* and *Don't Blame Me*, Bird is the only soloist, and the ballad is given a classic Parker treatment—complete with double-time, alternation of melody and improvisation, and long-lined ideas. The blues sounds very "alive," and Parker literally whizzes through the chords; he hints at a *Johnny One-Note* phrase at one point. Garcia does not seem to be on these two tracks and Moore certainly is not.

Wahoo is Benny Harris' riff on the *Perdido* chords, and Parker and Brew Moore play it in harmony with Bird improvising the bridge. Moore was known to have played sessions with Parker at the Open Door during 1953, but it is not known whether he was at any with Parker before the Montreal engagement. The line is so clean, however, that it almost sounds worked out. *Johnny One Note*, again and *Happy Birthday* creep into Bird's fluid solo, and Moore comes on ultra-masculine. There is a "fours" chorus with piano-drums-guitar-drums, and then someone yells "Bridge!" and Bird jumps right to it with improvisations. The harmonized riff takes it out.

Ex. 157 *Wahoo* Riff

Parker is not on *Bernie's Tune* even though it is included in most of the issues of this set of tunes. The tune had been recorded on August 16, 1952 by Gerry Mulligan and Chet Baker in one of their earliest recordings, and Moore and Garcia state the theme in the same type of harmony as the original record. The soloists—Moore, Garcia, and Bley—are all very good, although young listeners, if they are familiar with his later work, may be astounded to hear Bley play on conventional chord changes.

When one hears the excellence of the Canadian musicians, it is easy to see the impact made by the contributions of Parker and Gillespie. Eight years before only a handful of musicians could play correctly in the style, or handle the difficult material, whereas in 1953, in a foreign country, musicians at a session handled all the material with relative ease.

Recording—May 1953—Montreal, Canada—Session
Parker (as), Dick Garcia (gtr), Valdo Williams (p), Hal Gaylor (b), Billy Graham (d).

Ornithology	Jazz Showcase 5003
Embraceable You	Jazz Showcase 5003

This version of the Gershwin ballad must be heard, especially in comparison with the famous 1947 version. Here, Parker condenses the motif at times, uses unbelievably clean "double-time" ideas, and completely mesmerizes the listener throughout the 1¾ chorus solo (he returns to the second eight). Furthermore, the rhythm section is fine, and the piano player plays a tasty block-chord intro. If Garcia is playing (which is extremely doubtful), he is not audible.

Ornithology has a wild Bud Powell-like introduction and a good theme chorus, with Bird sounding very fresh. His solo gives the feeling of easy execution, and he quotes *Tenderly* and some other familiar phrases. He also develops the phrase from the *Fine and Dandy* live version of 1948 (Ex. 97). Garcia does solo on this tune but he can not be heard too well. There is a "cut" from Garcia's solo to the middle of the final theme chorus.

* * *

The Hi-Hat in Boston booked Parker several times during 1953 as a single; he worked with local musicians including Herb Pomeroy, trumpet and George Salano, drums. During two of these Massachusetts visits, Bird was a guest on Nat Hentoff's half-hour jazz radio show. The first time he was morose and reticent sometimes only nodding in response to Hentoff's queries (on a radio show!), but the second time, he talked incessantly about his new plans and his desire for perfection:

> Everytime I hear a record I've made I hear all kinds of things I could improve on...I'm always trying to develop, to find new and better ways of saying things...I'd like to do a session with five or six woodwinds, a harp, a choral group, and a full rhythm section. Something on the line of Hindemith's *Kleine Kammermusik*.[2]

He also talked of his liking for "legitimate" modernists Bartok and Stravinsky and traditionalists Bach and Beethoven and mentioned that jazz, after gaining a tradition comparable to classical music, would be taken more seriously.

The Granz recordings had given him a degree of public success (sometimes a dirty word in the jazz community), but something was still lacking. He continued to search; but was directionless. If he played ballads with strings, the "hip" community cried "sellout." If he stayed with his own boppish lines, he was accused of "sameness." There were ways, to be sure, but in order to find them, he needed time. Time for experiment; time for study; and time for thought. Time, however, was the one commodity that, for Bird, was fast disappearing.

Max Roach later told Bob Riesner:

> Bird...mapped out things for woodwinds and voices, and Norman Granz would holler, "What is this? You can't make money with this crazy combination. You can't sell this stuff."[3]

* * *

Recording—May 22, 1953—NYC—Charlie Parker and His Orchestra
Parker (as), Tony Aless (p). Hal McKusick (cl), Al block (fl), Tommy Mace (ob), Manny Thaler (bassoon), Junior Collins (Fr. Horn), Charles Mingus (b), Max Roach (dr), Dave Lambert Singers (vcl), Gil Evans (arr-cond).

In the Still of the Night	Verve 8009
Old Folks	Verve 8009
If I Love Again	Verve 8009

The instrumentation is that of a standard woodwind quintet plus a vocal group and rhythm, but it falls far short of Bird's Hindemithian ideal. The idea would not have had to fail as miserably as it did. One alternative would have been to turn Evans loose with the freedom to create original compositions with space for a soloist—such as the Stan Getz-Eddie Sauter *Focus* album of the 1960s.

But here, unfortunately, the vocal group does not even achieve a good blend within itself and has intonation and rhythmic problems. On *Love Again*, they do not adjust to the tempo at all. Bird's obligatos to the vocal group and his improvised solos, however, manage to shine despite all the fol-de-rol. Martin Williams, in his essay *The Listener's Legacy* in *Down Beat*, March 11, 1965, says of Parker's playing on *In The Still of the Night,* that "he shimmers and slithers around a tritely conceived group singing like a great dancer in front of a chorus doing simple time steps."

A horn solo over woodwinds opens the Porter standard, and the vocal group states the theme with Parker blowing obligatos on second and fourth sections. The next chorus is completely Bird—good Bird—with only the rhythm section for backing except for the woodwind chords at the third section. The tune returns to the second half with "Ah-Ah" vocals against Bird's blowing until the title line; the vocal group then returns to the words for the ending. Bird manages to get in *Three Blind Mice* on the final statements.

Parker's improvised phrase answers the flute on the introduction to *Old Folks,* and the voices begin the theme. Parker enters at the second eight, vainly trying to fit something tangible into the background. He finally jabs in *Pop Goes the Weasel* in mock seriousness. The bridge features Bird over "ah's" and "do-wa's" and then the vocal group returns for the final eight. The second chorus features Bird, but the "do-wa's" and other vocal accents tend to hamper rather than enhance, and it is actually a relief when the vocal returns at the bridge with Bird blowing behind. The "Amen" sounding ending is contrasted by Parker's flippant runs. The idea here is interesting, and one wishes it could have been perfected.

The final, little-known standard is the most unsuccessful, probably because of its unusual feel as to structure and the quickness of the tempo. Running woodwinds begin in the introduction, and Parker states the full theme with the vocal group behind him. The process is reversed for the second chorus, and here is where the vocal group strikes most of its afore-mentioned problems. Aless begins the third chorus with some nice piano, and woodwinds sneak in behind him during the second eight. Roach really adds something to the track with his sixteen-bar solo (eight alone-eight with woodwind backing) and perhaps saves it from complete mediocrity. There is excellent Bird on the last chorus—all improvisation—with the vocal group entering with words during the second half and singing a rhythmically-elongated ending. The singers are badly out of tune on the ending, but Bird helps them by outlining the top notes of the final 13th chord in his final figure.

* * *

Birdland bookings occupied some of Parkers time during the summer of 1953. He was there in late May, and, after a week's southern tour which supposedly included Rodney, he was also on an all-star bill at the Broadway club which included the groups of Gillespie, Powell, and, later in June, Ella Fitzgerald.

Sundays were spent at the Open Door sessions and Al Cohn, Zoot Sims, Brew Moore, and Don Joseph (trumpet) were frequent sitters-in. There were also Village sessions at Sherry Martinelli's apartment on Third Avenue at Fourth Street with Ted Wald (bass), and many of the men mentioned before. At the Open Door the rhythm section was often made up of Thelonious Monk, Charles Mingus, and Roy Haynes.

* * *

Recording—May 30, 1953—Birdland—NYC
Parker (as), Bud Powell (p), Charles Mingus (b), Art Taylor (d), Candido (bongo).

Moose the Mooche	Queen (It.) 002
Cheryl	Queen (It.) 002

These tracks are sometimes confused with the May 9th set, but the difference between Powell's and Lewis's style is obvious, and the presence of Candido on this version of Moose should leave little doubt for identification purposes. Powell can be heard playing the theme with Bird on the opening and closing choruses of both tunes (a display of Bud's irrepressible ego), but the group sounds very good despite this distraction and the bad recording.

Candido has long solos on both tunes, and Mingus plays a strong solo on *Cheryl*. In addition, Bud and Bird both sound very good; and Bird quotes *My Kinda Love, I Love You Truly, West End Blues,* and some more familiar tunes in *Cheryl*. There are four-bar exchanges between Parker and Candido on both tunes, and Parker begins the set on *Moose* with *Honey* and the other set with *The Song is You.* One can hear the group move into *Lullaby of Birdland* as the recording fades out.

Recording—C. 1953—N.Y.C.
Parker (as), Bud Powell (p), Charlie Mingus (b), Max Roach (d)

Dance of the Infidels	Queen (It) 002

This tune is probably from around the same period as the preceding recording, if one considers the over-all sound and some of the quotes.

The theme rendition is very well done, and Parker's solo includes *Why Do I Love You* (at two different places), *I Love You Truly,* and *The Song is You,* along with a constant flow of creative ideas. Powell grabs onto Bird's ending phrase as he dives into his excellent extended excursion. There are "fours" between Max and Bird before another clean theme chorus of the ingenious Powell blues composition.

* * *

The Sunday night Open Door sessions were frequented by many of Parker's former sideman, such as Al Haig and Max Roach, although most of Roach's time was occupied with a group of his own that included Hank Mobley (Mingus's label—Debut—recorded the Roach group during the year). The sessions were often "fun" battles of the Kansas City type, and Ira Gitler remembers a "musical goosing session" between Brew Moore and Bird in which they "played at each other behinds and finished up by playing to an old piece of chewing gum stuck to the floor."[4]

Parker and Reisner, however, often had business disagreements because of Bird's perverse behavior. He would leave the club and never return for the end of the engagement, or fall asleep on stand, or perhaps not even show up. He was always around, however, for an "advance" on his percentage.

The great moments in his playing were fast decreasing and during August, he made his last really excellent "studio" recording.

* * *

Recording—Aug. 4, 1953—NYC
Charlie Parker Quartet—Parker (as), Al Haig (p), Percy Heath (b), Max Roach (dr).

Chi-Chi—Take 1	Verve 8005
Chi-Chi—Take 3	Verve 8005
Chi-Chi—Take 4	Verve 8005
I Remember You	Verve 8005
Now's The Time	Verve 8005
Confirmation	Verve 8005

The rhythm team welds together to make this a polished—although not restricted—date. The bass and drum features on each tune add interest and strength to a set already rich in material; three Parker compositions and little-done standard.

Chi-Chi, a modern blues line, was supposedly named for one of Symphony Sid Torin's girl friends to whom Bird first gave this nickname. Parker is said to have written the line in a few minutes at Max Roach's kitchen table.[5]

Ex. 158—*Chi-Chi* Opening Bars

The sixth take was the original issue, and Bird's *Johnny One Note* quote is a good "identifier." One of the alternates has a slight break in the line at the end of the very first theme chorus. On the other one, however, Bird has horn problems, and the tempo is noticeably slower than the other two. This take also has an excellent understated Haig solo.

The inclusion of the beautiful standard, *I Remember You,* is a bonus on this fine group of tunes, and Parker handles the constantly changing tonal centers with ease.

The *Now's the Time* chorus in some ways is an accumulation of all the blues that Parker ever played. He opens the solo with his famous phrase from *Billie's Bounce* (1945-Ex. 27) and uses his other favorite "first four bar" figure to open the third chorus.

Ex. 159—*Now's The Time* Opening of 3rd Improvised Chorus

There is a reference to the *Bloomdido* solo and some outlines of substitute chords along with Parker's moving blues phrasing. The solo has been analyzed many times and will not be dealt with in depth in this work although phrases from it will be used in a comparative manner in the Analysis Section.

Martin Williams, again in "Listeners Legacy" (*Down Beat*, March 11, 1965) says of *Confirmation*:...

...An ingenious and delightful melody. For one thing, it is a continuous linear invention. Most pop songs and many jazz pieces that are in the song form have two parts: a main strain and a bridge (or release, or middle), the main strain repeated twice before the bridge and once after it, exactly or almost exactly. *Confirmation*, however, skips along beautifully with no repeats, though with one highly effective echo phrase, until the last 8 bars and these are a kind of repeat in summary to finish the line. In addition, Parker uses the bridge not as an interruption or interlude that breaks up or contrasts with the flow of the piece, but as part of its continuously developing melody. *Confirmation*, unlike many other Parker pieces, was not predetermined by the chord sequence of a standard tune; its melody dictates one of its own.

All of the above is true, but the harmony is similar in the first, second, and fourth eight-bar sections. The harmonic shift at the second section is very instructive, however.

Ex. 160—*Confirmation* Opening of First and Second Sections

This was Parkers only "studio" recording of *Confirmation*. Some "live" versions, however, were the Black Deuce recordings of the 1947 concert with Gillespie and the St. Nick's recording of Feb. 1950. Gillespie, of course, had recorded it in the West Coast session for Dial in 1946 that Parker did not make.

All things considered—the recording, rhythm section, solos, overall view—this set is the best one to own from the 1953-54 period if a single example is desired.

* * *

The string group was reactivated during the fall, and in October, played a concert at Jordan Hall in Boston hosted by disc jockey John McClellan. Bird also appeared at the Jazz Workshop as a guest and jammed with local musicians.

Back in New York, the Open Door expanded its jazz policy to four nights during this autumn season and Bird was frequently found on the scene. He was becoming a fixture on the Village scene and was well known to the "hip" artists and poets who were the Bohemian forerunners of the "Beat Generation" of the late 1950s.

Bird could hardly keep a group together, however, as the bookings were rather sparse, and he began doing more singles and scrounging up whatever jobs or package engagements he could find. He was fast becoming a forgotten man to the always fickle jazz public, but with the decline of his physical body through ulcers, heart trouble, liver problems, and general dissipation, he seemed to care little. He was living through his last, full, discontented winter.

* * *

Recording—December 19 and 20, 1953 Hi-Hat Club, Boston—Broadcast—WCOB—
"Symphony Sid" Torin
Parker (as), Herbie Williams (tpt) Rollins Griffith (p), Jimmy Woode (b), Marquis Foster (d).

Now's The Time	Phoenix LP10
Ornithology	Phoenix LP10
My Little Suede Shoes	Phoenix LP10
Groovin' High	Phoenix LP10
Cheryl	Phoenix LP10
Ornithology	Phoenix LP10
52nd Street Theme (Set Break)	Phoenix LP10

This is a prime example of Parker with a local "house band." His playing is especially inspired for this period. Technically the date is notable for Parker's use of ideas that imply substitute chords in the first four bars of the blues tune (*Now's the Time, Cheryl*—see example 147) and for his beautiful *developmental* usage of the quote and cliché.

Parker's second, third and fourth improvised choruses on *Now's The Time* are based upon material used in the previous (August, 1953) version of this blues (see Ex. 159 and Ex. 27), but from the fifth chorus on, he implies substitute harmony ("*Confirmation* chords") at the opening bars of each chorus. Chorus six also has substitute implications at bar eight (see Ex. 126). On *Cheryl* the same substitute implications at the beginning of each chorus occur regularly from the fourth improvised chorus on to the conclusion of Bird's solo.

Cheryl also has excellent examples of Bird's developmental skills. Chorus six has the *Habanera* phrase over the substitute harmony mentioned earlier; chorus seven opens with the *Swingin' on a Star* motif which Parker develops further at the same spot in chorus eight (he begins the motif, then turns into other thoughts); and chorus nine begins with *Let's Fall in Love* which Bird turns into *Johnny One Note* at the same spot in chorus ten.

The first *Ornithology* contains phrases from *Swingin' on A Star, Country Gardens, Minuet in G, Kerry Dancers*, and other Parker favorites. Again, most of these are not mere quotes but, more correctly, paraphrases. In other words, they are used as fragments of themselves and further developed into Parker's line of thought. This is different from the *Santa Claus is Comin' to Town* and *Tenderly* phrases that are used on the second *Ornithology*. In the latter case the quotes are there for their own sake, mostly as a comedic device, and not used developmentally.

Groovin' High also has Parker developing some of his own clichés in a highly original manner. These are good examples of clichés not being clichés in the hands of an artist.

Throughout the two sets Parker uses strange-sounding, sustained notes at the end of phrases (especially on *Now's the Time* and *Little Suede Shoes*) and also seems to have an especially good command of the flow of his ideas.

The supporting group (more will be said about them on the January 1954 date at the same club) is generally excellent although Williams is sometimes (understandably) unsure as to what Bird is going to do on the "head" choruses. The rhythm men have some excellent features; some of the best examples being: bass—*Now's the Time*; piano (including a block chordal section)—*Little Suede Shoes*; drums—second *Ornithology*. Williams is very Miles-like and quotes *Sippin' At Bells* (Aug. 1947—Miles) during his *Now's the Time* solo.

On the liner notes to the *Vol. 2* (Phoenix LP 12—includes the January 1954 Hi-Hat date), it is stated that there are some "cuts" made on *Cheryl* and the second *Ornithology* (a section of "fours" and one of the theme choruses—probably after the piano solo—on *Cheryl*; and most of the opening theme on the second *Ornithology*). The latter "cut" is done tastefully, but the first one creates a slight rhythmic lapse that is disturbing.

The recording is very well done for a "live" date of this period however, and the set is highly recommended as an example of Bird's better moments during the last sixteen months of his life.

Bird's conversation, comments, and announcements will also be of interest to collectors and "ornithologists." Interestingly enough, he mistakenly gives the date of the first recording of *Now's The Time* as 1944 (instead of 1945) in a humorous remark.

There is much here for both the novice and the musician to appreciate.

* * *

In January 1954, after fulfilling another engagement at the Hi-Hat, Parker joined the Stan Kenton Festival of Modern Jazz troupe which also included Gillespie, Candido, Erroll Garner and Slim Gaillard. Stan Getz had originally been the featured saxophonist, but the narcotics plague had gotten to him. He was later arrested in an unarmed attempt to hold up a drugstore. Getz was apprehended as he attempted, out of guilt, to apologize to the owner. He wrote a moving open letter to *Down Beat* from jail denouncing his own conduct and warning young musicians against drugs.

Bird joined the Kenton entourage in Wichita Falls, Texas and stayed with it through the tiring, month-long string of one-nighters that wound through the South, up the East coast, across the northern Midwest, and finally culminated at the Shrine Auditorium in Los Angeles. He was featured on *Night and Day* and *My Funny Valentine*, and Dave Schildkraut, a Kenton altoist, describes his behavior as being "exemplary and in the best tradition of musical knights of the road."[6]

* * *

Recording—Jan. 24, 1954—Hi-Hat Club, Boston—Charlie Parker All Stars

Parker (as), Herbie Williams (tpt), Rollins Griffith (p) Jimmy Woode (b), Marquis Foster (d)

Cool Blues	Phoenix LP12
My Little Suede Shoes	Phoenix LP12
Ornithology	Phoenix LP12
Out of Nowhere	Phoenix LP12
Jumpin' With Symphony Sid	Phoenix LP12

The All-Stars are the local Boston musicians mentioned on the previous Hi Hat date (Dec. 1953) and they assert themselves quite firmly on this recording. One can again see the profound influence that the early pioneers had on the "second line" boppers. Williams is directly out of Miles, and Griffith and Foster owe debts to Bud Powell and Max Roach.

This recording is another "air shot" recorded from one of the shows that "Symphony Sid" Torin (working in Boston since 1952) did from the Hi-Hat. It features some conversations between Bird and Torin that have reference to the Kenton tour and Bird's desire to study composition in Paris.

Cool Blues opens in unison for two choruses, but the recording misses the opening bars and Bird overpowers the trumpet (due to the miking at the source of the original recording). There are seven stimulating Parker choruses and an extended (nine-chorus) trumpet solo. Parker plays excellently—it is hard to believe this is the same man that is on the March studio recordings of this same year. During Parker's solo, Griffith states the "Confirmation" chords in the first four bars of the blues (as he did on the blues tunes of the last date—see also *Cool Blues*— March 1951) starting with the third chorus. The piano and bass solos are well done and the final bass chorus "walks" into the "fours" (alto and trumpet alternating with drums). The tune closes with two choruses of theme.

There is only about a half-chorus of Bird's solo and no opening theme contained on the *Little Suede Shoes* track. Both trumpet and piano solos make excellent use of "double time," however, and Williams uses many grace notes, a la Miles and Clifford Brown. After a bass solo, the theme is heard over Latin rhythm, with the horns breaking into harmony during the last half of each "A" section. Bird has the bridge alone.

Parker's *Ornithology* solo uses many of his favorite phrases and devices, but in an unusual manner and in unusual places. There is, for instance, a *Tenderly* quote in mid-fourth-chorus which is developed in a strange manner against the rhythm. Williams also uses a quote—*On the Trail*—and develops it in his Miles-ish solo. Griffith follows in the Powell tradition, and Woode "walks" two choruses. Bird is alone on the opening and closing themes.

The opening chorus of *Nowhere* is a Bird paraphrase of the melody including a development of the *Embraceable You* motif near the end of the chorus. Williams has a two-chorus solo in which he develops *Country Gardens* at one point, and Griffith's piano solo has some interesting chordal work at the beginning and a strumming left hand, a la Garner at various places. The closing chorus has Bird and Williams, but the trumpet is barely audible.

Jumpin' With Symphony Sid, used as a "chaser," has vibrant Bird—starting with double time—and some nice trumpet work which includes a *Gonna Wash That Man Right Outa My Hair* quote. The theme is performed in unison and then echoed in octave unison. Bird drops to the lower octave. The remastering of this recording was excellently done, and as a whole, the group can be heard in good balance (except for the aforementioned trumpet).

* * *

When the Kenton tour closed on February 28, Parker stayed on the coast for a week to join the back-up group of his friend from the McShann days, Al Hibbler. He visited the studio of sculptress Julie MacDonald during the afternoons and was the subject of a series of sculptural portraits. It was during this week that Parker was dealt one of the final knockout punches; his daughter Pree finally succumbed to pneumonia and died. Parker was crushed and sent telegrams to Chan all through the night. One of the shortest was also the most poignant:

"Chan, HELP. Charlie Parker."[7]

According to Julie MacDonald, Parker "...got very lushed on quadruple Alexanders; then, upon sobering, poured a bottle of Scotch down the john, gave away his heroin, and finally departed for the East a sober man."[8]

* * *

Recording—March 11, 1954—New York City—Charlie Parker Quintet
Parker (as), Walter Bishop (p), Jerome Darr (gtr), Teddy Kotick (b), Roy Haynes (dr).

I Get A Kick Out of You—Take 2	Verve 8007
I Get A Kick Out of You—Take 7	Verve 8007
Just One of Those Things	Verve 8007
My Heart Belongs to Daddy	Verve 8007
I've Got You Under My Skin	Verve 8007

These tracks were done soon after Pree's death and Parker himself had only a year and a day to live. It is evident in his playing that this is a sad Bird, a burdened man. At times his intonation fails him, although his ideas never do. He seems angry with himself. He just stops cold and does not play the final strain of *Just One of Those Things*. The same tune also has an added, "half-time," pseudo-Dixieland tag that sounds unreal. Bird seems to be parodying himself as well as the older form of music.

The melody on the original (probably Take 7) version of *I Get A Kick Out of You*, is played in such a mournful manner by Parker that the listener gets a personal glimpse of his anguish. This original issue also has a *Moon Over Miami* quote at the beginning of the bridge to Parker's improvised chorus and a full-chorus solo by Bishop as well as a half-chorus Darr offering. On the other take, however, there is no guitar solo and Bishop is reduced to 3/4 of a chorus. Nevertheless, both takes contain a "back-beat" intro with Darr participating. Darr is also on the Latin intro and coda to *I've Got You Under My Skin*—the tune is itself in straight-four—but is inaudible at all other times.

My Heart Belongs to Daddy also opens Latin, with Bishop stating *Hawaiian War Chant* figures behind, but moves to straight four for the second half. On the closing theme, however, where the above procedure is reversed, Bishop's Latin accompaniment clashes with Haynes on the first half of the tune. Bird's use of the *Woody Woodpecker* figure improvisationally seems to have a self-depreciating air.

As to the other soloists on the date, Bishop plays excellently throughout, and Haynes is heard to advantage on an eight-bar solo in *Just One of Those Things*. Although these contributions do not make up for the lack of great—or even good— Parker, they do add interest to a session that is only worth hearing for Bird's emotions.

* * *

After a short stint in mid-April at Philadelphia's Blue Note, Bird moved his family—Chan, Kim and Baird—to Brewster on Cape Cod for the summer. He worked a few weekend jobs at the local Red Barn and stayed close to the family except for a brief booking at the Crystal in Detroit in mid-July. In late August, he was booked into Birdland with the string group, on the same bill with Dinah Washington.

Dinah and Parker, both notorious drinkers, celebrated their combined birthdays backstage with much alcohol, and Bird was later involved in a hassle with his string musicians. Some reports say that Parker fired them on the spot after he began one tune and the strings played another but Bird's bassist for the evening, Tommy Potter, states:

> During one of the intermissions, he (Bird) went out in front of the club, opened the door of a cab, and sat down on the floor...he said he just wanted to sit there. There was a little tug of war and Bird rolled into the cab. The driver...drove over to a police station and left Bird there. With Bird gone there was no need of the string section so the Birdland management fired them.[9]

Depressed over his own behavior, Parker drank a bottle of iodine in an attempt at suicide after returning to his East Village apartment and violently arguing with Chan. He was rushed to Bellevue Hospital in an ambulance, treated for ingestion of the poison, and placed in the semi-agitative ward of the Psychiatric Division. The diagnosis, as mentioned before, was latent schizophrenia.

Before the Birdland booking, Parker had told a union official that he would "jump off the Empire State Building" if he did not make good, and the suicide attempt serves to point out how strongly Bird hated his own strange behavior. He later tried to pass the incident off as a "put-on" to legally absolve him of his debts, but, if anything, this story was a "self-put-on."

He was slated for a gigantic European package tour in October, but he cancelled out after his hospitalization and was replaced by Coleman Hawkins. After his release on September 10, however, he did work some concerts in the New York and Boston areas. The rhythm section of the Modern Jazz Quartet (Percy Heath, bass; John Lewis, piano; and Kenny Clarke, drums) which was on the same group of presentations, acted as his accompanying group.

On September 28, he committed himself into the hospital again and complained of severe depression which had caused him, he claimed, to return to his alcoholic pattern. The neurological examination proved negative, and Parker was discharged on October 15 in his own custody. Newspaperman Sol Weinstein met Bird on a train sometime after the Bellevue stay and states that Bird spoke of how depressed he was during his hospitalization until..."into the ward walks Roy Rogers in that Western get-up and carrying a guitar. When he started plunking that thing I was gassed."[10] Parker was a western fan, especially of Roy Rogers and Hopalong Cassidy. The latter hero, played by Bill Boyd, was on a TV series in the mid-1950s.

The Parker family moved to Bucks County, Pennsylvania where Chan's mother owned a farm a few miles away from the town of New Hope. Bird began commuting daily to the city for psychiatric treatment at Bellevue, and at the end of October, he performed excellently at a Town Hall concert presented by Bob Reisner. An ominous event happened at this concert, however. The stage hands' union regulations specified only so much time for the concert, and in the middle of Parker's last set the final curtain abruptly closed. It was truly a prediction of what was to come.

At the encouragement of Harvey Cropper, one of Bird's "Village" artist buddies, Parker took up painting. He lost 20 pounds and seemed to be again on the road to recovery. He soon started spending more time in the "Village" than at home with his family, however, and the drinking began again. Ahmed Basheer, a philosophical "Village" Muslim, and Ted Joans, another Bohemian character who dabbled in surrealistic art, beat poetry, trumpet playing, and party throwing, were two of his close associates. The January 1955 issue of *Our World* magazine pictured Parker at one of Joans' masquerade parties and described him as being "relaxed as a cool Mau Mau."

He jammed at Arthur's on 7th Avenue and also at the Village bistros, The Savannah, The Montmarte, and The Bohemia. His rhythm section often consisted of Ted Wald, bass; Warrick Brown, piano; and Bill Heine, drums. This group also appeared at the Open Door at the Sunday sessions.

He was slated to do some more recording to form an all-Porter album. At the end of December he did two tunes, it was the final studio recording of his life.

* * *

Recording—December 10, 1954—New York City. Charlie Parker and His Orchestra
Parker (as), Billy Bauer (g), Walter Bishop (p), Teddy Kotick (b), Art Taylor (d).

Love For Sale—Take 4	Verve 8007
Love For Sale—Take 5	Verve 8007
I Love Paris—Take 2	Verve 8007
I Love Paris—Take 3	Verve 8007

Bauer certainly lends more to this date than Jerome Darr did to the March one. He comps well, collaborates perfectly with Bishop, and adds some improvised contrapuntal lines behind Parker at times. One beautiful example occurs in the second section of the opening theme on the alternate take of *Love For Sale* (again there are no specific take listings).

Ex. 161—*Love For Sale*—Bauer's Contrapuntal Line

Parker's quote of *Nightingale* in his improvisation can also be used as an "identifier" for the alternate take.

Bird certainly does not sound like his best offerings of 1947 on the first tune, but he also does not sound bad. Bauer is pleasant and Bishop can be heard developing *Habanera* and few other favorite phrases in an original manner. Bishop had a characteristic way of using thirds in his right hand—almost like Bud Powell— at phrase endings and other spots. A characteristic example appears below (an invented one—not transcribed). A knowledge of this characteristic can be helpful in identifying him as other tapes from the end of Parker's career are found.

Ex. 162—Bishop's Characteristic use of Thirds

Both Bishop and Parker often developed the opening sequence of Gautier's *Le Secret* on record dates and live performances in which they participated together (hear Bishop's hint in the *Love for Sale* alternate).

Ex. 163—*Le Secret*

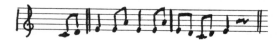

I Love Paris is usually performed as an AB tune (16 minor—16 major), but here it is done in the form of AAB. The "A" sections are in a Latin tempo in the exposition chorus, and the "B" section, the Latin tempo also returns for the "take-out." On the take not marked alternate, Bird's entrance to the final "B" section begins with the "They-all-ran-after-the-farmer's wife" figure from *Three Blind Mice* (he uses this on the other take also but not at this entrance). The Latin figure played behind Bird's melody by piano and guitar is slightly different on each take.

Ex. 164—*I Love Paris*—Backing Figure and Alternate

One of the less successful moments of the date is Kotick's "walking" half-chorus on *Love For Sale*; there is nothing wrong with Kotick's playing; the group merely sounds as if nothing is happening. Taylor is effective on the bridge of the same tune, however, although he and Bird do not quite jibe on the entrance of the final statement of the alternate take.

These tracks are much better than the March offering, even though they came later in Bird's life.

* * *

Indeed, there was only a short distance for the "Bird of Time...to flutter," as Parker so ominously predicted in his recitation of Stanza VII of Omar Khayyam's *Rubaiyat* to Bob Reisner on New Years Day, 1955.[11] But as one realizes that Bird was already on the wing, one is reminded of the many unfortunate circumstances which colored his life, which, in turn, remind this writer of another stanza (LXXXI) of the same poem:

> Oh Thou, who Man of baser Earth did make
> And ev'n with Paradise devise the Snake:
> For all the Sin wherewith the Face of Man
> Is Blacken'd—Man's forgiveness give—and take!

CHAPTER XXI

THE OUT-CHORUS
A Chaotic Death
(1955)

Fate shall yield
To fickle Chance, and Chaos judge the strife.
John Milton—Paradise Lost. Bk. II.

The year 1955 looked very promising for jazz in general. On national television, the *Tonight Show* featured the beautifully zany humor of the host, Steve Allen, who regularly used jazz musicians on his show; and the Dorsey Brothers and Stan Kenton had also jumped into the TV picture. Jazz recording was prolific (the Fifties produced more jazz records than all preceding decades combined), and the influence of the "boppers" was strong; Stan Getz had returned to the scene, and his former pianist Horace Silver was gaining a formidable reputation as a hard-swinging, "East Coast" musician through his 1954 recordings with Art Blakey's Jazz Messengers. Silver's *Doodlin'*, done at the end of 1954 with Kenny Dorham on trumpet, was fast becoming a classic composition. Both Getz and Silver had their roots in "bebop," but Getz moved toward the "cool" style while Silver gravitated to the hard-driving, blues-tinged style that came to be known as "funky." John Lewis and Milt Jackson formed the nucleus of the Modern Jazz Quartet, which would remain a working and recording combo until the mid-seventies; and Miles Davis was on the verge of becoming a major trend-setter (the Davis quintet recordings with John Coltrane began in October). The alliance of Max Roach with the brilliant young trumpeter, Clifford Brown, whose style evolved from Fats Navarro's, had produced several fine recordings during 1954, and the dually-led group would continue to extend the bop tradition until Brown's untimely death in June of 1956. Along with the television and recording industries, other media were also kind to jazz. Indeed, Dave Brubeck had been on the cover of *Time* magazine in November, 1954; and, in radio, there were some "personality" disc jockeys on far-reaching stations who favored a modern jazz policy on late night shows. It was on one such show— Daddy-O Daily's from Chicago—that this writer, living in Pennsylvania, first heard the later Parker sides described in this work. All things considered jazz seemed destined to reach a wider audience in the future.

As the year rolled on, however, the Rock revolution would roll in with big sales on Bill Haley's *Rock Around the Clock* and Mike Pedicin's *Shake A Hand*, both containing bleating, bluesy saxophone playing. The popular movement is generally ten to twenty years behind the underground in its pattern of "cultural lag," but a return to the 1930s "race" records seemed ridiculous. A Philadelphia-based TV Show, Bandstand, hosted by Bob Horn, kept alive the twanging guitars and one-note tenors, however, and in the midst of this retrogressive change, Charlie Parker was to die.

Bird worked on the road as a single in Detroit and at the Bee Hive in Chicago, even though his body had become severely bloated, and wracked by a cold. In addition, there was also a giant swelling at the back of his tongue. He returned east to Philadelphia's Blue Note in late February, and then came home to The Apple for a weekend two-nighter at Birdland in early March. He was not on hard drugs, but he was drinking profusely and continuously. Joe Segal, Chicago jazz authority and producer, describes Bird's behavior on the four-day Bee Hive engagement during January:

> On opening night, Bird retired to a back room, spent most of his time resting, and didn't emerge very often to play....The next night, Saturday, began fairly cool.... But by midnight Bird had retired to the back room and passed out....He had begun playing better on Sunday afternoon, and by the time the gig was over Monday night, he was wailing as of old....I'll always remember the last thing he said to me...though I still don't quite understand what he meant—he said, 'I'd tell you a joke, but you're too hip.'[1]

The group for the March Birdland gigs—Friday and Saturday (4th and 5th)—consisted of Dorham, Blakey, Powell, and Mingus. It should have been a "ball," but it wasn't. The first gig came off well except for the usual jibing by Bird and Bud, but on Saturday night the atmosphere was explosive. The childish behavior of both Powell and Parker set off firecrackers, and Bird ended up by stalking out of the club. Mingus lectured the audience over the PA system on how incidents of the type that was occurring were "killing jazz" and on how he did not want to be associated with the group. Bird, however, was later seen at Basin Street, around the corner, in a tearful, agonized state. He solved his problem, as usual with an enormous amount of alcohol.

Before leaving New York for his next scheduled engagement at Storyville, Bird decided to visit his friend of recent years, the Baroness Pannonica de Koenigswarter who lived in a suite at the posh Hotel Stanhope on Fifth Avenue. The Baroness, a devoted Afrophile, was the sister of the English diplomat Victor de Rothschild and was married to a French diplomatic official whom she had left in 1951 when she came to New York to live the life of the rich Bohemian. Her close associates in the jazz field were Thelonious Monk and Art Blakey, and she was often a patron of the Open Door when Monk worked there with Parker's quintet during 1953-1954.

Nica, as the Baroness was called by musicians, offered Bird a drink, which he refused, and she then tried to make him more comfortable by having him stretch out on the sofa. In a few minutes, however, Bird arose, made his way to the bathroom, and began vomiting blood. Nica had seen enough, she sent for her private physician,

Dr. Freymann, and he arrived quickly and advised hospitalization. Bird would not have this, however, and the doctor agreed to allow Bird to stay in the apartment under the care of the Baroness. Freymann warned Nica of the seriousness of Parker's condition. He felt that the ulcers plus advanced cirrhosis of the liver could lead to death at any moment.

After three full days of around-the-clock nursing by the Baroness and her daughter coupled with thrice daily visits by the doctor, however, Bird appeared to improve, and on Saturday, March 12, was told that he could sit up a bit during the evening and watch the Dorsey Brothers' eight o'clock television program. During the show, a juggling act miscued; Parker began laughing hysterically; choked; rose from his chair; and then fell back. When the doctor arrived at the suite, Parker was already dead. Doctor Freymann would not sign the death certificate, but diagnosed the cause of death as a heart attack. Later an autopsy report said it was lobar pneumonia caused by visceral congestion.

Although the cause of death still causes arguments, it seems to matter little; for any diagnosis would only include the immediate cause of death anyway and not all the contributing factors. The bleeding ulcers, unfunctioning liver, and a cold that was causing severe congestion certainly could have all combined to place a heavy strain on the cardiovascular system. Parker had not been using heroin for some time before his death, but the alcohol had actually depleted him worse and caused the eating away of the liver. It is perhaps best to think, therefore, that— as someone remarked—"Bird died of everything." The Baroness tried to keep the story quiet until Chan Richardson was notified, but news leaked out. Chan was finally located on Tuesday, March 15, but meanwhile, Parker's body had lain in the morgue unidentified. Many of the papers carried lurid headlines, and Bird became as fascinating in death as he was in life.

Here again there were reports of foul play, for Bird's age was given as 53 and his body was rumored to have been tagged "John Parker." There were also suspicions about Freymann not signing the death certificate and the Baroness's closed-mouth behavior. Realistically, however, one can understand the plight of the Baroness; she did not know where to locate Bird's family and the body had to be taken somewhere. The publicity, as many newspapers proved, could be extremely cruel, and she was probably trying to do the best thing for herself and Parker. Freymann, knowing that Bird should have been immediately hospitalized but giving in to his wishes, probably did not want to be associated with the death because of law suits and other professional jeopardies. Moreover, the hotel wanted the body removed as hurriedly as possible and Freymann's forced guess at the age and the possibility of a confused label are easily understood in the light of such haste. These are only guesses, but they do seem to make more sense than the invention of some fantastic mystery story. The discrepancies over the age, the wrong name on the body, and the other confusions over the death made good copy, but they were really unimportant. What was important, was the fact that the tragic man who had offered so much to the world of music was finally at peace with himself.

Doris, his third wife, and Chan, his common-law wife, haggled over the funeral arrangements, but finally the body was turned over to Doris and the viewing was held at the Unity Funeral Home. The funeral was held on March 21 from the

Abyssinian Baptist Church on 138th Street, and the body was sent to Kansas City to be buried. Parker left two sons—Leon, from his first wife; and Baird, from Chan. Several benefits were held to establish a trust for the boys, as Bird had died practically penniless; the Carnegie Hall benefit was sold out and raised over $5,000.00.

The estate was an unbelievably messy business, but Doris was named administratrix until 1960 when Geraldine, the second wife from the Hines period, turned up and proved that Parker had never divorced her. The estate was then divided between the legal wives and the sons, with Geraldine receiving the greatest share. Chan, who received nothing, continues to fight the decision to this day.

So ended the tragic life of Charles Parker, Jr. Perhaps the moving beauty that Parker, the musician, created would never have existed if it were not for the evil in Parker, the man. In other words, he was not frustrated because he was a musician, he was a musician because he was frustrated. But to those who heard his music, and understood the frustration, Parker will always be a model of the correct approach to art; he reminds us, time and time again, that music, in the larger sense, is not about notes or sounds, but rather, is about the people who create it.

* * *

Yet, Ah, that Spring should vanish with the rose!
That Youth's sweet-scented manuscript should close!
The Nightingale that in the branches sang,
Ah whence, and whither flown again, who knows!
Rubaiyat of Omar Khayyam
Stanza XCVI

APPENDIX I

A Numerical Listing of
Charlie Parker's Recordings

A number-identification system for all recordings by Charlie Parker could be a useful guide for discographers, researchers, musicologists, and listeners. The writer has developed the following system in his own Parker research. The listing is an attempt to be complete, but there may be inadvertent omissions or material newly released since its preparation.

The first two digits indicate the *year of recording* (45 for 1945). The following one or two digits (1 through 99) assign each recording its *individual number within a given year*. When the listing was first developed, numbers were assigned in date order within a year, but the system does *not* claim or seek to maintain completely accurate dating in this manner. Some recording dates are not certain, and a significant amount of unissued "live" material exists. It is therefore possible that subsequent determination of recording dates and/or the appearance of new live material will make the individual numbers inaccurate as precising dating devices, but it would be confusing to alter all subsequent numbers within a year each time a change occurs. It has therefore been the practice to add numbers within a year series, regardless of the date of the recording within that year.

The system is thus open-ended enough to allow for mistakes or new additions without having to revise the whole system. If, for example, an error in dating the year were found, the number would simply be deleted and placed in the correct year. The new individual number assigned, as with any new material, would be the next number after the last number previously used in the new year. The deletion of the old number would have no effect on the rest of the listing. The writer has, in fact, inserted a number of performances, dating from 1940 to 1953, in this manner and anticipates that more tapes of live performances will continue to emerge in the future. These insertions appear at the end of the appropriate year so that individual numbers remain in sequential order as assigned.

The *individual number* remains the same for different versions of the same tune at a given session; the final digit supplements it by indicating the *number of takes*. A final zero indicates that there was only one take (as would normally be the case in a live performance). If there were multiple takes of a tune on a given date, the final digit indicates the take number (e.g., 4411 is followed by 4412 and 4413, to indicate the three takes on "Tiny's Tempo" on September 15, 1944).

Studio performances are listed only if they have been issued. Some have been lost or destroyed, or are otherwise unavailable; this explains why some take numbers are missing.

The letter "T" immediately after the number indicates a tape made at a live performance; the absence of the "T" indicates a regular studio session.

A series of letter codes, set off from the number by a hyphen, provide information about the form or format of the tune where deemed necessary. These codes follow:

B—blues
R—*I Got Rhythm* pattern
H—*Honeysuckle Rose* pattern
RH—*I Got Rhythm* pattern with *Honeysuckle Rose* bridge
HR—*Honeysuckle Rose* pattern with *I Got Rhythm* bridge
RD—*I Got Rhythm* pattern with a different bridge
S—constructed on a *standard tune* pattern
OC—original construction
V—vocal
M—minor

At a glance, then, one can tell the year of recording, the individual number of the recording, the take number, whether it was taped at a live performance or a standard studio recording, and something about the form. Two examples follow:

1. *Scrapple From The Apple*—47422-HR: Recorded 1947; recording no. 42; second take (studio recording); *Honeysuckle Rose* pattern with the *I Got Rhythm* bridge.
2. *Scrapple From The Apple*—49180T-HR: Recorded 1949; recording no. 18; taped version; *Honeysuckle Rose* pattern with the *I Got Rhythm* bridge.

Some tunes on three Verve dates have been changed as to their "take" numbers (final digit) due to further research since their original publication in the Rutgers University *Journal of Jazz Studies*. These are:

Chi Chi—August 8, 1953—formerly 1-2-3, now listed 1-6-3.
I Get a Kick Out of You—March 11, 1954—formerly 1-2, now 7-2.
Love for Sale—December 30, 1954—formerly 1-2, now 4-5.
Love for Sale—December 30, 1954—formerly 1-2, now 3-2.

Other changes have been made in the numerical system since the original issue, but these were either the correction of misprints, or the addition of one of the "form" abbreviations at the end of some numbers for added clarity. The misprint corrections will be obvious to anyone who understands the system, and the added letters will only help in distinguishing the form rather than make any actual change in the basic number.

1940
November 30—McShann
I Found A New Baby—4010T
Body and Soul—4020T

December 2—McShann
Honeysuckle Rose—4030T
Lady Be Good—4040T
Coquette—4050T
Moten Swing—4060T
Wichita Blues—4070T-B

1941
April 30—McShann
Swingmatism—4110
Hootie Blues—4120-B
Dexter Blues—4130-B
November 18—McShann
One Woman's Man—4140-V

1942
July 2—McShann
Lonely Boy Blues—4210-B
Get Me On Your Mind—4220-V
The Jumpin' Blues—4230
Sepian Bounce—4240

Circa 1942—McShann
You Say Forward, I'll March—4250T-V
Lonely Boy Blues—4260T-V
Vine Street Boogie—4270T-B
Jump the Blues—4280T-B
One O'Clock Jump (theme)—4290T
Bottle It—42100T-B
Sweet Georgia Brown—42110T
Wrap Your Troubles in Dreams—42120T
One O'Clock Jump (theme)—42130T
   (Compiler's note: There is
   some doubt that Parker is the
   soloist on some of these sides.)
Circa 1942—probably at Monroe's
Cherokee—42140T

1944
September 15—Tiny Grimes
Tiny's Tempo—4411-B
Tiny's Tempo—4412-B
Tiny's Tempo—4413-B
Red Cross—4421-R
Red Cross—4422-R
I'll Always Love You Just The Same—4430-V
Romance Without Finance—4440-V

1945
January—Clyde Hart

What's The Matter Now—4510-V
I Want Every Bit of It—4520-V
That's The Blues—4530-V
4-F Blues—4541-V
G.I. Blues—4542-V
January-Trummy Young
I Dream of You—4550-V
Seventh Avenue—4560-V
Sorta Kinda—4570-V
Oh, Oh, My, My—4580-V
February 12—Cootie Williams
Floo-gee-boo—4590T-RH
February-March—Dizzy Gillespie
Groovin' High—45100-S
All The Things You are—45110
Dizzy Atmosphere—45120-RD
May 11—Dizzy Gillespie
Salt Peanuts—45130-R
Shaw 'Nuff—45140-R
Lover Man—45150-V
Hot House—45160-S
May 25—Sarah Vaughn
What More Can A Woman Do—45170-V
I'd Rather Have A Memory—45180-V
Mean To Me—45190-V
June 6—Red Norvo
Hallelujah—45201
Hallelujah—45202
Hallelujah—45203
Get Happy—45213
Get Happy—45214
Slam Slam Blues—45221-B
Sam Slam Blues—45222-B
Congo Blues—45231-B
Congo Blues—45232-B
Congo Blues—45233-B
Congo Blues—45234-B
Congo Blues—45235-B
September 4—Sir Charles Thompson
Takin' Off—45240
If I Had You—45250
20th Century Blues—45260-B (br)
The Street Beat—45270-R
November 26
Billie's Bounce—45281-B
Billie's Bounce—45282-B
Billie's Bounce—45283-B
Billie's Bounce—45284-B
Billie's Bounce—45285-B
Warming Up A Riff—45290-S

Now's The Time—45301-B
Now's The Time—45302-B
Now's The Time—45303-B
Now's The Time—45304-B
Thrivin' On A Riff—45311-R
Thrivin' On A Riff—45312-R
Thrivin' On A Riff—45313-R
Meandering—45320-S
KoKo—45331-S
KoKo—45332-S
December 29—Slim Gaillard
Dizzy's Boogie—45341-B
Dizzy's Boogie—45342-B
Flat Foot Floogie—45352-RH
Flat Foot Floogie—45351-RH
Poppity Pop—45360-R
Slim's Jam—45370
December 29—Dizzy Gillespie
Groovin' High—45380T-S
Dizzy Atmosphere—45390T-RD

1946
January 29—JATP
Sweet Georgia Brown—4610
February 5—Dizzy Gillespie
Diggin' Diz—4620-S
March 28
Moose The Mooche—4631-R
Moose The Mooche—4632-R
Moose The Mooche—4633-R
Yardbird Suite—4641-OC
Yardbird Suite—4644-OC
Ornithology—4651-S
Ornithology—4653-S
Ornithology—4654-S
Night in Tunisa (alto break)—4661
Night in Tunisa—4664
Night in Tunisa—4665
Early April—JATP
Blues for Norman—4670-B
I Can't Get Started—4680
Lady Be Good—4690
After You've Gone—46100
April 22—JATP
JATP Blues—46110-B
I Got Rhythm—46120
July 29
Max is Making Wax—46130-RD
Lover Man—46140
The Gypsy—46150

BeBop—46160-M
Early March—Finale Club
Blue and Boogie—46170T-B
Billie's Bounce—46180T-B
Anthropology—46190T-R
Ornithology—46200T-S
All the Things You Are—46210-T

1947
February 1
Home Cookin' I—4710T-SH
Home Cookin' II—4720T-S
Home Cookin' III—4730T-R
Yardbird Suite—4740T-OC
Lullaby in Rhythm—4750T
Blues—4760-B
Probably February—King Cole Trio
Cherokee—4770T
February 19
This is Always—4793-V
This is Always—4794-V
Dark Shadows—47101-V
Dark Shadows—47102-V
Dark Shadows—47103-V
Dark Shadows—47104-V
Bird's Nest—47111-RD
Bird's Nest—47112-RD
Bird's Nest—47113-RD
Cool Blues—47121-B
Cool Blues—47122-B
Cool Blues—47123-B
Cool Blues—47124-B
February 26
Relaxin' At Camarillo—47131-B
Relaxin' At Camarillo—47133-B
Relaxin' At Camarillo—47134-B
Relaxin' At Camarillo—47135-B
Cheers—47141-R (Altered) H
Cheers—47142-R (Altered) H
Cheers—47143-R (Altered) H
Cheers—47144-R (Altered) H
Carvin' The Bird—47151-B
Carvin' The Bird—47152-B
Stupendous—47161-S
Stupendous—47162-S
May
Donna Lee—47171-S
Donna Lee—47172-S
Donna Lee—47173-S
Donna Lee—47174-S

Chasin' The Bird—47181-R

Chasin' The Bird—47182-R

Chasin' The Bird—47183-R

Cheryl—47191-B

Cheryl—47192-B

Buzzy—47201-B

Buzzy—47202-B

Buzzy—47203-B

Buzzy—47204-B

Buzzy—47205-B

August—Miles Davis

Milestones—47211

Milestones—47212

Little Willie Leaps—47221-S

Little Willie Leaps—47222-S

Little Willie Leaps—47223-S

Half Nelson—47231

Half Nelson—47232

Sippin' At Bells—47241-B

Sippin' At Bells—47242-B

Sippin' At Bells—47244-B

September 13—Barry Ulanov-Broadcast

Hot House—47250T-S

Fine and Dandy—47260T

KoKo (theme)—47340T

September 29—Dizzy Gillespie

Night in Tunisia—47270T

Dizzy Atmosphere—47280T-RD

Groovin' High—47290T-S

Confirmation—47300T-OC

October 28

Dexterity—47351-R

Dexterity—47352-R

Bongo Bop—47361-B

Bongo Bop—47362-B

Dewey Square—47371-OC

Dewey Square—47372-OC

Dewey Square—47373-OC

Bird of Paradise—47381-S

Bird of Paradise—47382-S

Bird of Paradise—47383-S

Embraceable You—47391

Embraceable You—47392

November 4

Bird Feathers—47403-B

Klactoveedsedsten—47411-OC

Klactoveedsedstene—47412-OC

Scrapple From The Apple—47421-HR

Scrapple From The Apple—47422-HR

My Old Flame—47430

Out of Nowhere—47441

Out of Nowhere—47442

Out of Nowhere—47443

Don't Blame Me—47450

December 17

Drifin' On A Reed—47463-B

Drifin' On A Reed—47464-B

Drifin' On A Reed—47465-B

Quasimado—47471-S

Quasimado—47472-S

Charlie's Wig—47482-S

Charlie's Wig—47484-S

Charlie's Wig—47485-S

Bongo Beep—47492-B

Bongo Beep—47493-B

Crazeology—47501

Crazeology—47502

Crazeology—47503

Crazeology—47504

How Deep is The Ocean—47511

How Deep is The Ocean—47522

December

Another Hairdo—47521-B

Another Hairdo—47522-B

Another Hairdo—47523-B

Blue Bird—47531-B

Blue Bird—47532-B

Klaunstance—47540-S

Bird Gets The Worm—47551-S

Bird Gets The Worm—47552-S

March 9—Hi-De-Ho (Los Angeles)

Dee Dee's Dance—47560T

September 20—Broadcast-Barry Ulanov

KoKo (theme)—47570T

Sunny Side of the Street—47580T

How Deep Is The Ocean?—47590T

Tiger Rag—47600T

52nd Street Theme (theme)—47610T-RH

November—Broadcast-Barry Ulanov

52nd Street Theme (theme)—47620T-RH

Donna Lee—47630T-S

Fats Flat—47640T-S

Groovin' High—47650T-S

KoKo-Anthropology (theme)—47660T-S

1948

Spring 1948

52nd Street Theme—4810T-RH (long)

Shaw 'Nuff—4820T-R

Out of Nowhere—4830T

Hot House—4840T-S
This Time The Dream's On Me—4850T
Night in Tunisia—4860T
My Old Flame—4870T
The Way You Look Tonight—4880T
Out of Nowhere—4890T
Chasin' The Bird—48100T-R
This Time The Dream's On Me—48110T
Dizzy Atmosphere—48120T-RD
How High The Moon—48130T
52nd Street Theme—48140T-RH
Spring
These Foolish Things—48150T
There's A Small Hotel—48160T
Fine and Dandy—48170T
Hot House—48180T-S
August 29
Barbados—48191-B
Barbados—48192-B
Barbados—48193-B
Barbados—48194-B
Ah-Leu-Cha—48201-R
Ah-Leu-Cha—48202-R
Constellation—48211-RH
Constellation—48212-RH
Constellation—48213-RH
Constellation—48214-RH
Parker's Mood—48221-B
Parker's Mood—48222-B
Parker's Mood—48223-B
August-September
Perhaps—48231-B
Perhaps—48232-B
Perhaps—48233-B
Perhaps—48234-B
Perhaps—48235-B
Perhaps—48236-B
Marmaduke—48241-H
Marmaduke—48242-H
Marmaduke—48243-H
Marmaduke—48244-H
Marmaduke—48245-H
Marmaduke—48246-H
Steeplechase—48250-R
Merry Go Round—48261-RH
Merry Go Round—48262-RH
September 11
52nd Street Theme—48270T-RH
KoKo—48280T-S
December 11

Groovin' High—48290T-S
Big Foot—48300T-B
Ornithology—48310T-S
December 12
Hot House—48320T-S
Salt Peanuts—48330T-R
December 18
Out of Nowhere—48340T
How High The Moon—48350T
December 20—Machito
Mango Mangue—48360
Circa 1948—Neal Hefti
Repetition—48370
Circa 1948
The Bird—48380-M
December 25
Half Nelson—48390T
White Christmas—48400T
Little Willie Leaps—48410T-S
December 11
Slow Boat to China—48420T
Spring
52nd Street Theme—48430T (Talk)

1949
January 1
Slow Boat To China—4910T
January 3—Metronome All Stars
Overtime—4921-S
Overtime—4922-S
Victory Ball—4931-S
Victory Ball—4932-S
January 8
Cheryl—4940T-B
January—Machito
Okie-Doke—4950
Circa 1949—Machito
Mambo—4960
6/8—4970
Jazz—4980
January 15
Scrapple From The Apple—4990T-HR
Be Bop—49100T-M
Hot House—49110T-S
January 22
Oop Bop Sh' Bam—49120T-RH
February 5
Barbados—49130T-B
Salt Peanuts—49140T-R
February 12

Barbados—49150T-B
February 19
Groovin' High—49160T-S
February 26
Half Nelson—49170T
Night in Tunisa—49180T
Scrapple From The Apple—49190T-HR
March 12
Cheryl—49200T-B
Slow Boat To China—49210T
Chasin' The Bird—49220T-R
April
Cardboard—49230-OC
Visa—49240-B
May 5
Segment—49251-M
Segment—49252-M
Diverse (?)—49270-R
Passport (?)—49280-B
   (compiler's note: Titles are my
   conjecture; there is no way of telling
   them apart.)
May 8, 9, 14, 15—Paris
Scrapple From The Apple—49290T-HR
Out of Nowhere—49300T (Birthday)
Barbados—49310T-B
52nd Street Theme—49320T-RH
Salt Peanuts—49330T-R (sings French)
Allen's Alley—49340T-R
Out of Nowhere—49350T
Salt Peanuts—49360T-R
Blues—49370T-B
September 18—JATP
The Opener—49380-B
Lester Leaps In—49390-R
Embraceable You—49400
The Closer—49410-B
November 30—Strings
Just Friends—49420
Everything Happens To Me—49430
April in Paris—49440
Summertime—49450
I Didn't Know What Time It Was—49460
If I Should Lose You—49470
December 24
Bird of Paradise—49480T-S
Now's The Time—49490T-B
March 5—Broadcast-Waldorf
Barbados—49500T-B
Anthropology—49510T-R

December 24—Carnegie
KoKo—49520T-S
Cheryl—49530T-B
Ornithology—49540T-S
Circa 1949—Safranski-Lamond
Cool Blues—49550T-B
February 26—Roost
Deedle—49560T-V
What's This—49570T-V
March 5—Roost
Cheryl—49580T-B
Anthropology—49590T-R
May—Paris
52nd Street Theme—49600T-RH
   (No opening theme)

1950
February 18
52nd Street Theme—5010T-RH (short)
Ornithology—5020T-S
I Didn't Know What Time It Was—5030T
Embraceable You—5040T
Scrapple From The Apple—5050T-HR
Hot House—5060T-S
Now's The Time—5070T-B
Visa—5080T-B
Star Eyes—5090T
Confirmation—50100T-OC
Out of Nowhere—50110T
What's New?—50120T
Smoke Gets in Your Eyes—50130T
I Cover The Waterfront—50140T
52nd Street Theme—50150T-RH
March-April
Star Eyes—50160
Blues (fast)—50170-B
I'm In The Mood For Love—50180
May 15 (U.L.)
Rifftide (Street Beat)—50190T-R
Cool Blues—50200T-B
52nd Street Theme (3 chorus)
   50210T-RH
May 8 (U.L.)
Perdido—50220T-S (Wahoo)
'Round About Midnight—50230T
Move—50240T
May 29 (U.L.)
Ornithology—50250T-S
June 6—Gillespie
Bloomdido—50260-B

An Oscar For Treadwell—50273-R
An Oscar For Treadwell—50274-R
Mohawk—50283-B
Mohawk—50284-B
Melancholy Baby—50290
Leap Frog—50304
Leap Frog—50306
Relaxin' With Lee—50312-S
Relaxin' With Lee—50313-S
July 5—Strings
Dancing in The Dark—50320
Out of Nowhere—50330
Laura—50340
East of The Sun—50350
They Can't Take That Away From
   Me—50360
Easy To Love—50370
I'm In The Mood For Love—50380
I'll Remember April—50390
September 16—Concert
Repetition—50400
What is This Thing Called Love—50410
April in Paris—50420
Easy To Love—50430
Rocker—50440
October
Celerity—50450-R
Ballade—50460
November 24—Sweden—Folkets Park
Anthropology—50470T-R
Scrapple From The Apple—50480T-H
Embraceable You—50490T
Cool Blues—50500T-B
Star Eyes—50510T
All The Things You Are—50520T
Body and Soul—50530T
Fine and Dandy—50540T
Strike Up The Band—50550T
How High The Moon—50560T
Late November
Ladybird—50570T
Summer—Latin band
Bongo Ballad—50580T
Bird's Mambo—50590T
Circa 1950
I Can't Get Started—50600T
Malmo, Sweden-Nov.
Cheers—50610T-RH
Anthropology—50620T-R
Cool Blues—50630T-B

Lover Man—50640T
May 8 (U.L.)
This Time the Dream's On Me—50650T
Dizzy Atmosphere—50660T-RD
May 15 (U.L.)
Out of Nowhere—50670T
Night in Tunisia—50680T (no Parker)
May 22 (U.L.)
Little Willie Leaps—50690T-S
52nd Street Theme (no choruses)—
   50700T-RH
May 29 (U.L.)
I'll Remember April—50710T
52nd Street Theme (2 choruses)—50720-RH
Cafe Society
Just Friends ("Pop Goes the Weasel")—50730T
April in Paris ("Irish Washerwoman")—50740T
Just Friends—50750T
April in Paris—50760T
Moose the Mooche—50770T-R
Lover Come Back to Me—50780T
52nd Street Theme—50790T-RH
Wm. Henry Apartments
Half Nelson (lacking bass)—50800T
Cherokee—50810T
Scrapple From the Apple—50820-T-HR
Star Eyes—50830T
Bernie's Tune—50840T-M
Donna Lee—50850T-S
Out of Nowhere—50860T
Half Nelson—50870T
Fine and Dandy—50880T
Little Willie Leaps—50890T-S
All the Things You Are—50900T
Chubby Newsome Vocal
Embraceable You—50910T-V
August 23—Apollo
Easy to Love—50920T

1951
Au Privave—5112-B
Au Privave—5113-B
She Rote—5123-OC
She Rote—5125-OC
K.C. Blues—5130-B
Star Eyes—5142
March 12
My Little Suede Shoes—5150-OC
Un poquito de tu Amor—5160
Tico Tico—5170

Fiesta—5180

Why Do I Love You?—5192

Why Do I Love You?—5196

Why Do I Love You?—5197

March—Rockland Palace

Sly Mongoose—51100T

Moose The Mooche—51110T-R

Star Eyes—51120T

This Time The Dreams on Me—51130T

Cool Blues—51140T-B

Little Suede Shoes—51150T-OC

Lester Leaps In—51160T

March

Laura—51170T

Rocker—51180T

March 31—Birdland

Jumpin' With Symphony Sid—51190T-B

Blues 'n' Boogie—51200T-B

Anthropology—51210T-R

'Round Midnight—51220T

Night in Tunisa—51230T

April 7—Birdland Strings

Laura—51240T

April 12—Christy's Boston

Happy Bird Blues—51250T-B

Scrapple From The Apple

— 51260T-HR

Lullaby in Rhythm—51270T

I'll Remember April—51280T

July—Herman

You Go To My Head—51290T

Leo The Lion—51300T-B

Cubop Holiday—51310T-H

Nearness of You—51320T

Lemon Drop—51330T-R

The Goof and I—51340T-R

Four Brothers—51350T

August 8

Blues For Alice—51364-B

Si Si—51374-B

Swedish Schnapps—51383-R

Swedish Schnapps—51384-R

Back Home Blues—51391-B

Back Home Blues—51392-B

Lover Man—51402

March 24—Birdland—Strings

Jumpin' With Symphony Sid (opening)—
   51420T-B

Just Friends—51430T

Everything Happens to Me—51440T

East of the Sun—51450T

Laura—51460T

Dancing in the Dark—51470T

Jumpin' With Symphony Sid (closer)—
   51480T-B

April 7—Birdland—Strings

What is This Thing Called Love—51490T

Repetition—51500T

They Can't Take That Away From Me—
   51510T

Easy to Love—51520T

July—Herman

Laura—51530T

1952

January 22—Big Band and Strings

Temptation—5210

Lover—5220

Autumn in New York—5230

Stella by Starlight—5240

January 28

Mama Inez—5250

LaCucaracha—5260

Begin The Beguine—5270

Estrellita—5280

La Paloma—5290

March 28—Big Band

Night and Day—52100

Almost Like Being in Love—52110

I Can't Get Started—52120

What is This Thing Called Love?—52130

June—Session

Jam Blues—52140-B

Dearly Beloved—52150

Funky Blues—52160-B

What is This Thing Called Love—52170

November 14—Ellington Anniversary

Just Friends—52180T

Easy To Love—42190T

Repetition—52200T

Night in Tunisa—52210T

52nd Street Theme—52220T-RH

December 30

The Song is You—52230

Laird Bird—52240-B

Kim—52252-R

Kim—52254-R

Cosmic Ray—52262-B

Cosmic Ray—52265-B

June 16—West Coast

The Squirrel—52270T-B
They Didn't Believe Me
  (Be Careful, It's My Heart)—52280T
Indiana—52290T
Liza—52300T
TV Show—Early in Year
Hot House—52310T-S
Sept. 20—Birdland
Ornithology—52320T-S
52nd Street Theme—52330T-RH

1953
January 30—Miles Davis
Compulsion—5310-S
The Serpent's Tooth—5321-RH
The Serpent's Tooth—5322-RH
'Round About Midnight—5330
May 9—Birdland
Cool Blues—5340T-B
Moose The Mooche—5350T-R
Broadway—5360T
May 15—Massey Hall
Perdido—5370T
All The Things You Are—5380T
Salt Peanuts—5390T-R
Wee—53100T-R
Hot House—53110T-S
Night in Tunisa—53120T
May 22—Chorus
In The Still of the Night—53130
Old Folks—53140
If I Love Again—53150
August 8
Chi Chi—53161-B
Chi Chi—53166-B
Chi Chi—53163-B
I Remember You—53170
Now's The Time—53180-B
Confirmation—53190-OC
February 16
Your Father's Mustache—53200T-RD
March 23
Groovin' High—53210T-S
March 30—Bandbox (New York)
Star Eyes—53220T
Ornithology—53230T-S
Diggin' Diz—53240T-S
Embraceable You—53250T
May—Montreal—Sit in
Cool Blues—53260T-B

Don't Blame Me—53270T
Wahoo—53280T-S
May 30—Birdland
Moose The Mooche—53290T-R
Cheryl—53300T-B
Circa 1953
Dance of the Infidels—53310T-B
December—Hi Hat—Boston
Nows the Time—53320T-B
Ornithology—53330T-S
Little Suede Shoes—53340T-OC
Groovin High—53350T-S
Cheryl—53360T-B
Ornithology—53370T-S (Santa Claus)
52nd Street—53380T-RH
May 9—Birdland
Star Eyes—53390T
February 22—Washington, D.C.—Big Band
Fine and Dandy—53400T
These Foolish Things—53410T
Light Green—53420T-B
Thou Swell—53430T
Willis (Pennies from Heaven)—53440T-S
Don't Blame Me—53450T
Something to Remember Me by (in Medley)—
  53460T
Roundhouse (Out of Nowhere)—53470T-S

1954
January 24—Hi Hat—Boston
Cool Blues—5470T-B
My Little Suede Shoes—5480T-OC
Ornithology—5490T-S
Out of Nowhere—54100T
Jumpin' With Symphony Sid—54110T-B
March 11
I Get A Kick Out of You—5417
I Get A Kick Out of You—5412
Just One Of Those Things—5420
My Heart Belongs to Daddy—5430
I've Got You Under My Skin—5440
December 10
Love For Sale—5454
Love For Sale—5455
I Love Paris—5463
I Love Paris—5462

APPENDIX II

Suggested Verve Take Listings
For Future Reference

On the *Verve* recordings it is often impossible to tell which take was the original since most issues only bear the designation "alternate." The numbers and descriptions that follow are merely this author's suggested way of telling the "takes" apart. The "correctness" of these assumptions really matters little, for in the future, *identification* will be the problem and not documentation. If only one take of two (or two of three, etc.) is described, the remaining take with the absence of the description is, of course, assigned the other number. The descriptions are complete in the text portion, but this section will save time when looking to identify a particular *Verve* take.

Segment—49252—Dorham starts solo with sequences.
Passport—49280-B—Blues Form.
Diverse—49270-R—*I Got Rhythm* Form.
An Oscar for Treadwell—50273-R—Faltering ending.
Mohawk—50283-B—Faltering closing theme.
Leap Frog—50304—Mix-up on fours.
Leap Frog—50306—Complete Take (*Leap Frog* numbers are opposite of the listing on German Verve.)
Relaxin' with Lee—50312-S—Modulation for Gillespie's chorus.
Au Privave—5112-B—*Ornithology*-derived phrase at beginning of second chorus.
She Rote—5125-OC—Bird Hints at *Over There.*
Why Do I Love You—5192—Rhythmic confusion when going to "straight four" blowing section.
Why Do I Love You—5197—Blowing section Latin.
Why Do I Love You—5196—No confusion going to straight four.
Swedish Schnapps—51383-R—Parker's solo begins with same figure as the original *Moose the Mooche* solo.
Back Home Blues—51391-B—Trumpet begins to repeat after first theme statement.
Kim—52252-R—Bird quotes *High Society* and *Johnny One Note.*
Cosmic Rays—52262-B—Bass quotes *Blues in The Night*; *Temptation* ending.
Chi-Chi—53166-B—Bird quotes *Johnny One Note.*
Chi-Chi—53163-B—Slight break—Near end of first theme.
Chi-Chi—53161-B—Slower tempo—Slight horn problems.
I Get A Kick Out of You—5412—No guitar improvisation.

I Get A Kick Out of You—5417—Bird quotes *Moon Over Miami* at bridge to improvised chorus.

Love For Sale—5454—Bauer's contrapuntal line at 2nd eight of theme; Parker quotes *Nightingale*.

I Love Paris—5463—Bird begins final "B" section with "They-all-ran-after-the-farmer's-wife."

Latin backing—♩♩ ⁊ ♫♩ ♩ ♪♩ ♩ etc.

APPENDIX III

Alphabetical Listing of Parker Record Titles

The following list contains the number(s) of all versions of a given tune following the title. When used in conjunction with the numerical listing this should provide a helpful way of pinpointing any title and/or date in the quickest possible way. It also allows one to see at a glance all of the available versions and their year (from the number). The writer hopes that these systems will be useful rather than only being academic lists.

After You've Gone—46100 (JATP)
Ah-Leu-Cha—48201-R, 48202-R
Allen's Alley (Wee)—49340T-R, 53100T-R
All The Things You Are (Bird of Paradise)—45110, 46210T, 47381-S, 47382-S, 47383-S, 49480T-S, 50520T, 5380T, 50900T
Almost Like Being In Love—52110
Another Hair-Do—47521-B, 47522-B, 47523-B
Anthropology (Thrivin' on a Riff)—45311-R, 45312-R, 45313-R, 46190T-R, 47660T (with Ko Ko), 49510T-R, 51210T-R, 50620T-R, 50470T-R. 49590T-R
April In Paris—49440, 50420, 50740T, 50760T
Au Privave—5112-B, 5113-B
Autumn in New York—5230
Back Home Blues—51391-B, 51392-B
Ballade—50460
Barbados—48191-B, 48192-B, 48193-B, 48194-B, 49130T-B, 49150T-B, 49310T-B, 49500T-B
BeBop—46160-M, 49100T-M
Be Careful, Its My Heart—52280T (listed as They Didn't Believe Me)
Begin The Beguine—5270
Bernie's Tune—50840T-M
Big Foot—see Driftin' on a Reed
Billie's Bounce—45281-B, 45282-B, 45283-B, 45284-B, 45285-B, 46180T-B
Bird, The—48380-M
Bird Feathers—47403-B
Bird Gets the Worm (Lover Come Back)—47551-S, 47552-S, 51410T
Bird of Paradise (All the Things You Are)—45110, 46210T, 47381-S, 47382-S, 47383-S, 49480T-S, 50520T, 5380T, 50900T
Bird's Mambo (Mambo Fortunado)—50590T
Bird's Nest—47111-RD, 47112-RD, 47113-RD
Bloomdido—50260-B

Blue and Boogie—46170T-B, 51200T-B

Bluebird—47531-B, 47532-B

Blues ("Home Cookin' " recording)—4760-B (unissued at writing)

Blues (fast)—50170-B

Blues (Paris Festival)—49370T-B

Blues for Alice—51364-B

Blues for Norman (JATP)—4670-B

Body and Soul—4020T (McShann), 50530T (Sweden)

Bongo Ballad (Lament for the Congo)—50580T

Bongo Beep—47492-B, 47493-B

Bongo Bop—47351-B, 47352-B

Bottle It (McShann)—42100T-B

Broadway—5360T

Buzzy—47201-B, 47202-B, 47203-B, 47204-B, 47205-B

Cardboard—49230-OC

Carvin' the Bird—47151-B, 47152-B

Celerity—50450-R

Charlie's Wig (When I Grow to Old to Dream)—47482-S, 47484-S, 47485-S

Chasin' the Bird—47181-R, 47182-R, 47183-R, 48100T-R, 49220T-R

Cheers—47141-R(alt)H, 47142-R(alt)H, 47143-R(alt)H, 47144-R(alt)H, 50610T-RH

Cherokee (KoKo)—42140T, 45290-S (Warmin' Up a Riff), 45331-S, 45332-S (classic), 4720T-S, 4770T-S, 47660T (with Anthropology), 48280T-S, 49520T-S, 50810T

Cheryl—47191-B, 47192-B, 4940T-B, 49200T-B, 49530T-B, 53300T-B, 53360T-B, 49580T-B

Chi Chi—53161-B, 53163-B, 53166-B

Closer, The (JATP)—49410-B

Compulsion (Miles Davis)—5310-S

Confirmation—50100T-OC, 53190-OC, 47300T-0C

Congo Blues (Red Norvo)—45231-B, 45232-B, 45233-B, 45234-B, 45235-B

Constellation—48211-RH, 48212-RH, 48213-RH, 48214-RH

Cool Blues—47121-B, 47122-B, 47123-B, 47124-B, 49550T-B, 50200T-B, 50500T-B, 51140T-B, 5340T-B, 5470T-B, 50630T-B, 53260T-B

Coquette (McShann)—4050T

Cosmic Ray—52262-B, 52265-B

Crazeology—47501, 47502, 47503, 47504

Cubop Holiday (Woody Herman)—51310T-H

Dance of the Infidels—53310T-B

Dancing in the Dark—50320, 51470T

Dark Shadows—47101-V, 47102-V, 47103-V, 47104-V

Dearly Beloved—52150

Dee Dee's Dance—47560T

Deedle—49560T-V

Dewey Square—47371-OC, 47372-OC, 47373-OC

Dexter Blues (McShann)—4130-B

Dexterity—47351-R, 47352-R

Diggin' Diz (Lover)—4620-S, 53240T-S

Diverse—49270-R

Dizzy Atmosphere—45120-RD, 45390T-RD, 47280T-RD, 48120T-RD, 50660T-RD

Dizzy's Boogie (Slim Gaillard)—45341-B, 45342-B

Donna Lee (Indiana)—47171-S, 47172-S, 47173-S, 47174-S, 47630T-S, 52290T, 50850T-S

Don't Blame Me—47450, 53270T, 53450T

Dream of You (Trummy Young)—4550-V

Driftin' on a Reed (Big Foot)—47463-B, 47464-B, 47465-B, 48300T-B

East of the Sun—50350, 51450T

Easy to Love—50370, 50430, 52190T, 50720T, 51520T

Embraceable You—45320-S (Meandering), 47391 (classic), 47392, 47471-S (Quasimado), 47472-S, (Quasimado), 49400 (JATP), 5040T, 50490T, 53250T, 50910T-V

Estrellita—5280

Everything Happens to Me—49430, 51440T

Fat's Flats (What is This Thing Called Love)—47640T-S (Bird only on close—"Hot House")

Fiesta—5180

Fine and Dandy—47260T, 48170T, 50540T, 50880T, 53400T

Fifty-Second Street Theme—48430T (Talk), 47610T-RH, 47620T-RH, 4810T-RH (long), 48140T-RH, 48270T-RH, 5010T-RH, 50150T-RH, 50210T-RH, 52220T-RH, 53380T-RH, 50700T-RH, 50720T-RH, 50790T-RH, 52330T-RH, 49320T-RH, 49600T-RH

Flat Foot Floogie (Slim Gallard)—45351-RH, 45352-RH

Floo-Gee-Boo (Cootie Williams)—4590T-RH

Four Brothers (Woody Herman)—51350

Four-F Blues—4541-V

Funky Blues (Granz jam session)—52160-B

Get Happy (Red Norvo)—45213, 45214

Get Me on Your Mind (McShann)—4220-V

G.I. Blues—4542-V

Goof and I, The (Herman)—51340-R

Groovin' High (Whispering) 45100-S, 45380T-S, 47290T-S, 47650T-S, 48290T-S, 49160T-S, 53210T-S, 53350T-S

Gypsy, The—46150

Half Nelson—47231, 47232, 48390T, 49170T, 50800T, 50870T

Hallelujah (Red Norvo)—45201, 45202, 45203

Happy Bird Blues—51250T-B

Home Cookin' I—4710T-SH

Home Cookin' II (Cherokee)—4720T-S

Home Cookin' III—4730T-R

Honeysuckle Rose—4030T (McShann) See also Marmaduke and Scrapple from the Apple

Hootie Blues (McShann)—4120-B

Hot House—45160-S, 47250T-S, 4840T-S, 48180T-S, 48320T-S, 49110T-S, 5060T-S, 53110T-S, 52310T-S

How Deep is the Ocean—47511, 47512, 47590T

How High the Moon—48130T, 48350T, 50560T See also Ornithology

I Can't Get Started—4680, 50600T, 52120

I Cover the Waterfront—50140T

I Didn't Know What Time it Was—49460, 5030T

I'd Rather Have a Memory (Sarah Vaughan)—45180-V

If I Had You (Sir Chas. Thompson)—45250

If I Love Again—53150

If I Should Lose You—49470

I Found a New Baby (McShann)—4010T

I Get A Kick Out of You—5412, 5417

I Got Rhythm—46120 (JATP) The many derivatives are designated by an "R" following the number.

I'll Always Love You Just the Same—4430-V

I'll Remember April—50390, 51280T, 50710T

I Love Paris—5462, 5463

I'm in the Mood for Love—50180, 50380

Indiana—52290T See also Donna Lee

In the Still of the Night—53130

I Remember You—53170

I've Got You Under My Skin—5440

I Want Ev'ry Bit of It—4520-V

Jam Blues—52140-B

JATP Blues—46110-B

Jazz (Machito)—4980

Jumpin' Blues, The (McShann)—4230-B, 4280T-B (Jump the Blues)

Jumpin' with Symphony Sid—51190T-B, 54110T-B, 51420T-B, 51480T-B

Just Friends—49420, 52180T, 51430T, 50730T, 50750T

Just One of Those Things—5420

K.C. Blues—5130-B

Kim—52252-R, 52254-R

Klact-o-veed-sed-stene—47411-OC, 47412-OC

Klaunstance (Way You Look Tonight)—47540-S

KoKo (Cherokee)—45331-S, 45332-S (classic), 47340T (intro. section), 47570T (intro. section), 47660T-S (with Anthropology), 48280T-S, 49520T-S, See also Cherokee

La Cucuracha—5260

Lady Be Good—4040T (McShann), 4690 (JATP—classic)

Lady Bird—50570T (Paris)

Laird Baird—52240-B

Lament for the Congo (Bongo Ballad)—50580T

LaPaloma—5290

Laura—50340, 51170T, 51240T, 51460T, 51530T (Herman)

Leap Frog—50304, 50306

Lemon Drop (Herman)—51330T-R

Leo the Lion (Herman)—51300T-B

Lester Leaps In—49390-R (JATP), 51160T-R

Light Green—53420T-B

Little Willie Leaps—47221-S, 47222-S, 47223-S, 48410T-S, 50690T-S, 50890T-S

Liza—52300T

Lonely Boy Blues (McShann)—4210-B, 5260T-V

Lover—5220

Love for Sale—5454, 5455

Lover Come Back to Me—50780T, See also Bird Gets the Worm

Lover Man—45150-V (S. Vaughn), 46140 (collapse), 51402, 50640T

Lullaby in Rhythm—4750T, 51270T

Mama Inez—5250

Mambo (Machito)—4970

Mambo Fortunado (Bird's Mambo)—50590T

Mango Mangue (Machito)—48360

Marmaduke (Honeysuckle Rose)—48241-H, 48242-H, 48243-H, 48244-H, 48245-H, 48246-H

Max is Making Wax—46130-RD

Meandering (Embraceable You)—45320-S

Mean to Me (S. Vaughn)—45190-V

Melancholy Baby—50290

Merry-go-round—48261-RH, 48262-RH

Milestones (M. Davis)—47211, 47212

Mohawk—50283-B, 50284-B

Moose the Mooche—4631-R, 4632-R, 4633-R, 51110T-R, 5350T-R, 53290T-R, 50770T-R

Moten Swing (McShann)—4060T

Move—50240T

My Heart Belongs to Daddy—5430

My Little Suede Shoes—5150-OC, 51150T-OC, 53340T-OC, 5480T-OC

My Old Flame—47430, 4870T

Nearness of You, The (Herman)—51320T

Night and Day—52100

Night in Tunisia—4661 (alto break), 4664, 4665, 47270T, 4860T, 49180T, 52210T, 51230T, 53120T, 50680T (no Parker)

Now's the Time—45301-B, 45302-B, 45303-B, 45304-B, 49490T-B, 53180-B, 5070T-B, 53320T-B

Oh, Oh, My, My (Trummy Young)—4580-V

Okie Doke (Machito)—4950

Old Folks—53140

One O'Clock Jump (McShann)—4290T, 42130T

One Woman's Man—4140-V

Ooop Bop Sh'bam—49120T-RH

Opener, The (JATP)—49380-B

Ornithology (How High the Moon)—4651-S, 4653-S, 4654-S, 46200T-S, 48310T-S, 49540T-S, 5020T-S, 50250T-S, 53230T-S, 52320T-S, 5490T-S, 53330T-S, 53370T-S, See also How High the Moon

Oscar for Treadwell, An—50273-R, 50274-R

Out of Nowhere—47441, 47442, 47443, 48340T, 4830T, 4890T, 49300T, 49350T, 50110T, 50330, 54100T, 50670T, 50860T, 53470T-S (Roundhouse)

Overtime—4921-S, 4922-S

Parker's Mood—48221-B, 48222-B, 48223-B

Passport—49280-B

Pennies from Heaven—See Willis

Perdido—50220T-S (Wahoo), 5370T, 53280T-S (Wahoo)

Perhaps—48231-B, 48232-B, 48233-B, 48234-B, 48235-B, 48236-B

Poppity Pop (Slim Gaillard)—45360-R

Quasimado (Embraceable You)—47471-S, 47472-S

Red Cross—4421-R, 4422-R

Relaxin' at Camarillo—47131-B, 47133-B, 47134-B, 47135-B

Relaxin' with Lee—50312-S, 50313-S

Repetition—48370, 50400, 52200T, 51500T

Rifftide (Street Beat)—50190T-R Mistitle for Street Beat

Rocker—50440, 51180T

Romance without Finance (T. Grimes)—4440-V

Roundhouse (Out of Nowhere)—53470T-S

'Round Midnight—50230T, 51220T, 5330

Salt Peanuts—45130-R, 48330T-R, 49140T-R, 49330T-R, 49360T-R, 5390T-R

Scrapple from the Apple—47421-HR, 47422-HR, 4990T-HR, 49190T-HR, 49290T-HR, 5050T-HR, 50480T-H, 51260T-HR, 50820T-HR

Segment—49251-M, 49252-M

Sepian Bounce (McShann)—4240

Serpent's Tooth, The—5321-RH, 5322-RH

Seventh Avenue (T. Young)—4560-V

Shaw 'Nuff—45140-R, 4820T-R

She Rote—5123-OC, 5125-OC

Sippin' at Bell's—47241-B, 47242-B, 47245-B

Si Si—51374-B

Six-Eight (6/8) (Machito)—4970

Slam Slam Blues—45221-B, 45222-B

Slim's Jim (S. Gaillard)—45370

Slow Boat to China—4910T, 49210T, 48420T

Sly Mongoose—51100T

Smoke Gets in Your Eyes—50130T

Something to Remember Me By (in Medley)—53460T

Song is You, The—52230

Sorta Kinda (T. Young)—4570-V

Squirrel, The—52270T-B

Star Eyes—5090T, 50160, 50510T, 5142, 51120T, 53220T, 53390T, 50830T

Steeplechase—48250-R

Stella by Starlight—5240

Street Beat—45270-R, 50190T-R, See also Rifftide

Strike Up the Band—50550T (Sweden)

Stupendous—47161-S, 47162-S

Summertime—49450, 50930T (Cafe Society)

Sunny Side of the Street—47580T

Swedish Schnapps—51383-R, 51384-R

Sweet Georgia Brown—42110T (McShann), 4610 (JATP)

Swingmatism (McShann)—4110

Takin' Off (Sir Chas, Thompson)—45240

Temptation—5210

That's the Blues (Clyde Hart)—4530-V

There's a Small Hotel—48160T

These Foolish Things—48150T, 53410T

They Can't Take that Away from Me—50360, 51510T

They Didn't Believe Me—52280T (Real Title—Be Careful It's My Heart)

Thou Swell—53430T

Tiger Rag—47600T

This is Always—4793-V, 4794-V

This Time the Dream's on Me—4850T, 48110T, 51130T, 50650T

Thrivin' on a Riff—45311-R, 45312-R, 45313-R See also Anthropology

Tico Tico—5170

Tiny's Tempo—4411-B, 4412-B, 4413-B

Twentieth Century Blues (Sir Chas. Thompson)—45260-B (br)

Un Poquito de tu Amor—5160

Victory Ball (Metronome All Stars)—4931-S, 4932-S

Vine Street Boogie (McShann)—4270T-B

Visa—49240-B, 5080T-B

Wahoo (Perdido)—53280T-S, 50220T-S

Warmin' Up a Riff (Cherokee)—45290-S

Way You Look Tonight, The—4880T See also Klaunstance

Wee—53100T-R See also Allen's Alley

APPENDIX IV

A Guide to Supersax Harmonizations

A great labor of love undertaken by bassist Buddy Clark and altoist Med Flory created the most interesting Bird-based records of the early seventies: the two West Coast musicians transcribed Parker improvisations and harmonized them for a sax section. Their group, known as *SuperSax*, gives Bird's work an entirely different perspective, and hearing the Parker choruses harmonized gives one an aural thrill and an appreciation of the transcriptive and interpretive difficulties.

Below are listed the numbers (from the numerical system) of the versions which correspond with the *SuperSax* recordings. Some versions, however, are "composites"—various phrases from different versions linked together to form choruses.

SuperSax Plays Bird—Capitol ST-11177

KoKo	45332-S
Just Friends	49420
Parker's Mood	48223-B
Moose the Mooche	51110T-R
Star Eyes	50170
BeBop	49100T-M
Repetition	48370
Lady Be Good	4690
Hot House	1st improvised chorus from 45160-S, rest is "composite"

SuperSax Plays Bird, Vol. II, Salt Peanuts—Capitol ST-11271

Yardbird Suite—improvised chorus one—4641-OC   chorus 2 —4644-OC,   chorus 3—4740-OC.

Groovin' High	47290T-S
Embraceable You	47392
The Bird	4838-M
Lover	5220
Scrapple from the Apple—first improvised chorus from 47422—HR, rest is "composite"	
Lover Man	46140
Salt Peanuts—"composite"	

Super Sax Plays Bird with Strings—Capitol ST-11371

281

April in Paris, I Didn't Know What Time It Was, If I Should Lose You—These echo the original "string" recordings (49440, 49460, 49470) with new string settings and some added instrumental solos.

Ornithology (no strings)
First three improvised choruses—48310T-S
Chorus before final theme—4654-S
Opening Theme—as played from 1948 on
Closing Theme—as played on original (1946) recording
Cool Blues (no strings)—8 choruses—5340T-B
All The Things You Are (strings added)
 Bridge of opening chorus—45110
 The rest are choruses from 50520T
My Old Flame (strings added)—47430
Kim—52254-R
Blue and Boogie—51200T-B

APPENDIX V

Parker As A Composer

49 Compositions—Counting only those with some thematic material.

Blues	26
I Got Rhythm derivatives	10
Combination of *Honeysuckle Rose* and *I Got Rhythm* (chord patterns)	2
Standards (chord pattern base)	4
Original Construction	6
Minor	1

Three of the tunes listed under original construction are very close, harmonically, to standards, but do have some stamp of original harmony to them.

Out of the compositions, only twelve were used in "live" recordings that have so far been issued, and half of these were blues.

The *Charlie Parker Omnibook*, published by *Atlantic Music Corporation*, 6124 Selma Avenue, Hollywood California, includes the theme and solos on all but ten of the Parker originals plus solos on non-thematic improvisational frames.

APPENDIX VI

Labelology

Listed below are some of the smaller labels that have issued Parker material at various times. The larger or more definitive labels are listed in the text. Any known reissues of major labels, however, will be included here.

America (French)—St. Nicks and Onyx club recordings
Baronet—Some *Dial* takes
BYG (French)—The *Savoy's* in order
Charlie Parker—"Live" material and some *Dial* takes
ESP—"Live" material
Jazz Showcase—Montreal sit-ins, new "live" material
Jazztone—Some *Dial* takes, issued mid-Fifties
LeJazz Cool—Material later issued on Parker labels
Masterseal—Some "sideman" sides of 1945, Sarah Vaughan, etc.
Queen (It.)—"Live" material
Roost—*Some Dial takes, Black Deuce sides*
Royale—Some earlier 1945 sides with Diz
Saga—(English)—Several volumes, "live" material, *Shaw 'Nuff* from 1945, some Gillespie *Dials*
Society (English)—Product of *Saga*, some *Dials* including *Lover Man*
Vogue (French)—Bird with Sir Charles Thompson

The *Charlie Parker* label, owned by Doris Parker, also issued material by Duke Jordan and other Parker associates, but the accompanying information was often in error, especially on the issues of Bird material. Bird, for instance, is listed as Charles Christopher Parker, Jr, even though his birth certificate shows no middle name.

The German Verve label did the Granz recordings in chronological order, complete with matrix numbers, during the late 1960s, but unfortunately, these also had some wrong titles and faulty take numbers.

In recent years, a number of "bootleg" records have been issued containing "live" Parker material. Among these are *Okie Dokie, Richelieu, Main Man, Parktec* and *LeMere*, and the group of them are known in the trade as "Amalgamated Labels." Some of them have one name on the outside jacket and another on the label. The back of one *Partec* issue has a false picture of a supposed Dutch jazz expert, Dr. Claude Donke (Donkey?), with a photograph of Bird super-imposed upon it. This farce is humorous in a way, but it is also rather sad if one considers that someone of Parker's stature should be treated with more respect.

The *Savoys* have been reissued by *Arista* in two versions: a deluxe boxed set including all takes (S5J5500), and a set with only original takes (SJL2201). *Arista* has also reissued some of the "Roost" material (1107, 1108). *Verve*, too, has embarked on a Parker reissue program (although sometimes the same mistakes in listings were repeated), and *Warner Brothers* recently did a limited edition set of the *Dials*. *Columbia's* new issues at this writing consist of the Parker-Navarro "live" cuts (JG34808), the Bird and Diz Birdland set of 1951 (JC34831), and some "live" string group cuts from Birdland, Carnegie Hall, and the Apollo Theatre (JC3432).

Surely, more reissues will be done by major labels in the future, and furthermore, there are probably many small labels (mostly European) that already have issued Parker material, but which have been overlooked by this author.

Bibliography

Cohen, Maxwell. "With Care and Love," *Down Beat*, March 11, 1965.

Davies, Gordon. "Charlie Parker Chronology," *Discographical Forum*, March 1970, September 1971.

Feather, Leonard. "A Fist at the World" *Down Beat*, March 11, 1965.

Gillespie, John Birks. "The Years with Yard," *Down Beat*, May 25, 1961.

Gitler, Ira. *Jazz Masters of the Forties*. New York: MacMillan, 1966.

Granz, Norman. "Charlie Parker," accompanying booklet, *The Charlie Parker Story* (boxed set), Verve 8100-3.

Heckman, Donald. "Bird in Flight," *Down Beat*, March 11, 1965.

Hentoff, Nat. "The Charlie Parker Story," accompanying booklet *The Charlie Parker Story* (boxed set), Verve 8100-3.

Hentoff, Nat and Shapiro, Nat. *Here Me Talkin' to Ya*. New York and Toronto: Rinehart & Co., 1955.

Jepson, Jorgen Grunnet. *Jazz Records 1942-1965* (eight volume discography). Denmark: Karl Emil Knudson, 1965.

Levin, Michael and Wilson, John. "Interview with Charlie Parker," *Down Beat*, September 9, 1949.

Reisner, Robert. *Bird: The Legend of Charlie Parker*. New York: Citadel Press, 1962.

Russell, Ross. *Bird Lives*. New York: Charterhouse, 1973.

Segal, Joe. "Bird in Chicago," *Down Beat*, March 11, 1965.

Shaw, Arnold. *The Street That Never Slept*. New York: Coward, McCann & Geoghegan, 1971.

Ulanov, Barry. *A Handbook of Jazz*. Viking Press, 1960.

Williams, Martin. "The Listener's Legacy," *Down Beat*, March 11, 1965.

Williams, Tony. Liner notes, Spotlite Records, *Charlie Parker on Dial* series.

Woodward, Woody. *Jazz Americana*. Los Angeles: Trend Books, 1956.

Copyright Information

The following titles from which examples have been taken are the property of *Atlantic Music Corporation*, 6124 Selma Avenue, Hollywood, California; copyright 1978 as a solo collection (line plus improvisation)—*The Charlie Parker Omnibook* (see below for individual tune copyrights). The examples are used by the company's permission.

Ah-Leu-Cha
©1948
©renewed 1976

Another Hair-Do
©1948
©renewed 1976

Anthropology
©1946
©renewed 1974

Au Privave
©1956

Back Home Blues
©1956

Ballade
©1958

Barbados
©1948
©renewed 1976

Billie's Bounce
©1945
©renewed 1973

The Bird
©1956

Bird Gets the Worm

©1948
©renewed 1976

Bloomdido
©1953

Bluebird
©1948
©renewed 1976

Blues (fast)
©1977

Blues for Alice
©1956

Buzzy
©1947
©renewed 1975

Cardboard
©1956

Celebrity
©1958

Chasin' the Bird
©1948
©renewed 1976

Cheryl
©1947
©renewed 1975

Chi Chi
©1955

Confirmation
©1946
©renewed 1974

Constellation
©1948
©renewed 1976

Cosmic Ray
©1956

Dewey Square
©1958

Diverse
©1957

Donna Lee
©1947
©renewed 1975

K.C. Blues
©1956

Klaunstance
©1948
©renewed 1976

Laird Baird
©1956

Marmaduke
©1948
©renewed 1976

Merry-go-round
©1948
renewed 1976

Mohawk
©1956

Moose the Mooche
©1946
©renewed 1974

My Little Suede Shoes
©1956

Now's the Time
©1945
©renewed 1973

Ornithology
©1946
©renewed 1974

An Oscar for Treadwell
©1956

Parker's Mood
©1948
©renewed 1976

Passport
©1953

Perhaps
©1948
©renewed 1976

Red Cross
©1945
©renewed 1973

Relaxin' with Lee
©1953

Scrapple from the Apple
©1957

Segment
©1957

She Rote
©1956

Si Si
©1956

Steeplechase
©1948
©renewed 1976

Thrivin' from A Riff
©1945
©renewed 1973

Visa
©1953

Yardbird Suite
©1946
©renewed 1974

Analysis Section

ORNITHOLOGY:
A Study of Charlie Parker's Music

Reviewers are forever telling authors they can't understand them. The author might often reply: Is that my fault?

J.C. and A.W. Hare—Guesses at Truth

Most analyses of Charlie Parker's music deal with the melodic devices used by Parker as a composer and improviser. It is necessary, however, to relate these devices to their implied harmonies to gain an insight into the way Parker heard and thought.

The use of the flat sixth of the scale (Ab in the key of C, for instance) is a characteristic Parker melodic device, but we must note the chords against which he heard this note. In *Scrapple from the Apple*, it appears as the only important non-scale tone (the other non-scale tones are used as passing tones) and is used as the flat ninth of the dominant chord at the end of bar 3 (really an anticipation of bar 4).

In *Perhaps* it appears in bar 7 of a blues as the lowered fifth of the supertonic chord and again in bar 10 as the flat ninth of the dominant chord.

289

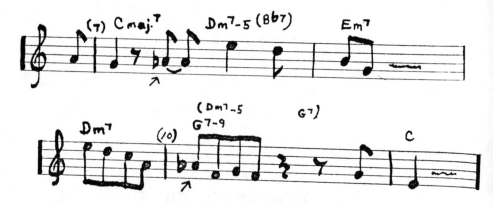

A most pronounced example is the blues theme *Barbados*. Here the device appears as important thematic material in bars 2 and 10 and can be harmonized with either a supertonic chord with a lowered fifth or a dominant with a flat ninth in both cases.

Barbados Bar 2 (1947)

Barbados Bars 9 and 10

Below are some other examples:

Cheryl: Bar 10—ii[7] with lowered fifth

Oscar for Treadwell: Bar 6 with Minor Subdominant (related to ii[7]—5)

Bloomdido: Bar 6 with Minor Subdominant (Related to ii⁷—5)

In many cases the bII⁷ or the bVII⁷ (Db⁷ and Bb⁷ in the key of C, respectively) can be substituted in places where Parker used the flat sixth of the scale.

Next is an example of an improvisational use of this device from bar 11 of the *Parker's Mood* solo. The first Gb suggests the minor subdominant and the second suggests the dominant flat ninth.

From the foregoing examples we can draw the following conclusions: (1) Parker usually used the flat sixth against supertonic or dominant chord structures. (2) The resolution of this device was to the tonic or tonic-sounding structures. (3) The flat sixth was often used in combination with the third of scale usually by leaping up to it. (*Perhaps, Barbados, Scrapple*). (4) Useful substitutes are the bII⁷ or the bVII⁷.

The Use of The Major Scale

Many jazz musicians before and after Parker have used various "blue notes" and "blues scales" in the opening bars of their blues themes, but Parker often used only the notes of the major scale for the first three bars of many of his blues themes.

Bloomdido (1950)

Perhaps (1948)

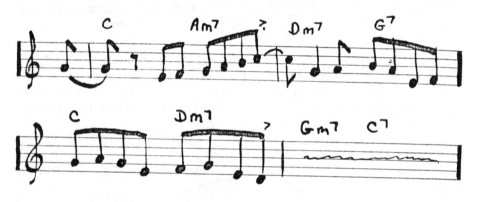

Bongo Beep (1947)

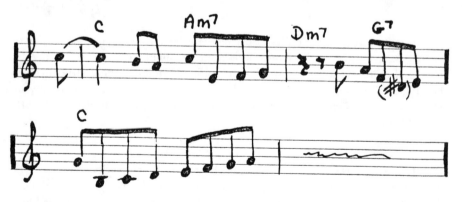

Driftin' on a Reed (1947)

In *Bloomdido* the major scale is used exclusively through the first three measures. This is also true of *Perhaps* and *Driftin'*. *Bongo Beep* uses only one other tone, the D# in bar 2, and that is in passing.

The use of the major scale is the prime reason for Parker's pianists to use parallel scalar chords in the opening bars of the blues. For example, in the key of C:

C maj⁷ Dm⁷/Em⁷ Dm⁷/Cmaj⁷Dm⁷.

In many cases, however, the line implied as best the progression:

I vi⁷/ii⁷V⁷/I ii⁷.

This resourceful use of the major scale is what sets the "bop" blues themes melodically apart from the blues of earlier years. The major scale, however, was not used exclusively in Parker's *improvised* excursions during the first few measures of the blues. Bird *often* used down-home "blue" notes, but we will touch upon that later. For now, an examination of the major scale in the improvisations is in order.

In *Bloomdido* it is used over the progression ii⁷-V⁷-I; *in Thrivin' From a Riff* over I-ii⁷-V⁷, in *Moose the Mooche* (the same general phrase as the one in *Bloomdido*) over ii⁷-V⁷-I; and in *Ornithology* over a tonic-sounding chord (not the tonic of the original key).

Bloomdido (1950)

Thrivin' From a Riff (1945)

Moose the Mooche (1946)

Ornithology (1946)

    Another interesting observation is that both of Parker's contrapuntal compositions, *Chasing the Bird* and *Ah-leu-cha*, use the major scale almost exclusively in the contrapuntal sections. They are constructed around the chords I-ii⁷-V⁷.

    We may conclude: (1) Parker often used the major scale compositionally in the opening bars of the blues and also over the progressions ii⁷-V⁷-I and I-ii⁷-V⁷; or plain tonic. (3) The phrase used in *Bloomdido* and *Moose* may be considered a motif which he used over ii⁷-V⁷-I.

Treatment of the Tonic

    When Parker did not treat the tonic chord scalewise, he treated it chordally, usually implying a major ninth chord.

Groovin' High (1945)

Groovin' High (1947)

Klact-oveeseds-tene: Take 2 (1947)

An example of the compositions which combine the chordal and scale approach is the opening bar of *Cardboard* from 1949:

Treatment Of The Dominant

Against a dominant chord Parker often used the higher chord intervals, most notably the ninth. The ninth was often raised or lowered or sometimes both in the same phrase. The thirteenth (or sixth if you will) and augmented fifth were also used extensively.

Thrivin' From a Riff: Solo, Take 3 (1945)

Yardbird Suite: Entrance to Solo (1946)

Cheryl: Entrance to Theme (1947)

Confirmation: Theme

Note that the flat ninth of the dominant is in fact the flat sixth of the scale mentioned earlier, which was used in the aforementioned combinations involving the third of the scale (thirteenth of the dominant). We now begin to see that Parker's simple explanation of "using the higher intervals of the chord as a melody" was perhaps the best and most easily understood explanation of his music.

Treatment Of The Progression ii⁷-V⁷-I

It has been shown already that Parker treated this progression: (1) with the use of the major scale; (2) with higher chord intervals on the dominant and sometimes a lowered fifth on the supertonic.

He also treated it with: (3) a chordal approach using some elements of (2); (4) a combined chordal and scalewise approach using some elements of (2) and perhaps some chromatic tones.

Klact-oveeseds-tene: Take 2 (1947) Combined Chordal and Scalewise Approach

Occasionally Parker implied the bIImaj[7] in place of the dominant. The following two examples were recorded within a few weeks of each other and in the same key.

Lady Be Good (April 1946)

Ornithology (March 1946)

This is a bit different from the use of the flat-seventh chord built a half-step above the tonic (bII[7]), which, because of Parker's use of higher chord intervals and altered tones on the dominant, could be substituted almost at random by the pianist. It created the chromatic progression Am[7]-Ab[7]-G instead of the usual Am[7]-D[7]-G. The relationship between the Ab[7] and D[7] is that the root of one is the lowered fifth of the other. This is what gave rise to all the talk of *flatted fifths* during the be-bop era.

It is obvious that Bird's study of the ii[7]-V[7]-I progression dates back to the McShann days, for the bridge of *Cherokee*, which he played often with McShann, is nothing more than successive repeats of this progression in different keys. Gene Ramey, the bassist, of the McShann band of that period, speaks of this usage in Robert Reisner's book, *Bird: The Legend of Charlie Parker*:

I am sure that at that time nobody else in the band could play, for example, even the channel [bridge] to *Cherokee*. So Bird used to play a series of *Tea For Two* phrases against the channel, and since, this was a melody that could easily be remembered, it gave the guys something to play during those bars.[1]

Tea For Two has a ii[7]-V[7]-I base. Parker also implied ii[7]-V[7] in his bridge figure to *Red Cross* in 1944 (in a secondary sense, of course, not the actual ii[7]-V[7] of the key).

Treatment of II[7]

Against the II[7] (a secondary dominant) Bird formulated a motif which later became a cliche and was over-used by imitators. It involved, descending the chord from the thirteenth through to the fifth and then leaping back to the ninth. He also used this against chords but not so extensively.

He used this figure compositionally in his *Dewey Square* line:

His other treatments usually involved the ninth and the thirteenth of chord as the most important notes. The examples illustrate his other usages.

Groovin' High (1945)

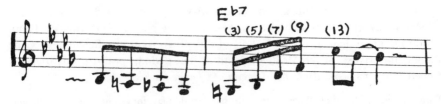

The above is an example of a chordal approach beginning with the third and culminating with the thirteenth.

Yardbird Suite: Take 4 (1946)

This is a usage which approaches the ninth by skips from tones of the basic chord.

Groovin' High: Concert (1947)

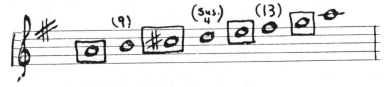

This is the same as the first example, only leaping downward to the thirteenth.

When he approached the II⁷ scalewise, the scale used was constructed from the chord:

The following is an example using mostly a scalewise approach, with a hint at the motif (mentioned earlier) at the end. There is also some chromatic inflection.

Just Friends—2nd ad lib chorus (1949)-Alto key

Treatment of Other Secondary Dominants

Basically, Parker treated the other common secondary dominants in the same way as the II[7]—chordally, with emphasis on the ninth and thirteenth (sometimes eleventh); scalewise, with the scale built from the chord; and sometimes implying the related secondary supertonic in shifting accents. These chords can best be examined in the *I Got Rhythm* bridge pattern: III[7]-VI[7]-II[7]-V[7].

Moose the Mooche: Take 2

The first measure implies the related secondary supertonic and resolves to the thirteenth and eleventh of the D[7]

On the G[7] he uses part of the motif, then creates a scalewise approach which leads smoothly to chordal treatment of the C[7]. It becomes obvious now that these basic elements were not really the key to Bird's genius. It was the way he used them that was so unique. An understanding of the basic elements is necessary, however, before looking at the works as a whole.

The following two examples from *Yardbird Suite* show Parker's uses of the VI[7] in a different setting. The first implies the related secondary supertonic and uses both the flat and raised ninth against the VI[7], which the second is a strict chordal approach using the unaltered ninth.

Again, note the smooth movement into the II⁷ chord, which is achieved in the first example. Parker achieved this smooth transition between chords by using sound musical principals, such as building a line that ends with the seventh of the first chord resolving to the third of the next (first example) or using tones which are common between the two chords as melodic material (second example).

The following examples all show an implied related secondary supertonic to the VI⁷ chord with a flat ninth. The phrases are all similar and have either the seventh of one chord resolving to the third of the next or the flat ninth of one resolving to the fifth of the next. The examples are from the solo on the second take of *Klactoveeseds-tene:*

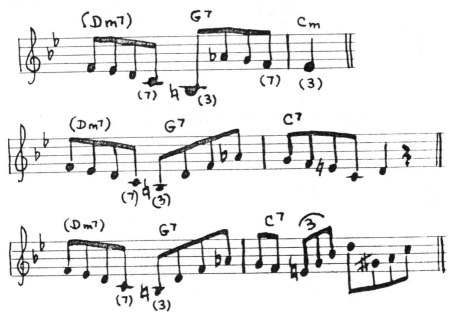

Note that the seventh of the implied Dm⁷ also resolves downward to the third of the G^7. It can be seen that Parker used all the sound basic principles of traditional harmony in his playing and did not base his music on rule-breaking, as is commonly assumed. In fact, he paid more heed to the intellectual utilization of these principles than did earlier jazz musicians, and yet he was called *revolutionary*. Again, it was the way in which he utilized these principles and the fact that he applied them in a jazz sense that was unique, not the principles themselves.

Treatment of the bVI⁷

An interesting use of this chord occurs in the composition *Cardboard* (1949). The tune is constructed somewhat like *Don't Take Your Love From me*, except for the use of this chord. It occurs in bar 3 in an unusual place. The spot can also be harmonized with a diminished chord (C-Eb-Gb), carried over, which would make it more commonplace. Pianist Haig seems to state the bVI⁷ only in bar 3 during the improvised section, and the soloists all seem to have a different conception about where it should resolve.

The Cdim and the Ab⁷ are related, and so this choice of harmony is both logical and confusing. It has the effect of making one want to hear a different progression.

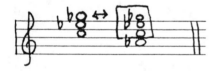

Treatment of bVII⁷

In the theme to *Dewey Square*, Parker used this chord as the second chord change resolving back to the tonic.

As mentioned before, this chord is a useful substitute and should always be considered in melodic passages where Parker used the flat sixth of the scale. It resolves well to tonic and tonic-substitutes.

Yardbird Suite offers three clear examples—one compositional and the others improvisational—and the usage is exactly the same as *Dewey Square*.

Yardbird Suite: Theme

Yardbird Suite: Solo-Take 4

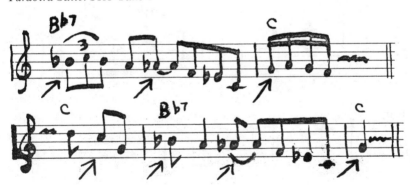

In all of the above examples, there is a hidden descending line which indicates the harmony (see arrows).

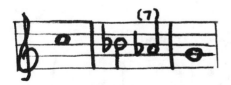

The seventh of the chord (Ab) (again the flat sixth of the scale) is used as an important "pull" tone to the fifth of the scale (G). In the first *Yardbird* example, Parker goes directly to the seventh and in the others he approaches it chromatically.

On various publications and transcriptions of *Yardbird Suite*, this chord is sometimes given as "Ab^7" (bVI^7). This harmonization fits well with the line, and one often has difficulty distinguishing it from the original chord, even after several hearings. (Indeed, this writer erroneously analyzed it as such in the first publication of this study in the Rutgers *Journal of Jazz Studies!*)

Further use of the bVII^7 chord will be covered in the sections titled *Substitute Chords* and *Blues*.

Approach To The Minor Chord

When the minor chord was used as a true tonic, Parker often added the raised sixth of the minor scale to the triad. He played in the minor rather infrequently, considering the bulk of work; only one composition exists that is in this mode. The composition is from the title-confused May 5, 1949, recording, but is generally called*"Segment."* The main theme figure is made up of a broken tonic triad stated rhythmically, and in bar 3 Parker uses the raised sixth of the scale against the triad.

Segment: Alto Key

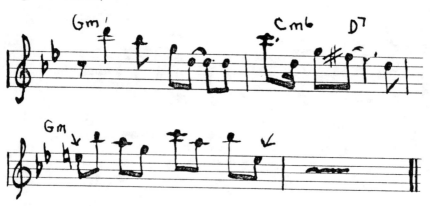

In a momentary minor excursion in *Yardbird Suite*, he uses the melodic minor scale against the triad in his improvisation.

Treatment Of The Progression iii⁷ to biii⁷

This progression is often used in the eighth bar of the blues form and as a substitute progression in standard tunes where there is a need for a smooth progression to the supertonic. It became a harmonic cliche during the be-bop days and was over-used by amateurs.

Parker often approached it strictly chordally:

Lady Be Good: Solo (1946)

Klact-oveeseds-tene: Solo-Take 2

In *Klact-oveeseds-tene* Bird only suggests this progression once—and then only in the final bar of his solo. The rest of the time his solo line suggests the "fifth" progression iii⁷ to VI⁷ instead of the parallel chords. Examples can be found in the section on the VI⁷ chord.

Treatment Of The Progression I-I⁷-IV-iv

In *Thrivin' From A Riff* (Take 3) he approaches the seventh of the I⁷ chord chromatically and treats both subdominants chordally.

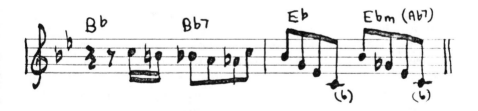

With sixths being employed in both subdominants, they can truly be called ii⁷ and ii⁷b⁵. Keep in mind that in this harmonic cycle bVI⁷ can always be substituted for ii⁷b⁵ or iv. The same approach is used in one place in *Moose the Mooche* with slight changes. In another spot in *Moose* he implies a iv⁷ or a #IVdim⁷ as the final chord of the progression.

Moose the Mooche

In the theme to *Oscar for Treadwell*, he leaps from the seventh of the I[7] to the thirteenth and on the iv chord, he again employs the leap of the flat sixth of the scale to the third.

Substitute Chords

Anyone studying Parker's music should look seriously at the implications in the melodic line before choosing a chord pattern or patterns. His playing was mostly done on familiar chord bases, but, as has been shown, there were implications of substitute chords and in many cases they were very open-ended and allowed a freedom of choice by the pianist.

Perhaps—Theme (1947)

The example above gives a few choices which can be used in various combinations in bars 7-8 of this particular blues theme.

The two most important substitutes are the bII[7], usually with +9 (third of scale), and the bVII[7], but they should be used tastefully and not overdone.

The related bII[7] may be used as a substitute for a secondary dominant, but again, if it is done indiscriminately a sterile chromaticism results: D[7]Db[7]C[7]B[7]. Parker's music does not demand this device as much as is sometimes supposed. His higher chord intervals alone give a polytonal feeling, and it is not necessary to overstate the chromatic chords. He would use this principle with the related ii[7] at certain places in some of his favorite vehicles, such as *How High The Moon*. It usually occurred in the form iii[7]-bIII[7]-ii[7]-bII[7]; in the key of G-/Bm[7] Bb[7]/Am[7] Ab[7]/. Again, however, it would generally occur only at one spot in the line and was not overdone. This is why it was effective.

Shifting Harmonic Accents

Because of Parker's unique sense of rhythm, which was at the root of his genius, the implied harmony would often shift abruptly and unusually. For instance, if a progression was /Am⁷/D⁷/he might state/Am⁷D⁷/Am⁷D⁷/or/D⁷Am⁷/Am⁷D⁷. A passage from "Grooving High" (1945) illustrates the point.

It is not necessary for the pianist to state all the implied chords, but a study of Parker's improvisations will provide any pianist with a deeper insight into "comping." Another example is from the *Yardbird Suite* solo (1946). The basic progression was/D⁷/G⁷/.

In the theme to *Relaxin' at Camarillo*, which provided much difficulty in recording because of its shifting rhythms, it is perhaps best to have the chords with the line, at times, instead of the more usual half note movement:

Bars 1, 2 and 3 (Blues)

Bars 7 and 8

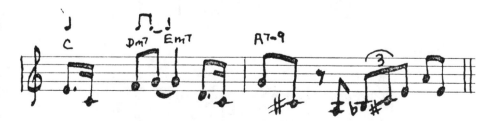

Bongo Bop (1947) offers two other examples of shifting harmonies in its theme:

Bars 3 and 4 (Blues)

Bars 7 and 8 (Blues)

In bars 3 and 4, the b7th of the scale is hinted at in the third bar instead of the usual bar 4. The early entrance can be harmonized with a Gm7 (the related secondary ii7); then the true seventh chord (C7); and finally the Gb9 (the related secondary bII7) on the Ab melody note. The second example is another instance where moving the chords with the melody notes is perhaps the best approach.

Use of Rhythm

The basic unit of rhythm in Parker's music is the eighth note, with sixteenth notes and even thirty-second notes being used in the "double-time" passages in the improvisations. The compositions show little use of sixteenth notes, however, and are usually based upon short, anticipated rhythmic motifs.

The motif which made *Moose the Mooche* so famous, for instance, can also be found in many other compositions:

Moose the Mooche

Billie's Bounce

Bongo Bop

Driftin' on a Reed

Perhaps

Following are some other examples of Parker's recurring rhythmic motifs:

Perhaps

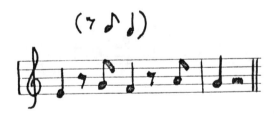

Cardboard

Au Privave

Bloomdido

Mohawk

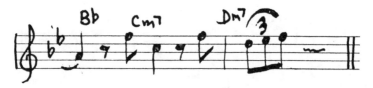

Perhaps

Visa

Chi Chi

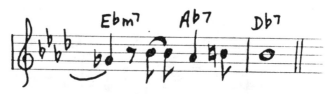

Bongo Beep

Mohawk

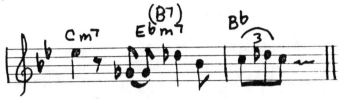

Scrapple from the Apple

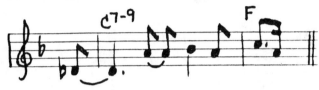

Bongo Beep

Au Privave

An Oscar for Treadwell

These short motifs used ingeniously and coupled with lines of eighth notes interspersed with triplets is what gave Parker's personal stamp to a composition. His improvisations, however, are not so easy to define rhythmically. Here are found the flowing ideas in eighth notes and triplets, the "double-time" (sixteenth notes) bursts of invention, and the shifting syncopated accents.

Improvisationally, Parker often began phrases with sixteenth notes or an eighth note falling after a beat

The following is an example of a "double-time" passage from *Thrivin' On a Riff* which begins this way and also implies a substitute chord.

In "Lady Be Good" (1946), we find the use of triplets in a "double-time" passage which culminates in a syncopated figure.

Much of Parker's "drive" was gained by a "breath push" or pulse on the second half of the beat, which cannot be notated. It is a rhythmic feeling rather than a usage and is of extreme importance in the interpretation of Bird's music.

Parker's phrasing, "double-timing," and rhythmic patterns left an indelible mark on the language of jazz—a mark used as an improvisational yardstick by all jazz improvisors up to the present time.

Superimposition

Parker sometimes superimposed one familiar harmonic sequence (implying it in his melodic line) on another familiar harmonic base. This device differed from "shifting harmonic accents" in that it implied a completely new harmony against a given set of chords rather than implying logical substitute chords to the original harmony. An interesting example is from *Dizzy Atmosphere* (February-March 1945) (bars 9-10-11).

The chords are the *I Got Rhythm* sequence, and Parker melodically superimposes a sequence of diminished chords. Running diminished chords was a common improvisational practice during the "swing" period and was still in vogue at this time, but Bird shifts the rhythmic accents so the beginning of each chord falls on a weak beat rather than the common strong beat accents. This example again shows the need for tasty "comping" by the pianist. Chords should be stated after the pianist hears where the soloist is going, not before, so as not to force the nature of the improvisation.

A strange thing happens in the bridge section to this tune. The section is based on chromatically descending seventh chords, and Bird, judging from his fine reading of the theme, is thoroughly familiar with them. In his solo, however, the notes chosen seem to imply a completely different progression. The sound of the solo is excellent, nevertheless, and this is probably because the implied chords form a logical sequence in themselves, again giving the effect of superimposition. Whether this was intentional or whether Bird simply started on a sequence differing from the original chords is beyond the judgment of this writer.

In bars 17 and 18, the chosen notes could fit with the original chords (implying, of course, the related secondary supertonic Am7), but at each succeeding chord, the presence of the major seventh of the chord against the flat-seventh chord in the harmony certainly implies another sequence. The major scale used in bars 19 and 20 is also indicative of a different key, as has been shown in earlier examples.

The Blues Form: Improvisational Treatment

A great amount of Parker's recorded material is based on the form of the twelve-bar blues. An investigation of his work would therefore be incomplete without a thorough detailing of his improvisational efforts on this form. For this purpose several different blues choruses, each of a different nature, will be dissected.

1. Bars One to Four

The beginning four bars of blues have undergone many harmonic changes since the early days of jazz, and many of these changes can be directly attributed to Parker's *melodic* ideas. The traditional form was usually I/I/I/I7; or I/IV7/ I/I7; or even I/IV7 #IVdim.7/I/I7. Although Bird sometimes kept melodically within these basic chords, for he was an excellent traditional blues player, he also often stated melodic ideas which implied a much different harmonic approach. Some of these have already been discussed (for example the major scale, implying scalar chords). A common approach which is rarely discussed in analyzing Bird's music is the suggestion of I vi7/ii7V7 in the first two measure; in other words a transference of the common "I Got Rhythm" opening bars to the blues. Two examples from "Driftin' on a Reed" (December 17, 1947) illustrate this point. The examples are from the final take, choruses one and two.

Chorus I

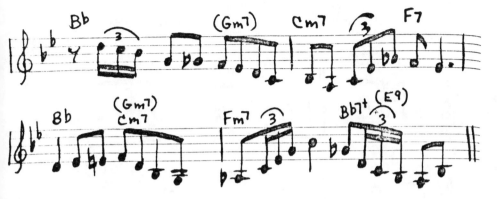

Chorus II

In the second measure of both examples, the V^7 is alluded to melodically before it appears harmonically. This is another example of Parker's "shifting harmonic accents" which fit perfectly when used with the "comping" style of piano accompaniment. We also see again the use of the flat sixth of the scale as important melodic material (used in both cases as the flat-nine of the dominant).

The fourth bar of the blues is the traditional place to emphasize the flat-seventh of the key, thereby creating the "bluesy" effect. Parker also emphasized this tone but did so in many varied and sophisticated ways. In the first example above, Bird plays the flat-seventh as the first note in the measure, but from the subsequent intervals it is clear that he intended it as part of the related secondary ii^7. On the final two beats of the measure (the actual place of the I^7 chord), he uses the flat-sixth of the scale as the augmented fifth of the Bb^7 chord or the ninth of its logical substitute the E^7 (see *Substitute Chords*).

In the second example above, the flat-seventh is approached by chromatic inflection. He holds back the seventh until the final two beats of the measure, again implying that the secondary dominant (I^7) is to be preceded by its related secondary supertonic seventh. Note that the final resolution of the flat-seventh of the scale is to the third of the subdominant in classical theoretical fashion. This characteristic of building lines so that they result in perfect musical resolutions is evident through all of Parker's improvisations.

Another example is from the fourth improvised chorus on *Perhaps* (August-September, 1948).

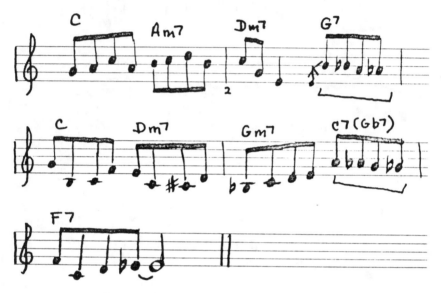

While this example does not imply the exact progression as emphatically as the preceding ones, it is again striking to see what Parker could do with only scale tones and chromatic inflection. Again it should be noted that Parker built his melodic ideas on where they were going and on using sound musical principles to get there. In other words, the mind is constantly thinking ahead, using a sound knowledge of chord patterns combined with rhythmic invention to create constantly moving patterns, much in the pattern of Bach and other great Baroque improvisors.

This example also gives us some insight into Bird's use of his favorite melodic devices. The chromatic figure in bars 2 and 4, which can be considered a Parker cliche, usually appears over dominant-type harmony, with the chromatic tones forming altered chord intervals. In the first case above, it begins on the third of the chord and descends through sharp 9—natural 9—flat 9 to resolve on the fifth of the next chord. In the second case, it begins on the thirteenth (sixth) of the chord and descends through sharp 5—natural 5—flat 5 to the root of the next chord. Again we see that a study of Parker's melodic genius is meaningless unless it is compared to the probable underlying harmony.

An example using a more traditional approach is the final chorus of *Parker's Mood* (August 29, 1948).

The second bar uses the traditional IV⁷ which Parker treats chordally but glisses from the thirteenth of the chord to end the measure. A traditional player might have played all the other notes in the measure but probably would not have thought of the "C" against the Eb⁷. In bar 4, we see the flat sixth of the scale playing a prominent role once more; after a scalar passage, he leaps to the natural sixth, then the flat sixth, and glisses to the flat seventh. Here again the flat sixth of the scale is used as the raised fifth of the chord or the ninth of the substitute chord.

On two occasions in his recording career Parker treated the first four bars of blues with the substitute chords I/vii⁷III⁷/vi⁷II⁷/v⁷I⁷, or in the key of F:F/Em⁷A⁷/Dm⁷G⁷/Cm⁷F⁷. The tunes were "Laird Baird" (December 30, 1952) and *Blues for Alice* (August 8, 1951). This chord structure is identical with *Confirmation*, one of Parker's early compositions, and, of course, is a succession of secondary ii⁷ V⁷ progressions. This progression was implied improvisationally on two different "live" versions of *Cool Blues* (March 1951—Rockland Palace and May 9, 1952—Birdland).

On a JATP date of September 18, 1949, pianist Hank Jones states a substitute progression on *The Closer* which Parker follows beautifully. The progression in Bb would be B⁷E⁷/A⁷D⁷/G⁷C⁷/F⁷Bb⁷ or a string of secondary dominants. Bird seems to refer to this progression in the chorus before and Jones states it partially, so one will never know whether the idea was Bird's or Jones' or partly talked over beforehand. Nevertheless, it is Bird's only use of this progression on record.

Another simple but unusual harmonization is on *Backhome Blues* (August 8, 1951). This was/I/Iaug./I⁶/I⁷. An example is found in the text of Chapter XVII.

2. *Treatment of the IV*(Bars 5-6)

The important note in this chord is its seventh, or the flat third of the scale. Parker accented this note most of the time in his own ingenious manner. He often entered bar 5 of the blues with a motif which culminated a long line from the previous measure (the I⁷ bar) approaching the seventh from below.

Driftin' on a Reed— Chorus 3

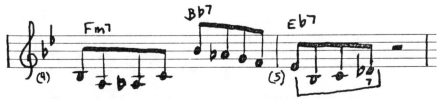

Perhaps: Chorus 3

Perhaps: Chorus I

The next three examples show an interesting parallel: the first shows a decorative approach to the seventh of IV⁷; the second is a combination scalar-chordal approach; and the third, done a year later, combines the best elements of one and two.

1. *Driftin' on a Reed*: Chorus I

2. *Driftin' on a Reed*: Chorus 2

3. *Parker's Mood*: Chorus 2

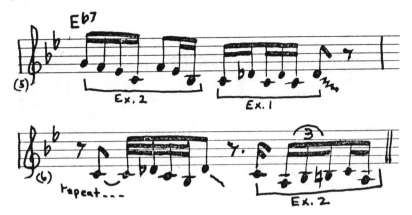

In *Bongo Beep* (December 17, 1947), Parker uses scalar tactics, chordal tactics, uses the motif approaching the seventh from below and the motif which ends the third example above.

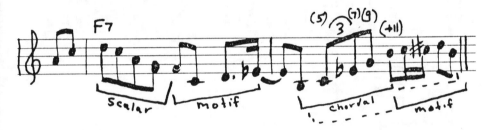

Again it is striking that the essence of Parker's genius is not in the individual elements which we are investigating, but in the way that he combined these elements into an artistic whole. All of bar 2 above can be considered a Parker motif because he used it against other harmonies (notably the Imaj[7] with the natural scale third). It can also be considered a chordal motif because it states all the intervals of the chord(s) with which it was used.

An interesting example is from *Parker's Mood* (Chorus 3) which involves the alternation of the chord seventh and thirteenth (sixth).

3. *The Tonic Return* (Bars 7 and 8)

Parker generally used these two measures to create a smooth sequence to the cadence chords in bars 9 and 10. The chord patterns suggested were usually Iii[7]/iii[7]VI[7] or Iii[7]/iii[7]biii[7] occasionally I/VI[7] or iii[7]/biii[7] and iii[7]VI[7]/biii[7]bVI[7].

Below are some examples:

Driftin' on a Reed: Chorus 1

Driftin' on a Reed: Chorus 2, shifting harmonic accents

Bongo Beep: Chorus 1

Bongo Beep: Chorus 2

Perhaps: Chorus 3

Now's the Time: Chorus 4

Now's The Time: Chorus 2

Note the coupling of the two previous motifs in the final example from *Now's The Time*. Again we see the remarkable synthesizing quantity of Parker's mind.

4. *The Cadence Bars (9 to 12)*

In the cadence Parker usually held back the dominant until the final two beats of bar 10 and treated the ii-V[7] progression with the elements discussed earlier in this work (under *Treatment of Progression* ii[7]-V[7]). He also made extensive use of the flat sixth of the scale on the beats where the true dominant would fall.

On the final tonic bars (11 and 12) of an early chorus in an improvisation of several choruses, he sometimes formulated a motif ending on the scale fourth, giving a feeling of continuance. Otherwise he treated the tonic as discussed earlier (chordal, scalar, motif or combinations).

Perhaps: Chorus I

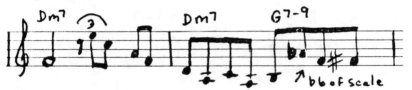

Driftin' on a Reed: Chorus 1

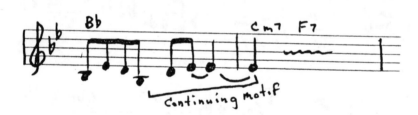

Driftin' on a Reed: Chorus 2

Bongo Beep: Final Chorus

Bongo Beep: Chorus 1

Now's The Time: Chorus 2 (1953)

Some of the other slight variations which Bird used in his blues playing were covered in the analysis of some blues themes. While these analyses do not cover all of Parker's prolific inventiveness, they should show, in a general way, his approach to the blues form. This form, perhaps older than jazz itself, is the backbone of jazz, and Parker certainly demonstrated many possibilities within its seemingly simple structure (besides showing us the emotional strength which surges from every good blues player.)

The Melodic Motif

From previous examples it is obvious that the motif, both melodic and rhythmic, was an important part of Birds thinking. It is one of the factors which made an organized whole out of his ideas. Some of the best examples for analysis lie in his improvisational phrases on the opening bars of Gershwin's *Embraceable You*.

Embraceable You: Take 1 (October 28, 1947)

Meandering: Actual Key-Eb (November 26, 1945)

Quasimado: Actual Key-Eb (December 17, 1947)

Embraceable You: Live at St. Nick's Arena (February 18, 1950)

The first *Embraceable* and *Meandering* are done as slow ballads, the last *Embraceable* at a moving ballad tempo, and *Quasimado* in a "medium bounce" vein. Examples two and three, which are actually in the key of Eb, are given in F for ease of examination.

The same general motif is used throughout but developed differently in each. The major seventh and ninth of the scale are the principal notes in the motif when used against the tonic, and it is interesting to note that Parker also used these two scale steps as the principal notes against the diminished chord in the second measure. This is another example of Parker's "using the higher chord intervals as a melody."

In the first example, the motif is used against the tonic, repeated against the diminished chord, then transposed up a perfect fourth, used against the supertonic, and repeated with embellishment. Stripped of everything but the important higher chord intervals the phrase would look like this:

It now can be seen that Parker's ability to combine the higher chord intervals with their neighboring tones into interesting melodic patterns, in which the higher chord intervals occupied the principal places, was at the root of his melodic invention.

The second example uses the major seventh as the principal tone in Bar 1 and the ninth or scale second as the principal tone in Bar 2.

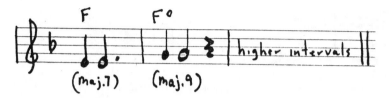

Quasimado, taken "up," gives an example of a scalar passage incorporating the motif.

   The final example is closely related to the first, but, because of the poor quality of the recording and the fact that the tape cuts in abruptly on Bird's solo, it is difficult to hear exactly what is happening. The writer has tried to notate it as closely as possible. On a JATP recording of September 1949, Bird also begins his *Embraceable* solo with this general motif in his entrance to the second bar following Lester Young's chorus and audience applause. He alludes to this motif again in his Swedish recording of November 1950, using it at the beginning of the second sixteenth bar section on the tonic and at the end of this first chorus on the dominant. Bird obviously thought of this motif as a tool for development on the *Embraceable You* chords, as much a part of his thinking as the original melody or the chords. He did not, however, always use this motif on every reading of the tune. The second take of October 28, 1947, or the second *Quasimado* take do not have the motif and both are well-formulated choruses. Another fantastic use of motivic design was often put to use in Bird's versions of *Out of Nowhere*. The following example, the first take of November 4, 1947, begins on bar 9 of the tune.

The tempo is slow, and Bird's thoughts are in double time. The motif first appears in bar 10 and continues throughout, broken only by an earthy phrase outlining the minor chord in bar twelve. In the final bar there is a coupling with the motif discussed earlier for approaching the seventh of a chord. It should be noted that Parker used the motif on successive notes of the basic chord involved. In bar 11 for instance, he used it on the root, then the fifth, then the third of the minor chord. The Eb⁷ chord is anticipated at the final half-beat of bar 12 beginning on the third, then using the motif on the fifth and root in bar 13.

The second take of November 4, 1947, again has the motif in two significant places, but the third take does not use it at all. Note can be made of the use of this motif in some of Parker's live versions of the tune. The recording at St. Nick's on February 18, 1950 has the motif at places close to those in the example, even though the tempo is fast. The spring 1948 recordings, possibly from the Onyx Club, have the motif on both versions near the end of the first chorus, and one of the versions from the Paris Jazz Festival in 1949 has the motif near the end of the second chorus.

The two motifs mentioned seem to be used *only* on these particular tunes, never on other ballads (at least not in a developmental sense; they were sometimes alluded to, however). In other words, they were almost thematic material for Parker to develop. They serve to point out the very organized pattern of Parker's thought, rather than his much-abused image as a chaotic genius, beyond analysis. It is this writer's opinion that Bird was the most organized, logical improviser of all time, and it is the organization coupled with the flash of invention that made him a genius among improvisors.

Embraceable You—Study of a Complete Solo
(From a first take, October 28, 1947)

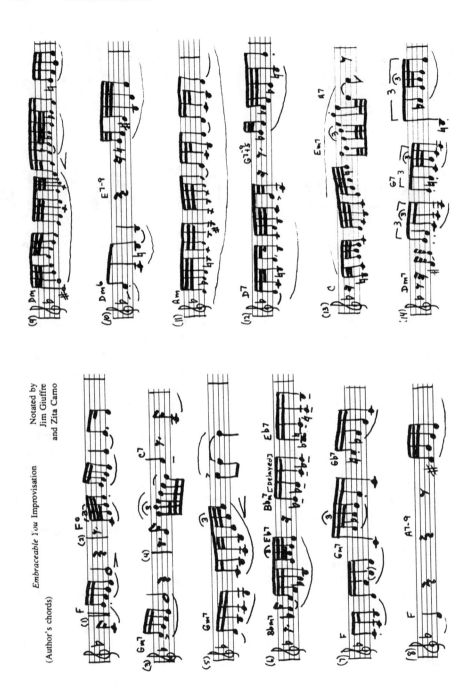

Embraceable You Improvisation

Notated by
Jim Giuffre
and Zita Camo

(Author's chords)

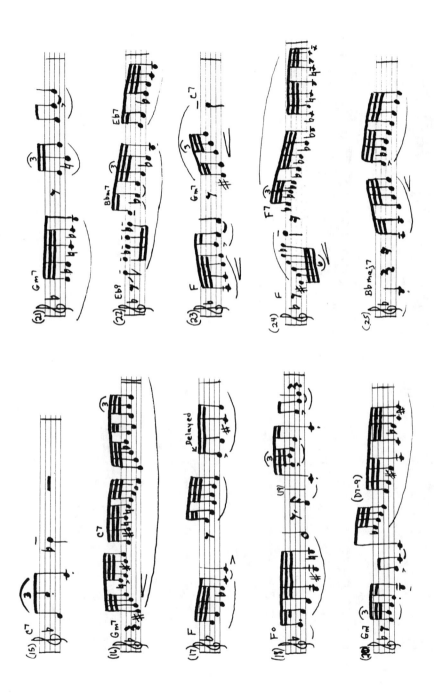

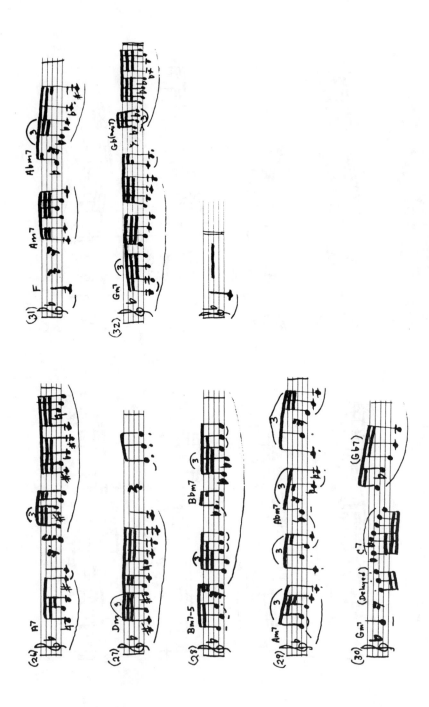

Parker's complete *Embraceable You* solo demonstrates all of the elements mentioned earlier in this essay:

Bars 1-4. Use of motif; motif formulated only from the notes in the major scale; higher chord tones used as the principle melodic notes.

Bar 5. Begins with the motif and blends into an ascending chordal treatment leading to a climax of the phrase.

Bar 6. Implies the related secondary supertonic; uses chromaticism coupled with the scale built from the chord.

Bar 7. Hints at *Cool Blues* motif; uses chromatic decoration; uses chordal treatment on the dominant, suggesting a substitute chord.

Bars 8-10. The phrase beginning at the end of bar 8 is an example of "shifting harmonic accents." The beginning notes of bar 9 obviously belong, in thought, to the A^7 chord which is stated in bar 8. The phrase continues scalewise, embellished by a chromatic slide, and comes to rest on the natural sixth of the minor chord. It is interesting that Bird used the chromatic tones both for embellishment and to create a smooth logical line to another chord or scale tone.

Bars 10-12. Chordal treatment of the secondary dominant (end of 10) approached by scalewise movement after the beat. The notes used against the dominant imply a flat ninth chord. The phrase continues (bar 11) with combinations of scalar and chordal treatment with chromatic tones and then takes an ingenious turn of melodic and rhythmic repetition that climaxes with a rhythmic diminution.

Bars 12-13. Chordal treatment of secondary dominant using altered tones (bar 12). Note the relationship to the end of bar 10; use of only *related* major scale notes (C) in bar 13. Hints at opening motif (rhythmically).

Bars 14-15. Chordal treatment of a secondary supertonic; leap upward to the flat ninth of the secondary dominant; rhythmic, decorated sequences culminating in an undecorated triplet, which leaps to the seventh of the true dominant. Note that the opening eighth notes on beats two and three of bar 14 are the exact scale tones used in the opening motif, or the motif with harmonic embellishment.

Bars 16-18. The flow of the phrase at half-cadence (bar 16) continues right through to the tonic beginning the next section. The phrase contains chordal treatment, a sequence, scalar movement, and the chromatic tones for smooth movement. The phrase beginning in bar 17 makes use of the opening motif again in bar 18, this time chordally embellished.

Bars 19-21. The sequence in bars 19-20 is beautifully conceived, the phrase in bar 20 sounding like an afterthought for emphasis. The next phrase implies a secondary dominant and is used to break the monotony of the same harmony; it is also used as a decorative effect culminating in a chromatic motif also used in many other improvisations (bar 21). After this comes a decorated hint at the melody, as if to say to the listener "Here is where we are."

Bars 22-23. The phrase begins with weighted notes gleaned from a scale derived from the chord, then directly implies the related secondary supertonic, and continues with scalewise movement culminating in a chordal treatment of the tonic (bar 23). Note that the seventh of the implied related supertonic (Ab) really resolves to the third of the dominant structure (G) on beat four of bar 22, even though the other chord tones are in between. These other chord tones can be considered as embellishment. This facet of Parker's playing occurs often.

Bars 23-24. The phrase ending on beat one of bar 23 is imitated chordally first on the dominant and then the tonic. The beginning chromatic notes are, of course, lower neighboring tones. The next phrase begins with an altered tone arpeggio suggesting an altered I and culminates with a sequence leading to the subdominant.

Bars 25-27. The related major scale (Bb) dominates bar 25, except for the lone chromatic tone (Cb), and moves smoothly to the next chord change (bar 26). The next phrase begins with a favorite Parker melodic device, which is imitated on the first beat of bar 27.

Bars 28-29. What begins as scalewise movement in bar 27 merges into a melodic motif, which is repeated a half-step lower with the change of harmony. This in turn merges into a harmonically derived motif, which is also repeated with the change of harmony, finally coming to rest in bar 30. This is a prime example of how Parker used chromatic harmony (Bm^7-Bbm^7-Am^7-Abm^7) without sounding trite.

Bar 30. The cadence bar uses both b9 and the #9 of the dominant and suggests an alteration or substitution before resolving to the tonic.

Bars 31-32. These are "turn-around" measures, but Bird really uses them as an elongated cadence, extending one beat into the next chorus. Here again we find a beautifully conceived, harmonically derived sequence which subtly hints at the opening motif, chromatically implies an altered dominant, and finally comes to rest on the fifth of the scale.

The beauty of these elements is that it is usually impossible to see exactly where one stops and the next begins. They are fused together into a logical and artistic whole. And added to them is an emotion which cannot be analyzed or examined but which moves all these elements beyond the realm of exercise and makes them into beautiful, living music. The emotion can only be felt. Upon hearing this performance, there is no doubt that the listener will *feel* what Bird was feeling, for much of his genius lay in his ability to communicate emotion universally.

And so it is with Parker's music as a whole: no amount of examination can make one feel its' *intensity*. This writer hopes, however, that this analytical study will help *understand* it, at least intellectually.

Notes

Introduction

[1]Robert Reisner, *Bird: The Legend of Charlie Parker* (New York: Citadel Press, 1962), p. 233.

[2]Ross Russell, *Bird Lives* (New York: Charterhouse, 1973), p. 324.

[3]Reisner, p. 20.

[4]Reisner, p. 51.

Chapter One

[1]Most authorities agree on this maiden name, although Parker's birth certificate lists the name as "Bailey."

[2]Robert Reisner, *Bird: The Legend of Charlie Parker* (New York: Citadel Press, 1962), p. 159.

[3]Reisner, p. 130.

[4]Reisner, p. 41.

[5]Reisner, p. 214.

[6]Taped Interview *Okey Doke Records* ("Bootleg" recording)

[7]Reisner, p. 185.

[8]Bird, in a later taped interview on *Okey Doke Records* speaks of a spinal fracture and mentions that everyone feared that he wouldn't be able to walk erect. There is no mention of this, however, by Daniels or Mrs. Parker when they speak of the accident in the Reisner book. The date of the accident has been rumored to have been a year earlier and some sources even say a year later. Daniels sets it rather emphatically as 1936, however, and he seems the most reliable source at present.

[9]Nat Hentoff and Nat Shapiro, *Hear Me Talkin' to Ya* (New York: Rinehart & Co., 1955), p. 353.

[10]Reisner, p. 214.

[11]Some researchers state that Parker came to New York in early 1938, directly from Chicago, and returned to Kansas City via Annapolis in 1939 for the funeral. According to his mother, he was seventeen yeas old at the time of the funeral and was found in Chicago. His mother's statements plus Buster Smith's testimony that Charlie found him after Smith had been in New York for seven months (Smith left Kansas City in early 1938), support the version given here. The other version is certainly not beyond the realm of possibility, however, and if this was the actual case, the Harlan Leonard stint probably came later, just before he rejoined Jay McShann. The Leonard band was made up of many Parker cronies and evolved from earlier bands in which Bird played. Even firsthand sources, therefore, easily mistake the date of Bird's stay with Leonard.

Chapter Two

[1]Robert Reisner, *Bird: The Legend of Charlie Parker* (New York: Citadel Press, 1962), p. 187.

[2]Reisner, p. 150.

[3]Reisner, p. 188.

[4]Nat Hentoff, Accompanying booklet, *Charlie Parker Story* (Verve Records, MGV 8100-3—boxed set), p. 11.

[5]Ross Russell, *Bird Lives* (New York: Charterhouse, 1973), p. 128.

[6]Reisner, p. 150.

[7]Reisner, p. 150.

Chapter Three

[1]Robert Reisner, *Bird: The Legend of Charlie Parker* (New York: Citadel Press, 1962), pp. 110, 114.

Chapter Five

[1]Nat Hentoff and Nat Shapiro, *Hear Me Talkin' To Ya* (New York: Rinehart & Co., 1955), p. 360.

[2]Arnold Shaw, *The Street That Never Slept* (New York: Coward, McCann & Geoghegan, Inc., 1971), p. 261.

[3]Robert Reisner, *Bird: The Legend of Charlie Parker* (New York: Citadel Press, 1962), p. 79.

Chapter Six

[1]Arnold Shaw, *The Street That Never Slept* (New York: Coward, McCann & Geoghegan, Inc., 1971), p. 261.

[2]Ira Gitler, *Jazz Masters of The Forties* (New York: The MacMillan Company, 1966), pp. 30, 31.

[3]Robert Reisner, *Bird: The Legend of Charlie Parker* (New York: Citadel Press, 1962), p. 87.

[4]Shaw, p. 261.

Chapter Seven

[1]Robert Reisner, *Bird: The Legend of Charlie Parker* (New York: Citadel Press, 1962), p. 42.

[2]Ross Russell, *Bird Lives* (New York: Charter House, 1973), p. 213.

[3]Russell, p. 213.

[4]Russell, p. 236-237.

[5]Reisner, p. 144.

[6]Russell, p. 223.

[7]Reisner, p. 98.

[8]Russel, p. 226.

[9]Russell, pp. 236-238—Chan Richardson's letter to Russell.

Chapter Eight

[1]Robert Reisner, *Bird: The Legend of Charlie Parker* (New York: Citadel Press, 1962), p. 154.

[2]Reisner, p. 195.

[3]Reisner, p. 125.

[4]Reisner, p. 224.

[5]Reisner, p. 170.

[6]Reisner, p. 183.

[7]Reisner, p. 94.

[8]Reisner, p. 219.

Chapter Nine
[1]Ross Russell, *Bird Lives* (New York: Charterhouse, 1973), p. 249.
[2]Liner Notes *Spotlite* LP 106.
[3]Robert Reisner, *Bird: The Legend of Charlie Parker* (New York: Citadel Press, 1962), p. 126.

Chapter Ten
[1]Robert Reisner, *Bird: The Legend of Charlie Parker* (New York: Citadel Press, 1962), p. 125.

Chapter Eleven
[1]Liner Notes, *Capitol* M11026, Miles Davis, *Birth of the Cool.*
[2]Ira Gitler, *Jazz Masters of the Forties* (New York: MacMillan Company), p. 46.
[3]Robert Reisner, *Bird: The Legend of Charlie Parker* (New York: Citadel Press, 1962), p. 224.

Chapter Thirteen
[1]Robert Reisner, *Bird: The Legend of Charlie Parker* (New York: Citadel Press, 1962), p. 174.
[2]Accompanying booklet, *The Charlie Parker Story,* (boxed set, Verve Records, MGV-8100-3), p. 2.
[3]Ira Gitler, *Jazz Masters of the Forties* (New York: MacMillan Company, 1966), p. 101.

Chapter Fourteen
[1]Bassist Tommy Potter gives 1951 as the date of the plane incident (see next note for source) which is possible since Bird was in Kansas City and St. Louis during the summer of that year. Potter also mentions Roach and Jordan as the other rhythm men, however, which is highly improbable at a 1951 booking. Since Rodney was definitely on the JATP tour and Potter was still a regular member of the rhythm section during 1950 (with Haynes and Haig), it seems logical that the incident took place during the Spring of 1950.
[2]Robert Reisner, *Bird: The Legend of Charlie Parker,* (New York: Citadel Press, 1962), p. 183.
[3]Reisner, p. 211.
[4]Reisner, p. 155.

Chapter Seventeen
[1]Robert Reisner, *Bird: The Legend of Charlie Parker* (New York: Citadel Press, 1962), p. 46.
[2]Reisner, p. 145.
[3]Reisner, p. 109.
[4]Ross Russell, *Bird Lives* (New York: Charterhouse, 1973), p. 309.

Chapter Eighteen
[1]Robert Reisner, *Bird: The Legend of Charlie Parker* (New York: Citadel Press, 1962), p. 107.
[2]Reisner, p. 88, 89.

Chapter Nineteen

[1]*Note to musicians—Liza* with its quick chord changes is always difficult to play on in linear improvisation—to achieve the *sound* (suggestion) of these changes. Notice Parker's tendency to suggest II7-V7 (half cadence) at the end of each "A" section (instead of ii⁷-V⁷-I). This makes the tune much more difficult to "hear" for the listener.

[2]Ira Gitler, *Jazz Masters of the Forties* (New York: MacMillan Co., 1966), p. 53.

Chapter Twenty

[1]Ross Russell, *Bird Lives* (New York: Charterhouse, 1973), p. 313.

[2]Nat Hentoff, accompanying booklet, *The Charlie Parker Story* (Verve Records MGV 8100-3, boxed set), p. 23.

[3]Robert Reisner, *Bird: The Legend of Charlie Parker* (New York: Citadel Press, 1962), pp. 194, 195.

[4]Ira Gitler, *Jazz Masters of the Forties* (New York: MacMillan Co., 1966), p. 51.

[5]Reisner, p. 19, p. 219.

[6]Reisner, p. 207.

[7]Russell, p. 328.

[8]Reisner, p. 141.

[9]Reisner, p. 16.

[10]Hentoff, p. 26.

[11]Reisner, p. 15.

Chapter Twenty-One

[1]Joe Segal, "Bird in Chicago," *Down Beat*, May 11, 1965.

Analysis Section

[1]Robert George Reisner, *Bird: The Legend of Charlie Parker* (New York: Citadel Press, 1962), p. 188.